THE JAZZ GUITAR

TO BARNEY KESSEL

THE JAZZ GUITAR

Its Evolution,
Players and Personalities
Since 1900

By
MAURICE J. SUMMERFIELD

First Edition 1978
Second Edition 1979
Third Edition 1993
Fourth Edition 1998

ASHLEY MARK PUBLISHING COMPANY

FIRST EDITION JULY 1978

SECOND EDITION APRIL 1979

THIRD EDITION DECEMBER 1993

FOURTH EDITION MAY 1998

ISBN 1 872639 31 3 SOFT COVER

ISBN 1 872639 26 7 HARD COVER

THE JAZZ GUITAR

CONTENTS

FOREWORD

I have known Maurice Summerfield since he first wrote to me in 1957. He was a guitarist then and still is. He has combined his passionate interest in the multitudinous aspects of the guitar, a curiosity into the full spectrum of music and a keen business sense, into a fruitful life. Tempered by the mutual exchange of love with his wife Pat, his children and his many friends, he is the man who should have written this book and, thank goodness, he wrote it.

It has been great fun, extremely interesting, and yes— even exciting for me to read about my musical ancestors, become better acquainted with my contemporaries, and learn about the new performers in the world of jazz guitar, through reading this book.

I hope that you also will draw much pleasure from the information and photographs included in this work. Personally, I can't wait to start locating some of the records and written music that was produced by some of the guitarists, material that I did not know existed.

I intend to track down these musical treasures with the sleuthing expertise of Sherlock Holmes. Maurice Summerfield thank you for the time and effort you have given and the dedication you have shown, to produce this book that we can experience over and over again with joy and delight.

Barney Kessel

ACKNOWLEDGEMENTS

I would like to thank all the jazz guitarists and personalities who have supplied photographs and information for their biographical entries in all four editions of this book, and also the following companies and individuals. Without their help completing this new edition would have been impossible.

Jamey Aebersold-Double Time Records
Accent Records
Laurindo & Didi Almeida
Absolute Artists-Thembisa S.Mshaka
Atlantic Records

William A.Bay
Bob & Cindy Benedetto
Berklee College of Music-Toni Ballard
Blue Note Records
Peter Broadbent
Chris Burden-String Jazz

Capitol Records
Mike Carr
Cannonball Recordings-Lori Morrow
Chiaroscuro Records-Hank O'Neal
Alan M.Collins
Concord Records-David Ginochio/Jennifer Jaime
Contemporary Records
Colin Cooper
Crescendo Jazz Magazine-Dennis Matthews
Criss Cross Records-Gerry Teekens

Charles Delaunay
Denon Records
John D'Addario Jnr-J.D'Addario Co.Inc.
Denon Records-Melanne Mueller
Downbeat Magazine
Dreyfus Records-Jim Eigo

Encore Jazz Promotions-Maureen Hopkins
Enja Records- Matthias Winckelman
ECM-Records-Steve Lake

Famous Door Records
Fantasy Records-Terri Hinte
Leonard Feather
Fender Guitars-Richard Siegle
Jim Ferguson
Frank Forte
Fret Records-Ian Cruickshank

Geffen Records
Gibson Guitars
GM Recordings-Marc Lambert
GRP Records
GSP-Dean Kamei
Guild Guitars-Neil Lilien

Guitar Player Magazine-Jim Crockett

A. Holberry

Ibanez Guitars
Adrian Ingram
June Ingram
Ike Isaacs

Jazz Journal-Nevil Skrimshire
Just Jazz Guitar-Ed Benson

Barney & Phyllis Kessel

Graham Langley-BIJS
Peter Larter
Lipstick Records-Jeanine Troisi

Mario Maccaferri
Melody Maker
Robert Masters
Hans Meelen
Monmouth Evergreen Records

R.G.Nolting

Ostinato Records-Randy Cole

PIT Productions-Mirande Voskuylen
PolyGram International–Marina Detienne
PolyGram Jazz-Cees Schrama
Rounder Records

Charles E.H.Smith
Spotlite Records-Tony Williams

Telarc International-Kathy De John
The Jazz Tree-Maya Newton

Vanguard Records
Velvet Swan Music-Dale Langel
Verve Records-Dahlia Ambach

Warner Bros Records-Ron Carter
Terry Whitenstall
Gordon Wright

Xanadu Records-Don Schlitten

Robert Yelin

THE JAZZ GUITAR

PREFACE

It is almost 20 years since the first edition of this book was published. That edition was the first book to cover comprehensively the subject of the guitar's role in jazz. Since that time there has been a great improvement in the availability of books, music, methods and recordings for jazz guitarists. Indeed there is now a relative cornucopia of such material. I have realised for many years that a further complete update and revision of my original book was necessary. Now, after several years of research and study, I am delighted to finally see this new edition in print.

Since 1978 over 35 important jazz guitarists featured in the biographical section of the original book have died. Fortunately since the late 1970s many great new jazz guitarists have appeared on the international scene. Over 200 of these are included in the biographical section of this fourth edition. The fusion and free areas of jazz, fairly new in 1978, are now firmly established in the jazz world of the 1990s. This fact is reflected in many of these new biographies. At the same time several outstanding young guitarists have crossed many of the boundaries of jazz and then firmly established themselves into the mainstream roots of swing and bebop.

The last 20 years has also seen the unprecedented growth in educational opportunities for the aspiring jazz guitarist. Establishments such as the Berklee College of Music in Boston, the Guitar Institute of Technology (GIT) in Los Angeles, and similar institutions in other parts of the USA and in other parts of the world, now provide an invaluable service in educating young musicians. Today there are many talented and prolific authors of jazz guitar methods and music books for guitarists to teach themselves. The most important of these scholars are included in the biographical section of this new edition as a tribute to their very important contribution to the evolution of the jazz guitar.

At time of going to press I am confident that this new book is the most comprehensive, and factually correct, book available on the guitar in jazz. As with the first edition there is a comprehensive 'Sources of Supply' section. Through this the reader can obtain most of the books, music and recordings listed throughout the book. With the arrival of the CD recording format many rare, and some newly discovered, jazz guitar recordings have become generally available. The recordings detailed in the 'Selected Recordings' listings of the book are in the main from my personal collection built up over 40 years. Some of these are LPs but most are CD releases, they have the letters CD as part of the record number. Many of the LPs are now available on CD so check with a specialist dealer for availability.

The collection of photographs in this book is a unique one. It is certainly the most comprehensive photograph collection of jazz guitarists published in one book. Many of these are from my personal collection or have been supplied by the guitarists, their agents or record companies. When known the photographer's name is shown. I would like to take this opportunity of thanking all those who have helped in supplying photographs for this new edition.

Without writing a book of encyclopaedic proportions it would be impossible for me to cover in any comprehensive way the enormous area now inhabited by the jazz guitar. My selection has therefore been made according to my own feelings and beliefs, and to those who will inevitably criticise it on the grounds that certain (and no doubts numerous) names have been omitted that should have been included, I can only say that I agree wholeheartedly, and wish that the book could have been big enough to encompass them all. Nevertheless I am confident that this book does give a clear outline of the jazz guitar's development since 1900 in terms of its players, scholars and makers.

MAURICE J. SUMMERFIELD
April 1998

The author with four legendary jazz guitarists at the launch of the first edition of this book on 20 October 1978 in London.   Left to right;   Charlie Byrd, Joe Pass, Herb Ellis, Barney Kessel and Maurice Summerfield.

THE JAZZ GUITAR
Its Evolution

THE EVOLUTION OF THE JAZZ GUITAR

		In the U.S.A	Outside the U.S.A.
1895	The Blues	†Big Bill Broonzy/Hudson (Leadbelly) Leadbetter Blind Willie McTell/Blind Lemon Jefferson	
1900	New Orleans	The Banjo } Bud Scott	
1910	Dixieland Chicago	Johnny St Cyr	
		Snoozer Quinn *Eddie Lang/*Lonnie Johnson	
1930	Kansas City	*Carl Kress/*Dick McDonough *George Van Eps/Teddy Bunn Freddie Green (rhythm guitar) Allan Reuss	*Django Reinhardt Oscar Aleman
1940	Swing	Al Casey/Tiny Grimes *Charlie Christian Oscar Moore/George Barnes/Les Paul	
1945	Bebop	*Barney Kessel *Tal Farlow/*Chuck Wayne	
1950	Modern/West Coast	*Jimmy Raney/Herb Ellis *Jim Hall	Réne Thomas
	Cool	Billy Bauer/Johnny Smith Kenny Burrell/*Wes Montgomery	
	Bossa/Nova	*Laurindo Almeida/Charlie Byrd *Joe Pass/George Benson	Baden Powell Attila Zoller
1960			Gabor Szabo
1970	Jazz Fusion Jazz/Rock/Soul Indo/African/Free	Larry Coryell/Al Di Meola Lee Ritenour/*Lenny Breau	John McLaughlin Derek Bailey
1980-1998		John Scofield/Pat Metheny Earl Klugh/*Bill Frisell Stanley Jordan/Howard Alden	Philip Catherine Martin Taylor Bireli Lagrene

†These artists' recordings give a true representation of the music of the blues singer/guitarists of this period.

*THE MAJOR INNOVATORS

A chart showing those guitarists who have had an important influence on the evolution of the jazz guitar from the beginning of jazz music to the present day.

THE JAZZ GUITAR
ITS EVOLUTION

Many books have been written about the origins of jazz. The authors have varying concepts and theories about these origins but most agree that the beginnings of jazz, as we know it today, happened around 1895. Few would disagree that the guitar, albeit in many cases in a primitive form, was the first instrument of jazz. The first organized jazz began in the form of marching bands in New Orleans and a photograph of the earliest known jazz group, Buddy Bolden's band circa 1894, shows guitarist Brock Mumford as part of the line-up. The early black blues singers, prior to and after 1895, used the guitar for their accompaniment. Those singer/ guitarists who had developed their technique on the instrument were able to interject their accompaniments with single note lines and riffs to add colour and impetus to their performance. Although we obviously have no recorded proof of what these artists sounded like there seems little doubt that the records made by singer/guitarists such as Big Bill Broonzy, Leadbelly, and Blind Willie McTell give us a true representation of the first sounds of jazz and the jazz guitar.

As a real solo voice in its own right the guitar eventually became one of the last instruments of jazz. This was mainly due to the guitar's lack of volume and carrying power. Until the arrival of microphones, recording, and the first primitive amplification in the mid 1920s the guitar was relegated to the rhythm section in organized jazz, felt rather than heard. The banjo, because of its bright, loud and cutting sound was the preferred instrument in many early jazz groups, although the guitar was still the primary instrument used for accompaniment by blues singers. There were important jazz artists such as Bud Scott, often heard with Kid Ory, and Johnny St Cyr who played with Louis Armstrong, who doubled on both banjo and guitar, but their prime role was as part of the rhythm section.

One of the first jazz guitarists who could solo in an articulate manner, comparable to performers on other instruments of jazz, was the black blues singer Lonnie Johnson. He was featured as a backing artist on many records in the mid 1920s and was a soloist on a 1928 recording by Duke Ellington and his orchestra called `The Mooche`. Johnson had early musical training on the violin and there seems little doubt that this training combined with his special natural talents made him aware of the single note capabilities of the guitar as a solo voice. There is also no doubt that it was Johnson's playing that directly inspired Eddie Lang the brilliant white guitarist from Philadelphia, who incidentally also had an early training on the violin. Lang picked up the blues style of Johnson's guitar playing very quickly, and reached international fame within a relatively short period of time. Fame that black artists like Johnson could not have access to at that time due to racial predjudice in the USA. Yet Lang fully realized Johnson's genuine musical talents and

Brock Mumford, guitarist with Buddy Bolden's jazz band, circa 1894.

not only played with him in private but recorded several ageless guitar duos with him, usually under the pseudonym Blind Willie Dunn.

Virtually all the recordings made by Johnson and Lang, both their solos and duos, are now fortunately available once more and bear full testimony to the genius of both guitarists. Lang was a virtuoso of the guitar and mixed authentic blues lines with long and exciting flowing arpeggios, chords and runs. His guitar was often heard with the other jazz masters of the 1920s including Bix Beiderbecke and Joe Venuti. From 1929 Lang was also a prominent soloist with the Paul Whiteman Orchestra. The only other guitarist of note at that time was Snoozer Quinn. He had a fine reputation amongst jazzmen in the New York area but due to illness and other reasons never achieved lasting fame. Eddie Lang at the height of his career, having become the full time accompanist of his friend the singer Bing Crosby, died suddenly in 1932 after a tonsillectomy. His death was a tragic loss that almost certainly held up the evolution of the jazz guitar in the USA for a short while.

Carl Kress, Dick McDonough, and George Van Eps stand out as being the most important jazz guitarists in America during the early 1930s, particularly after the death of Eddie Lang. They were great rhythm guitarists and their solo style was a happy mixture of single note lines and punchy, rhythmic chords, a derivation of the solo banjo style developed in jazz bands

Dick McDonough

during the 1920s. Kress, McDonough and Van Eps were all originally banjoists. The black guitarist Teddy Bunn, featured with the vocal group `The Spirits of Rhythm`, continued and extended the blues influenced guitar style of Lonnie Johnson.

But it was to Europe that jazz lovers in 1934 turned their attention when the everlasting genius of Django Reinhardt exploded on to the scene. Reinhardt, a Belgian-born Gypsy, had overcome a terrible disability with the virtual total loss of the use of his third and fourth fingers of his left hand. This occured after a fire in his caravan in 1928. He developed a new technique which enabled him to portray fully on the guitar his fantastic mixture of improvised music, fired by his Gypsy background and love for the American jazz that he heard on early records.

His virtuoso guitar playing carried to a new high level the standards of solo jazz guitar playing which had been set by Eddie Lang. His artistry virtually overshadowed the American jazz guitarists of that time, particularly after the early death in 1938 of Dick McDonough. Prior to Lang and Johnson the guitar had been an integral part of the rhythm section in many jazz bands. This tradition, started by artists such as Johnny St Cyr and Bud Scott, was continued into the 1930s and early 1940s by George Van Eps, Allan Reuss,

Bud Scott

Eddie Lang with the Mound City Blues Blowers.

Eddie Condon and Freddie Green. Condon, who played a four-string guitar (an instrument which facilitated the changeover to guitar for banjo players) through the years until his death in 1973, was one of the greatest promoters of Chicago style jazz. Van Eps, a brilliant musician, taught Reuss and recommended that he should take his place in the Benny Goodman Band. In the late 1930s Reuss taught Freddie Green for a while at his studio in New York. The amazing Freddie Green became the pulse and driving force of the legendary Count Basie band's rhythm section from 1937 with hardly a break until his death in 1987. For fifty years Green set unsurpassed standards in the art of rhythm guitar.

The next important step in the evolution of the jazz guitar came in 1939 when jazz promoter John Hammond discovered the Oklahoma born black guitarist Charlie Christian. Christian's genius, in a very short period of time, opened new horizons for not only the guitar but for jazz itself. But it was certainly the inventive and enquiring mind of trombonist/guitarist /arranger Eddie Durham that speeded the transformation of the acoustic guitar to its amplified state. Durham had experimented for a few years with amplifying the guitar. At first he tried by attaching a resonator to his instrument and with this device recorded the attractive solo `Hittin' the Bottle` with the Jimmy Lunceford band in 1935. In 1937 whilst working with the Count Basie band on trombone, Durham also played and recorded with a small group out of the band called `The Kansas City Six` on one of the first electric guitars. It was Durham who made Charlie Christian aware of the electric guitar as early as 1937. The young guitarist quickly realized the potential which the electric guitar offered. He saw that notes could be sustained on the amplified instrument so that a saxophone style of single note playing, which he so admired, could be obtained. He also saw that the volume of the guitar could now equal any other instrument in the band. Many early observers of Christian's playing, who were not familiar with the sound of the electric guitar, often thought at first they were listening to a saxophone. As the 1940s approached there were other fine jazz guitar soloists making their mark in the USA, but they were mainly acoustic guitar players. Al Casey with Fats Waller's sextet and Allan Reuss with the Benny Goodman and Jack Teagarden bands were amongst the best of these. But it was the combination of the amplified guitar and Christian's advanced and brilliant harmonic concepts that suddenly opened the doors wide, not only for the jazz guitar, but for jazz itself. On the recommendation of John Hammond, Christian was hired in 1939 by Benny Goodman. Within a very short time Christian was featured as a main soloist with Goodman's big band and sextet.

In the same way that banjo players at the beginning of the 1930s changed virtually en

15

Guitarmen, Wake Up and Pluck!

Wire for Sound; Let 'Em Hear You Play

BY CHARLIE CHRISTIAN
(Featured Guitarist, Benny Goodman Orchestra)

Guitar players have long needed a champion, someone to explain to the world that a guitarist is something more than just a robot plunking on a gadget to keep the rhythm going. For all most band-leaders get out of them, guitarists might just as well be scratching washboards with sewing thimbles.

There are dozens of guitar players around the country—and I mean *good* guitar players—who have resigned themselves to a life of playing for nothing but cookies or just their own kicks, because they've had no alternative if they wanted to continue playing guitar.

Bernard Addison, formerly with Stuff Smith's band, in the August '39 DOWN BEAT, said:

Git-men Get Short End

"Guitarists are goats. In the present day band's setup, it's the guitar player who gets the short end. Leaders don't appreciate the possibilities of the instrument."

I've been inclined to agree 100 per cent with Addison, although

CHARLIE CHRISTIAN
Thinks amplification gives guitarists new lease on life.

naturally there are leaders who have been exceptions to this generality (and not out of fear for my job do I say that Benny is one of them).

With an appalling ignorance of the effective use to which they could put the instrument, most leaders, including those in the radio and movie studios, have demanded a guitarist who can fiddle, arrange or pick his teeth walking a tight rope every other chorus. The fact that he might have been truly an artist on the guitar was negligible.

A New Era Dawning

And arrangers seem either to have neglected to learn anything about the guitar or else have found that arranging for it is beyond their ability.

But the dawn of a new era is at hand for all these fine guitarists who had become resigned to playing to feed their souls but not necessarily their stomachs.

Electrical amplification has given guitarists a new lease on life.

Allan Reuss, with Jack Teagarden's band, was one of the first well-known men to attach an amplifier to his guitar. Musicians have been aware of Reuss's ability for several years, but the instrument is subtle and the public probably never would have realized his ability if they'd had to strain their ears to catch the niceties of his technique and the beauty of his improvisations. Allan's recent work on Jack Teagarden's Brunswick record, *Pickin' for Patsy*, his own number, proved to the record companies as well as to musicians and public alike that as a solo jazz instrument the guitar is far from stillborn. Reuss's guitar was amplified on the session.

Smith Gains Prominence

Then there's Georgie Barnes, the 17-year-old Chicagoan, who, with an amplified instrument, set that town on its ear at Chicago's Off-Beat club last spring. Barnes has just been added to the staff of the Chicago NBC studios. A year ago he had a tough time booking his own Chicago Heights combo for Saturday nights.

And Floyd Smith, the colored guitar player with Andy Kirk's band. With an amplified guitar he has been acclaimed widely as one of the greatest guitarists of all time, particularly in the blues idiom. His work on the Decca record, *Floyd's Blues*, with the Kirk band, forces his ability and the value of the guitar smack into the consciousness and ears of the public.

Needless to say, amplifying my instrument has made it possible for me to get a wonderful break. A few weeks ago I was working for beans down in Oklahoma and most of the time having a plenty tough time of getting along and playing the way I wanted to play.

Practice Solo Stuff

So take heart, all you starving guitarists. I know and so does the rest of our small circles, that you play damned fine music, but now you've got a chance to bring the fact to the attention of not only short-slighted leaders but to the attention of the world. And I don't think it'll be long before you're feeding your stomach again as well as your heart. Practice solo stuff, single string and otherwise, and save up a few dimes to amplify your instrument.

You continue to play guitar the way it should be played and you'll make the rest of the world like it.

Johnny Dodds is Slowly Recovering

Chicago — Johnny Dodds, early day New Orleans jazz clarinet player, who was stricken with a severe illness in August, is slowly recovering at his home on the south side here. According to his

When Bix Was with Goldkette in 1927

these pictures were taken for Red Ingle, who also was with the band at the same time. Picture on the left, taken at Castle Farms, Cincinnati, shows Bix and Ingle (who now is with Ted Weems' band in Chicago). The shot of Bix on the right was taken later the same year, outside a spot the band played on the shores of Lake Erie at Fremont, Ohio. (Photos courtesy of Ingle).

Reprinted with the permission of Downbeat magazine..

masse to the guitar the beginning of the 1940s saw virtually every jazz guitar soloist changeover from acoustic to electric guitar. The 1930s heralded the big band era and the boom of swing music. The early part of the decade had seen guitarists such as McDonough, Kress and Van Eps fitting into the big band scene in a relatively subordinate role, despite their genuine virtuoso talents on the instrument. It is fortunate that most of these artists` outstanding solos and duets are once more available on record. Their style of playing was carried on by other white guitar players including Carmen Mastren and Allan Reuss, and in a more blues influenced way by the black guitarist Al Casey. These guitarists were virtually unaffected by the style of jazz being played at that time in Europe by Django Reinhardt, and the less known but brilliant Argentinian guitarist Oscar Aleman. We do know that Charlie Christian greatly admired Django Reinhardt and as a teenager would often play the gypsy's recorded solos note for note when playing in jazz clubs in Oklahoma.

After joining Goodman, Christian tragically lived for only a little more than two years but in that short time he transformed the position of the guitar in jazz. The styles and ideas that he developed set new standards in jazz music that were unsurpassed for many years to come.

The early 1940s saw national prominence for two guitarists from Chicago, one was Les Paul, a great Django Reinhardt fan, and the other George Barnes, who attributed his distinctive style to various reed players rather than guitarists. Paul was one of the first guitarists to experiment with the development of the electric guitar and in fact played an amplified instrument as early as 1937. Both Paul and Barnes were really not affected by Charlie Christian but virtually all the other new guitarists to come to the fore in the 1940s were. Oscar Moore, and later Irving Ashby and John Collins, all fea-

Charlie Christian

tured guitarists with pianist Nat `King` Cole`s trio, were all inspired by Charlie Christian. The only female guitarist to make an impression on the jazz scene in the 1940s, Mary Osborne, was also a Christian devotee particularly after she had met and befriended him.

With the enormous success of Benny Goodman's big band and small groups, most other big bands were anxious to have an electric guitarist in order to try and emulate the same type of success. In 1944 the great jazz promoter Norman Granz produced his historic film `Jammin' The Blues` which featured some of the top black jazz stars of the day. The only white musician to be featured in this film was Barney Kessel, a twenty one year old guitarist from Muskogee, Oklahoma. Like Mary Osborne he had also met and befriended Charlie Christian. Kessel`s driving, blues influenced style on the guitar, so obviously an authentic extension of Christian's playing, was soon recognised by many jazz critics as making him the true successor to Charlie Christian. For the next few years, right up to his entry into the Hollywood studios in the 1950s, Barney Kessel was generally regarded as the leading jazz guitarist in the USA.

As the 1950s approached a multitude of world class jazz guitarists appeared on both coasts of North America. They set standards which were virtually unsurpassed by any guitarists outside the USA for many years, with the exception of Django Reinhardt. Particularly prominent amongst these were Tal Farlow, Jimmy Raney, Jim Hall, Herb Ellis, Mundell Lowe, Johnny Smith, Chuck Wayne, Billy Bauer, and Sal Salvador. These and many other American gui-

Teddy Bunn (bottom left) with the Spirits of Rhythm .

17

tarists were fortunate that important small groups of the late 1940s and early 1950s, led by other jazz instrumentalists, were to prove valuable training grounds for the development of their skills on the guitar. Vibraphonist Red Norvo, pianists Nat `King` Cole, Art Tatum, Oscar Peterson and George Shearing, drummer Chico Hamilton, saxophonists Stan Getz and Jimmy Giuffre were amongst the most important of these. The first hints of avant garde/free jazz were intimated at that time by a group led by saxophonist Lee Konitz, pianist Lennie Tristano and guitarist Billy Bauer. In Europe Django Reinhardt still reigned supreme at the beginning of the 1950s, his natural musical genius effortlessly absorbed and accepted all the new movements and changes in jazz.

The stage was now set for a new development in the evolution of the jazz guitar. The amplified guitar had enabled Charlie Christian and his followers to put their instrument on an equal footing with all the other single note instruments in jazz. The acoustic `F` hole archtop guitar was often still used as an essential part of the rhythm section playing four in the bar chords. But the power of amplification for a time made many guitarists forget that the guitar was more than a single note instrument. They were often quite content to play long flowing improvised single note lines, many in the manner of saxophonists Lester Young and Charlie Parker, neglecting the chordal and other harmonic aspects of the guitar. In California during the late 1940s George Van

Django Reinhardt and Barney Kessel 1953

Eps, who had come to international prominence as the guitarist with several big bands in the 1930s, was still fascinated by the overall harmonic possibilities that the guitar offered. Even though he still used an acoustic guitar as late as 1949, his recorded solos during this period show that he had an amazing modern harmonic concept of music. He also had an incredible technique on the guitar to display these concepts. Eps showed that the guitar could solo not only with single notes, but in a piano like manner with a mixture of chords, octaves, double and single notes.

Van Eps`s approach to the guitar proved a great influence on Barney Kessel the `heir` to Charlie Christian`s throne. Kessel realised that he had the ability and the desire to play his own individual style of jazz rather than a replica of the style of Christian. He also saw that

Django Reinhardt and the Quintet of the Hot Club of France

Charlie Byrd

PHOTO: COURTESY GUILD GUITARS

with the right technique the guitar was a 'small orchestra', so that in a small group format the guitarist could only display its full chordal and rhythmic potential by excluding the piano. His experiments led to the release in 1957 of his first 'The Poll Winners' recording. This trio was made up of Kessel on guitar, Ray Brown on bass and Shelly Manne on drums. This first recording and other 'Poll Winners' recordings that followed were a great success. The format of the trio, although now a very standard one for jazz guitarists, was a great innovation at that time. Kessel showed that if a guitarist had the right technique, musical concepts and talent, he could fill the role of soloist and accompanist on an equal level to the pianist. From that time the guitar had a freedom of performance and expression previously unknown in jazz.

In 1953 Django Reinhardt died suddenly after a heart attack at his home in France. He was only forty-three years old. Fortunately his music lives on through the availability of virtually every recording he ever made and he remains an inspiration to most guitarists of all styles. Many groups playing in the 'Hot Club of France' style have continued on both sides of the Atlantic to emulate the style of the original 1930s quintet. In 1953 a new sound was added to the jazz guitar repertoire in the USA. Brazilian guitarist Laurindo Almeida, who had settled in the USA in 1947 and played in the Stan Kenton orchestra, conceived the idea of mixing traditional Brazilian melodies and rhythms with jazz improvisations. He formed the quartet 'Brazilliance' with saxophonist Bud Shank. They subsequently made several best selling recordings. On all of these Almeida played a classical guitar. With the use of high quality microphones and amplification Almeida proved that the nylon string instrument, played with classical right hand fingerstyle technique, could be an effective sound in jazz. He also showed that the horizons of jazz music itself could be broadened with the introduction of South American melodies and rhythms. Although Almeida's quartet enjoyed success amongst jazz lovers its conception was premature. It took another classically trained fingerstyle guitarist, Charlie Byrd, to pick up and succeed on an enormous international scale with Almeida's original concepts. Byrd had for several years succesfully played jazz on the classical guitar with his trio in East coast clubs. This in itself was a great innovation. Today there are many guitarists playing jazz with classical right hand fingerstyle technique on both nylon and steel string instruments. Charlie Byrd was the first to introduce the concept in the 1950s. In 1961 Byrd and his trio were hired by the US State Department to play in Brazil. Whilst he was on tour Byrd realised the potential of fusing the melodies and rhythms of several popular Brazilian songs of the day, written by composer/guitarists Antonio Carlos Jobim, Joao Gilberto, Luiz Bonfa and others with jazz. On his return to the USA Byrd formed a quartet with saxophonist Stan Getz. Together they helped begin the bossa nova boom with their recordings and concert performances of 'Desafinado', 'O Pato', 'Wave', 'Girl From Ipanema' and other Brazilian songs which have now achieved the status of becoming jazz standards. The success of bossa nova swept throughout the world appealing to an audience outside the fringes of the usual jazz audience. Byrd's enormous success helped bring to the attention of jazz lovers the

Joe Pass

PHOTO: GEORGE CLINTON/COURTESY GUITAR

talents of other Brazilian guitarists including Baden Powell and Bola Sete. Charlie Byrd is still an important figure in the jazz world of the 1990s, recording and playing in concert all over the world.

By the beginning of the 1960s jazz and the jazz guitar had for many years enjoyed great popularity and relative prosperity. But with the rise of rock and roll in the early 1960s the demand for jazz rapidly declined. With a few exceptions most of the world's best jazz guitarists had to take financial refuge in the film, television and recording studios. The enormous success of popular groups such as 'The Beatles' and 'The Rolling Stones', singers Elvis Presley, Buddy Holly and others slowed down the development and the demand for jazz for several years.

Nevertheless at that time the jazz world had talented and individual guitarists who helped keep jazz alive and well. There were several guitarists continuing the mainstream tradition started by Charlie Christian including Barney Kessel, Jimmy Raney, Tal Farlow, Kenny Burrell, Grant Green, Jim Hall and Herb Ellis. The rhythm guitar tradition was continued by Freddie Green, Steve Jordan and others. Fingerstyle guitarists Laurindo Almeida, Charlie Byrd and Bola Sete playing on classical guitars added new dimensions to jazz. Johnny Smith's 1952 recording of 'Moonlight in Vermont' with saxophonist Stan Getz had been a best seller and he continued to enjoy great popularity. Smith's virtuoso single string technique and block chording made many guitarists rethink their approach to the guitar. George Van Eps continued to make new inroads with his development of the electric seven-string guitar. These were taken up later by Bucky Pizzarelli

George Benson

PHOTO: T.H. ADKINS/COURTESY JAZZ JOURNAL

Freddie Green

and others. Many prominent blues singer/guitarists such as Lonnie Johnson were once more in demand for concert and club appearances.

It was Wes Montgomery, a black guitarist from Indianapolis, who in 1960 gave the jazz guitar a much needed shot in the arm. Montgomery had developed an individual warm sound on the guitar by using the thumb of his right hand instead of a pick. This was a technique he originally used to keep the volume of his electric guitar down whilst practising at home. Montgomery's playing never lost interest due to a wonderful mixture of chords, long flowing lines of single notes, and an unusually articulate use of octaves. His brilliant solo style was so attractive that his later recordings produced by Creed Taylor, usually with a large orchestral backing, enjoyed great popular success. Wes Montgomery's genius became an inspiration to a new wave of young guitarists who emulated his original jazz guitar style. The most important of these were Pat Martino and George Benson. Over the years fate had already dealt the evolution of the jazz guitar severe blows with the premature deaths of Eddie Lang at 29, Charlie Christian at 23, Dick McDonough at 34 and Django Reinhardt at 43. In 1968 it decided in its own way to take Wes Montgomery at the age of 44. But, like all these other legendary giants of the jazz guitar, Montgomery left a deep and lasting mark in jazz history, one that has never been forgotten.

By the end of the 1960s jazz guitar had come a long way since the early performances of the primitive blues singer/guitarists of the late nineteenth century. The standards of technique that had been set on this most difficult of

PHOTO: COURTESY IBANEZ GUITARS

all instruments were not conceivable at the beginning of this century. The incredible international rise and wide popularity of rock and roll, soul, and rhythm and blues music of the 1960s had on the one hand caused a temporary decline in the popularity of jazz. On the other hand vast numbers of people were being attracted to the guitar and other instruments because of their interest in popular music. Many of these were inspired by popular rock guitarists such as Jimi Hendrix, and blues guitarists such as Eric Clapton. These young guitarists progressed technically to a stage that they wanted to play a style of music that offered them more musical depth than could be found in the basic forms of popular music. As the 1970s approached a new worldwide interest in jazz began. This allowed the great jazz masters of the 1950s and 1960s to leave the commercial studios, or virtual retirement, to once again make a successful full time career in jazz. Guitarists such as Barney Kessel, Tal Farlow, Jimmy Raney, Herb Ellis, Jim Hall and Kenny Burrell appeared once more all over the world in jazz clubs, concerts and festivals, setting new standards that pushed the boundaries of jazz guitar to even wider limits.

In the first fifty years of this century most jazz guitarists were usually self-taught or had lessons privately with established guitarists. Many of the top players gained priceless experience playing in the big swing bands or small jazz groups. Their association with other excellent instrumentalists in these bands gave them an education in the art of jazz that was second to none. In 1948 the Berklee College of Music in Boston started to offer specialised jazz degree courses, including one for guitarists. It took several years to establish itself but since the 1960s many of the best jazz guitarists of the day have graduated from Berklee. John Abercrombie, John Scofield, Mike Stern, Bill Frisell and Leni Stern are amongst these. Over the years many other colleges in the USA, and other parts of the world, have added jazz courses to their curriculum. In 1976 the Guitar Institute of Technology (GIT) was founded in Los Angeles. It has also produced many outstanding jazz guitarists. The establishment of these courses coincided with the decline of the big bands and many small jazz groups. As a result most jazz guitarists from the 1960s onwards received their early jazz education in a very different way to their predecessors.

Wes Montgomery

PHOTO: MICHAEL SALTER/COURTESY JAZZ JOURNAL

Since the 1960s rock and roll, and other forms of contemporary music made a great impression on the new generation of jazz guitarists. Many were influenced by the whole spectrum of music including Avant Garde, Soul, Latin, Indian, African, Oriental, Arab, Free and Classical music. Amongst the first jazz guitarists whose playing was affected by some, if not all, of these idioms were Larry Coryell, Ralph Towner, John McLaughlin, John Abercrombie, Pat Metheny, John Scofield, Al Di Meola and Lee Ritenour. They added many new dimensions to jazz in the 1970s. At around the same time the English guitarist Derek Bailey became one of the prime instigators of the movement of free jazz, as did Sonny Sharrock in the USA. This movement has gained a growing audience throughout the world since the 1970s. All these guitarists were familiar with the traditions established by mainstream jazz guitarists from the 1940s to the 1960s but were determined to achieve fresh ideas in jazz.

Whilst this new generation of guitarists extended the limits of jazz in the 1970s the jazz world also saw the rise of Joe Pass (1929-1994), an outstanding mainstream jazz guitar virtuoso. This amazing guitarist`s talents were already recognised in the early 1960s by many jazz

lovers, but his genius only gained international recognition, and commercial success, after he came under the exclusive management of jazz promoter Norman Granz in 1973. Through many recordings on the Pablo label, and international jazz club and concert appearances, Granz made the world aware of Joe Pass`s unique ability on the guitar. Like most great jazz musicians, Pass developed his individual style on the foundations laid down by earlier jazz artists, but he evolved an incredible and individual solo technique. Using a classical right hand fingerstyle technique Pass gave countless solo concerts, setting once again new standards in the field of jazz guitar. These standards were extended by another genius, Lenny Breau who was tragically murdered in 1984 at the age of forty three. Breau blended country and flamenco styles into a unique jazz guitar style which was greatly influenced by pianist Bill Evans. Admired by his peers, because of his tragic circumstances Breau never gained the recognition from jazz critics and fans that his enormous talent deserved. In recent times British guitarist Martin Tayor has fused and refined the jazz guitar fingerstyle techniques of Pass, Breau and others. An enormous jazz talent Taylor is universally recognised as one of the great jazz guitarists of the day.

John Abercrombie (left) and Ralph Towner

22

The 1980s saw the emergence of several outstanding new jazz fusion guitarists including Bill Frisell, Mike Stern, Steve Khan and Leni Stern. They added many new colours and ideas to the foundations of jazz fusion guitar laid down in the previous decade by John Abercrombie, John Scofield, Pat Metheny and Lee Ritenour. From Australia came the young virtuoso guitarist Frank Gambale. He settled in Los Angeles and after studying at the GIT came to international prominence as guitarist with pianist Chick Corea`s quartet. The 1980s also saw a new approach to jazz guitar playing with the arrival on the scene of Stanley Jordan. He picked the strings simultaneously with both hands achieving a piano like approach on the guitar. This technique was facilitated by a very low string action on his solid body electric guitar and the high sensitivity of its pickups. Jordan has enjoyed great success, although the complexities of this new technique have to date deterred any other guitarists from following in his footsteps. During the 1980s several brilliant young guitarists established themselves in successful careers maintaining the jazz guitar styles of previous generations. Howard Alden, Bruce Forman and Joshua Breakstone are oustanding players following in the footsteps of Kessel, Farlow and Raney. George Benson discovered Earl Klugh, a fingerstyle guitarist from Detroit. He has achieved a lot of popular success but some of his many recordings confirm he is a great jazz talent. Klugh has extended the tradition of playing jazz on the classical guitar established by Charlie Byrd and Laurindo Almeida. From Brazil came Toninho Horta, an excellent guitarist continuing and extending the traditions of Bola Sete and Baden Powell. The 1980s also saw many brilliant young Gypsy guitarists emerge on to the European jazz scene. They dazzled audiences with incredible techniques inspired by the virtuoso style of the legendary Django Reinhardt. Amongst the best of these are Boulou Ferre, Raphael Fays, Bireli Lagrene and Stochelo Rosenberg.

Now, as the late 1990s come to a close it can be said without a doubt that the world of jazz guitar is thriving. It has never been so varied. Virtually every style of jazz is being performed on the guitar to appreciative and discerning audiences throughout the world. With the recent introduction of the CD recording format record companies are reissuing at an incredible pace every old jazz recording of worth in their catalogues. Jazz guitar enthusiasts of the 1990s have the unique opportunity to hear recordings of most of the all time jazz greats from every era, and so study and learn from them. In the past fifteen years there has also been a proliferation in the availability of jazz guitar music, methods and instructional videos

Martin Taylor

from publishers all over the world. There are excellent jazz courses, short and long term, available at educational establishments in the USA and other countries. As the twentieth century draws to a close we can be sure this will be the most exciting period that jazz has ever known, a period in which the guitar will have a major role in the further evolution of jazz.

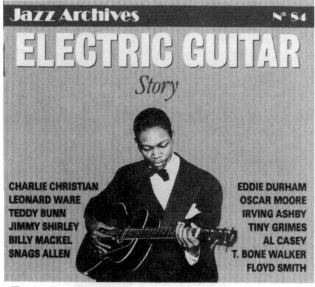

From the Pioneers to the Masters 1935/1945

23

SELECTED BOOKS -
for a general appreciation of the history of jazz and the jazz guitar.

The Book of Jazz	Leonard Feather	Horizon (1957)
The Encyclopaedia of Jazz	Leonard Feather	Horizon (1960)
The Encyclopaedia of Jazz in the Sixties		
	Leonard Feather	Horizon (1967)
The Encyclopaedia of Jazz in the Seventies		
	Feather/Gitler	Horizon (1976)
The Jazz Book Joachim	Berendt	Paladin (1976)
Jazz Masters of the Twenties	R.Hadlock	McMillan/Collier (1966)
Jazz Masters of the Forties	Ira Gitler	McMillan/Collier (1966)
Jazz Masters of the Fifties J.Goldberg		McMillan/Collier (1965)
Jazz Masters of the Fifties J.Goldberg		McMillan/Collier (1965)
Jazz Masters of the Transition	Williams	McMillan/Collier (1966)
Jazz Masters of New Orleans	Williams	McMillan/Collier (1967)
Who's Who of Jazz	John Chilton	Chilton Book Co. (1970)
The Making of Jazz	James Lincoln Collier	Granada (1978)
Jazz Now-edited Roger Cotterell		Quartet Book (1976)
A Pictorial History of Jazz	Keepnews/Grauer	Spring Books (1959)
Esquire's World of Jazz	L.W.Gillenson	Barker Co.(1963)
Combo USA	Rudi Blesh	Chilton Book Co.(1971)
The Devils Music-History of the Blues	Oakley	BBC Publications (1976)
Shining Trumpets	Rudi Blesh	Cassell (1958)
Early Jazz Gunther Schuller		Oxford University Press (1968)
The Story of Jazz	M.Stearns	Oxford University Press (1958)
Jazz Guitarists		Guitar Player Productions (1975)
Modern Jazz	Morgan & Horricks	Gollancz (1957)
The Art and Times of the Guitar	Grunfeld	Macmillan (1969)
Guitars Tom and Ann Mary Evans		Paddington (1977)
The Guitar Players	James Sallis	Quill (1982)
History of the Guitar in Jazz	Norman Mongan	Oak Pub.(1983)
The Jazz Guitarists	Stan Britt	Blandford Press (1984)
Swing to Bop	Gitler	Oxford University Press (1985)
Great Guitarists	Rich Kienzle	Facts On File (1985)
The New Grove Dictionary of Jazz		Macmillan (1988)
Jazz-The Essential Companion		Grafton Books (1987)
The Swing Era Gunther Schuller		Oxford University Press (1989)
Jazz Gitarristen (in German)	A.Schmitz	Oreos Verlag (1992)
Jazz John Fordham		Dorling Kindersley (1993)
The Guitar in Jazz-Anthology ed. James Sallis		
		University of Nebraska (1996)
Jazz Hot Magazine – May 1972 is devoted to jazz guitarists (in French)		

SELECTED RECORDINGS -
For a general appreciation of jazz guitar from the 1920s to the present day.

Pioneers of the Jazz Guitar	Yazoo 1057CD
Fun on the Frets-Early Jazz Guitar	Yazoo 1061CD
Fifty Years of Jazz Guitar	(2LPs) Columbia CG 33566
The Jazz Guitar Album	(2LPs) Verve 2683-065
Guitar Player	(2LPs) MCA 2-6002
The Guitarists (3LP/Book Set)	Time Life STL-J12
Jazz Guitar Anthology (6 LPs)	Joker SM 4023-4028
Great Blues Guitarists	Columbia 467894-2 CD
The Jazz Guitar	Jazz Roots CD 56007
Legends of Guitar Jazz Vol.1	Rhino R2 70717 CD
Legends of Guitar Jazz Vol.2	Rhino R2 70722 CD
Jazz Guitar Classics	Prestige OJC CD-6012-2 A
String of Guitars	Premier Jazz CD JA 10
Classic Jazz Guitar (3 CD Set)	Sequel Jazz NXT CD 174
Guitar Fire-Jazz Fusion Anthology	GRP GRP97082 CD
The Jazz Guitar Vol.1	Jazz Portraits CD14528
The Jazz Guitar Vol.2	Jazz Portraits CD14535
The Jazz Guitar Vol.3	Jazz Portraits CD14538
The Jazz Guitar Vol.4	Jazz Portraits CD14541
The Great Jazz Guitars	Fantasy OJCGS1
Jazz-Club Guitar	Verve 840035-2CD
Guitar Fire	GRP 97082CD
Blue Guitar	Blue Note CDP7 96581 2
Jazz Guitar	Columbia 481263 2 CD
Jazz Café-Guitar	RCA 1-26369 2 CD
Totally Jazz Guitar	VSOP CD240
Kings of Jazz Guitar	Hallmark 302832CD
Jazz Guitar-Sunday Times Collection	STCD 251
The Electric Guitar Story	Jazz Archives (84) 158522CD
Legends of Jazz Guitar (1) Video	Vestapol 13009
Legends of Jazz Guitar (2) Video	Vestapol 13033
Legends of Jazz Guitar (3) Video	Vestapol 13043

Leadbelly (Hudson 'Huddie' Leadbetter) with trumpeter Bunk Johnson.

Top British guitarists of 1937 at Abbey Road Studios, London. Left to right: Harry Pike, Don Stutely (bass), Sam Gelsley, Albert Harris and Ivor Mairants.

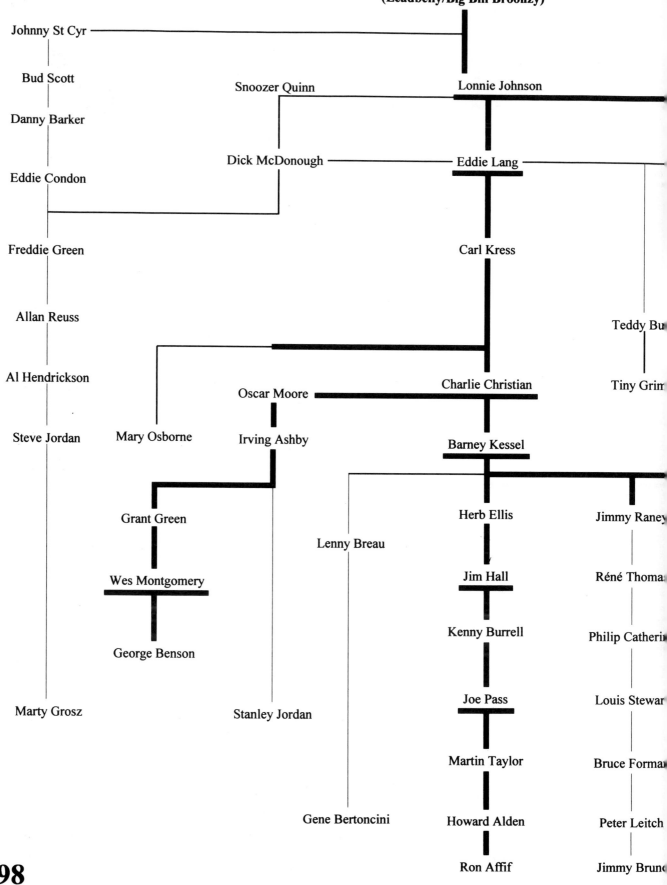

THE BLUES SINGERS/GUITARISTS
(Leadbelly/Big Bill Broonzy)

Johnny St Cyr

Bud Scott

Danny Barker

Snoozer Quinn

Lonnie Johnson

Dick McDonough

Eddie Lang

Eddie Condon

Freddie Green

Carl Kress

Allan Reuss

Teddy Bu

Al Hendrickson

Oscar Moore

Charlie Christian

Tiny Grim

Steve Jordan

Mary Osborne

Irving Ashby

Barney Kessel

Grant Green

Herb Ellis

Jimmy Raney

Lenny Breau

Wes Montgomery

Jim Hall

Réné Thoma

Kenny Burrell

Philip Catheri

George Benson

Joe Pass

Louis Stewar

Marty Grosz

Stanley Jordan

Martin Taylor

Bruce Forma

Gene Bertoncini

Howard Alden

Peter Leitch

1998

Ron Affif

Jimmy Brun

A Family Tree of the Jazz Guitar showing the main
stylistic influences from 1895-1998

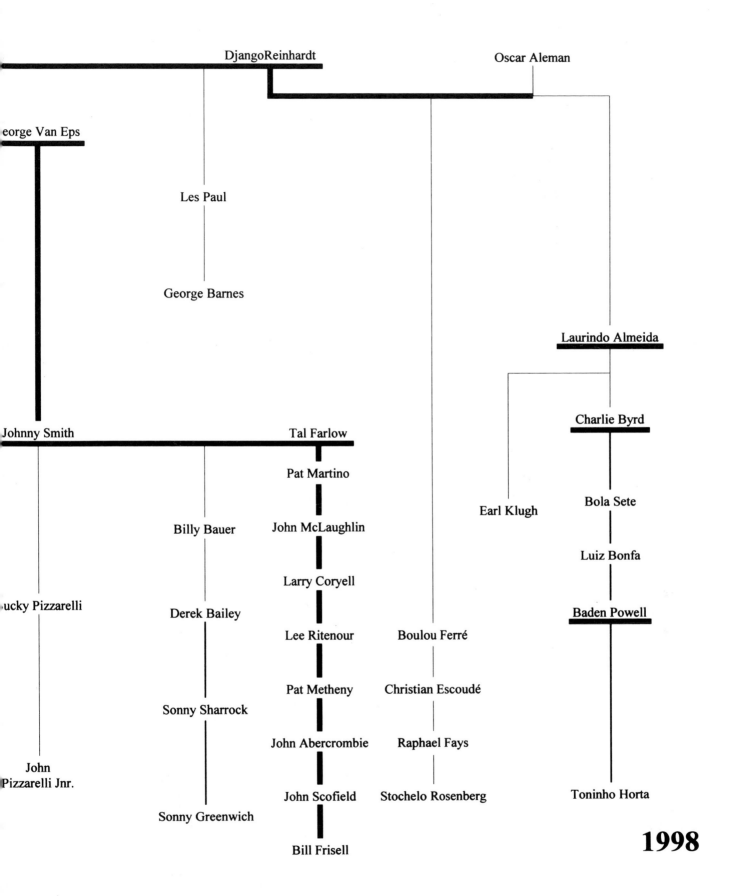

AFTER THOUGHTS Part I

DECCA RECORD No. 23136A

A MODERN GUITAR SOLO
WITH PIANO ACCOMPANIMENT
by

CARL KRESS

OTHER SOLOS
HELENA
LOVE SONG
PEG-LEG SHUFFLE
SUTTON MUTTON
(Taking It On The Lamb)
AFTER THOUGHTS Part II
AFTER THOUGHTS Part III

PRICE $100 IN U.S.A.

4/-

Clifford Essex Music Co. Ltd.
20 EARLHAM STREET, Cambridge Circus,
LONDON, W.C.2.

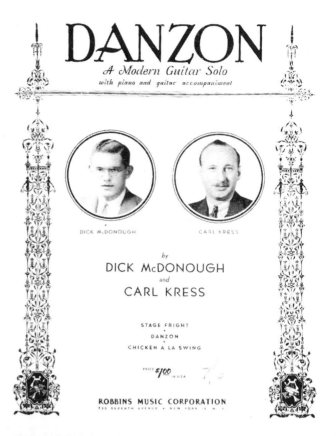

DANZON
A Modern Guitar Solo
with piano and guitar accompaniment

DICK McDONOUGH   CARL KRESS

by
DICK McDONOUGH
and
CARL KRESS

STAGE FRIGHT
DANZON
CHICKEN A LA SWING

PRICE $100 IN U.S.A.

ROBBINS MUSIC CORPORATION
799 SEVENTH AVENUE • NEW YORK 19 N.Y.

FEELIN' MY WAY
MODERN GUITAR SOLO
WITH PIANO OR GUITAR ACC.

by
EDDIE LANG
AMERICA'S FOREMOST GUITARIST

OTHER GUITAR SOLOS
PERFECT
MELODY MAN'S DREAM
EDDIE'S TWISTER
RAINBOW'S END
FEELIN' MY WAY
PICKIN' MY WAY
APRIL KISSES

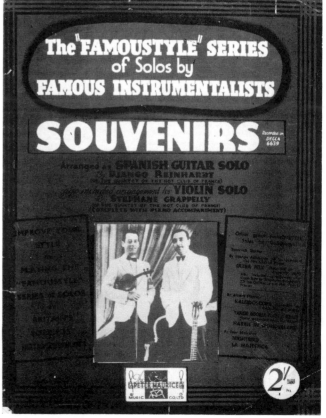

The "FAMOUSTYLE" SERIES
of Solos by
FAMOUS INSTRUMENTALISTS

SOUVENIRS

Arranged as SPANISH GUITAR SOLO
by DJANGO REINHARDT

VIOLIN SOLO
by STEPHANE GRAPPELLY

2/-

Examples of pre 1940 jazz guitar music.

28

THE JAZZ GUITAR
Its Players

DOWNBEAT MAGAZINE READERS 1936-1997
AND CRITICS 1953-1997 POLL WINNERS.

	READERS Winner	CRITICS Winner	Talent Deserving Wider Recognition
1936	Eddie Lang		
1937	Carmen Mastren		
1938	Benny Heller		
1939	Charlie Christian		
1940	Charlie Christian		
1941	Charlie Christian		
1942	Eddie Condon		
1943	Eddie Condon		
1944	Allan Reuss		
1945	Oscar Moore		
1946	Oscar Moore		
1947	Oscar Moore		
1948	Oscar Moore		
1949	Billy Bauer		
1950	Billy Bauer		
1951	Les Paul		
1952	Les Paul		
1953	Les Paul	Barney Kessel	Johnny Smith
1954	Johnny Smith	Jimmy Raney	Tal Farlow
1955	Johnny Smith	Jimmy Raney	Howard Roberts
1956	Barney Kessel	Tal Farlow	Dick Garcia
1957	Barney Kessel	Tal Farlow	Kenny Burrell
1958	Barney Kessel	Freddie Green	Jim Hall
1959	Barney Kessel	Barney Kessel	Charlie Byrd
1960	Barney Kessel	Kenny Burrell	Wes Montgomery
1961	Wes Montgomery	Wes Montgomery	Les Spann
1962	Wes Montgomery	Wes Montgomery	Grant Green
1963	Charlie Byrd	Jim Hall & Wes Montgomery	Joe Pass
1964	Jim Hall	Jim Hall	Gabor Szabo & Attila Zoller
1965	Jim Hall	Jim Hall	Bola Sete
1966	Wes Montgomery	Wes Montgomery	Rene Thomas
1967	Wes Montgomery	Wes Montgomery	George Benson
1968	Kenny Burrell	Kenny Burrell	Larry Coryell
1969	Kenny Burrell	Kenny Burrell	Pat Martino
1970	Kenny Burrell	Kenny Burrell	Sonny Sharrock
1971	Kenny Burrell	Kenny Burrell	Dennis Budimir
1972	John McLaughlin	Kenny Burrell	Tiny Grimes & Pat Martino
1973	John McLaughlin	Kenny Burrell	George Benson & Attila Zoller
1974	John McLaughlin	Jim Hall	Ralph Towner
1975	Joe Pass	Joe Pass	John Abercrombie
1976	George Benson	Jim Hall	John Abercrombie
1977	Joe Pass	Jim Hall	Derek Bailey
1978	Joe Pass	Joe Pass	Pat Metheny
1979	Joe Pass	Jim Hall	Philip Catherine
1980	Joe Pass	Joe Pass	James 'Blood' Ulmer
1981	Joe Pass	Joe Pass	James 'Blood' Ulmer
1982	Joe Pass	Jim Hall	Emily Remler
1983	Pat Metheny	Jim Hall	Bruce Foreman & Emily Remler
1984	Joe Pass	Joe Pass	Emily Remler
1985	Stanley Jordan	Jim Hall	Emily Remler
1986	Pat Metheny	John Scofield	Bill Frisell
1987	Pat Metheny	Jim Hall	Bill Frisell
1988	Pat Metheny	Jim Hall	Bill Frisell
1989	Pat Metheny	John Scofield	Emily Remler
1990	El: Pat Metheny	Bill Frisell	Sonny Sharrock
	Ac: Jim Hall	Jim Hall	Emily Remler
1991	El: Pat Metheny	John Scofield	Kevin Eubanks & Sonny Sharrock
	Ac: John McLaughlin	Jim Hall	Egberto Gismonti
1992	El: John Scofield	John Scofield	Sonny Sharrock
	Ac: John McLaughlin	John McLaughlin	Howard Alden
1993	El: John Scofield	John Scofield	Mike Stern
	Ac: John McLaughlin	John McLaughlin	Howard Alden
1994	El: John Scofield	John Scofield	Mike Stern
	Ac: John McLaughlin	John McLaughlin	Fareed Haque
1995	El: John Scofield	John Scofield	Mark Whitfield
	Ac: John McLaughlin	John McLaughlin	Howard Alden
1996	John Scofield	Bill Frisell	Howard Alden
1997	Bill Frisell	John Scofield	Charlie Hunter

* From 1990-1995 Downbeat included both electric and acoustic guitar categories.

JOHN ABERCROMBIE
Born-Portchester, New York, USA
16 December 1944

John Abercrombie

PHOTO: JIM BENGSTON/COURTESY ECM

John Abercrombie first became interested in music during his school years in Greenwich, Connecticut.   Originally influenced by popular artists of the day including Bill Haley and Elvis Presley, he took up the guitar at the age of fourteen. By the late 1950s he was already playing in various rock bands at high school. It was at this time that Abercrombie heard his first jazz guitar records. The jazz artistry of Barney Kessel, Tal Farlow, Jimmy Raney, and Johnny Smith, in particular, caused a deep impression on him. As a result he decided to enter the Berklee College of Music in Boston from 1962-1966 to study the guitar and music in depth. Whilst he was at Berklee he studied with Jack Petersen and Herb Pomeroy.

After leaving Berklee Abercrombie spent eight years in Boston gaining experience with various local jazz groups. His first significant job was in 1967-68 with organist Johnny `Hammond' Smith. At this time he was influenced by the guitar style of Jim Hall. In 1969 Abercrombie left Boston and moved to New York. He played for a short while with drummer Chico Hamilton's group. After returning to Boston for a short while he rejoined Hamilton in 1971 to play at the Montreux Jazz Festival in Switzerland. He was then given the opportunity to write on a regular basis for this group which helped broaden his musical ability. In New York Abercrombie became much in demand as a session musician recording with Gil Evans, Gato Barbieri, Barry Miles, the Brecker Brothers and other top jazz artists. He first gained real international recognition when he joined drummer Billy Cobham's 'Spectrum' jazz/fusion band, which also featured the Brecker Brothers.

Abercrombie was then fortunate to meet Manfred Eicher of ECM records. He was given a contract to record for this important company and his first release , 'Timeless', a collaboration with Jan Hammer and Jack DeJohnette, was a big success. In November 1975 ECM released his first 'Gateway' recording with bassist Dave Holland and DeJohnette. Since that time Abercrombie has made many recordings for ECM both as leader of his own groups and as a sideman. Many of these have received high critical acclaim. His collaboration with Ralph Towner in a guitar duo was particularly outstanding.

Since the 1980s John Abercrombie has developed into one of the most influential and innovative jazz guitarists of the day. His guitar style reflects many of the best trends of contemporary rock and jazz/fusion, yet retains the swing and bebop traditions of earlier years.

SELECTED RECORDINGS

Sorcery w/Jack DeJohnette	Prestige P10081 LP
Timeless	ECM 1047 CD
Gateway	ECM 1061 CD
Gateway II	ECM 1105 CD
Saragossa Sea with Ralph Towner	ECM 1080 CD
Characters	ECM 1117 CD
Arcade	ECM 1133 CD
John Abercrombie Quartet	ECM 1164 CD
M	ECM 1191 CD
Night	ECM 1272 CD
Current Events	ECM 1311 CD
Getting There	ECM 1321 CD
Abercrombie Trio	ECM 1390 CD
Animato	ECM 1411 CD
Nosmo King	SteepleChase SCCD 31301
Now It Can Be Played	SteepleChase SCCD 31314
Hymn Owl	R2 79250 CD
Works	ECM 837 275-2 CD
While We're Young	ECM 1489 CD
Emerald City	Pathfinder PTF 8701-CD
November	ECM 1502 CD
Speak of the Devil	ECM 1511 CD
Tactics	ECM 1623 CD
While We Were Young w/Andy La Verne	Double Time Records CD-110

Jazz Guitar – Instructional Video	Homespun Tapes

SELECTED READING

Interview	Downbeat, February 1976
Interview	Guitar Player, February 1976
Profile	Guitar, November 1977
Interview	Guitar Player, November 1986
Profile	Jazz Times, August 1993
Article	Downbeat, November 1994
Interview	Guitar Player, February 1995
Article	Jazz Times, December 1995

SELECTED MUSIC

Jazz Guitar Solos-John Abercrombie	Advance Music

BERNARD ADDISON
Born-Anapolis, Maryland, USA
15 April 1905

As a teenager Addison co-led a band with Claude Hopkins in Washington D.C. He then moved to New York where he joined the house band at Small's Paradise Club. He remained there until 1929 after which he worked for many years in various big bands and small groups. Addison worked as a sideman with some of the biggest names of the day in jazz including Louis Armstrong, Fletcher Henderson, Jerry Roll Morton, Fats Waller, Adrian Rollini and Art Tatum. For a while he worked as an accompanist to both 'The Mills Brothers' and ' The Ink Spots'. Right through to the 1940s Addison continued to work with prominent jazz musicians including Teddy Bunn, Mezz Mezzrow, Sidney Bechet and Stuff Smith. He took part in many recording sessions including one in London in 1936 with saxophonist Benny Carter.

Bernard Addison continued to take an active part in jazz until the early 1960s. After that time he was mainly involved in teaching the guitar until his retirement.

Bernard Addison

SELECTED RECORDINGS

Bernard Addison All Stars	77 Records 77LA 12/8 LP
Bechet/Mezzrow Feetwarmers	Storyville SLP 4028 LP
Louis Armstrong Orchestra	Black & Blue BLE 59.226-2 LP

RON AFFIF
Born-Pittsburgh, Pennsylvania, USA
30 December 1965

Ron Affif first studied guitar at the age of 12 with his uncle Ron Anthony, the leading West Coast guitarist. Affif's father was a professional boxer who had a great love of jazz and was a friend of Miles Davis. For a while Ron Affif studied with Pittsburgh guitarist Joe Negri and when he was 18 he decided to become a professional musician moving to the West Coast to live near his uncle. Affif worked with Jack Sheldon, Pete Christlieb, Dick Berk, Sherman Ferguson and bassist Andy Simpkins.

In 1989 Affif returned to New York. There he has worked with a wide variety of jazz artists including singer Sheila Jordan, pianist Billy Mays and saxophonist Ralph LaLama. Ron Affif , a Pablo recording artist, is now regarded as one of the USA's finest jazz guitarists.

SELECTED RECORDINGS

Ron Affif	Pablo PACD 2310-948-2
Ron Affif - Vierd Blues	Pablo PACD 2310-954-2
Ron Affif Trio - 52nd Street	Pablo PACD 2310-958-2
Ringside-Ron Affif Trio	Pablo PACD 2310-962-2

SELECTED READING

Profile	Jazz Times, July/August 1996
Profile	Downbeat, May 1997
Profile	Guitar Player, December 1997

Ron Affif

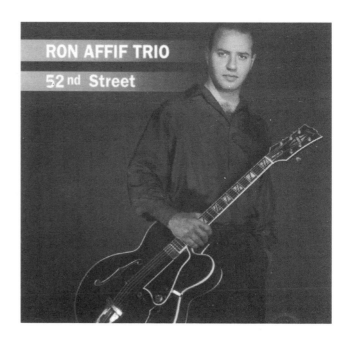

HOWARD ALDEN
Born-Newport Beach, California, USA
17 October 1958

Howard Alden began to play the guitar at the age of ten. He was originally self taught, inspired by the recordings of leading jazz musicians, including those of guitarists Charlie Christian, Barney Kessel and George Van Eps. By his early teens he had progressed to a level that allowed him to play professionally in the Los Angeles area. At the age of sixteen he took some formal lessons with guitarists Jimmy Wyble and Joe Diorio. He then teamed up with trombonist Dan Barrett and they played together for a while in many of Los Angeles' jazz nightspots.

In 1979 Alden was hired by Red Norvo for a season in Atlantic City. The young guitarist decided to live in New York City in 1982. Since that time Alden has proved to be one of the most talented jazz guitarists around, playing with a wide variety of jazz artists including Warren Vache Jnr, Ruby Braff, Woody Herman, Joe Bushkin, Monty Alexander, Flip Philips and George Van Eps. Since signing for the Concord label he has made many excellent recordings both as leader and sideman. In the last few years Alden has toured throughout the world appearing in important jazz festivals and at many leading jazz clubs. He has now gained recognition as one of the most outstanding and creative jazz guitarists of the day. In 1990 Alden was voted 'Best Emerging Talent - Guitar' in the 1st Annual Jazz Times magazine Critic's Poll. Most recently his association, both on the concert platform and in the recording studio, with veteran guitarist George Van Eps has been particularly significant.

Howard Alden

PHOTO: NORMAN WILSON

SELECTED RECORDINGS

Swing Street w/ Dan Barrett	Concord CCD-4349
Howard Alden Trio plus Guests	Concord CCD-4378
Howard Alden Trio w/Monty Alexander	Concord CCD-4424
The ABQ Salutes Buck Clayton	Concord CCD-4395
Swinging into Prominence	Famous Door HL 152 CD
Ruby Braff- Me, Myself And I	Concord CCD-4381
Ruby Braff- Bravure Eloquence	Concord CCD-4423
No Amps Allowed	Chiaroscuro CR(D)-303
13 Strings w/ George Van Eps	Concord CCD-4464
Mysterioso	Concord CCD-4487
Duo w/Harry Allen	Master Mix CHECD 00106
Hand-Crafted Swing w/ George Van Eps	Concord CCD-4556
Seven & Seven w/George Van Eps	Concord CCD-4584
Plays Bill Evans	Concord CCD-4621
Encore! – Duo with Ken Peplowski	Concord CCD-4654
Concord Jazz Collection	Concord CCD-4672
Keepin' Time w/George Van Eps	Concord CCD-4713
Take You Pick	Concord CCD-4743
A Good Likeness	Concord CCD-4544
Duo w/Ken Poplowski	Concord CCD-4556
Just The Two Of Us w/Richard Carr	Audiophile 253 CD

SELECTED READING

Interview	Jazz Journal, February 1989
Interview	Guitar Player, January 1990
Profile	Jazz Times, August 1992
Interview	Just Jazz Guitar, February 1995
Profile	Guitar Player, November 1996
Profile	JAZZIZ, August 1997

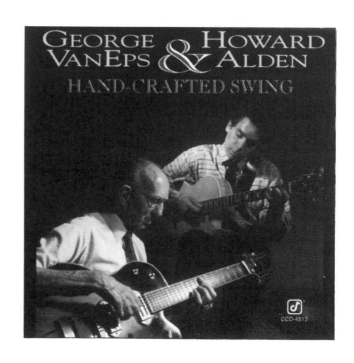

OSCAR ALEMAN
Born-OSCAR MARCELO ALEMAN
Resistencia, Province of El Chaco, Argentina
20 February 1909
Died-Buenos Aires, Argentina
10 October 1980

Oscar Aleman

Little is known today of the brilliant guitarist who earned a well-deserved reputation in Europe from 1928-39. It is interesting to note that many leading jazz critics in the 1930s wrote of their very high regard for Oscar Aleman. There is no doubt on listening to some of the recordings made in Paris during the late 1930s that he was a jazz guitarist of considerable talent.

Oscar Aleman's father, Jorge Aleman Moreira, was a guitarist who led a professional folk group. As a child Aleman appeared with this group as a dancer. His first musical instrument was the four-stringed Brazilian ukulele, the cavaquinho, after which he took up the guitar. By the time he was twelve Aleman was already a star performer. He was hired to play with a group called the Moreira Sextet. With this group Aleman went to Brazil and it was there that he heard his first jazz record. In 1925 Aleman and guitarist Gaston Bueno Lobo formed a duo called 'Les Loups'. In 1927 they worked in and around Buenos Aires. Though times were not easy the guitarists were given the opportunity to tour Spain backing dancer Harry Fleming. At the end of this tour both Bueno Lobo and Aleman decided to stay on in Spain working in a Belga orchestra. In 1932 the duo decided to split up. Josephine Baker, who at that time was the number one cabaret artiste in Paris, heard of Aleman's exceptional musical talent. She offered him the guitar seat in her accompanying band at the Cafe de Paris. Through working with Baker in Paris, Aleman's guitar talent became well known. He worked and recorded for a time with violinist Svend Asmussen. At one time he replaced Django Reinhardt in Freddy Taylor's orchestra. It is obvious from listening to their recordings that both these great guitarists had some influence on each other's playing. Aleman, who said that Eddie Lang and Bill Coleman were also important influences, made several records with Danny Polo under the supervision of Leonard Feather.

In 1941 Aleman, who was not happy with the German occupation of France, returned to Buenos Aires. For eighteen years Oscar Aleman had devoted his career to the jazz guitar but as time went on popular demand had swung towards Latin American music rhythms and Aleman appeared mainly in diverse popular dance bands for the rest of his professional career.

An example of the respect that Aleman had amongst leading jazzmen was shown when Duke Ellington, on a visit to Buenos Aires in September 1968, requested the U.S. Ambassador there to find out where Aleman lived as he wished to meet him.

Aleman took part in an unsuccessful tour of Spain and Portugal in 1959. After his return to Argentina Oscar Aleman lived in Buenos Aires where he devoted the last years of his life to teaching and playing the guitar.

SELECTED RECORDINGS

The Guitar of Oscar Aleman	The Old Master TOM 31 LP
Oscar Aleman Vol 2	The Old Master TOM41 LP
Oscar Aleman '72	Redondell SL-10508 LP
Oscar Aleman w/Jorge Anders	Redondell SL-10511 LP
Oscar Aleman Swing Guitar Legend	Rambler 106 LP
Special Guitares	Jazz Time EMI 798997-2CD
Buenos Aires-Paris 1928-1943	Night and Day FA 020 CD

SELECTED READING

Jazz Solography	Vol.4 Jan Evensmo
Profile	Jazz Journal International, April & May 1982

PHOTO: COURTESY OSCAR ALEMAN

Laurindo Almeida

LAURINDO ALMEIDA

Born-LAURINDO JOSÉ ALMEIDA NOBREGA NETO
Prainha, Santos, Brazil, 2 September 1917
Died – Los Angeles, USA, 26 July 1995

Laurindo Almeida was one of the most important guitarists of the 20th century. He was one of the few musicians to achieve great success in both the classical and jazz fields of music. He was the total musician, not only a brilliant soloist and accompanist, with a distinctive warm sound, but also an outstanding composer and arranger. His overall musical talent and original concepts gained him enormous international respect amongst his peers in the 60-plus years of his professional career.

Almeida received his early music tuition from his mother, who was a concert pianist. She hoped that he too would become a pianist, but Almeida fell in love with a guitar owned by his sister Maria. In a short time it was evident to all around him that he was on the way to being a master guitarist. In 1936 he signed on as guitarist on a Brazilian cruise liner, the 'Cuyaba'. During the voyage to Europe he absorbed a wide variety of musical styles including his first exposure to jazz. On a visit to Paris he heard the 'Hot Club of France' string quintet, starring the Gypsy virtuoso guitarist Django Reinhardt. This group made a great impression on him. On his return to Brazil he settled in Rio and took on the post of staff guitarist/arranger with Radio Mayrink Veiga. By 1944 Almeida had reached the heights of his profession in Brazil. In 1947 he decided to move to the USA, settling in Hollywood. Here he worked as a studio musician in films, and as a classical soloist with violinist Elizabeth Waldo. His interest in jazz helped him get the guitar seat in the famous Stan Kenton orchestra, which became a legend over the whole world for its innovations in jazz music. His most outstanding recordings with Kenton were his solo work in Pete Rugolo's *Lament*, and his own composition *Amazonia*. In 1950 Almeida left the Kenton orchestra to lead a more diverse musical career.

In 1953-54 Almeida joined forces with saxophonist Bud Shank and, with the addition of bass and drums, recorded three brilliant recordings entitled 'Brazilliance'. These recordings were the forerunners of bossa nova, mixing Brazilian rhythms with American jazz. Almeida's impeccable taste as a composer, arranger and guitarist shines through on all these recordings. It was during this time he made the first of many solo guitar albums of both classical and popular music for the Capitol and Decca labels. In 1963-64 he toured the world as a featured soloist with the Modern Jazz Quartet. This association originally began as a project for the 1963 Monterey Jazz Festival. In 1966 he made the American debut recordings of Radamés

Gnattali's *Concerto de Copacabana* (Capital SP 8625), and the Villa-Lobos Guitar Concerto (Capital SP 8638). Throughout his career Almeida was years ahead of his peers in his promotion of the music of Barrios, Gnattali, Villa-Lobos and other outstanding South American composers. From the 1960s he performed, recorded and published (through his Brazilliance Publishing Company) the guitar works of these and other great South American composers.

In the 1970s Almeida once more gained great international popularity with his 'LA Four' quartet, which featured saxophonist Bud Shank, bassist Ray Brown and drummer Shelley Manne. This group was a direct continuation of his original Brazilliance quartet.

From the 1970s right up to the time of his death Laurindo Almeida remained one of the most sought-after guitarist/composer/arrangers in Hollywood. He often concertised and recorded with his wife Deltra (Didi) Eamon, the talented Canadian soprano, whom he married in 1971.

Laurindo Almeida won ten Grammy Awards and, as well as performing on the guitar, had a long list of film scores to his name including, amongst others, *Viva Zapata, The Godfather, A Star is Born, Camelot* and *The Agony and The Ecstasy*. He was a prolific composer. One of the Grammy Awards was for his composition *Discantus* which tied with Igor Stravinsky in 1961 for best contemporary composition. His many original works included concertos for guitar and orchestra (he recorded his first concerto on the Concord Concerto label CC-2001 – in November 1979) and his classical guitar quintet. Almeida received an Oscar for composing the music to the animated fable *The Magic Tree*. In October 1977, he was awarded the Certificate of Appreciation from the American String Teachers Association for 'a lifetime of dedicated and distinguished service to the guitar in the United States'. He also published many valuable books of arrangements of classical and jazz standards for guitar, and an excellent tutor. These works are an enormous contribution to the 20th century repertoire of the guitar. He donated his unique collection of over 1000 items of music and original scores to the California State University at Northridge.

Laurindo Almeida was one of the busiest and most popular guitarists in the United States. There is no doubt that through his enormous output of records, publications and many concert appearances, he was one of the most influential guitarists on the North American Scene for over forty years.

SELECTED RECORDINGS

Brazilliance 1	Capitol/World Pacific 96339 CD
Brazilliance 2	Capitol/World Pacific 96102 CD
The Guitar Artistry of Laurindo Almeida	Guitar Masters GNR 104-97CD
Guitar from Ipanema	Capitol ST2187 LP
Modern Jazz Quartet	Atlantic ATL 1429 CD

Duo with Ray Brown	Century City CCR80102 LP
Sammy Davis Jnr	Sandstone CD 233081
Stan Getz/Bossa Nova	Verve 823 149-2 CD
L.A.Four Scores	Concord CCD-6008
L.A.Four Concierto	Concord CCD-4018
Latin Guitar	Dobre DR1000
Virtuoso Guitar	Laserlight 15-296CD
Guitar Player Collection	MCA MCA2-6002
L.A.Four-Pavane	East Wind EW10003
L.A.Four-Watch What Happens	Concord CCD-4063
Chamber Jazz	Concord CCD-4084
Brazilian Soul	Concord CCD-4150
L.A. Four-Just Friends	Concord CCD-4199
Latin Odyssey	Concord CCD-4211
Artistry in Rhythm	Concord CCD-4238
Brazilian Masters	Concord CCD-4389
Otra Vez	Concord CCD-4497

SELECTED READING

Profile	Downbeat, July 1958
Profile	Guitar Player, August 1968
Profile	Guitar, July 1974
Profile	Frets, June 1979
Profile	Guitar, November 1979
Profile	Jazz Journal, August 1990
Profile	Classical Guitar, April 1992
Interview	Acoustic Guitar, September/October 1993

SELECTED MUSIC

Guitar Method	Criterion Music Corp.
Guitariana Vol 1	Brazilliance Music
Guitariana Vol 2	Brazilliance Music
Bossa Guitarra Six Solos	Criterion Music Corp.
Contemporary Moods	Robbins Music Corp.
Guitar Tutor	Gwyn Publishing Co.
Popular Brazilian Music	Brazilliance Music
Broadway Solo Guitar	CPP/Belwin

Laurindo Almeida with the Modern Jazz Quartet.

PETER ALMQVIST
Born-Lund, Sweden
17 July 1957

Peter Almqvist's first musical interest was in The Beatles and other rock and pop groups. His father, a former executive for the Levin and C.F. Martin guitar companies, is an enthusiastic jazz guitar fan. He encouraged his son to listen to his recordings of Barney Kessel, Tal Farlow, Jim Hall and Wes Montgomery. Whilst still at high school Almqvist decided to make music and the guitar his career.

He met fellow Swedish guitarist Ulf Wakenius in 1978, and in 1980 they formed the jazz duo 'Guitars Unlimited'. This brilliant duo won international recognition through their many concert and television performances.

In recent years Peter Almqvist has established himself as one of Sweden's best jazz guitarists appearing in concert and on recordings with his jazz trio.

Peter Almqvist

PHOTO: KARL JANTZEN

SELECTED RECORDINGS

Dig Myself & I - Peter Almqvist Trio	Storyville STCD 4201 CD
Peter Almqvist Trio with Horace Parlan	Storyville STCD 4205 CD

WITH GUITARS UNLIMITED

Introducing Guitars Unlimited	Sonet SNTF-923 LP
Acoustic Shokk	Sonet SNTF-953 LP
Lets Vamos	Sonet SNTF-978 LP
Three for the Road	Sonet SNT 1006 CD
Phraserace	COOP 8303 CD
Extraordinaire	Musik Musik MM 18CD

PETER ALMQVIST TRIO

WITH HORACE PARLAN

STORYVILLE

TUCK ANDRESS
Born-Tulsa, Oklahoma, USA
28 October 1952

Tuck Andress's first interest in music began as a child studying classical music on the piano. At the age of fourteen he began to play rock music on the guitar. After he joined the high school stage-band Andress was exposed to the jazz artistry of Wes Montgomery, George Benson, Miles Davis and others. After leaving school he entered Stanford University where he finally majored in Music. He also studied classical guitar there with Stanley Buetens and Charles Ferguson.

While still a student at Stanford, Andress joined a well known soul group in Oklahoma called the Gap Band. Another guitarist in this group, Odel Stokes was to be a great influence on Andress, as was another guitarist from Tulsa, Tommy Crook. For some time the young guitarist commuted back and forth between California and Oklahoma. After leaving university in the mid 1970s he joined a show band in San Francisco. In the band was a young singer Patti Cathcart. After the band split up the two decided to form a vocal/guitar duo playing a mixture of jazz, pop, blues and other fusion music. Within a relatively short time Tuck and Patti enjoyed considerable commercial success with their recordings, club and concert appearances.

Tuck Andress has emerged into the 1990s as one of the most talented and original jazz guitarists of the day. He has fused jazz pick technique together with classical right-hand finger style, and, both as a soloist and accompanist, developed a unique melodic and rhythmic jazz style.

Tuck Andress

PHOTO: MAURICE J. SUMMERFIELD

SELECTED RECORDINGS

Tears of Joy	Tuck & Patti	Wyndham Hill	WH-0111 CD
Love Warriors	Tuck & Patti	Wyndham Hill	WH-0116 CD
Reckless Precision	Tuck Andress	Wyndham Hill	WH-0124 CD
Dream	Tuck & Patti	Wyndham Hill	WH-0134 CD
Hymns, Carols and Songs	Tuck Andress	Wyndham Hill	WH-0135 CD

Tuck Andress	Instructional Video	Hot Licks

SELECTED READING

Tuck Andress	Private Lesson	Guitar Player, April 1988
Profile		Jazz Times, June 1991
Profile		Jazziz, April/May 1991
Profile		Guitar Player, June 1995
Interview		Fingerstyle Guitar, Nov/Dec 1995

RON ANTHONY
Born-Pittsburgh, Pennsylvania, USA
16 December 1933

Ron Anthony studied at the Fillon School of Music, and then Duquesne University where he majored in string bass and minored in piano. He worked as a musician for five years in the New York area. He played with pianist George Shearing's quintet in 1962 and 1963, and for a further four years from 1971. In 1965 Anthony moved to Los Angeles and in 1966 and 1967 worked with singer Vic Damone. Around this time he also played with Les Brown's and Stan Kenton's bands. From 1986 to 1995 Ron Anthony worked almost exclusively for Frank Sinatra.

A stylish jazz guitarist Ron Anthony is also a talented singer, composer and educator. From his home in Toluka Lake, California he teaches privately and plays with his jazz trio in local clubs. He has also taught at Pierce College, MIT and Los Angeles Music Academy. His nephew Ron Affif is one of the best of the current generation of USA jazz guitarists.

Ron Anthony

SELECTED RECORDINGS

Rare Form - George Shearing	Capitol
Road to Morocco - Frank Marocco	Discovery DS 854 LP
Same Time, Same Place	Digital Fixed Medium DFM 5017CD

SELECTED MUSIC

Comping	Dale Zdenek Publications

DON ARNONE
Born-Elizabeth, New Jersey, USA
2 December 1920

Don Arnone began to play the guitar at the age of thirteen. He studied briefly with two guitar teachers, including Harry Volpe, but then decided to teach himself. He listened to, and studied, the recordings of acoustic jazz guitar greats Eddie Lang, Carl Kress and Django Reinhardt. But his biggest influence at that time was George Van Eps.

Arnone first started playing professionally at the age of eighteen in commercial groups around New Jersey. In 1941 he entered the US Army and for a time played in the army band. In 1946, after leaving the services, Arnone returned briefly to New Jersey. He then decided to move to New York. Here with the help of Al Caiola he started to work on a regular basis in the CBS studios.

Arnone retained an interest in jazz and in 1958 met Tal Farlow and Johnny Smith. Farlow hired him to play on his first recording as leader, together with Joe Morello on drums, and Clyde Lombardi on bass. Over the years Arnone has been very involved in studio work. He has played on many national radio and television shows including those hosted by Ed Sullivan, Steve Allen, Jack Benny, Fred Waring and Jack Paar. Arnone has had a long professional association with guitarists Al Caiola and Tony Mottola, making numerous recordings with them on the Command and other record labels. He has recorded with Mundell Lowe on a RCA jazz release, and also with singers Bette Midler and Barbra Streisand.

Don Arnone

SELECTED RECORDINGS

Serenade in Blue	Golden Crest CR 3003 LP
Tal Farlow Quartet	Blue Note 5042 LP
Mundell Lowe Quintet	RCA LJM 3002 LP
Tony Mottola And The Quad Guitars	Project 3 5078 LP
Billy Eckstine-At Basin Street East	Emarcy 832592 CD LP
Guitars, Guitars, Guitars-Al Caiola	United Artists UAS 6077 LP
Percussion And Guitars	Time 52000 LP

SELECTED READING

Interview	Guitar Player, February 1978
Interview	Just Jazz Guitar, February 1995

Don Arnone, 1960

IRVING ASHBY
Born-Somerville, Massachusetts, USA
29 December 1920
Died-Perris, California, USA
22 April 1987

Irving Ashby was born into a musical family. His mother was a pianist and his brother played the tenor guitar. Ashby taught himself the rudiments of guitar playing on this four-stringed instrument. For a time he became interested in guitar construction and worked as an assistant in the workshops of the Boston guitar maker, Stromberg. In 1938 Ashby played in various local dance groups. He planned to enter Boston University to major in Art and Writing but received an offer to join the Lionel Hampton band. He decided this offer was too good to turn down. Although the standard of his music sight reading was not too good at the time, Ashby had an excellent ear. With this natural ability he was able to follow the band's many written arrangements. His featured solo with the band was his arrangement of 'Prelude in C Sharp Minor' by Rachmaninoff. He had received a scholarship several years earlier on the basis of this solo when he was at the New England Conservatory of Music. His guitar style at the time was greatly influenced by Charlie Christian whom he had met and befriended.

During World War II Irving Ashby spent his service in the US Army Band. In 1946, after the end of the war, Nat 'King' Cole offered him the guitar seat in his famous trio. This had recently been vacated by Oscar Moore and was at that time the prize job for guitarists. Ashby worked with Cole's trio for four and a half years. As the singer/pianist became more and more commercial Ashby felt musically stifled. He decided to quit the trio and in 1951 became the first guitarist with the then newly formed Oscar Peterson trio. In 1952 he toured as Peterson's guitarist with Norman Granz's 'Jazz at the Philharmonic' and this period probably marked the peak of Ashby's jazz career. Although not an innovator on his chosen instrument Irving Ashby was a fine musician and his talents have really been underestimated by guitarists and the jazz world as a whole. He lived the last years of his life in Perris, California, teaching the guitar and occasionally recording, but spent most of his time sign painting and drawing architectural plans.

Irving Ashby

| Guitar Player Collection | MCA MCA 2-6002 LP |
| Memoirs | Accent AGS 5091 LP |

SELECTED READING

| Interview | Guitar Player, September 1974 |

SELECTED MUSIC

| Guitar Work Book | Trebla Publishing Co. |

SELECTED RECORDINGS

Nat King Cole Trio	Swing House SWH-12 LP
Oscar Peterson Trio	Columbia 33C 1037 LP
Andre Previn Trio Plays Ellington	Monarch LP 204
J.A.T.P.Concert	Verve 2610024 LP
California Guitar	Famous Door HL102 LP

GUITAR

All the best to:
Maurice Summerfield
1/14/79

WORK BOOK

STAN AYEROFF
Born-STANLEY AYEROFF
Culver City, California, USA
16 February 1950

Stan Ayeroff is well known to jazz guitar lovers throughout the world by his many books of excellent arrangements for jazz guitar.

Ayeroff currently works as a freelance musician and composer in the Los Angeles area. He plays in jazz clubs, is involved in the recording studios and writes music for films and advertising. Included amongst the many well known musicians he has worked with are singer Vicki Carr and rhythm and blues artist Delbert McClinton. Ayeroff has also worked with the West Coast Pop Art Experimental Band.

SELECTED MUSIC

Jazz Masters: Charlie Christian	Music Sales Corporation
Jazz Masters: Django Reinhardt	Music Sales Corporation
Play It Again, Stan	Warner Brothers
Best In Contemporary Standards	Warner Brothers
Best of Gershwin for Guitar	Warner Brothers
Cavatina & 20 Movie Themes for Guitar	Warner Brothers

Stan Ayeroff

PHOTO: COURTESY STAN AYEROFF

Al Avola c.1938, guitarist with the Artie Shaw Band for many years.

PHOTO: COURTESY JAZZ JOURNAL

ELEK BACSIK
Born-Budapest,Hungary
22 May 1926

Elek Bacsik, a Hungarian Gypsy, started playing the violin at the age of four. As a youth he played both Gypsy and classical music on the violin. He went on to study the violin at the conservatory in Budapest with George Cziffra.

During World War II he was in the Hungarian army. After the war he left Hungary for Vienna and then Switzerland. There he played in 'continental' style light music groups. In 1945, he took up the guitar. Within a few years Bacsik was already regarded as one of Europe's finest jazz guitarists. In 1949 he joined the Hazy Osterwald band in Switzerland. He went on a long European tour with this band. In 1959 he ended up in Paris and played at the renowned 'Mars' jazz club with pianist Art Simmons and bassist Michael Gaudry. This engagement lasted for two years. For the next few years, until 1966, Bacsik played with many visiting U.S. jazzmen including trumpeter Dizzy Gillespie. In 1962, he recorded in Paris an excellent session entitled 'The Eclectic Elek Bacsik'. This recording which fully displays Bacsik's instrumental virtuosity and inventive mind, is still one of the best European jazz guitar records of the period.

Elek Bacsik

In 1966 Elek Bacsik decided to move to the U.S.A. At first he spent much of his time in Las Vegas doing commercial work in hotel bands with little involvement in jazz. In 1974 promoter Bob Thiele encouraged him to come out of the obscurity of Las Vegas and he once again devoted some time to jazz. In 1974 a recording, produced by Bob Thiele, was released featuring Bacsik's jazz artistry on both violin and guitar. He was accompanied by pianist Hank Jones, bassist Richard Davis and drummer Grady Tate.

SELECTED RECORDINGS

The Eclectic Elek Bacsik	Fontana 834 449-2 CD
Elek Bacsik	Fontana 460 112 LP
Dizzy Gillespie on the French Riviera	Philips 600-048 LP
Bird & Dizzy- Musical Tribute	Flying Dutchman BDL1-1082 LP
Blue Rondo A la Turk	Phonogram PG 250(2LP)
Elek Bacsik-I Love You	Bob Thiele BBL1-0556 LP

SELECTED READING

Profile	Just Jazz Guitar, May 1996

DEREK BAILEY
Born-Sheffield, England
29 January 1932

Derek Bailey is today regarded as one of the pioneers of free jazz. He had a traditional musical background as his grandfather was a professional pianist/banjoist, and his uncle a professional guitarist. As a youth he studied music with C.H.C. Biltcliffe and guitar with John W. Duarte and George Wing. Bailey started his professional career as a band guitarist working in theatres and popular night spots of London including the 'Talk of the Town'. He also worked in recording, radio and television studios.

Bailey found that after ten years of playing commercial music he was not getting any musical satisfaction. He found himself becoming fascinated more and more by the sounds of freely improvised music, and gradually he became one of the first generation of British free improvisors.

In 1963 Bailey formed a trio with Gavin Bryars and drummer Tony Oxley. They played regularly at a Sheffield pub called 'The Grapes'. The group developed a small but loyal following. All three musicians decided to further their musical careers in jazz by moving to London in 1966. In 1970 Bailey founded Incus Records, with Tony Oxley and Evan Parker, the first independent, musician owned record company in Britain. In 1976 he formed 'Company', a changing ensemble of improvising musicians from many backgrounds including Europe, North and South America, Africa and Japan. This group has performed all over the world.

In 1977 Bailey had the distinction of winning the Downbeat magazine's critics' poll for the jazz guitarist deserving wider recognition. In 1980 his book 'Improvisation; Its Nature and Practice in Music was published. Originally written in 1974-76 it has been transalated into several languages. A revised edition of this book was published in 1992 by the British Library. A series of television films called 'On The Edge', based on this book, were shown on Britain's Channel 4.

Derek Bailey has recorded over one hundred albums on different labels. He is today recognised internationally as one of the foremost exponents of free jazz.

PHOTO: COURTESY DEREK BAILEY

Derek Bailey

Company 3	Incus LP 25
Company 4	Incus LP 26
Time	Incus LP 34
Compatibles	Incus LP 50
Cyro	Incus CD 01
Han	Incus CD 02
Drops	Incus CD 03
Company	Incus CD 04
Figuring	Incus CD 05
Village Life	Incus CD 09
Solo Guitar Vol 1	Incus CD 10
Solo Guitar Vol 2	Incus CD 11
Moment Precieux	Victo 02
Aida	Dex 5 CD
Guitars, Drums n' Bass	AVAK 60 CD
Music and Dance	REVN 201 CD
Wireworks w/Henry Kaiser	SHAW 5011 CD
Yankees w/John Zorn	CELL 5006 CD
Will w/Will Change	Incus Video 01
Mountain Stage w/Min Tanaka	Incus Video 02
Company in Japan	Incus Video 03
Gig w/John Stevens	Incus Video 04

SELECTED READING

Profile	Guitar, July 1974
Profile	Impetus /6 1977
Improvisation its Nature and Practice in Music	
Moorlands Publishers(1980)/British Library(1992)/De Capo (1997)	
Profile	Jazz Journal, March 1978
Profile	Jazz Magazine,March 1974
Profile	Guitar, May 1978
Interview	Wire, May 1985
Profile	Guitar Player, April 1988
Profile	Guitar Player, January 1997
Article	Jazz Times, August 1997
Article	Coda, January/February 1998

SELECTED RECORDINGS

Improvisation	Cramps CRSLP6202 LP
Guitar Solos	Virgin/Caroline C1518 LP
Improvisations for Cello & Guitar	ECM Records ECM 1013 LP
The London Concert	Incus LP 16

DUCK BAKER
Born-RICHARD ROYALL BAKER IV
Richmond, Virginia, USA
30 July 1949

Duck Baker is recognised as one of world's foremost fingerstyle guitarists. He plays in many jazz styles from ragtime through to modern jazz. He began to play the guitar as a teenager playing in local rock and blues bands. He then became interested in fingerpicking blues and a major influence was ragtime pianist Buck Evans.

Baker moved in the early 1970s to San Francisco where he joined a local bluegrass band and also played in the local swing jazz scene. His association with Stefan Grosman in the late 1970s meant that Baker's unique talents were heard by an international audience. His many concert appearances and recordings for Grossman's Kicking Mule Company led to him being much in demand, particularly in Europe. As a result Baker moved to Europe for nine years before returning to San Francisco in 1987. During the late 1970s Baker became associated with the free music scene performing with Eugene Chadbourne and John Zorn in New York, and Bruce Ackley and Henry Kaiser in San Francisco. He has also played on the soundtracks of several films.

Duck Baker

Duck Baker's recordings since 1980 have been mostly of his own compositions which reflect the influence of pianists Thelonious Monk, Randy Weston, Horace Silver and others. As an educator he has written several books on fingerstyle guitar and made several tutorial videos.

SELECTED RECORDINGS

The King of Bong	Kicking Mule SNKF 137 LP
Opening The Eyes of Love	Shanachie 97025 CD
The Clear Blue Sky	Acoustic Records 319.1106.2 CD
Ms. Right	Acoustic Records 319.1130.2 CD
Duck Baker Plays Herbie Nichols	Avant 040 CD

Fingerstyle Jazz: Swing to Bop	Tutorial Video	Vestapol
Fingerstyle Jazz: Bop to Modern	Tutorial Video	Vestapol
Fingerstyle Jazz: Improvisation	Tutorial Video	Vestapol
The Music of Thelonious Monk	Tutorial Video	Vestapol

SELECTED READING

Interview	Fingerstyle Guitar, January/February 1996

SELECTED MUSIC

A Thousand Words	Acoustic Music
A Clear Blue Sky	Acoustic Music
Opening The Eyes of Love	Acoustic Music
Fingerstyle Jazz Compositions	Acoustic Music

MICKEY BAKER
Born-McHOUSTON BAKER
Louisville, Kentucky, USA.
15 October 1925

Mickey Baker's reputation amongst many guitarists is mainly as an author of various guitar books and tutors. But he has also been a professional guitarist mainly in the field of rhythm and blues music. He is still musically active and now lives in Paris with his wife Sylvia.

As a boy Baker lived in an orphanage and it was in this institution's marching band that he first developed an interest in music. At the age of sixteen he ran away from the orphanage and ended up in New York paying his way as a labourer. By the time he was nineteen, having listened to many leading jazz musicians, including Charlie Parker and Dizzy Gillespie, Baker decided that he wanted to be a jazz musician. The trumpet was his first choice but the finance needed to purchase this instrument was too high, so at the age of nineteen he decided to buy a guitar.

After a few years study, including a short spell at the New York School of Music, Mickey Baker developed the ability, in 1949, to form his own jazz group. This venture was not a financial success so he decided to move to California. There the reception to his progressive style of jazz music was even less successful. While he was trying to earn the money needed to get back to New York Baker heard blues guitarist, Pee Wee Creighton. He liked what he heard and saw that Creighton was earning a good living. The result was that Baker changed his guitar style and returned to New York as a blues guitarist. His decision proved correct as Mickey Baker, blues guitarist, found himself much in demand for the Atlantic, Savoy and King labels as a backing artist for top blues artists, including Ray Charles, Big Joe Turner, Ruth Brown, and The Drifters.

During the mid 1950s Baker felt he could improve his financial status by emulating the chart topping duo of guitar wizard Les Paul and singer Mary Ford. He joined forces with an ex-student of his called Sylvia and in 1957 they had a smash hit with a song called 'Love is Strange'. Their popularity lasted right through to 1961. With this success behind them the Bakers were financially able to establish their own publishing and recording companies, as well as their own night club.

Since the early 1950s Mickey Baker had been working on his tutors and music albums and

Mickey Baker

now through his own publishing company he achieved world-wide distribution for these works.

Despite his success as a blues and popular guitarist Baker felt that he still wished to play jazz guitar again. He therefore decided to move with his wife to Europe where he hoped he could develop a more fulfilling musical life.

He bought a home in Paris and established permanent French residency there. Since that time Mickey Baker has prospered writing, arranging, leading various groups and has to a great extent fulfilled his desire to continue playing his own distinctive style of jazz and blues guitar.

SELECTED RECORDINGS
The Wildest Guitar of Mickey Baker	Atlantic 8035 LP
Blues & Jazz Guitar-Mickey Baker	Kicking Mule SNKF127 LP
Blues, Candy & Big Maybell	Savoy Jazz SJL 1168 LP
Listen To My Song	Savoy Jazz SJL 1182 LP
The Blues and Me	Black & Blue BB 507-2 CD

SELECTED READING
Profile	Guitar Player, January 1976
Profile	Guitar World, April & May 1988

SELECTED MUSIC
Analysis of the Blues	Baker Publishing Co.
Jazz Book 1	Lewis Music Publishing Co.
Jazz Book 2	Lewis Music Publishing Co.
Guitar Method 1-3	Lewis Music Publishing Co.
Many Shades of the Blues (with CD)	Mel Bay Publications

DAVE BARBOUR

Born-DAVID MICHAEL BARBOUR
Long Island, New York, USA
28 May 1912
Died-Malibu, California, USA
11 December 1965

Dave Barbour started his career on the banjo but in common with many other banjo players of that time he changed to the guitar. Early on in his career he was featured with various small groups including Wingy Manone's band in 1934 and Red Norvo's band 1935-36. In the late 1930's Barbour, who was recognized as one of the most able jazz guitarists of the time, was regularly featured with top jazz artists including Bunny Berigan, Teddy Wilson, Mildred Bailey and Louis Armstrong. He also worked in the big bands of Artie Shaw and Benny Goodman. It was during the time he was with the Goodman orchestra that Barbour met, and later married in 1943, the outstanding vocalist Peggy Lee. He worked with her for a few years and during that time they wrote several hit songs together, including 'Manana' and 'It's a Good Day'. In 1951 their marriage broke up. The next year marked the end of Barbour's career as a jazz guitarist, and as a full-time professional musician. In the last thirteen years of his life he was virtually retired from music with the exception of some recording sessions with singers Jeri Southern and Nellie Lutcher. He occasionally played at charity concerts and in 1962 appeared on a recording session with Benny Carter.

Dave Barbour appeared as an actor in several films during the 1950s. In one film, 'The Secret Fury', he took the part of a jazz guitarist.

SELECTED RECORDINGS

Mildred Bailey	Brunswick LA8692 LP
Benny Goodman Orchestra	CBS 88130 LP
B.B.B.& Co.	Swingsville 2032 LP
Easy Listening	Artistic ART 005 LP
Benny Carter Orchestra	Prestige MPP 2513 IMS LP
Meet The Singers Video	Charly VID JAM 18

Dave Barbour

DANNY BARKER

Born-DANIEL BARKER
New Orleans, Louisiana USA
13 January 1909
Died-New Orleans, Louisiana, USA
13 March 1994

Danny Barker

Danny Barker was a nephew of drummer Paul Barbarin. His first instrument was the clarinet. His uncle then taught him the drums but Barker finally chose to play the ukulele, then the banjo and guitar.

In the late 1920s Barker was featured with Lee Collin's ragtime band. In 1930 he decided to move to New York and for the next few years played with many famous jazz names including Albert Nicholas, Lucky Millinder and James P. Johnson. In 1938 he joined Benny Carter's big band and then from 1939 to 1949 he played with Cab Calloway. Barker had married singer Blue Lu Barker and in 1946 formed a backing group for her. Through the late 1940s and the 1950s Barker freelanced with many of the leading traditional jazz musicians including Bunk Johnson, Paul Barbarin and Albert Nicholas. At this time he played the banjo again, rather than the guitar. Barker had played successfully on both American coasts but in the late 1950s he decided to settle in New York. He appeared at the Newport Jazz Festival in 1960 with Eubie Blake, and led his own banjo group at the New York World Fair in 1964.

In May 1965 Barker decided to return home to New Orleans. Here he became Assistant to the Curator of the New Orleans Jazz Museum. He remained in New Orleans from that time playing, and also lecturing on traditional jazz. In 1969 he was a Grand Marshall for the New Orleans Jazz Festival. Barker received a Lifetime Achievement Award for the Humanities in 1991. He died of cancer in March 1994.

SELECTED RECORDINGS

Bunk Johnson Band	Nola LP3
Sidney Bechet Album	Saga Pan 6900 LP
Edmund Hall Quintet	Queen Disc 020 LP
Prestige Blues Swingers	Prestige P 24051 IMS LP
Mezzrow/Bechet Septet	Storyville SLP 326
A Memorial Mary Osborne	Stash ST-CD 550
Save The Bones	Orleans Records OR 1018CD

SELECTED READING

Bourbon Street Black Barker & Buerkle	Oxford Univ. Press (1973)
A Life In Jazz Autobiography	Oxford University Press(1986)
Profile	IAJRC Journal, Winter 1993

EVERETT BARKSDALE
Born-Detroit,Michigan, USA
28 April 1910
Died-California, USA
January 1986

Everett Barksdale's first professional job as a musician was in Chicago in the early 1930s with the Erskine Tate band. He then played with violinist Eddie South from 1932 for a period of almost ten years. During the 1940s he was featured with many leading jazz players, including alto-saxophonist Benny Carter. He also worked for nineteen months for the C.B.S. radio network in New York. In 1949 he joined the Art Tatum trio. Barksdale worked and recorded on and off with this world famous group until 1955. His admirable guitar work came to international prominence during his time with this jazz piano legend. In 1956 he took a break to become musical director for the popular vocal group 'The Inkspots' but then rejoined Art Tatum's trio until the pianist's death on 4 November 1956. Barksdale went back to working as staff musician for the ABC network in New York City. He also played electric bass for the Buddy Tate band in the late 1950s.

Everett Barksdale was also much in demand for studio recording sessions backing top singers including Lena Horne, Sammy Davis Jnr., Dinah Washington and Sarah Vaughan. In the late 1970s he moved to California where he

Everett Barksdale

continued to play regularly until shortly before his death.

SELECTED RECORDINGS

Art Tatum Trio-Live	Jazz Anthology 30-JA5138
Tatum Trio Capitol Recordings Vol 1	Capitol CDP 7928662 CD
Tatum Trio Capitol Recordings Vol 2	Capitol CDP 7928672 CD
Benny Carter Orchestra	RCA PM 42406
'Red' Allen Band 1957	RCA Bluebird ND 82497 CD

Everett Barksdale with the Eddie South Orchestra.

George Barnes with Carl Kress

GEORGE BARNES

Born-Chicago Heights, Chicago, Illinois, USA
17 July 1921
Died-Concord, California, USA
5 September 1977

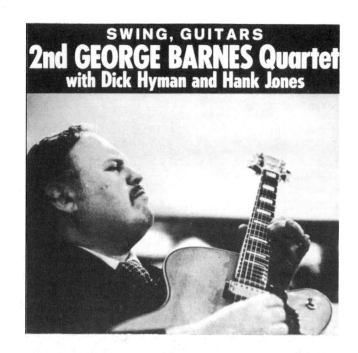

George Barnes came from a family of musicians. He began to play the guitar at the age of nine. His father was his first teacher. Barnes was brought up in Chicago, a city that had become a main centre of jazz development. He claimed that his main musical influences were Jimmy Noone (in whose band he played at the age of sixteen), Benny Goodman and Louis Armstrong.

As a youth Barnes was associated with the great blues guitarist Lonnie Johnson who obviously influenced him. He also listened to many records by Django Reinhardt. At the age of 14 Barnes had his own jazz quartet. He won a Tommy Dorsey Amateur Swing Contest when he was sixteen, and at the age of 17 was working on the Chicago NBC staff as guitarist, conductor, and arranger - a remarkable achievement. Barnes held this position for five years until 1942 when he was drafted into the army. During the seven years up to 1942 George Barnes was often featured in recording sessions with many legendary Folk/Blues artists including Big Bill Broonzy, Washboard Sam, and Blind John Davis.

On leaving the army after the war, Barnes returned to a life which became one of the busiest in jazz history. In 1951 he moved from Chicago to New York. Here his exceptional musical ability won him a contract with Decca Records as guitarist, composer and arranger. Because of his multiple talents Barnes was much in demand over the years as a backing artist for top singers and jazz artists including Frank Sinatra, Bing Crosby and Louis Armstrong. He made many historic jazz recordings with his own various quartets and quintets but his greatest contribution to jazz guitar history were his unique guitar duos with Carl Kress (and then Bucky Pizzarelli after the death of Kress), and the quintet he led jointly with cornetist Ruby Braff.

Always a great individualist George Barnes had a very distinctive sound partly due to his personally designed archtop guitar constructed without the usual 'F' soundholes. This instrument was made especially for him by the Guild Guitar Company. He also usually used an unwound third string, which was unusual for a guitarist of his generation. In 1975 Barnes moved to Concord, California. There he devot-

ed his time to playing in jazz clubs, recording, and teaching until his death following a heart attack in September 1977.

SELECTED RECORDINGS

Jazz Renaissance Quintet	Mercury MG 20605 LP
Guitars A'Plenty	Mercury SML 30002 LP
Guitar Galaxie	Wing/Mercury SRW 16392 LP
Country Jazz	Colortone C33-4915 LP
George Barnes Octet	Hindsight HSR-106 LP
Something Tender with Carl Kress	United Artists UAJ 14033 LP
Two Guitars And A Horn	Stash JSC CD636
Town Hall Concert with Carl Kress	United Artists UAS 6335 LP
Guitars Anyone with Carl Kress	Carney LPM 202 LP
Smokey & Intimate with Carl Kress	Carney LPM 201 LP
Braff/Barnes Quartet	Chiaroscuro CR 121 LP
Braff/Barnes Quartet play Gershwin	Concord CCD 6005
Braff/Barnes salute Rodgers & Hart	Concord CJ 7
Braff/Barnes To Fred Astaire	RCA SF 8442
Guitars-Pure and Honest	A & R Records 7100-077
The Guitar Album	CBS CBS 67275
Barnes/Venuti Quintet – Gems	Concord CCD 6014
Blues Going Up	Concord CJ 43
Plays So Good	Concord CCD 4067
Braff/Barnet Quartet Live at the New School	Chiaroscuro CR126 CD

SELECTED READING

Profile	B.M.G., December 1966
Profile	Guitar Player, February 1975
Profile	Guitar, June 1975

SELECTED MUSIC

George Barnes Electric Guitar Method	Wm.J.Smith Music Co.
10 Duets for 2 Guitars w/Carl Kress	Music Minus One MM03613CD

JOHN BASILE
Born-Dedham, Boston, Massachusetts, USA
5 March 1955

John Basile

John Basile's father played the guitar. Basile was attracted by the music of Count Basie at the age of nine. He began to play the guitar at the age of 16 and attended the Berklee College of Music, studying with William Leavitt, throughout high school. In 1976 He went on to study music at the New England Conservatory in Boston. He also studied privately with composers George Russell and Jackie Byard, and guitarists Barry Galbraith and Jim Hall.

Basile became a professional musician on leaving the conservatory. He gained early professional experience working with Rhythm & Blues showbands, and with various organ trios, in the Boston area. He relocated to the New York area in 1979. He worked as an accompanist performing and recording with singers Peggy Lee, Rosemary Clooney, Morgana King and Sylvia Sims. In 1984 he released his first recording as leader on the Seabreeze label. He worked for a while in a duo with clarinetist Brad Terry. In 1988 Basile won the Hennessey Jazz Search competition. This success resulted in a recording contract for the Musical Heritage label and performances in concerts and clubs throughout the USA.

Over the last few years John Basile has appeared with several major jazz artists including Tom Harrell, George Mraz, Cecil Payne and Pepper Adams. Basile also toured Europe in 1987 for bassist Red Mitchell in an all-star band of Count Basie veterans including Harry 'Sweets' Edison and Clark Terry.

SELECTED RECORDINGS

Very Early	Seabreeze 2024 LP
Quiet Passage	Pro Jazz CDJ 627
Sunnyside Up	Pro Jazz CDJ 641
John Basile/Brad Terry Duo	Musical Heritage 512744 A CD
Frankly Speaking	Jazz Heritage 513446K CD
For All Time	Philology PLOG 103 CD
Desmond Project	Chesky Jazz JD 156 CD

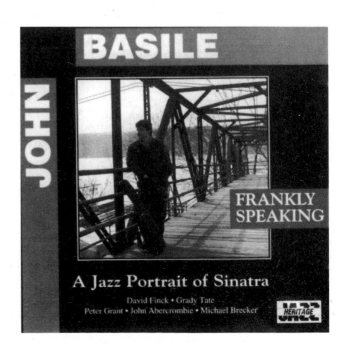

54

BILLY BAUER
Born–WILLIAM HENRY BAUER
New York City, USA
14 November 1915

Billy Bauer was originally a banjo player but changed to the guitar in the 1930s when he joined the Jerry Wald Orchestra. Over the next few years he played with various bands including those led by Carl Boff, Dick Stabile and Abe Lyman. He reached international prominence in 1944 when he took over the guitar seat in the Woody Herman band. After the Herman band disbanded in 1946, Bauer freelanced around New York with top jazz artists including Benny Goodman and Chubby Jackson. It was at this time that he first met pianist Lenny Tristano. His association with Tristano was to prove to be Billy Bauer's most important contribution to the development of the jazz guitar. His individual jazz style was an ideal match for the new cool/free improvisation style of Tristano, and also that of alto-saxophonist Lee Konitz. Together they made some historic recordings which added new ideas and dimensions to jazz as it was then known. These recordings proved to be a milestone in jazz history. In 1949 and 1950 Bauer won the jazz guitarist poll in Downbeat magazine. He won the jazz guitar poll in Metronome magazine for five years running from 1949.

In 1950 Bauer taught at the New York Conservatory of Music for three and a half years. From the early 1960s to the 1970s he was mainly involved in studio and session work. He appeared at the jazz club in McGurl's

Sherwood Inn, Long Island with his own group from 1961-63. Bauer also worked for a period as a staff guitarist with 'Ice Capades'. Much of his time since then has been devoted to freelance work, teaching at his guitar school in Roslyn Heights, and with his own publishing company.

SELECTED RECORDINGS

Barry Ulanov's All Stars	Jazz Anthology JA5108 LP
Rare Jazz Broadcasts	Jazz Anthology JA5164 LP
Billy Bauer-Plectrist	Norgran 1082 LP
Cross Currents with Tristano	Capitol M11060 LP
First Sessions	Prestige P 24081 2LP
Lenny Tristano Sextet	Jazz Records JR-9 CD
Jazz Renaissance Quintet	Mercury MH 20605 LP
Lee Konitz-Ezzthetic	Prestige 7827 LP
Billy Bauer/Anthology	Interplay IP 8603 LP

SELECTED READING

Profile	Guitar Player, April 1972
Profile	Guitar, April 1975
Interview	Just Jazz Guitar, February 1996
Sideman – Autobiography	Bauer Publications 1997

Billy Bauer with Tony Aless (piano), Arnold Fishkind (bass).

BILL BAY
Born-WILLIAM ALAN BAY
Pacific, Missouri, USA
25 April 1945

Bill Bay is President of Mel Bay Publications Inc founded by his father in 1947. From the late 1980s Bay took over the management and product development of the company. As a result the company now has one of the most important catalogues of jazz guitar music books and methods.

Bill Bay began playing the trumpet at the age of seven. By the time he was eleven he was playing with a number of jazz bands throughout the St Louis area, and soloing with a number of concert symphonic bands. In his teens he fronted a thirteen piece jazz band which included several notable musicians including saxophonist David Sanborn. Bay took up the guitar whilst at college and soon took an active interest in the many facets of the instrument. After completing his master's degree he joined the family publishing company. At that time the company had 25 books in print. Today it has over 2000 products including videos and audio recordings.

Bill Bay's close personal association with jazz guitarists such as George Van Eps, Joe Pass, Sal Salvador, Jerry Hahn, Johnny Smith, Joe Puma, Allen Hanlon, Al Hendrickson, Jimmy Stewart, Alan de Mause, Lenny Breau, Larry Coryell, Tommy Tedesco, Tom Bruner, Vincent Bredice, Ronnie Lee and other guitarists has led to the publication by Mel Bay Publications of some of the most important jazz guitar music books and methods available. Bay's endeavours in recent years have made an enormous, and valuable, contribution to the evolution of the guitar in jazz.

SELECTED READING
Interview   Guitar Player, November 1982

SELECTED MUSIC
Building Right Hand Techniques   Mel Bay Publications
Complete Book Of Guitar Chords, Scales and Arpeggios
                                                        Mel Bay Publications
De Luxe Encyclopedia of Guitar Chords   Mel Bay Publications

Bill Bay

Mel Bay (1913 - 1997)

BILLY BEAN
Born-WILLIAM FREDERICK BEAN
Philadelphia, Pennsylvania, USA
26 December 1933

Billy Bean

Billy Bean was born into a musical family. His father was a guitarist and his mother a pianist, so Bean had the right environment for the serious study of his chosen instrument. After gaining a lot of experience with various bands in and around Philadelphia, Bean joined the Charlie Ventura Quartet in 1956. Following in the footsteps of many of his fellow musicians Bean moved to California in 1958. Here he freelanced with various groups in and around the Los Angeles area. These groups often featured top jazz artists such as Buddy Collette, Paul Horn, Calvin Jackson, Bud Shank and Buddy de Franco.

His jazz recordings in the 1950s and 1960s, particularly those in a guitar duo with John Pisano, reveal Billy Bean to be a jazz guitarist of the highest calibre. Yet he has not at this time received the recognition in jazz circles that his talent deserves. Since the 1970s Bean has not been involved professionally as a musician.

SELECTED RECORDINGS

The Trio-Bean/Norris/Gaylor	Riverside RLP 380 LP
Take Your Pick	Decca DL 9212 LP
Making It	Decca/Brunswick LAT 8272 LP
Fred Katz-Folk Songs	Warner Bros 1277 LP
A Gasser! Annie Ross	Pacific Jazz CDP 7468542

Herb Ellis and Tommy Tedesco

57

JOE BECK
Born-Philadelphia, USA
29 July 1945

Joe Beck

Joe Beck became interested in the guitar at the age of five after hearing a recording by classical master guitarist, Andrés Segovia. Beck's mother was a piano teacher. He then heard some recordings by Chet Atkins and George Van Eps. By the time he was thirteen Beck was playing electric guitar and bass professionally in various local lounges.

After graduating from high school, Beck moved from New Jersey to New York City. By the time he was twenty he began a long period of working with many top jazz musicians including Charles Lloyd, Gary McFarland, Chico Hamilton and Gil Evans.

In 1971 Beck decided to become a dairy farmer and for a period of two years he gave up playing the guitar professionally. In 1973 he returned to an active life as a recording artist, session man and busy jazz/rock fusion guitarist. In recent times Beck has his own company which produces music for television and radio commercials. It also produces web sites for major musical instrument companies.

SELECTED RECORDINGS

Beck	Kudu KU-21S1
Nature Boy	Verve Forecast FTS 3081
Empathy Joe Beck/Red Mitchell Duo	Gryphon G-2 911
Joe Beck w/Jay Leonhart	Sunnyside SSC 1006
Double Cross w/Jay Leonhert	Sunnyside SSC 1032
Joe Beck – Back to Beck	DMP CD-464
The Journey	DMP CD-481
Joe Beck/Red Mitchell Duo – Live	Capri 74033-2 CD
Jazz Chord Workout Instructional Video	Hot Licks

SELECTED READING

Interview	Guitar Player, September 1977
Profile	Guitar World, February 1989
Profile	Jazz Times, August 1995
Profile	Guitar Player, April 1996

Empathy*/JOE BECK, guitar and RED MITCHELL, bass — as it happened at Bradleys in New York, August 1980

2 RECORD SET

*EM·PA·THY (empa·thē) understanding so intimate that the feelings, thoughts, and motives of one are readily comprehended by another.

ED BENSON
Born-EDWARD BENSON
New York, USA
20 May 1940

Ed Benson, although not a professional musician, has made a major impact on the world of jazz guitar as publisher of Just Jazz Guitar magazine.

Benson's father was a doctor, and he also considered medicine as a career. Whilst studying dentistry in 1958 at Western Reserve University, Cleveland, Ohio, Benson began to take an interest in the guitar. His first teachers included Dick Lurie and Van Moretti. Benson went on to play as a semi-professional with various bands but finally made his career in business. He eventually became a senior vice president of Macy's Department Store, a position he held until his retirement in 1994.

Ed Benson maintained an interest in the jazz guitar throughout his business career. In 1994, whilst making the video 'Building an Archtop Guitar' with Bob Benedetto, the suggestion was made by the famous luthier, and his wife Cindy that Benson should publish a newsletter for jazz guitarists. With the encouragement of the Benedettos and others, Ed Benson published the first issue of his quarterly magazine Just Jazz Guitar in November 1994. He is the senior editor. Amongst the magazine's regular conributor's are Van Moretti, Adrian Ingram, Arnie Berle and Andy Mackenzie.

SELECTED READING
Just Jazz Guitar Magazine Issue 1 to date

PHOTO: NORMAN WILSON

Ed Benson

George Benson

GEORGE BENSON
Born-Pittsburgh,Pennsylvania, USA
22 March 1943

In 1976 George Benson was voted by several popular and jazz polls as the world's number one jazz guitarist. During that same year world-wide sales of his record 'Breezin' passed the 2,000,000 mark. Since that time Benson has become one of the most successful popular singers of the day. The bulk of Benson's current record sales are to a non-jazz audience who purchase his recordings for his singing and unique guitar sound. Yet there is no doubt that through these recordings he has opened the ears of many of his fans to his fine jazz guitar playing. As a result Benson has created an interest for them to listen to other jazz guitarists.

Benson's stepfather, Thomas Collier, was a fan of Charlie Christian. He taught Benson to play the ukulele at an early age. By the time he was eight Benson was already working in nightclubs with his stepfather, singing, dancing and also playing the ukulele. In 1954 he began to study the guitar, borrowing guitars at friends' houses and then playing an electric guitar made for him by his stepfather. In the same year Benson made his first recording for a rhythm and blues label. By the time he was seventeen he was already leading his own rock and roll group. After hearing recordings by various jazz artists, including those of Hank Garland, Grant Green, Charlie Parker and, in particular, the late Wes Montgomery, Benson was encouraged to turn his musical talent towards jazz.

In 1962 Jack McDuff, on the recommendation of Don Gardner, hired Benson. This association lasted for three years. Playing with McDuff gave Benson valuable experience playing with top jazz artists. In 1965 he formed his own quartet featuring Lonnie Smith on organ. After the death of Wes Montgomery in 1968, Benson was an obvious choice for record producer, Creed Taylor, to fill the gap for A & M Records left by Montgomery's early demise. Taylor hoped that Benson's guitar sound, so similar at that time to Montgomery's, would also achieve popular success for A & M. Creed Taylor's choice would prove right, but the success did not actually happen until 1976 when Benson's Warner Brother's record 'Breezin' surpassed the highest record sales that Wes Montgomery had ever achieved.

A talented and highly successful singer, Benson's guitar style on his popular recordings is usually a mixture of jazz/funk, soul, and rhythm and blues. Some of his recent recordings have a strong jazz content and these show that George Benson remains one of the great jazz guitarists of the day who can produce wonderful single note and chordal improvisations. His special ability to play improvised lines on the guitar in unison with his 'scat' singing is very distinctive. George Benson's 1990 recording with the Count Basie Band shows that he is determined to retain his contact with the world of jazz.

SELECTED RECORDINGS

New Boss Guitar	OJC 461 CD
Benson/McDuff (2LPs)	Prestige P24072 LP
Its Uptown	Columbia 52976 CD
George Benson's Cookbook	Columbia 52977 CD
In Concert Carnegie Hall	Columbia 44187 CD
Benson & Farrell	Columbia 44169 CD
Miles In The Sky w/Miles Davis	Columbia 48954 CD
Shape of Things to Come	A & M Records SP3014 LP
The Other Side of Abbey Road	A & M Records SP3028 LP
White Rabbit	Columbia 64768 CD
Breezin	Warner Bros. 3111 CD
In Flight	Warner Bros. 2983 CD
Weekend in L.A. (2LPs)	Warner Bros. 3139 CD
Tenderly	Warner Bros. 25907-2 CD
Big Boss Band	Warner Bros. 26295 CD
Collaboration with Earl Klugh	Warner Bros 25580 CD
Talkin' Verve Jazz	Verve 553780 CD
Best of George Benson	Warner 46050 CD
I Like Jazz	Columbia 52921 CD
That's Right	GRP 98242 CD
Verve Jazz Masters (21)	Verve 21861 CD

SELECTED READING

Profile	Downbeat, June 1967
Profile	Downbeat, June 1973
Interview	Guitar Player, January 1974
Interview	Guitar, May 1974
Profile	Guitar Player, August 1976
Interview	Downbeat, September 1976
Interview	Guitar, August 1978
Interview	Crescendo, August 1978
Profile	Wire, May 1985
Interview	Downbeat, May 1987
Profile	Downbeat, May 1988
Interview	Downbeat, January 1991
Profile	Jazziz, November 1993
Profile	Jazz on CD, November 1993
Article	Jazz Times, August 1996

SELECTED MUSIC

The Very Best of George Benson/Recorded Versions	Hal Leonard

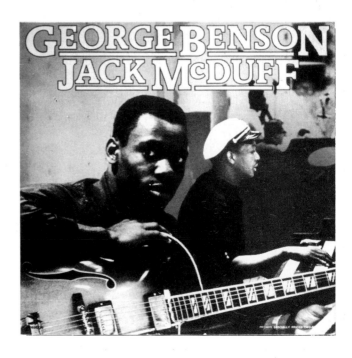

ARNIE BERLE
Born-New York City, USA
29 May 1929

Arnie Berle began playing the clarinet, flute and saxophone while he was in high school. n the 1950s he toured with the Johnny Long dance band. During that time he became seriously interested in the guitar and then studied with Hy White, Barry Galbraith, Howard Morgen and Jim Hall. While continuing his studies he worked in night clubs and theatres accompanying popular artists including Tony Bennett, Jerry Lewis and Alan King.

Berle was also much in demand as a private teacher and it was in this area of music that he decided to devote his career. His first two books for the guitar were published by the Amsco Publishing Corporation in the late 1960s and early 1970s. In 1974 he began to write for Guitar Player magazine and in 1977 he began a monthly column for the same magazine which lasted for almost fourteen years. He also contributed over fifty interviews of famous jazz and studio guitar players to Guitar Player.

Since 1977 Berle has been a professor of music at Mercy College in Dobbs Ferry, New York. He earned a BA degree from Empire State College. He has written more important books for jazz guitarists in recent years and is currently working on several others. He is a regular contributor to Just Jazz Guitar magazine.

Arnie Berle

PHOTO: COURTESY ARNIE BERLE

SELECTED MUSIC

Chords & Progressions For Popular & Jazz Guit.	Amsco Publications
Complete Handbook of Jazz Improvisation	Amsco Publications
New Guitar Techniques for Sightreading	CPP/Belwin
New Techniques for Chord Melody Guitar	CPP/Belwin
How To Create and Develop A Jazz Solo	Mel Bay Publications
Jazz Licks, Patterns and Phrases	Mel Bay Publications
Fretboard Basics	Mel Bay Publications

PETER BERNSTEIN
Born-New York City, USA
3 September 1967

Peter Bernstein's first musical instrument was the piano which he studied for four years from the age of eight. He began to play the guitar at the age of 12. His first influences were Jimi Hendrix and other rock guitarists. He then became interested in the blues style of B.B. King. It was some recordings by Wes Montgomery that finally made Bernstein decide to concentrate on jazz. He studied for one year at Rutgers College, one year at William Paterson College and then for two years at the New School from which he graduated with a BA in Music. His teachers included Attila Zoller, Gene Bertoncini, Ted Dunbar and Jim Hall.

Since 1988 Peter Bernstein has been one of the busiest jazz guitarists in the New York area. He has recorded or worked with many top jazz artists including Lou Donaldson, Larry Goldings, Cecil Payne, Lee Konitz, Clifford Jordan, Melvin Rhyne, Joshua Redman and Junior Cook. Since 1992 he has recorded for the Criss Cross Jazz company and other leading jazz record labels.

Peter Bernstein

SELECTED RECORDINGS

Somethin's Burnin'	Criss Cross	CRISS 1079 CD
Signs of Life	Criss Cross	CRISS 1095 CD
Brain Dance	Criss Cross	CRISS 1130 CD
The Legend w/Melvin Rhyne	Criss Cross	CRISS 1059 CD
Brian Lynch Quintet	Criss Cross	CRISS 1070 CD
Melvin Rhyne Quartet	Criss Cross	CRISS 1080 CD
Ralph Lalama Quartet	Criss Cross	CRISS 1132 CD
Caracas w/Lou Donaldson		Milestone MCD 9217-2
Whatever It Takes w/Larry Goldings		Warner 45996 CD
Jim Hall Invitation MusicMasters		Limelight 820 843-2 CD
Freedom In The Groove w/Joshua Redman		Warner 46330 CD

GENE BERTONCINI
Born-New York City, USA
6 April 1937

Gene Bertoncini began to play the guitar at the age of seven. His family were very musical including his father who played both the guitar and harmonica. As a youth Bertoncini received some lessons from Johnny Smith and then later he studied for a while with Chuck Wayne. It was only after graduating from Notre Dame University with a degree in architecture that he decided to play the guitar for a living.

After a short spell with drummer Buddy Rich's quintet (1961-62) the young guitarist was to become very involved with the New York studio scene. Bertoncini's television, radio and recording work saw him with the position of staff guitarist on several popular programmes including Merv Griffin's 'Play Your Hunch', Johnny Carson's 'Tonight Show' and 'The Jack Parr Show'.

Gene Bertoncini has also worked with many well known jazz musicians including Hubert Laws, Clark Terry, Ron Carter, Wayne Shorter, Paul Desmond, Billy Taylor and singers Tony Bennett and Morgana King. His main jazz club and recording work for many years has been in a duo with the bassist Michael Moore. In this duo the two musicians include classical, Brazilian and popular music into their usual jazz repertoire. Bertoncini is as at home on the classical nylon strung guitar, played with the right hand fingers, as he is with the steel strung archtop electric, played with a pick. He is one of the few guitarists to master both jazz styles with success.

Bertoncini also includes in his work schedule time for teaching jazz guitar in various colleges including the Eastman School of Music in New York, the New England Conservatory, New York University and the Banff School of Fine Arts in Alberta, Canada.

As he has not often travelled professionally outside the USA Bertoncini is not too well known to international jazz audiences. Through his recordings, including several in his duo with Michael Moore, there is no doubt that he is a creative jazz artist.

Gene Bertoncini

Tribute to Wes Montgomery Vol 1	King Records KICJ 112CD
John Frigo – Debut of a Legend	Chesky JD 119 CD
Acoustic Romance	Bellaphon KICJ 155 CD
Jiggs and Grave w/Jiggs Whigham	AZICA AJD-72204 CD

SELECTED READING

Interview	Guitar Player, September 1977
Interview	Just Jazz Guitar, May 1997

SELECTED MUSIC

Approaching The Guitar. A Method	Kjos Music (1990)

SELECTED RECORDINGS

Hubert Laws at Carnegie Hall	CTI 6025 LP
Evolution! Gene Bertoncini	Evolution Records 3001
Bridges. Duo with Michael Moore	MPS 0068.176
Close Ties. Duo with Michael Moore	Omnisound GJB 3334
O Grande Amor. Duo with Michael Moore	Stash ST 258
Strollin. Duo with Michael Moore	Stash ST 272
Two In Time. Duo with Michael Moore	Chiaroscuro CR(D)308CD
Roger Kellaway Meets The Duo	Chiaroscuro CR(D)315CD

SKEETER BEST
Born-Kingston, North Carolina, USA
20 November 1914
Died-New York, USA
27 May 1985

Skeeter Best

Skeeter Best received his first musical education from his mother who was a piano teacher. He took up the guitar as a youth and started to work professionally with a local band, led by Abe Dunn in the early 1930s.

In 1940 he joined the Earl Hines orchestra after working for a short time in Philadelphia with the Slim Marshall band. He then served in the US Navy. In 1945, after leaving the US forces, Best was featured in various jazz groups playing for US servicemen in Japan and Korea. One of these groups, in 1951-52, was led by the famed jazz bassist Oscar Pettiford.

After that time Best freelanced around the New York area playing and recording with many top jazz men including saxophonist Paul Quinichette, trumpeter Dizzy Gillespie and drummer Kenny Clarke. Although Skeeter Best never gained real international recognition the musicians he was associated with regarded him as a very able jazz musician.

SELECTED RECORDINGS

Earl Hines Orchestra	RCA PM 43266 LP
Sir Charles Thompson Trio	Vanguard PPT 12020 LP
Modern Jazz Sextet (w/Dizzy Gillespie)	Columbia 33CX 100048 LP
Paul Quinichette Sextet 'Blow Your Horn'	Brunswick LAT 8099 LP
Quinichette/Gonsalves	Communication CO 300 LP
The Chase and The Steeplechase	MCA 510127 LP
Ray Charles/Milt Jackson	Atlantic 50914 LP

ED BICKERT
Born-EDWARD ISAAC BICKERT
Hochfield, Manitoba, Canada
29 November 1932

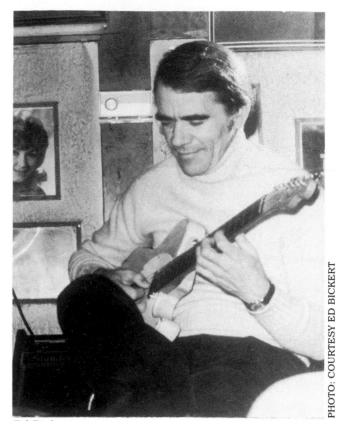

Ed Bickert

Ed Bickert grew up in Vernon, British Columbia, and started to play the guitar at the age of eight. Both his parents were musicians who played in a country music band. Bickert occasionally played with them at dances.

By the time he was twenty Bickert had moved to Toronto. Here he worked for a local radio station, as well as doing studio and jazz work. In the mid 1950s Bickert's musical approach was greatly influenced by the jazz guitar styles of Tal Farlow and Barney Kessel. He was fortunate to meet them both when they played in Toronto clubs.

Bickert was often heard as the featured guitarist with the Moe Koffman Quintet and Rob McConnell's Boss Brass. For many years he played at the well known jazz spot, the Bourbon Street Club in Toronto. Here he had the opportunity to back many visiting USA jazz musicians including Red Norvo, Chet Baker, Paul Desmond, Frank Rosolino and Milt Jackson. Bickert was often featured at this club fronting his own trio.

Ed Bickert still continues to spend much of his professional time working in the radio, television and recording studios of Toronto. In recent years he has also made many jazz recordings for the Concord Record label in California. This association has brought Ed Bickert well deserved international recognition. He is, without doubt, one of Canada's leading guitarists in both the commercial and jazz areas of music.

SELECTED RECORDINGS

Pure Desmond	CTI Records CTI 6059 LP
Paul Desmond Quartet	A & M Horizon SP 850 LP
Moe Koffman Quintet	GRT 9230-107 LP
I Like To Recognise The Tune	United Artists UALA 747G LP
Ed Bickert	PM Records PMR 101 LP
Ruby Braff w/ Ed Bickert Trio	Sackville 3022 LP
Ed Bickert/Don Thompson Duo	Sackville 4005 LP
Ed Bickert/Don Thompson Duo	Sackville 4010 LP
Ed Bickert 5	Concord CJ 216 LP
Ed Bickert-Bye Bye Baby	Concord CJ 232 LP
I Wished on the Moon	Concord CCD-4284
Trio Sketches	Concord CCD-4591
Duo w/Bill Mays	Concord CCD-4626
Ed Bickert Trio w/Dave McKenna	Concord CCD-4380
Ed Bickert/Lorne Lofsky	Concord CCD-4414
Ed Bickert & Rob McConnell Duo	Jazz Alliance TJA-10003 CD
Paul Desmond Quartet	Telarchive CD-83319
Portraits in Jazz	Radioland RACD 10006

SELECTED READING

Profile	Downbeat, May 1976
Profile	Guitar Player, September 1978
Interview	Guitar, November 1979

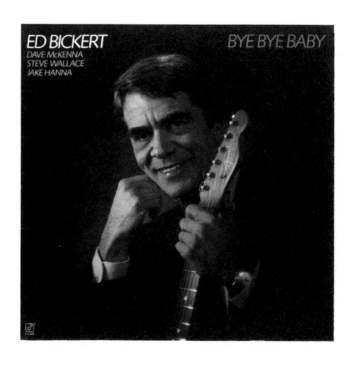

ED BICKERT
DAVE McKENNA
STEVE WALLACE
JAKE HANNA

BYE BYE BABY

PAUL BOLLENBACK
Born-Hinsdale, Illinois, USA
6 June 1959

Although born in Illinois Paul Bollenback was raised in Hastings-on-Hudson near New York City. He began to take an interest in music at the age of seven. From 1974 he played in guitar in various rock bands, his guitar style influenced by a two and a half stay in New Delhi, India. In 1976 Bollenback moved to the Washington, D.C. area.

Bollenback spent two years as a performance major at the University of Miami, Florida. He followed this with eight years of private study in composition and ear training with Asher Zlotnik. During that time, and up to the present day Bollenback has established himself as an important guitarist playing with a wide variety of jazz artists including; Joey DeFrancesco, Stanley Turrentine, Jack McDuff, David "Fathead" Newman, Herb Ellis, James Moody, Keter Betts, Ethel Ennis, Jimmy Bruno, Charlie Byrd and Arturo Sandoval. He was featured on the 1991 recording "Reboppin" with organist Joey DeFrancesco, for which SESAC awarded him an Outstanding Composer of the Year Award. Bollenback has also appeared frequently on top television shows with DeFrancesco including 'The Today Show', 'Good Morning America' and the 'Joan Rivers Show'. He has also toured extensively thoughout the USA and Europe with DeFrancesco.

In 1991 Bollenback received a grant from the Virginia Commission on the Arts and the National Endowment to compose and perform 'New Music for Three Guitars' which premiered at Washington's Blues Alley. He continues to live in New York City where he is a frequent performer and clinician at the city's top jazz spots. Paul Bollenback is also a prominent endorsee for the Guild Guitar company, a divison of Fender Musical Instruments.

Paul Bollenback

PHOTO: COURTESY GUILD DIVISION/FENDER INC.

SELECTED RECORDINGS

Original Visions	Challenge	CHR 70022 CD
Double-Gemini	Challenge	CHR 70046 CD
Part Three w/ Joey DeFrancesco	Columbia	47063 CD
Reboppin' w/ Joey DeFrancesco	Columbia	48624 CD
Exile's Gate w/Gary Thomas	JMT	514009-2 CD
Scorcher w/ Ron Holloway	Milestone	9257 CD

SELECTED READING

Profile	Jazz Times, October 1995
Profile	Just Jazz Guitar, August 1997

LUIZ BONFA
Born-LUIZ FLORIANO BONFA
Rio de Janeiro, Brazil
17 October 1922

Luiz Bonfa

Luiz Bonfa's greatest contribution to the jazz world has been his original compositions. In particular his musical score for the film 'Black Orpheus' included several songs that have now become jazz standards. 'Manha de Carnival', and 'Samba de Orfeu' are just two of the songs that are today known by most jazz lovers throughout the world.

Luiz Bonfa is also, as can be heard on his many recordings, a very fine guitarist in the traditional Brazilian style. He began to play the guitar at the age of eleven. He was initially taught by his father who was also a guitarist. He continued his studies under Isaias Savio, a master classical guitarist. Bonfa achieved a very high standard on the classical guitar but decided, after giving several concert recitals, to devote his career to the field of popular music. In 1946 he started his professional career in Brazil. A major influence on Bonfa was the legendary Brazilian guitarist Garoto (Anibal Augusto Sardinha). Garoto, who is regarded by most Brazilian musicians to be the 'father' of bossa nova, was instrumental in Bonfa getting his first job with Radio Nacional in Rio. In a short time he became one of Brazil's top musicians both on the radio and the stage. At one time he sang and played the guitar in a group called the 'Quitandinha Singers'.

In 1958 Bonfa decided to move to the USA where his arrival coincided with the bossa nova boom. The popular singer Mary Martin was greatly impressed by Bonfa's guitar artistry and hired him to accompany her for several concerts in 1958-59. During this time Bonfa had his first real exposure to jazz. He made several very successful recordings with saxophonist Stan Getz. Bonfa also made several recordings with his wife, Brazilian singer Maria Toledo.

For many years Luiz Bonfa continued to lead a highly successful career as a guitar player, singer, and composer based in California. His multi-talented musical talents being much in demand for the film, television and recording industries. In recent times Bonfa has returned to live in Brazil but continues to spend some time of each year in the USA.

Fabulous Guitar of Luiz Bonfa	Atlantic 8028 LP
Le Roi de la Bossa Nova	Fontana 680-228 LP
Bossa Nova	Verve SVLP 9209 LP
Luiz Bonfa	Dot DLP 25804 LP
Black Orpheus Impressions	Dot DLP 28548 LP
Bonfa	Dot DLP 25881 LP
Braziliana w/Maria Toledo	Philips BL7703 LP
Luiz Bonfa En Rio	Philips 11056 LP
The Brazilian Scene	Philips SBL7727 LP
Jazz Samba/Stan Getz'	Verve 823 613 2 CD
Jacaranda	Ranwood R8112 LP
The New Face of Bonfa	RCA LSP4376 LP
A Arte Do Encontro	RGE 310.60002 LP
Non Stop to Brazil	Chesky JD29
The Bonfa Magic	Milestone MCD-9202-2

SELECTED READING

| Profile | Guitar Player May 1983 |

SELECTED MUSIC

| Four Guitar Solos | GSP Publications |
| Music of Luis Bonfa | Tropical Music |

SELECTED RECORDINGS

Melodias Das Americas	IMP-30.009 LP
Violao Boemio	IMP-30.109 LP
Alta Versatilidade	Odeon MOFB 3.003 LP
Meu Querido Violao	Odeon MOFB 3076 LP
O Violao E O Samba	Odeon MOFB 3295 LP
Softly...Luiz Bonfa	Epic BN 26124 LP

JOSHUA BREAKSTONE

Born-Elizabeth, New Jersey, USA
22 July 1955

Joshua Breakstone

As a youth Joshua Breakstone was drawn to the guitar by rock guitarists such as Jimi Hendrix. It was after hearing some recordings of Charlie Parker and other leading jazz artists when he was fifteen, that Breakstone decide to study and play jazz.

Breakstone studied privately with Sal Salvador in New York and then went on to study at the Berklee College of Music in Boston. In 1975 he was awarded a degree in jazz studies from Berklee. In 1977 he joined reed player Glen Hall for a tour of Canada and in 1979 was featured on Hall's Sonora label record release, 'Book Of The Heart'. From 1979-81 Breakstone was Professor of Non-Classical Guitar and Jazz Studies at the Rhode Island Conservatory of Music. This gave him the opportunity to play in New York area jazz clubs with many jazz artists including Warne Marsh, Emily Remler, Dave Schnitter, Aaron Bell, and Vic Juris. In 1983 Sonora, a Canadian record company, released Breakstone's first recording as leader featuring pianist Barry Harris. Since that time Breakstone has enjoyed a growing reputation as one of the best young guitarists continuing the bebop jazz guitar tradition.

Joshua Breakstone has played and recorded with many important jazz artists including Tommy Flanagan, Kenny Barron, Pepper Adams and Jimmy Knepper. He now records for the Double Time label.

SELECTED RECORDINGS

4+4 = 1	Mobile Fidelity MFCD CD
Echoes	Contemporary C-14025 CD
Evening Star	Contemporary C-14040 CD
Self-Portrait in Swing	Contemporary C-14050 CD
9 by 3	Contemporary C-14062 CD
Compositions of the Beatles (Vol. 1)	Bellaphon KJCJ 122 CD
Compositions of the Beatles (Vol. 2)	Bellaphon KJCJ 123 CD
Sittin' on the Thing with Ming	Capri 74042 2 CD
Walk Don't Run	Evidence 22058 2 CD
Remembering Grant Green	Evidence 22146 2 CD
Let's Call This Monk	Double Time DTRCD-121

SELECTED READING

Profile	Jazz Times, December 1994
Interview	String Jazz, July/August 1995

Lenny Breau

LENNY BREAU

Born-LEONARD BREAU
Auburn, Maine, USA
5 August 1941
Died-Los Angeles, USA
12 August 1984

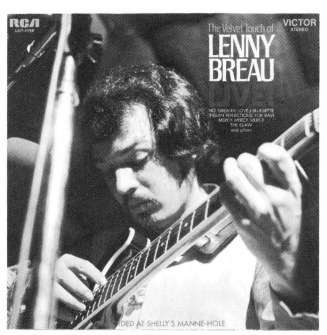

Lenny Breau was discovered by top country guitarist Chet Atkins in Winnipeg, Canada. Regarded by many jazz guitarists to be the most innovative guitarist to have appeared on the jazz scene in the 1960s, Breau lived for most of his life as a recluse. This was mainly due to his drug addiction and the related physical and mental problems. His recordings certainly prove that he was a brilliant, versatile and individual jazz guitar stylist.

Breau started to play the guitar at the age of seven. By the time he was twelve he was able to play professionally with his parents, country and western singers Hal 'Lone Pine' Breau and Betty Cody. He first became interested in jazz at the age of seventeen. Breau listened to the recordings of most of the leading guitar innovators of the 1950s including Barney Kessel, Tal Farlow and Johnny Smith. But the unique style of guitar playing which he finally developed was mainly influenced by the finger-style approach of country guitar legend, Chet Atkins, and the jazz piano approach of Bill Evans. When Chet Atkins heard Breau in Winnipeg he immediately recognized the young player's unique ability and signed him to record for the RCA label. After the success of his first recording for RCA Breau spent some time in Los Angeles. Here he gained prominence in jazz circles when he played at drummer Shelley Manne's jazz club, 'The Manne Hole', and other jazz spots.

In the late 1960s Breau returned to Toronto, moving to Winnipeg in 1973 until 1975. For some years he lived in Killaloe, Ontario, Canada, but rarely gave any public performances. With the persuasion of Chet Atkins and others, he did spend some time in Nashville, teaching and playing occasional club dates. From 1977-81 Breau made a few recordings which once again reveal his enormous talent. By this time he was playing a seven-string guitar built to his own design. This instrument had an extra treble string, a high A, rather than the extra bass string as introduced by George Van Eps on his seven-string guitar. In November 1983 Breau moved to Los Angeles where he taught privately and gave seminars. He also wrote a regular column (edited by Jim Ferguson) for Guitar Player magazine. In August 1974 he was found dead in what was

originally thought to be a swimming pool accident. Later evidence suggests that he was murdered.

Lenny Breau, although little known to the average jazz lover, is regarded by guitarists, and those jazz musicians who worked with him, as one of the most influential and original jazz guitarists of all time.

SELECTED RECORDINGS

Guitar sounds from Lenny Breau	RCA 4076 CD
Velvet Touch of Lenny Breau	One Way ON29315 CD
Lenny Breau	Direct-to-Disk DD 112
Lenny Breau...Now	Soundhole NR 10462
When Lightn' Strikes	Tudor TR 113004
Five O'Clock Bells	Genie 5006 CD
Lenny Breau Mo' Breau	Adelphi AD 5012
Last Sessions	Genes GCD 5024
Living Room Tapes	DOS 7503 CD
Standard Brands w/Chet Atkins	One Way 29316 CD
Buddies	Flying Fish 041 LP
Minors Aloud	Flying Fish 088 LP
Live at Bourbon Street	Guitarchives GR 0001 CD
Cabin Fever	Guitarchives GR 0002 CD
Chance Meeting w/Tal Farlow	Guitarchives GR 0003 CD

SELECTED READING

Profile	Guitar Player, September, 1974
Interview	Guitar Player, October, 1981
Profile	Guitar International August, 1987
Article	Just Jazz Guitar, November 1995
A Lost Lenny Breau Lesson	Guitar Player, March 1996
Article	Fingerstyle Guitar, Sept/Oct 1997

SELECTED MUSIC

Lenny Breau Jazz Guitar Style	Mel Bay Publications

BOBBY BROOM

Born-New York City, USA
18 January 1961

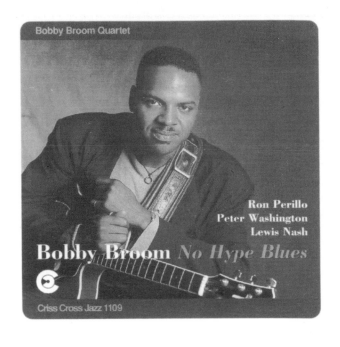

Bobby Broom started to play the guitar at the age of 13. He attended the High School of Music and Art in Manhattan and soon made excellent progress. By the time he was 16 he had already played in groups supporting top jazzmen including Sonny Rollins, Al Haig and Donald Byrd.

Broom studied music at Coumbia College, the School of Music in Chicago, Berklee School of Music in Boston and Long Island University. He earned a BA from Columbia College. He has taught at Jackie McLean's Afro-American Music Department at the Hartt School of Music at the University of Hartford and at the American Conservatory of Music in Chicago.

In recent times Bobby Broom has been one of the busiest jazz musicians in the New York area working and touring with organist Mel Rhyne. Broom has also toured with Sadao Watanabe, Art Blakey, Stanley Turrentine, Dave Grusin and Tom Browne. Broom has also given a series of workshops and master classes for the Yamaha Corporation of America. Since 1995 he has recorded for Criss Cross the leading jazz label based in the Netherlands.

SELECTED RECORDINGS

The Tip w/Dave Murray	D1W 891 CD
Jug-a-Lug w/Dave Murray	D1W 894 CD
Jazz Guitar Band w/Kenny Burrell	Blue Note 7902602 CD
No Hype Blues	Criss Cross CRISS 1109 CD
Eric Alexander in Europe	Criss Cross CRISS 1114 CD
Waitin' and Waitin'	Criss Cross CRISS 1135 CD

SELECTED READING

Interview	Jazz Journal, October 1993

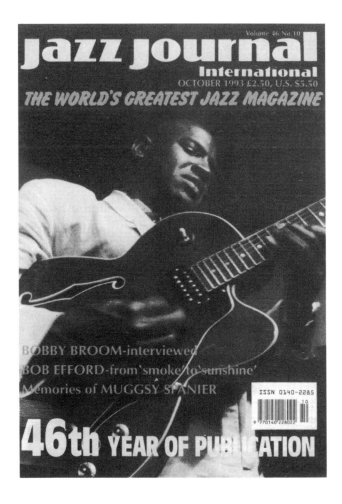

BIG BILL BROONZY
Born-WILLIAM LEE CONLEY BROONZY
Scott, Mississippi, USA
26 June 1898
Died-Chicago, Illinois, USA
14 January 1958

Big Bill Broonzy the legendary singer/guitarist whose music is the very essence of the blues and early jazz, was raised in Arkansas. His parents were born into slavery, and as a young man Broonzy made his living as a farm worker. In 1916 he worked as a coal miner for a year. In 1917 he worked with the American Expeditionary Forces in Europe.

Exposed to the music of many early blues guitarists, Broonzy developed a moving, blues style on the guitar which he used to accompany his voice and other musicians and singers.

In 1920 Broonzy moved to Chicago where he worked as a labourer. He became a member of the local black Community and as a result associated with many legendary blues singers and instrumentalists including Tampa Red, Memphis Minnie, Lonnie Johnson, Memphis Slim and Leroy Carr. He also took guitar lessons from Papa Charlie Jackson. His talents were obvious and in 1926 he was hired by Paramount to record as a guitar accompanist for various blues singers.

By the late 1930s Broonzy had already established himself as a top blues singer/guitarist in his own right and was recording regularly. In 1938-39 he was a featured artist in John Hammond's `From Spirituals to Swing` concerts.

During World War II Broonzy dropped out of the limelight and worked as a janitor at the Iowa State College. Fortunately he was still able to maintain a musical career in Chicago and as a result his whereabouts were known to jazz lovers throughout the world.

In 1951-52, because of popular demand, Broonzy was hired for concert tours of Europe and the United Kingdom. These tours were so successful they ensured that Broonzy's great talent was internationally recognized. Further concert tours followed in 1955 and 1957. A lung operation in late 1957 brought Broonzy's singing career to an end and he died of cancer the following year.

The importance of Big Bill Broonzy's contribution as a blues singer is undisputed. But it is perhaps not generally realized by jazz fans

Big Bill Broonzy

that his guitar playing was a great influence and inspiration for many jazz guitarists. He was without doubt one of the finest, and most influential, of the early blues guitar stylists.

SELECTED RECORDINGS

Big Bill Broonzy	Queen Disc Q-023
Big Bill Broonzy	MSI Disc 30JA5127
Big Bill Live	Storyville 670143
Remembering Big Bill	Mercury 60905
Big Bill Broonzy	Mercury 842 743-2
Big Bill Broonzy	Black & Blue 33-012
Big Bill Sings Country Blues	XTRA 1093
Trouble In Mind	Spotlight SPJ1900
The Young Big Bill Broonzy	Yazoo L-1011
See See Rider	Jazz Anthology 30 JA 5127
Big Bill Broonzy	Mercury 842 743 2 CD

SELECTED READING

Big Bill Broonzy-A Biography as told to Yannick Bruynoghe	
	Cassell & Co (1955)
Big Bill - This is Jazz p.89-96 Y.Bruynoghe	Newnes (1960)
Article	Guitar Player, April 1973
Profile	Guitar Player, August 1986

SELECTED MUSIC

Six Black Blues Guitarists	Oak Publications
Ragtime Blues Guitarists	Oak Publications
The Guitar of Big Bill Broonzy	Stephan Grossman Guitar Workshop

DALE BRUNING
Born-Carbondale, Pennsylvania, USA
8 November 1934

Dale Bruning served in the US Navy 1953-57. During that time he was a guitarist and arranger, and at times also played piano, bass and vibraphone. After leaving the Navy in 1957 Bruning studied at Temple University from where he graduated with a bachelor of arts degree in pyschology. He also studied music at that time with the well-known educator Dennis Sandole.

In 1961 Bruning was appointed the leader of the house band for The Del Shields Show a popular Philadelphia radio programme. In 1964 he moved to Denver. In 1988 Bruning suffered a serious accident to his left hand. Fortunately after a long period of recuperation he managed to regain his former technical ability.

He taught in the 1970s in the guitar departments of the University of Northern Colorado and The University of Colorado. He has also taught privately for over forty years. Bill Frisell was one of his students. Bruning has been a clinician at dozens of music seminars. He has won several important music awards including Best Guitarist - Denver Area 1983-86, and played with many top jazz artists including Jim Hall, Red Norvo, Dizzy Gillespie, Peanuts Hucko, Billy Bean, Chet Baker, Nancy Wilson, Art Van Damme and Johnny Smith.

A respected performer, composer, arranger and teacher Dale Bruning lives and works from Longmont, Colorado.

Dale Bruning

PHOTO: JUDE HIBLER

SELECTED RECORDINGS
Tomorrow's Reflections - Dale Bruning Quartet Jazz Link JLECD 4001

SELECTED READING
Profile   Just Jazz Guitar, November 1997

SELECTED MUSIC
Jazz Guitar Instruction Series   Jazz Link Enterprises

JIMMY BRUNO
Born-Philadelphia, Pennsylvania, USA
22 July 1953

Jimmy Bruno's father was a professional guitarist. His hit recording 'Guitar Boogie Shuffle' with Frank Virtue and The Virtues sold two million copies.

Jimmy Bruno began to play the guitar at the age of seven. Completely self taught he joined the Buddy Rich Band when he was nineteen. Since that time Bruno has led a busy career as a studio guitarist backing popular and jazz artists including Lena Horne, Frank Sinatra, Tony Bennett, Elvis Presley, Barbra Streisand and B.B. King. He studied with Tommy Tedesco, and more recently collaborated on Tedesco's book 'The Anatomy of a Guitar Player'.

Bruno recently signed a contract with the Concord record company and on his first release for them is featured with a trio playing in the style of the jazz masters of the 1950s and 1960s. Bruno currently teaches guitar at the Community College of Philadelphia.

Jimmy Bruno

PHOTO: NORMAN WILSON

SELECTED RECORDINGS

Carnival Time w/Tommy Tedesco	Trend TRCD 534 CD
A Hollywood Gypsy w/Tommy Tedesco	Discovery DSCD 928 CD
Sleight Of Hand	Concord CCD-4532
Burnin'	Concord CCD-4612
Concord Jazz Collective	Concord CCD-4672
Like That	Concord CCD-4698
Live at Birdland	Concord CCD-4768

SELECTED READING

Interview	Just Jazz Guitar, November 1994
Profile	Jazz Times, August 1995
Interview	20th Century Guitar, August 1997

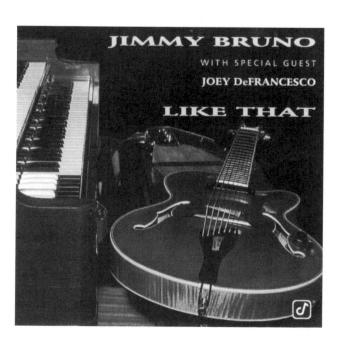

Right to left: Jimmy Bruno, Howard Alden and Jack Wilkins. New York, June 1997.

PHOTO: RICH RAEZER

75

MIKE BRYAN
Born-MICHAEL NEELY BRYAN
Byhalia, Mississippi, USA
1916
Died-Los Angeles, California, USA
20 August 1972

Mike Bryan

Mike Bryan was brought up in Germantown, Tennessee. After leaving school he taught himself to play the guitar. He was soon playing in clubs around the Memphis area. For a short while he moved to Chicago where he played with the Red Nichols band. In 1938 he formed his own band in Greenwood, Mississippi.

From November 1940 until May 1941 Mike Bryan played with the Benny Goodman band. He then played with diverse groups including those led by Bob Chester, Jan Savitt and Artie Shaw. Bryan then served in the US Army from March 1942 until November 1944. On his return to civilian life he went to New York where he played briefly with the Slam Stewart trio.

In January 1945 Bryan was once again hired by Benny Goodman. He left this famous band in September 1946 and moved to California, where he became involved in the studios. In 1962 he toured parts of Europe as musical director of the 'Goodyear Band'. He then stopped being a full time professional musician and in the mid 1960s became involved in the automobile business. He later ran his own music shop.

SELECTED RECORDINGS

Mike Bryan Sextet	Storyville SLP 234
Mike Bryan Sextet	Storyville SLP 825
Mike Bryan Sextet Video	Virgin/Storyville

DENNIS BUDIMIR
Born-DENNIS MATTHEW BUDIMIR
Los Angeles, California, USA
20 June 1938

Dennis Budimir

PHOTO: COURTESY REVELATION RECORDS

At the age of nineteen Dennis Budimir's reputation on the guitar had already earned him a place in the Harry James band. Following his stay with this famous big band Budimir returned to California where he worked with drummer Chico Hamilton's jazz group. After leaving Hamilton Budimir began a successful association with saxophonist Eric Dolphy. The experience gained with these groups helped Budimir develop an individual jazz guitar style which is more orientated to the style of saxophonists Sonny Rollins and John Coltrane, than other guitarists. Following his work with Dolphy's quintet Budimir worked for two years in the Los Angeles studios, mainly backing singer Peggy Lee. He replaced Billy Bean for a while in the Bud Shank Quartet but left in 1961 when he was drafted into the army. In 1963 Budimir joined pianist Bobby Troup for a tour of Japan. Since that time he has worked as a highly respected studio musician in the Los Angeles area, working with a very wide variety of famous artists including, Quincy Jones, Lalo Schiffrin, Don Ellis, Julie London and Marty Paich. Much admired by other West Coast guitarists Budimir won 'Downbeat' magazine critics' poll in 1971. In 1975 he won the first of four consecutive 'Most Valuable Player' awards from the National Association of Recording Arts And Sciences. After his fourth win in 1979 Budimir was given this prestigious association's Emeritus Award. Because of Budimir's many years spent working in the studios his fine guitar work is little known today to the general jazz listener. His recordings as leader of his own jazz group on the Revelation Label, out of production for many years, are available once again.

SELECTED RECORDINGS

Alone Together	Revelation Rcv 1 LP
A Second Coming	Revelation Rev 4 LP
Duo with Gary Foster	Revelation 5 LP
Sprung Free	Revelation Rev 8 LP
Session with Albert	Revelation Rev 14 LP
The Creeper	Fontana TL 5307 LP
Chico Hamilton Quintet	Warner WB56239 LP

SELECTED READING

Profile	Guitar Player, May 1981

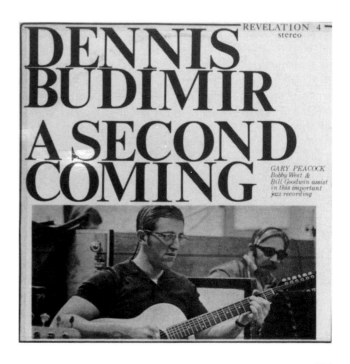

REVELATION 4
stereo

DENNIS BUDIMIR A SECOND COMING

GARY PEACOCK Bobby West & Bill Goodwin assist in this important jazz recording

TEDDY BUNN
Born-THEODORE LEROY BUNN
Freeport, Long Island, New York, USA 1909
Died-Lancaster Hospital, California, USA
20 July 1978

Teddy Bunn was a mainstay of the world famous 1930's vocal/instrumental group 'The Spirits of Rhythm'. His unique guitar style greatly infuenced guitarists of the period. Although never really featured as a guitar soloist, his technical ability, swing, and inventiveness on the guitar have always been admired by jazz lovers.

Bunn was a self-taught player but had an excellent ear which helped him quickly master his chosen instrument. In the mid 1920s he accompanied various blues singers and in 1928 he was featured with the 'Washboard Serenaders'. It is not generally known that for eighteen months he temporarily replaced Freddie Guy as guitarist with the Duke Ellington orchestra. In the 1930s he came to international prominence when he replaced Buddy Blanton in the 'Spirits of Rhythm'. At that time they were regularly featured at the 'Onyx Club' the famous 52nd Street jazz night club in New York City. A feature of Bunn's solo playing was that he often used his right hand thumb instead of pick.

In 1937 Bunn worked for a time with the original John Kirby Band but in 1939 rejoined the 'Spirits of Rhythm'. In 1944 this great guitarist led his own group called the 'Waves of Rhythm' and in the following years fronted his own small bands in Sacramento and Los Angeles.

After the war Bunn freelanced mainly on the West Coast of the USA with traditional jazz artists such as Johnny Dodds, Jimmie Noone, and Mezz Mezzrow. In the mid 1950s he worked with Edgar Hayes, Jack McVea and Louis Jordan. In the late 1950s he played for a time with a rock and roll band. In 1970 he worked in a night club in Honolulu but poor health forced him to stop working. After a long illness Teddy Bunn died at the age of 69 in the summer of 1978.

Teddy Bunn

PHOTO: PETER TANNER/COURTESY JAZZ JOURNAL

SELECTED RECORDINGS

The Spirits of Rhythm	Caete LP-1 LP
Johnny Dodds-Blues Galore	MCA 510-106 LP
Teddy Bunn (1930-1939)	RST BD-2069 LP
Sidney Bechet Jazz Classics Vol 1	Blue Note 1201 LP
50 Years of Jazz Guitar	Columbia 33566 LP
Kings of the Guitar	Beppo 14800 LP
Ladnier/Mezzrow/Bechet	RCA FXM 1-7132 LP
The Spirits of Rhythm 1933-34	JSP 307 CD
Teddy Bunn 1929-40	RST JPCD-1509-2

SELECTED READING

Teddy Bunn on Record Part 1	Jazz Journal, June 1971
Teddy Bunn on Record Part 2	Jazz Journal, July 1971
Profile	Guitar, May 1973
Teddy Bunn Today	Jazz Journal, October 1976

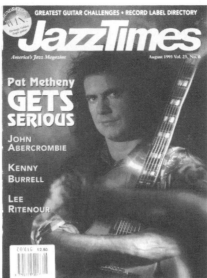

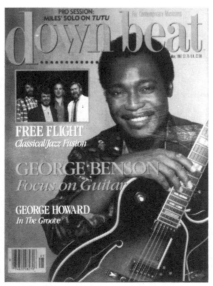

Jazz magazines with guitarists as their cover artists.

Kenny Burrell

KENNY BURRELL
Born-KENNETH EARL BURRELL
Detroit, Michigan, USA.
31 July 1931

Kenny Burrell's music career began in his home town of Detroit. He started to play the guitar at the age of twelve when he was taught by his elder brother Billy. Burrell originally wanted to play the saxophone, but the high cost of this instrument influenced him to take up the guitar instead.

Burrell was fortunate to have a musical background. His father was a banjoist, his mother a pianist, and both brothers were guitarists. Many of Burrell's friends at the Miller High School in Detroit were musicians, including jazz pianist Tommy Flanagan and bassist Calvin Jackson. His music adviser at school was Louis Cabrara and he proved most influential in shaping Burrell's musical career. It is interesting to note that other ex-pupils of Miller High School were vibraphonist Milt Jackson, and saxophonists Yusef Lateef and Pepper Adams.

Burrell's early influences were Charlie Christian and Oscar Moore. By 1948 he already was well known locally for his guitar talent. He played in many groups in the Detroit area including a spell in 1951 with trumpeter Dizzy Gillespie at the Club Juana. In 1955 he led his own group but left to replace Herb Ellis in the Oscar Peterson Trio. Burrell stayed with Peterson for only six months but having left Detroit decided to settle in New York.

After arriving in New York in 1956 Burrell was first hired by pianist Hampton Hawes. He then worked with saxophonist Frank Foster and trumpeter Thad Jones. Over the years he has enjoyed great success fronting his own groups in various New York jazz clubs. He also gained wide international recognition through his many recordings made there. Although Burrell did spend some time playing with Broadway theatre orchestras (including the popular shows, 'Bye Bye Birdie' and 'How To Succeed In Business Without Really Trying') he managed to maintain a continuous career in jazz for almost eighteen years on the East Coast.

From 1952-53 Burrell studied the classical guitar with Joe Fava, and now sometimes incorporates this technique as part of his jazz performance. He also decided to study music theory and composition, and in 1955 earned his Bachelor of Music degree from Wayne State University. In 1957 he played with Benny Goodman's band.

Kenny Burrell's interest in promoting the guitar is seen by his involvement for several years with a jazz club in New York called 'The Guitar'. This venture, now closed, was the brainchild of fellow Detroiter Fred Hayes with whom he had studied at Wayne University.

In 1973 Burrell moved to Los Angeles where he became involved in studio work. At the same time he also maintained a rigorous schedule of jazz club, concert performances and teaching which continues to this day. Since 1978 he has taught the History of Jazz and American Music at UCLA during the winter term.

Kenny Burrell continues to be one of the most successful jazz guitarists on today's scene. He has won many jazz magazine readers and critics polls and continues to record prolifically. It is said that Duke Ellington let it be known that Kenny Burrell was his favourite jazz guitarist.

SELECTED RECORDINGS

Ronnell Bright Trio	Savoy SV-0220 CD
Introducing Kenny Burrell	Blue Note 1523
Kenny Burrell	Blue Note 1543
Blue Lights Vol 1 & 2	Blue Note 57184 CD
Soul Call	Prestige OJCCD-846-2
Midnight Blue	Blue-Note CDP 746399-2
Kenny Burrell Quintet	Blue Note 4021
Two Guitars Burrell/Raney	Prestige 7119
Weaver of Dreams (Vocal)	Columbia 1703
Kenny Burrell	Prestige 7088
Kenny Burrell/John Coltrane	Prestige P24059 (2LPs)
The Best of Kenny Burrell	Prestige 7448
All Day Long, All Night Long	Prestige PR24025 (2LPs)
Asphalt Canyon Suite	Verve OK
Blues - The Common Ground	Verve SVLP 9217
Guitar Forms	Verve 314-521-403 CD
Night Song	Verve VLP 9246
Cool Cooking	Checker 6467-310
Ode To 52nd Street	Cadet LPS 798
Both Feet On The Ground	Fantasy 9427
Ellington Is Forever Vol 1	Fantasy F7-9005(2LPs)
Ellington Is Forever Vol 2	Fantasy F-5944 (2LPs)
Up The Street	Fantasy 9458
Tin Tin Deo	Concord CCD-4045
When Lights Are Low	Concord CCD-4083
Moon And Sand	Concord CCD-4121
Heritage	AudioSource ASD-1
Hand Crafted	Muse MR 5144 CD
Live At The Village Vanguard	Muse MR 5216 CD
Kenny Burrell In New York	Muse MR 5241 CD
Listen To The Dream	Muse MR 5264 CD
Groovin' High	Muse MR 5281 CD
A La Carte	Muse MR 5317 CD
The Jazz Guitar Band Generation	Blue Note BT 85137 CD
The Jazz Guitar Band Blues	Blue Note BT 90260 CD
Kenny Burrell Quartet – Guiding Spirit	Contemporary C-14058 CD
Sun Up To Sundown	Contemporary CCD-14065-2
Tribute To Wes Montgomery Vol 1	Evidence 22049 CD
Tribute To Wes Montgomery Vol 2	Evidence 22051 CD
From Vanguard with Love	Paddle Wheel KICJ 212 CD
Live at the Blue Note	Concord CCD-4731
For Charlie and Benny	Verve 831087 2 CD
No Problem w/Ray Bryant	EM ARCY 522 387 2 CD
Kenny Burrell – Verve Jazz Masters (45)	Verve 527 652 2 CD

SELECTED READING

Profile	Downbeat, August 1963
Profile	Downbeat, July 1966
Profile	BMG, October 1969
Profile	Downbeat, June 1971
Interview	Guitar Player, March 1971
Profile	Jazz Journal, November 1978
Profile	Coda, October 1979
Interview	Guitar Player, April 1981
Profile	Jazz Times, August 1993
Interview	Downbeat, September 1993
Article	Just Jazz Guitar, November 1995

SELECTED MUSIC

Jazz Guitar Solos Kenny Burrell	Chas. Colin Music
Jazz Guitar	Elliot Music Co.

BILLY BUTLER
Born-WILLIAM BUTLER
Philadelphia, Pennsylvania, USA
15 December 1924
Died-Teaneck, New Jersey, USA
20 March 1991

Billy Butler

Billy Butler first began to play the guitar professionally in 1940 with a group called 'The Three Tones'. He had taken up the guitar at the age of thirteen and was virtually self-taught. Although originally inspired by acoustic guitarists Eddie Lang and George Van Eps, it was the electric guitar sounds of Charlie Christian, George Barnes and Oscar Moore that were to prove to be his major influences.

In 1943 Butler joined the Army and was put into a military band as a drummer. After his discharge he returned to Philadelphia where he was featured with a vocal quartet called 'The Harlemaires' from 1947-49. He spent three years with a band called 'Daisy May and the Hepcats' and in 1952 formed his own group. It was in 1954 that popular success came to Butler, now regarded as a top blues guitarist, when he joined a band led by organist Bill Doggett. They made a record called 'Honky Tonk' which sold a million copies. Following on this success Butler stayed with Doggett for almost eight years.

After leaving Doggett, Butler established himself as a successful studio artist in New York. He recorded with many famous artists including Dinah Washington, King Curtis, Johnny Hodges, Jimmy Smith and David 'Fathead' Newman. He also played in the pit bands of several Broadway theatres. At the same time he was still involved in making records with jazz artists including Houston Preston (1969-71), Al Casey (1974), and Norris Turney (1975). From 1976 Butler played on a regular basis at USA and European jazz venues.

SELECTED RECORDINGS

That Healin' Feelin'	Prestige 7601
This is Billy Butler	Prestige 7622
Guitar Soul	Prestige 7734
Guitar Odyssey with Al Casey	Jazz Oddysey 012
Don't Be That Way	Black & Blue 33-014

SELECTED READING

Profile	Guitar Player, March 1975

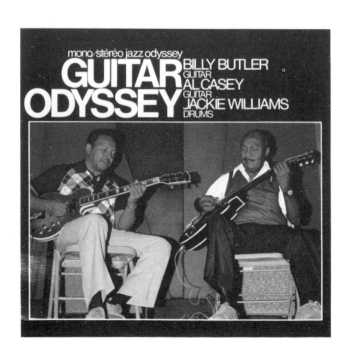

CHRIS BUZZELLI
Born-Trenton, New Jersey, USA
15 September 1959

Chris Buzzelli started to play the guitar at the age of ten. Over the years he studied with Jack Petersen, Denis Sandole, Frank Hipp and classical guitarist Alice Artzt. Whilst still at high school Buzzelli was already working as a professional guitarist and teacher. At the age of 16 he played in the Philadelphia area with many top jazz musicians including saxophonist Richie Cole. After earning two music degrees Buzzelli established himself as a leading guitar teacher and composer of music for student guitar ensembles.

Over the years Chris Buzzelli has appeared in concert and jazz clubs with fellow guitarists Joe Pass, Herb Ellis, Tal Farlow, Cal Collins and Joshua Breakstone. He has also played with diverse jazz musicians including Clark Terry, Peter Erskine, Stanley Cowell , Ira Sullivan and Slide Hampton. In 1993 he made the first of his recordings for the Schoolkid's Record label.

Chris Buzzelli is currently Associate Professor of Guitar and Jazz studies at Bowling Green State University, Ohio.

Chris Buzzelli

PHOTO: NORMAN WILSON

SELECTED RECORDINGS
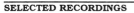
Boss of the B-3 w/Jack McDuff   Schoolkid's Records
What Goes Round   Scoolkid's Records 48775-1563
So Easy to Love NTSU Jazz Guitars   Mark Records MJS 57604

SELECTED READING
Article   Just Jazz Guitar, August 1996

Charlie Byrd

CHARLIE BYRD

Born-CHARLES L. BYRD
Chuckatuck, Nr Suffolk, Virginia, USA
16 September 1925
Died-Annapolis, Maryland, USA
1 December 1999

Charlie Byrd

PHOTO: COURTESY JAZZ JOURNAL

Charlie Byrd started to play the guitar at the age of nine. He studied with his father who played several fretted instruments, including the mandolin. Byrd's first professional work was in a dance band at the Virginia Polytechnic Institute. Later he toured Europe with an Army show band under the direction of Marty Faloon. Whilst he was in Paris he had the opportunity to hear and play with the legendary Gypsy jazz guitarist, Django Reinhardt.

After leaving the Army, Byrd remained in the New York City area from 1946 for four years playing jazz with many groups which included various well-known jazz artists including Joe Marsala.

Although a plectrum guitarist at the time Byrd began to take a serious interest in classical music and the classical guitar. Bill Harris, the jazz/classical guitarist from Washington DC, recommended he take lessons from Sophocles Papas a noted guitarist/educator and a resident of Washington. In 1950 Byrd, now a resident of Washington, decided to devote himself to the classical guitar. He studied guitar with Papas, and theory and harmony with musicologist, Thomas Simmons. Byrd also took part in a master class given by Andres Segovia in Siena, Italy.

On his return to the USA Byrd toured for a short while as guitarist with the Woody Herman band. But it was his love of the classical guitar that would eventually bring Charlie Byrd's name to the forefront of jazz fans all over the world. He had at one time decided to give up jazz, but after some experimentation he founded his historic jazz trio comprising of himself on classical guitar, Keeter Betts on bass ,and Bertel Knox on drums. They played sessions most nights of the week to packed houses at Byrd's Washington jazz club, 'The Showboat Lounge'. The bulk of the music played by the trio was jazz but Byrd usually included several classical guitar solos as part of the programme.

This new trio, which featured Charlie Byrd's original fingerstyle jazz guitar made an enormous impact on the jazz world. In 1961 the USA State Department sponsored a tour for Byrd's trio to South America. During this tour the idea occurred to Byrd to mix jazz improvisation and harmony with the samba, and other popular Brazilian rhythms. On his return to the USA in 1962, Byrd made a historic best selling recording with saxophonist Stan Getz. Despite the fact that a few years earlier Bud Shank and Laurindo Almeida's quartet had produced similar recordings entitled 'Brazilliance', Byrd's choice of music, with many compositions by top Brazilian guitarist/composers Antonio Carlos Jobim, Luiz Bonfa, Joao Gilberto and others, proved a winning formula. Their wonderful melodies and harmonies helped achieve enormous commercial success for their first recording. The unique combination of Getz's saxophone and Byrd's nylon-strung classical guitar marked the start of a fantastic bossa nova boom in the USA, and eventually throughout the rest of the world.

After this success Byrd made many recordings which sold in large quantities. With their popular appeal they outsold most recordings by other top jazz guitarists of the day. In 1965 Byrd was chosen to play for President Johnson in the White House. He was also a winner of several annual international jazz polls during the 1960s.

Charlie Byrd continued to maintain a high profile in the jazz world right up to the time of his death. Over the years he toured with his own trio and also with 'The Great Guitars', a successful group which originally included Barney Kessel and Herb Ellis. In recent years he made many recordings for the Concord Record company in California.

SELECTED RECORDINGS

Jazz Recital	Savoy SV-0192 CD
Midnight Guitar	Savoy MG12116
Byrd In The Wind	OffBeat OJ-3005
Jazz At The Showboat	OffBeat OLP 3001
Latin Impressions	Riverside 9427
Bossa Nova Pelos Passaro	Riverside 9436
Mr.Guitar	Riverside 9450
Byrd's Word	Riverside 9448
Byrd in the Wind	Riverside 9449
Blues Sonata	Riverside 9453
Byrd at the Gate	OJC/Riverside 262 2 CD
Byrd Song	Riverside 9481
Solo Flight	Riverside 9498
Once More Charlie Byrd	Riverside 9454
At the Village Vanguard	Riverside 9452
The Guitar Artistry of Charlie Byrd	Riverside 9451
Brazilian Byrd	Riverside 673027
In Greenwich Village	Milestone M-47049 (2LPs)
Byrd Swings Downtown	Improv 7116
Jazz Samba	Verve 810 061-1
Travellin'Man	Columbia 2435
Stroke of Genius	Columbia 30380
Guitar/Guitar	Columbia 9130
Great Guitars Vol 1	Concord CCD-6004
Great Guitars Vol 2	Concord CCD-4023
Great Guitars at the Winery	Concord CCD-4131
Great Guitars at Charlie's	Concord CCD-4209
Great Guitars – Straight Tracks	Concord CCD-4621
Crystal Silence	Fantasy 9429
Top Hat	Fantasy F9496
Blue Byrd	Concord CCD-4082
Sugarloaf Suite	Concord Picante CCD-4114
Brazilian Soul	Concord Picante CCD-4150

Charlie Byrd Trio Live	Concord Picante CCD-4173
Byrd & Brass	Concord CCD-4304
It's A Wonderful World	Concord CCD-4374
Bossa Nova Years	Concord Picante CCD-4468
Music to Dine By	Leisure 04900-91050 CD
Moments Like This	Concord CCD-4627
Hot Club de Concord	Concord CCD-4674
Return of the Great Guitars	Concord CCD-4715
Au Courant	Concord CCD-4779
Charlie Byrd Trio Live-Video	Leisure Jazz MV 1059-3
Charlie Byrd – Instrumental Video	Hot Licks
Great Guitars at the Maintenance Shop (Vol. 1) Video	
	Shanachie/Kay
Great Guitars at the Maintenance Shop (Vol. 2) Video	
	Shanachie/Kay
Great Guitars at the Maintenance Shop (Vol. 3) Video	
	Shanachie/Kay

SELECTED READING

Profile	Downbeat, July 1960
Interview	Classical Guitar, March 1986
Profile	Acoustic Guitar, May/June 1994
Profile	Jazz Times, July/August 1994
Profile	Jazziz, September 1994
Article	Just Jazz Guitar, May 1995
Interview	Fingerstyle Guitar, Jan/Feb 1996

SELECTED MUSIC

Charlie Byrd's Melodic Guitar Method	Hollis Music
Jazz 'n' Samba Album	Hollis Music
Charlie Byrd/Bossa Nova	Peter Maurice Co.
Three Classic Guitar Blues	Columbia Music Co.
Great Movie Themes for Guitar	Edward B. Marks Co.

The Great Guitars– Charlie Byrd, Barney Kessel and Herb Ellis.

ROYCE CAMPBELL
Born-Seymour, Indiana, USA
7 June 1952

Royce Campbell

Royce Campbell first became interested in the guitar through listening to Elvis Presley recordings. He began to play the guitar at the age of nine studying with a teacher at a local music store. Within a short while he was playing in a local rock band. At the age of eleven he began to take an interest in jazz after hearing a Wes Montgomery recording.

After leaving high school Campbell lived for a while with his uncle Carroll DeCamp who at one time arranged for the Stan Kenton and Les Elghart orchestras. His uncle gave him important music tuition, and in his late teens he began to play for local dance bands. In 1975 he took a three day job working with the famous composer Henry Mancini. The composer was so impressed with Campbell that he hired him on a permanent basis. Campbell went on to work with Mancini both in the USA and all over the world until the composer's death in 1994.

Over the years Royce Campbell has had the opportunity to work with many top jazz artists including Cab Calloway, Jack McDuff, Sarah Vaughan, James Moody, Nancy Wilson, Dave Brubeck, Cleo Laine and Mel Torme. He has also backed many top popular singers including Julie Andrews, Petula Clark, Perry Como and Englebert Humperdinck.

Campbell's first love has always been jazz and since 1983 he has made many jazz recordings both as leader or co-leader. He has also devoted time to teaching jazz guitar at Cincinnati and Purdue University, and is the guitarist for the Indianapolis Symphony Orchestra.

SELECTED RECORDINGS

Solo Guitar	Redbud
Around The Town	Raised Eyebrow
Nightime Daydreams	Timeless CD SJP 337
Vista	Sin-Drome 8896 CD
Tribute to Wes Montgomery	Evidence ECD 22101-2 CD
Elegy to A Friend	Raised Eyebrow RE 1003 CD
Gentle Breeze	Timeless SJP 389 CD
6 x 6	Paddlewheel KICJ 220 CD
Make Me Rainbows	Positive 78024 CD
Waltz For Debby	Paddlewheel KICJ 248 CD
A Tribute to Henry Mancini	Episode ESP-1001-2 CD
Pitapat	A Records AL 731 26 CD
Hands Across The Water w/Adrian Ingram	String Jazz SJRCD 1002

SELECTED READING

Article	String Jazz, January/February 1996

LARRY CARLTON
Born-LAWRENCE EUGENE CARLTON
Torrance, California, USA
2 March 1948

Larry Carlton began to play the guitar at the age of six. He soon developed a strong interest in jazz and even at an early age was influenced by jazz greats such as Barney Kessel, Joe Pass, Wes Montgomery and John Coltrane. As he went into his teens Carlton became influenced by a wide variety of other guitar styles. At the age of sixteen he became interested in the blues guitar style of B.B. King, Albert Collins and Robben Ford.

Larry Carlton started playing with several important artists, including George Shearing and the Fifth Dimension, while studying at Long Beach State University in the late nineteen sixties. In late 1969 he became musical director for the NBC children's programme. His exposure on this show made the Los Angeles studios aware of Carlton's talent and he soon became one of the busiest studio guitarists in that area. At the same time he became a member of the Jazz Crusaders, recording thirteen albums with them from 1971 to 1976. Carlton also toured throughout the USA and internationally with this popular group. As a sideman in the studios his guitar work can be heard on the recordings of a multitude of top stars including Quincy Jones, Ray Charles, Joni Mitchell, Diana Ross, Steely Dan, Michael Jackson, Linda Ronstadt, Art Garfunkel and Glen Campbell. He received a Grammy Award in 1981 for his performance on the theme music of the television programme, Hill Street Blues.

In 1976 Carlton decided to spend less time in the studios and concentrate on developing his own career as a jazz rock guitarist and vocalist. He built a studio in his house and made many of his recordings for Warner Brothers there. He recorded exclusively for Warners from 1978 to 1983. In 1985 he signed for MCA. This new association gave Carlton a wider audience outside of the jazz field. In 1988 he was shot by an intruder at his home and was incapacitated for several months. Carlton fortunately recovered and is now once again fully active as one of the USA's most distinctive and influential guitarists.

SELECTED RECORDINGS

Larry Carlton	Warner Bros BSK 3221
Larry Carlton Strikes Twice	Warner Bros BSK 3380
Mr 335 Live In Japan	Warner Bros
Sleepwalk	Warner Bros
Kid Gloves	GRP 96832 CD
Collection	GRP 96112
Discovery	GRP 01032

Larry Carlton

PHOTO: COURTESY GRP RECORDS

Alone, But Never Alone	GRP 01052
Friends	GRP 01042
On Solid Ground	GRP 01062
Larry Carlton	GRP 01242
Last Nite	GRP 01252
All Strings Attached	Verve 841 291-1
Renegade Gentleman	GRP GRD-973
The Gift	GRP 98542 CD
Larry Carlton Instructional Video	Starlicks Videos

SELECTED READING

Interview	Guitar Player, September 1986
Profile	Guitar World, November 1986
Interview	Frets, February 1988
Interview	Guitar Player, June 1989
Interview	20th Century Guitar, Nov/Dec 1994

SELECTED MUSIC

Larry Carlton	PMP Publishing
Original Larry Carlton	Amsco Publications

LARRY CARLTON Discovery

DIGITAL MASTER

JOE CARTER
Born-Bridgeport, Connecticut, USA
13 February 1955

Joe Carter

Joe Carter began to play the guitar at the age of nine. Whist studying at the University of Bridgeport he took lessons with Sal Salvador and pianist John Mehegan. Carter graduated with a degree in music performance and moved on to New York University to study for a masters degree. During this time he studied with guitarists John Scofiels and Allen Hanlon.

Carter currently divides his career between teaching and performance. He teaches at New York University and Manchester Community College in Connecticut. He has performed in the New York and Connecticut areas with diverse jazz musicians including Andy LaVerne, Don Friedman and Bill O'Connell.

SELECTED RECORDINGS	
Too Marvellous For Words	Empathy 1001 LP
Chestnut	Empathy 1002 LP
My Foolish Heart	Empathy 1004 LP

SELECTED READING	
Profile	Just Jazz Guitar, May 1995

SELECTED MUSIC	
Tonal Colors for Guitar	CPP Music
Chordal Colors for Guitar	CPP Music

JOSEPH CARTER III
Born-Brooklyn, New York, USA
17 July 1962

Joseph Carter III

PHOTO: COURTESY VELVET SWAN MUSIC

Joseph Carter III was inspired to play the guitar at the age of fifteen after hearing Jimi Hendrix. He went on to become a blues player performing with Ko Ko Taylor and Ruth Brown. Carter then turned his attention to jazz studying with Jim Hall, Tal Farlow and Joe Diorio.

Carter took a course in composition at Long Island University. There he studied under Raoul Pleskow, eventually receiving a masters degree in composition. Since that time Carter, a left-handed guitarist who plays a special-order guitar made by the late Jimmy D'Aquisto, has played and recorded with diverse jazz musicians including organist Bill Doggett, keyboardist Stu Waters and drummer Walter Perkins.

SELECTED RECORDINGS	
Straight Ahead Backwards	Velvet Swan VS-001

SELECTED READING	
Interview	Just Jazz Guitar, November 1994
Article	Vintage Guitar Magazine, January 1998

AL CASEY
Born-ALBERT ALOYSIUS CASEY
Louisville, Kentucky, USA
15 September 1915

Al Casey's father was a professional drummer. He and other members of his family helped make up the famous spiritual group 'The Southernaires'. They were regularly featured on radio broadcasts from Cincinatti in the early 1930s.

Casey first started to play the violin, under the tutelage of his mother, from the age of five. He played the ukulele for a while and then took up the guitar in 1930 when he moved to New York City. He was able to take lessons at the Martin-Smith Music School. He first came to prominence when he became the guitarist with the highly successful combo led by pianist/singer Fats Waller. He had been introduced to Waller when the pianist appeared with 'The Southernaires' on a radio show. The pianist showed genuine interest in the young guitarist and promised him a job when he finished high school. In late 1933 Casey graduated at the age of seventeen and as promised, joined Waller's band. He appeared regularly with Fats Waller from 1934 to 1943, and the sound of his guitar was an integral part of both Waller's small and large groups. Casey did have a break from playing with Waller in 1939-40 when he played with the Teddy Wilson band.

Waller was to be a major influence on Casey's approach to jazz. Casey often said he regarded the pianist as his second father. After Fats Waller's death in 1943 Casey led his own jazz trio in New York clubs, and then worked as a sideman with other groups, including those of Louis Armstrong, Billy Kyle and Clarence Profit.

In 1949 Al Casey joined the King Curtis rock and roll band and then Curley Hamner's group. Casey changed to a solid electric guitar for this commercial work. In 1973 he returned to playing jazz, gigging and recording both in the U.S.A. and Europe. He has continued to maintain a busy schedule working and recording all over the world with top jazz musicians including Bob Wilber, Milt Buckner and Jay McShann.

Al Casey

SELECTED READING

Profile	Downbeat, July 1962
Interview	Guitar Player, November 1981
Profile	Downbeat, December 1990

SELECTED RECORDINGS

Ain't Misbehavin-Fats Waller	RCA Victor LPM1246
Buck Jumpin	Prestige OJCCD-675 2 CD
Slamboree	Black and Blue 33-049
Jumpin with Al	Black and Blue 33-056
Guitar Odyssey w/Billy Butler	Jazz Odyssey 012
Six Swinging Strings	JSP Records 1026
Best Of Friends w/Jay McShann	JSP Records 1051
Genius Of The Jazz Guitar	JSP Records 1062
A Tribute to Fats	Jazzpoint JP 1044 CD

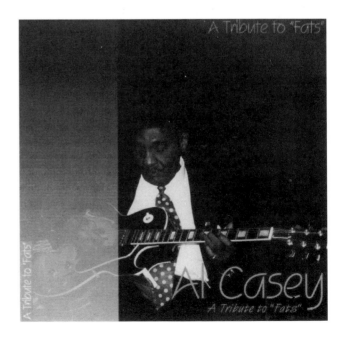

OSCAR CASTRO-NEVES
Born-Rio de Janeiro, Brazil
15 May 1940

Oscar Castro-Neves

Oscar Castro-Neves grew up in a musical envirorment. He studied both the guitar and the piano from the age of seven. At the age of twelve he became interested in jazz harmonies through the influence of an uncle. By the time he was in his mid teens Neves was already playing professionally in a group with his brothers. They played in local clubs and also appeared on radio and television programmes. By the time he was seventeen Neves had become a full time professional musician. He not only played the guitar and the piano, but was composing and arranging for studios in Rio de Janeiro.

In 1962 bossa nova exploded onto the world music scene. It became the rage in the USA. Castro-Neves and his quartet were invited to play in November 1962 in an 'All Star Bossa Nova' concert at the Carnegie Hall in New York. He shared the bill with Antonio Carlos Jobim, Luiz Bonfa, Stan Getz, Sergio Mendes and many more of the biggest names in bossa nova. After this concert the Oscar Castro-Neves quartet toured to selected major USA cities in the company of the Laurindo Almeida Quartet, the Lalo Schifrin Trio, the Stan Getz Quartet and the Dizzy Gillespie Quintet.

In 1963 Castro-Neves returned to Brazil to resume a busy life as a musical director, arranger and producer. In 1967 he returned to the USA as the musical director of the vocal quartet, 'The Girls From Bahia'. The following year he decided to settle in Los Angeles with his wife Regina. He worked with Quincy Jones and then Sergio Mendes. In 1971 he joined the highly successful Mendes group on a permanent basis until January 1979. He then decided to concentrate on studio work, arranging and teaching. He also started to play in local jazz spots with various groups.

Oscar Castro-Neves continues to live and work in the Los Angeles area. He has taught at the Guitar Institute of Technology (GIT) and at Dick Grove Music Workshops, and continues to record both as leader and as sideman.

SELECTED RECORDINGS

Oscar! Oscar Castro-Neves	Living Music LM0010
Edu Lobo	A & M Records AMLS 63035
Getz & Gilberto	Columbia PC 33703
Tudo Bem Joe Pass	Pablo 2310824
Lee Ritenour in Rio	JVC VIJ 6312
Brazilian Scandals	JVC CD 2018-2
Maracuja	JVC CD 2019-2
Simpatico w/John Klemmer	JVC CD 9025-2

SELECTED READING

Interview	Guitar Player June 1981

PHILIP CATHERINE
Born-London, England
27 October 1942

Philip Catherine

Philip Catherine was born to an English mother and a Belgian father. His grandfather played first violin with the London Symphony Orchestra. He took up the guitar at the age of fourteen when he heard some recordings by the popular singer/guitarist Georges Brassens. Catherine was inspired to play jazz after hearing some recordings by Django Reinhardt. He then began to listen to the recordings of all the great jazz musicians of the 1950s. The Belgian jazz guitarist Rene Thomas was a major influence on Catherine.

By the late 1950s Catherine was already playing with various jazz groups in Belgium including those led by Fats Sadi and Jack Sels, and broadcasting on Belgian Radio. In 1960 he toured Europe with organist, Lou Bennett, whilst still a college student. In 1971 he decided to become a professional musician after he was offered the chance to join violinist Jean-Luc Ponty's quintet.

During the early 1970s Catherine's jazz guitar style was influenced by the playing of guitarists John McLaughlin, Larry Coryell, and other jazz/rock musicians. After leaving Ponty, Catherine decided to go to the USA. He spent a year there studying at the Berklee School of Music. In 1973 he formed his own jazz/rock group called 'Pork Pie' which he co-led with saxophonist Charlie Mariano.

Since that time Philip Catherine has become one of the busiest jazz guitarists of the day. He lives in Brussels from where he has become one of Europe's most important jazz artists. Over the years he has led several different groups and also accompanied many of the all-time great jazz musicians, including Charles Mingus, Benny Goodman, Dexter Gordon, Stephane Grappelli, Chet Baker, Toots Thielmans and Didier Lockwood. He has appeared often in concert, and also recorded with fellow guitarist Larry Coryell. In recent times he has formed a successful trio with trumpeter Tom Harrell.

I Remember You	Criss Cross 1048 CD
Moods Vol 1	Criss Cross 1060 CD
Moods Vol 2	Criss Cross 1061 CD
Barney Wilen Trio	IDA 029 CD
Strollin' w/Chet Baker	Enja ENJ 5005 2 CD
Spanish Nights	Enja ENJ 7023 2 CD
In Concert w/Kenny Drew	Steeplechase SCS C3 1106 CD
Art of the Duo	Enja ENJ 8016 2 CD
Philip Catherine Quartet 'Live'	Dreyfus FDM 36587 2 CD

SELECTED RECORDINGS

Grapelli/Ponty	Inner City 1005 LP
Guitars-Philip Catherine	Atlantic K50 193 LP
Twin House Duo with Larry Coryell	Atlantic 50 342 LP
September Man	Atlantic 40 562 LP
Babel	Elektra 52 244 LP
Coryell Catherine Kuhn	Elektra 52 232 LP
End of August	WEA K 58 450 LP
Splendid Duo with Larry Coryell	Electra K520 LP
The Viking	Pablo 2310 894 LP
Catherine/Escoude/Lockwood Trio	JMS 031 LP
Transperance	Timeless SJP 242 LP
Oscar	Igloo 060 CD

PHOTO: PATRICK GRIES/COURTESY PHILIP CATHERINE

GREG CHAKO

Born-GREGORY THOMAS CHAPOPOULO
Cincinatti, Ohio, USA
12 June 1958

Greg Chako first studied the guitar at the age of 10 at the Helen Hoffman Music Studios. In 1969 he won second place in an American Guild Guitar Contest, moving on to attend Berklee College of Music from 1976-79 as a performance major. For a while Chako gave up playing the guitar, but after a short while studying classical guitar began to gain some professional experience playing jazz in Amherst, Massachusetts and Cincinatti. From 1987 - 92 Chako went into the real estate business and gave up playing altogether.

It was after moving to Hong Kong in 1992 that Chako returned to working as a full time professional musician. There he led his own jazz trio in many prestigious locations throughout the former UK colony. He has appeared at the Heineken Jazz Festival in Singapore and now lives and works from Singapore.

SELECTED RECORDINGS

Everything I Love - Greg Chako Trio	CP Productions CP 88-1
Sudden Impact - Greg Chako	CP Productions CP 88-2

SELECTED READING

Profile	Just Jazz Guitar, May 1995

Greg Chako

PETE CHILVER
Born-PETER WILLIAM CHILVER
Windsor, UK
19 October 1924

Pete Chilver is regarded as on of the finest jazz guitarists to have emerged out of Britain since 1945. He retired into the hotel business in 1950 and as a result is today not known to most jazz fans.

Chilver started to play the ukulele at the age of seven. In 1938 he changed over to the guitar after hearing some Django Reinhardt records. By the time he was nineteen Chilver was playing in a five piece band led by pianist Ralph Sharon. Chilver won the 'Best Guitarist' award in the 1942 Melody Maker jazz poll.

Chilver who was a draughtsman by profession first started working as a full-time professional musician in 1946 as a member of the Ray Ellington Quartet. In 1947 he joined accordionist Tito Burn's Sextet. He also played at that time with many leading jazz musicians including Stephane Grappelli, Ralph Sharon, George Shearing, Ronnie Scott, Art Pepper, Frank Weir and John Dankworth. Chilver also had the opportunity on several occasions to jam privately with Django Reinhardt. The gypsy guitar genius would often make a point of visiting the flat Chilver shared with Dave Goldberg each time he visited London.

In 1948 Pete Chilver joined the Ted Heath Big Band. In 1949 he played with the Benny Goodman Orchestra in concert at the London Palladium. In the same year he played frequently with the Bert Ambrose Orchestra.

In 1950 Chilver moved to Edinburgh where for the next twenty years he managed the family hotel and restaurant business. He maintained an involvement in jazz through regularly featuring jazz artists, including Tubby Hayes, Sandy Brown, John Dankworth and Ralph Sharon, at his 'West End' restaurant in Edinburgh.

Pete Chilver

PHOTO: COURTESY PETE CHILVER

SELECTED READING
Interview   Archtop Magazine, May/June 1988

Gibson Guitar 1960s advertisement featuring prominent jazz guitarists of the day.

Charlie Christian

CHARLIE CHRISTIAN

Born-CHARLES HENRY CHRISTIAN
Bonham, Texas, USA
29 July 1916
Died-New York City, USA
2 March 1942

Charlie Christian grew up in Oklahoma City. His father was a singer/guitarist, his mother a pianist, and they played in a Dallas cinema when he was a child. His two brothers were also musicians. Christian started his musical career on the trumpet but due to a serious chest condition changed to the guitar at the age of twelve. He also had some knowledge of the bass and the piano. Following the family's move to Oklahoma City in 1921 Christian senior lost his sight. To make a living he eventually became a street musician accompanied by his three sons, Clarence on violin and mandolin, Edward on string bass, and Charlie on guitar.

During the early 1930s Christian played acoustic guitar in his brother Edward's band, 'The Jolly Jugglers'. He first gained wider recognition for his obvious talent in 1937 when he joined the Anna Mae Winburn Orchestra. He then played in 1938 with the Alphonso Trent Sextet. Christian became fascinated with the electric guitar when he met Eddie Durham, who played an early version of the amplified instrument. Christian decided to experiment with the amplified guitar. He soon mastered what was then a very new instrument. His reputation on the electric guitar grew very quickly and jazz lovers came from far and wide to hear his new and original guitar style. His amplified single note lines sounded at times like a tenor saxophone. Christian began to develop many original ideas into his jazz improvisations. He used augmented and diminished chords in a way which in the not too distant future would transform the world of jazz. Though his ideas were very individual he was a great fan of Django Reinhardt's guitar style. He enjoyed playing Reinhardt's improvised choruses, note-for-note, on numbers like 'St.Louis Blues', and then adding several of his own improvised choruses.

In 1939 whilst playing with the Leslie Sheffield Band he was heard by the influential jazz promoter, John Hammond. He had been persuaded by pianist Mary Lou Williams to travel to Oklahoma City to hear Christian. Hammond was so impressed he persuaded his brother-in-law, band leader Benny Goodman, to hear Christian. Although Goodman was originally reluctant to listen to the young guitarist he finally agreed to give him an audition on August 16 1939, in Los Angeles. It only took a few bars of Charlie

THE ART OF THE JAZZ GUITAR
CHARLIE CHRISTIAN

Edited by
DAN FOX

Includes a biography of Charley Christian and complete analyses of his solos

Price $2.00

REGENT MUSIC CORPORATION
1619 BROADWAY · NEW YORK 19, N. Y.

Christian soloing on 'Rose Room' for the great clarinetist to recognise the young guitarist's genius. Christian was signed up on the spot.

In the two years that followed Charlie Christian became a major influence, not only in the Benny Goodman Big Band and Sextet, but also on the history of jazz. After playing at night with the Goodman band, Christian would go on to play into the early hours of the morning at Minton's jazz club in Harlem. Here he played for hours on end, his exciting improvisations directly influencing other jazz musicians who came to the club including Thelonious Monk, Dizzy Gillespie, Kenny Clarke, Joe Guy and others. Some of these historic jam sessions fortunately were recorded for posterity by Jerry Newman.

Tragically the late nights and Christian's love of the New York night life did not help his health. He had suffered from poor health for most of his life. In the spring of 1940 he was admitted to hospital where diagnosis showed that he had tuberculosis. Despite the doctors warnings he failed to take proper care of his health. In July 1941 he suffered a serious relapse and entered the Seaview Sanitarium on Staten Island. He died there in March 1942.

The following extract from sleeve notes on a Philips' vinyl record release of Charlie Christian, written by Al Avakian and Bob Prince, gives a clearer picture of Christian's vital contribution to jazz; "His improvisations sound simple and effortless but when analysed, prove complex and daring in their explorations of musical principles. These complexities were not contrived, but were the result of Christian's natural inventiveness and drive, bringing forth a new mobile swinging jazz that resulted in a basic influence on modern musicians. His greatest asset was his command of rhythm. He had a natural drive to swing at all costs, and this, coupled with his spontaneous explorations of rhythmic principles, led him to a flexibility of beat that was unique. This flexibility became a prerequisite in all forms of jazz to follow. Christian's basic beat was the modern, even four-four, but his solos are full of metric denials. They are remarkable illustrations of mobile swing. Christian had complete and easy control over rhythm and on the basis of this rhythmic freedom, he constructed his phrasing. A singular aspect of his phrasing is the unusual length of his melodic lines, consisting of even and clearly executed notes. His meter was delineated by the subtle accent of certain of these eighth notes. Charlie Christian considered no interval wrong. In his eighth-note phrases, running up and down the basic chords, he extended the chords to include other intervals such as the ninth, flattened ninth, eleventh, augmented eleventh, thirteenth and flattened thirteenth. In addition, his partiality for the diminished seventh chord over basic harmonic progressions, can be heard in any number of his solos."

Charlie Christian's legacy to the advancement of jazz music as a whole is indisputable. His style of playing has directly influenced the major jazz guitar artists of 1940-60 including Barney Kessel, Jim Hall, Tal Farlow and Herb Ellis. There can be few jazz guitarists today that have not been influenced by Charlie Christian in some way.

SELECTED RECORDINGS

LXXIX. Charlie Christian Airchecks and Private Recordings
The Golden Age of Jazz JZCD 379
Solo Flight. Charlie Christian with the Benny Goodman Sextet
Vintage Jazz Classics VJC-1021-2
Charlie Christian Live   Music Memoria 34009 CD
Benny Goodman 'The Rehearsal Sessions' (1940-41)
Jazz Unlimited JUCD 2013
Ida Cox. I Can't Quit My Man   Affinity CD AFS 1015
Charlie Christian. Solo Flight   Topaz Jazz TPZ 1017 CD
Charlie Christian. Genius of the Electric Guitar
Giants of Jazz CD 53049
Charlie Christian with Benny Goodman (1939-41)
Jazz Portraits CD 14545
Charlie Christian with Benny Goodman (1939-41)
Jazz Roots CD 56059
Charlie Christian Guitar Wizard   Le Jazz CD 11
Charlie Christian. The Genius of the Electric Guitar
CBS 460612 2 CD
Benny Goodman Sextet featuring Charlie Christian (1939-41
CBS 465679 2 CD
Benny Goodman Sextet featuring Charlie Christian (1939-41)
CK 45144 CD
Charlie Christian and Lester Young Together
Archives of Jazz 3801062 CD
Charlie Christian and the Benny Goodman Sextet. Live. (1939-41)
Archives of Jazz 3801232 CD
Charlie Christian (Vol. 1) (1939)   Masters of Jazz MJCD 24
Charlie Christian (Vol. 2) (1939)   Masters of Jazz MJCD 29
Charlie Christian (Vol. 3) (1939-40)   Masters of Jazz MJCD 40
Charlie Christian (Vol. 4) (1940)   Masters of Jazz MJCD 44
Charlie Christian (Vol. 5) (1940)   Masters of Jazz MJCD 67

Charlie Christian (Vol. 6) (1940-41)   Masters of Jazz MJCD 68
Charlie Christian (Vol. 7) (Feb-Mar 1941)   Masters of Jazz MJCD 74
Charlie Christian (Vol. 8) (Mar-Jun 1941)   Masters of Jazz MJCD 75
An Introduction to Charlie Christian (1939-41) Best of Jazz 4032 CD

Solo Flight   Video   View Video

SELECTED READING

Modern Jazz p30-42 Morgan & Horricks,   Gollancz (1957)
The Jazz Makers p316-331   Grove Press (1958)
Article   Downbeat, August 1966
Combo U.S.A p 161-186   Rudi Blesh Chilton Book Co(1971)
Jazz Solography Vol.4   Jan Evensmo
Article   Downbeat, June 1970
Article   Jazz Magazine, July 1970
Discography 1939-41 J.Callis   Middleton Publication(1977)
Article   Guitar Player, February/March 1977
Profile   Guitar World, July 1981
Charlie Christian Special Issue   Guitar Player, March1982
The Guitar Players p97-120 James Sallis   Quill(1982)
The Swing Era p562-578 Gunther Schuller Oxford Univ. Press (1989)
Charlie Christian Peter Broadbent   Ashley Mark Publishing (1997)
Charlie Christian (Booklet and CD)   Jazz Greats (1997)
Charlie Christian – Photo Collection. T. Arnold   Black Arts (1995)
Tales of Second Street – Arnold   Black Arts (1995)

SELECTED MUSIC

The Art of Jazz Guitar   Regent Music Corporation
Charlie Christian Bop Guitar   Smith Tharp Publishing Co
The Swingiest Charlie Christian   Charles Colin Music Co
Six Charlie Christian Solos   Downbeat, July 1961
Charlie Christian Blues Solo   Downbeat, June 1970
Charlie Christian Jazz Masters   Music Sales

JOE CINDERELLA
Born-JOSEPH CINDERELLA
Newark, New Jersey
14 June 1929

Joe Cinderella began to play the guitar at the age of nine. His first jazz guitar influences were Django Reinhardt and Charlie Christian. His father, a musician who worked in the music publishing business, gave him his first guitar. It was during his late teens and early twenties that Cinderella, whilst serving in the US army, began to seriously study music and composition. He had studied guitar with Frank Staffa for five years and then attended Essex University graduating with a degree in music. Further formal education continued by learning the Schillinger System with Edwin Bave, followed by private studies in film writing with composer/arranger Kermit Leslie, musical director of The Hit Parade.

Cinderella began a career as a jazz guitarist in the early 1950s. In 1954 he recorded an album with singer Chris Connors which received high critical acclaim. He went on to play with many leading jazz musicians including Teddy Charles, Zoot Sims, Donald Byrd, Vinnie Burke, Joe Newman, Roger Kellaway and Gigi Gryce. Cinderella came to further prominence when he joined baritone saxophonist Gil Melle's jazz quartet.

Joe Cinderella moved into the world of radio and television session work in the early 1960s.

He had a 22 year career in the studios. As a skilled arranger and composer his talents were much in demand. He was staff guitarist for Channel 13, Newark's PBS station for many years. Cinderella backed many top popular singers , including Judy Garland, Neil Diamond, The Byrds, Della Reese and the Beach Boys, both in concert and in the recording studios. He scored and played on many films including 'Barbarella' and 'Midnight Cowboy', and also played guitar in the theatre orchestra for many top Broadway musicals.

Joe Cinderella has for many years been a prominent teacher. In 1969 he was appointed Adjunct Professor of Music at William Paterson College in New Jersey. In 1982 he decided to give up studio work and devote most of his time to teaching, and also in experimenting with new guitar tunings. Since 1981 he has played an eight-string guitar made to his own design. A solid body version was made for him in 1981 by the late Sam Koonz. More recently an archtop version of his guitar has been made by Gary Mortoro.It is tuned E, A, C, E, G, B, D and F# (low to high).

SELECTED RECORDINGS
Lullabys of Birdland w/Chris Connors	Bethlehem BTM 6823 LP
Gils Guests - Gil Melle Quartet	Prestige OJCCD 1753-2
Patterns in Jazz w/Gil Melle	Blue Note 8709683 LP

SELECTED READING
Article	Guitar World, May 1991
Article	Vintage Guitar Magazine, May 1995

SELECTED MUSIC
Chord Melody Playing for the Guitarist Musician	
	Warner Bros GF 0342
Jazz Arpeggios for Guitar	Camerica

Joe Cinderella

PHOTO: STEVEN LUCAS

BRUCE CLARKE
Born-ALFRED BRUCE CLARKE
Melbourne, Australia
1 December 1925

Bruce Clarke began to play the guitar at the age of seventeen in a Hawaiian band. In the mid 1940s he began to play jazz in various groups in the Melbourne area. From 1949-52 he played in local nightclubs, but maintained an interest in jazz broadcasting with Don Bank's Boptet, and playing in local jam sessions.

In 1956 Clarke started a long and successful career in the film and television studios. In 1963 he established his own studio and production company. From 1963-75 Clarke wrote and directed over 3000 television and film soundtracks for Australian and foreign producers. Throughout this period he continued to maintain his interest in jazz, improvisation and contemporary music. For several years Clarke was president of the International Society Of Contemporary Music.

In 1974 Clarke joined the music board of the Australia Council, and became Kenneth Myer Music Fellow to the Victoria Institute of Colleges. In 1977 he instigated the Jazz Studies programme at the Victorian College of Arts. In 1976 he founded his own guitar school and since that time has written several guitar instruction books. In 1984 he formed a jazz quintet which played in local clubs and restaurants.

Bruce Clarke is one of the most important guitarists to have come from Australia. He continues to be a major force in music education, and in the promotion of the jazz guitar.

PHOTO: COURTESY PROM MUSIC

Bruce Clarke

SELECTED RECORDING

In Memory Of Charlie Christian	PROM Music POL 056 LP

SELECTED MUSIC

Bruce Clarke-Jazz Guitar Solos	Allans Music
Jazz Studies 1	Allans Music

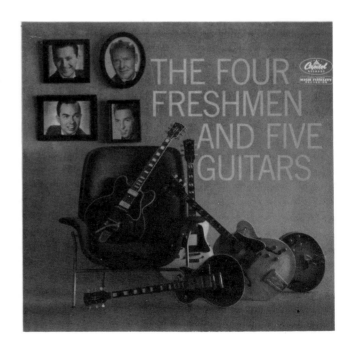

GREG CLAYTON
Born-Montreal, Canada
21 September 1951

Greg Clayton loved music as a child. He began to play the guitar at the age of twelve, but it was not until he was 20 that he began to take an interest in jazz. His first jazz influences were some recordings by Charlie Parker and Wes Montgomery. Clayton is virtually self-taught although he did attend two summer semesters at Berklee in 1973 and 1974. He had the benefit of seeing and hearing two Montreal jazz guitarists Nelson Symonds and Ivan Symonds on a regular basis, and he also studied briefly with Ed Bickert, Joe Pass and Tal Farlow.

Greg Clayton, now regarded as one of Canada's finest jazz guitarists, teaches jazz improvisation at Montreal's McGill University and gives private lessons. He has over the years made numerous television and radio appearances and cites Jimmy Raney, Tal Farlow, Wes Montgomery and Joe Pass as his main stylistic influences. He concentrates on the American popular songbook as a vehicle for his straight-ahead jazz improvisations in both concert and recording performances.

Greg Clayton

PHOTO: RANDY COLE

SELECTED RECORDINGS

Live at Boomers - The Greg Clayton Trio	Ostinato OST 001-2 CD
Kevin's Heaven - Kevin Dean Quartet	Double-Time DTRCD-103

SELECTED READING

Article	Planet Jazz Magazine, Fall 1997

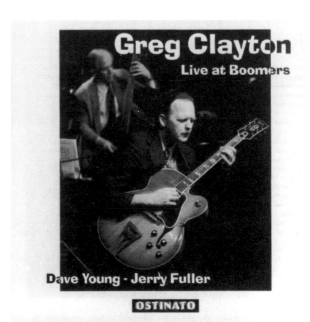

DAVE CLIFF
Born-DAVID JOHN CLIFF
Hexham, Northumberland, UK
25 June 1944

Dave Cliff began to play the guitar at the age of fourteen. By the time he was 19 he was playing professionally in a rhythm and blues band in the Newcastle upon Tyne area. In 1967 he enrolled at the City of Leeds College of Music to study on its full-time jazz course under bassists Peter Ind and Bernie Cash. Cliff was fortunate to befriend Ind whilst at the college. Ind had studied in the USA with jazz pianist Lennie Tristano and also worked with Lee Konitz and Warne Marsh. Ind introduced Cliff to the jazz styles of these famous musicians, and they were to prove a major influence on him.

After leaving college Cliff moved in 1971 to London and worked there with Ind and a wide variety of local jazz musicians. In 1975 Cliff had the opportunity to make up the backing group, with Ind, for a UK concert and club tour by Konitz and Marsh.

Since that time Dave Cliff has established himself as one of Britain's foremost jazz guitarists working and recording with many top jazz artists including Mike Carr, Bob Wilber, Warren Vache, Dick Pearce, Kenny Davern, Howard Alden, Humphrey Lyttleton, Bruce Turner, Kenny Davern and Bob Wilber. Cliff has also played at leading European Jazz Festivals including Brecon 1994 with the Davern/Vache Sextet and Jersey 1996 with Ken Peplowski.

Dave Cliff

PHOTO: PETER SYMES

SELECTED RECORDINGS

Dave Cliff Quintet-The Right Time	Miles Music	MM 074 LP
No Kidding-Peter Ind Quartet		Wave 9 LP
Lee Konitz Quartet		Horo HLL 101-32 LP
Konitz/Marsh Quintet	Storyville	SLP 1028 CD
Peter Ind Sextet		Wave 13 LP
Great Jazz Solos Revisited-Bernie Cash Orchestra		Wave 18 LP
Bruce Turner Group-The Dirty Bopper	Calligraph	CLG 003 LP
Bill le Sage Quartet		Marc 501 LP
Altitude-Jamie Talbot		Move MVLP 21
Michael Moore Trio	Mixmaster	CHELD 00110
Warren Vache Quintet		Nagel-Heyter CD012
Sipping at Bells		Spotlite SPJ-CD 553
Dave Cliff/Geoff Simpkins 5		Spotlite SPJ CD 560
But Beautiful w/Brian Lemon		ZEPHYR ZECD 1
When Lights are Low		ZEPHYR ZECD 18

SELECTED READING

Profile	Guitarist, February 1990
Interview	String Jazz, November/December 1995

guitar

Geoff Simkins
Simon Woolf
Mark Taylor

Dave **Cliff**
Duo & Quartet
sipping at **bells**

JOE COHN
Born-JOSEPH COHN
Flushing, New York, USA
28 December 1956

Joe Cohn is the son of the late jazz saxophonist Al Cohn. He started to play the guitar during his senior year in high school. With his father's encouragement he studied with Allen Hanlon. He first became interested in jazz through the recordings of pianist Dave McKenna, and the Thad Jones - Mel Lewis Big Band. Cohn is also a talented pianist, bassist and trumpeter.

After leaving high school Cohn went to the Berklee College of Music in Boston. After leaving Berklee he began his career as a professional musician free-lancing in the Boston area on string-bass. He then played for six years as guitarist with the Artie Shaw Orchestra and followed this by playing with trombonist Al Grey for ten years. In recent years Cohn has established himself as one of the best guitarists in the new York area. Double Time Records recently released his first recording as leader. His quintet on this release also features guitarist Doug Raney.

SELECTED RECORDINGS

Overtones w/Al Cohn	Concord CCD-4194
Chip Off The Old Bop w/Buddy DeFranco	Concord CCD-4527
Two Funky People	Double Time DTR-129 CD

SELECTED READING

Profile	Jazz Times, August 1997

SELECTED MUSIC

Jazz Conception/Snidero for Guitarists (Joe Cohn plays on the companion CD)	Advance Music # 14726

Benedetto Players in Concert– Melville, New York, May 17, 1997. Back row, left to right: Gerry Beaudoin. Ed and Phyllis Benson, Andy MacKenzie, Cindy and Bob Benedetto, Randall Kremer (Smithsonian Institution) Front row, left to right: Jack Wilkins, Howard Alden, Jimmy Bruno, Frank Vignola and Adrian Ingram.

PHOTO: JOHN BUSCARINO

CAL COLLINS
Born-CALVIN CECIL COLLINS
Medora, Indiana, USA
5 May 1933

Cal Collins' first musical influences were country and bluegrass music and these sounds still colour his distinctive jazz guitar sound. Although the guitar was his chosen instrument his first jazz influences were pianists Fats Waller, Art Tatum, Nat 'King' Cole and George Shearing.

In the 1950s he moved to Cincinatti, Ohio, where he played in local clubs giving him the opportunity to play with visiting jazzmen including Harold Jones and Aby Simpkins. In 1976, after a recommendation by Jack Sheldon, he joined the Benny Goodman band for a period of three years. During a concert given by the Goodman band at the 1977 Concord Jazz Festival in California he was heard by the executive producer of Concord Records, Carl Jefferson. Collins so impressed Jefferson that he was signed up for Concord record label as their 'house guitarist'.

Since that time Cal Collins has made many recordings for the Concord label both as leader and sideman. Throughout the 1980s and 1990s Collins toured extensively in the USA, and internationally, with several all-star groups. He has been featured with many important jazz instrumental soloists and singers including Al Cohn, Marshall Royal, Buddy Tate, Warren Vache Jnr, Herb Ellis, Scott Hamilton and Rosemary Clooney. In 1991 he joined the Woody Herman All Stars, led by vibraphonist Terry Gibbs, for a tour of Germany. He was also featured in 1991 in a California concert tour entitled, 'Masters of Swing Guitar'.

Cal Collins

SELECTED RECORDINGS

Milestones	Pausa PR 7159 LP
Ohio Boss Guitar	Famous Door HL 123 LP
Cincinnati to LA	Concord CJ 59 LP
Cal Collins in San Francisco	Concord CJ 71 LP
Blues On My Mind	Concord CJ 95 LP
Cal Collins By Myself	Concord CJ 119 LP
Interplay with Herb Ellis	Concord CJ 137 LP
Cal Collins Cross Country	Concord CJ 166 LP
Crack'd Rib	Mopro M 107 LP
Ohio Style	Concord CCD 4447CD

SELECTED READING

Interview	Guitar Player April 1980
Interview	Just Jazz Guitar, May 1995

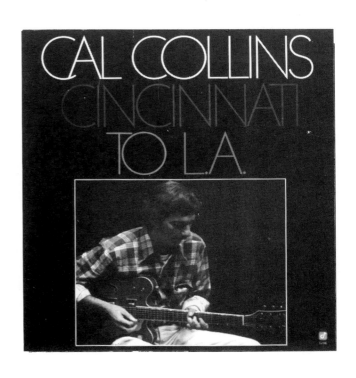

104

HOWIE COLLINS
Born-New York, USA
3 September 1930

Howie Collins' first instrument was the banjo which he began to study at the age of ten in 1940. Four years later, attracted by the guitar styles of Tony Mottola, George Van Eps and others Collins began to study the guitar. He took lessons from a local teacher, Al Peterson. By the time he was sixteen he was playing professionally in hotel bands in New York's Catskill Mountain region. Collins studied at Hofstra University from where he graduated in accounting. At that time he played the guitar on many evening club dates in New York.

Collins' career in music came to a halt for a while as after graduation he joined the US Marine Corps whilst the Korean war was in progress. He left the army in 1953 and worked in a bank during the day and as a musician at nights. At this time he became friendly with Barry Galbraith, playing and studying with this great guitarist. It was Galbraith who persuaded Collins to make the guitar his career. In 1955 he began working with several big bands, including that of trumpeter, Ralph Marterie. He also worked on a USA tour with the popular British orchestra led by Mantovani. Following this time Collins played many evenings in jazz clubs He took over Jimmy Raney's seat with pianist Jimmy Lyon at New York's Blue Angel club for a while. From 1956 to 1958 he studied classical guitar at the Manhattan School of Music with Albert Valdes Blaine.

From 1955 to 1961 Howie Collins once again worked with many bandleaders including Neil Hefti, Skitch Henderson and Warren Covington. 1955 also marked the beginning of a fifteen year period of studio work including a spell working on singer Pat Boone's ABC Television shows. At the same time Collins continued playing jazz including two years (1960-61) wth pianist George Shearing and singer Nancy Wilson. In 1961 he joined the Benny Goodman band for a South American tour.

In recent years Howie Collins has spent most of his time teaching and playing club dates in the New York area. He has also played in the pit orchestras for several Broadway shows. In 1971 he took up the seven-string guitar originally developed by George Van Eps, and also for a while studied the viola.

SELECTED RECORDINGS

Bucky Pizzarelli Guitar Quintet	Monmouth/Evergreen MES 7066
Desafinado Coleman Hawkins	Impulse A28
Jazz And Samba	Impulse A70

Howie Collins with Benny Goodman.

Ruby Braff Quartet Plus Three	Chiaroscuro CR 115 LP
The Vibes of Peter Appleyard	Fidelity 1901 LP

SELECTED READING

Interview	Guitar Player, October 1979

JOHN COLLINS
Born-JOHN ELBERT COLLINS
Montgomery, Alabama, USA
20 September 1913

John Collins originally studied music with his mother Georgia Gorham, a professional band leader. In the mid 1920s his family moved to Chicago. There Collins studied with the respected guitar teacher, Frank Latham. When he was fifteen he began to play with his mother's band. In 1934 he was heard by the legendary pianist Art Tatum who offered him a job with his band.

After leaving Tatum, Collins went on to play for three years with trumpeter Roy Eldridge. From 1940-42 he worked in New York City with many top jazz men including Benny Carter, Fletcher Henderson, Lester Young and Dizzy Gillespie. After four years in the US Army Collins played with bassist Slam Stewart from 1946-48, and pianist Billy Taylor from 1949-51. In 1947 he won Esquire magazine's New Star Award. After a recommendation from Irving Ashby, Collins was hired in 1951 to fill the guitar seat in the Nat 'King' Cole trio. He stayed with Cole until the singer's death in 1965.

Always respected as a fine soloist by his fellow musicians, John Collins was relegated to a background role for the fourteen years he was with Nat 'King' Cole. From 1965-71 he toured with pianist Bobby Troup's quartet and this gave Collins the opportunity to once more display his talented guitar work.

In recent times Collins has freelanced around the Los Angeles area leading his own quartet, and backing star singers such as Sammy Davis Jnr, Ella Fitzgerald, Frank Sinatra, and Nancy Wilson. A wonderful tribute was made to John Collins when the Mayor of Los Angeles, Tom Bradley, proclaimed September 15, 1985 'John Collins Day' in the city of Los Angeles. A sign of the high esteem in which the guitarist is held.

John Collins with Nat 'King' Cole

PHOTO: COURTESY MELODY MAKER

SELECTED RECORDINGS
Esquire's All American Hot Jazz	Vintage LPV544 LP
Browns Bag	Concord CJ19 LP
Guitar Player	MCA MCA2-6002 LP
After Midnight Nat'King'Cole	Capitol W-782 LP
The Incredible John Collins	Nilva NQ 3412 LP

SELECTED READING
Interview	Guitar Player, January, 1985

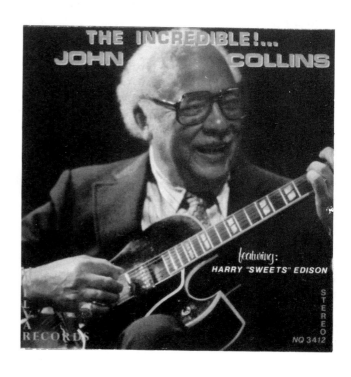

EDDIE CONDON
Born-ALBERT EDWIN CONDON
Goodland, Indiana, USA
16 November 1905
Died-New York City, USA
4 August 1973

No one denies Eddie Condon's importance in the history of jazz as a band leader. As a guitarist Condon really made no influence on jazz music for he did not solo, and his rhythm playing, although felt by the musicians in his bands, was always very discreet.

Eddie Condon was brought up in Momence in Chicago Heights, Illinois. He was self-taught on the ukulele and banjo and from the age of 15 was already working professionally with various local groups. At the age of 17 he was banjoist with Hollis Peavey's Jazz Bandits. As a Chicago based musician in the 1920s he was closely associated with other top jazzmen including drummer, Gene Krupa and saxophonist, Bud Freeman. In 1928 he recorded with 'The Chicagoans' led by Red McKenzie and himself. Recordings made by this group are today recognized as being some of the most authentic 'Original Chicago Style' jazz.

In 1928 Condon moved to New York City. Here he played with Red McKenzie's 'Mound City Blues Blowers', and recorded with Fats Waller and Louis Armstrong. In 1929 he toured with trumpeter Red Nichols. For several years he was often featured as sideman with some historic bands, including those of Bobby Hackett and Joe Marsala, and many other small groups on the now legendary 52nd Street. It was in 1942 that he first established himself as a jazz promoter. He organised the first television jam session and started to promote concerts at the New York City Town Hall. In December 1945 he opened his own club in Greenwich Village. This moved premises over the years and closed in 1967.

The combination of Condon's love for Chicago style jazz, and his exceptional organizing ability, became well known and a recipe for his international success. In 1948 he had his own television show, 'The Eddie Condon Floorshow'. His passion for, and devotion to, Dixieland Music brought happiness and pleasure to both player and listener alike.

Eddie Condon never pretended to be a guitar master. Having changed from banjo to the four-string guitar in the late 1920s his rhythm guitar playing became an integral part of all his groups. From 1954-57 he toured throughout

Eddie Condon

the USA, and the United Kingdom. In 1964 he took his band to Japan, Australia and New Zealand. In 1971 he toured with Barney Bigard, Wild Bill Davison and Art Hodes. Until his death in 1973 Eddie Condon was actively engaged in concerts and club work, and with the promotion of the special type of jazz that he loved.

SELECTED RECORDINGS

Jazz As It Should Be Played	Jazzology J50 LP
Condon A La Carte	Commodore FL30-010 LP
Eddie Condon Orchestra	Trip TLP5800 LP
A Night at Eddie Condon's	Decca 8281 LP
Confidentially, It's Condon	Gala GLP 342 LP
We Dig Dixieland	Savoy 197 CD
Ringside at Condon's	Savoy 231 CD
Dixieland All Stars	Decca GRD-637 CD
Complete CBS Recordings	Mosaic MD5-151

SELECTED READING

Profile	Downbeat, December 1956
Eddie Condon's Scrapbook of Jazz	St.Martins Press(1973)
We Called It Music	H.Holt (1947)
Eddie Condon's Treasury of Jazz	Dial Press (1956)
Article	Downbeat, February 1965
Article	Guitar Player, November 1975

BILL CONNORS
Born-WILLIAM A. CONNORS
Los Angeles, USA
24 September 1949

Bill Connors was first attracted to the guitar in his mid teens by blues-oriented rock. He was particularly inspired by Eric Clapton's guitar style. He then began to listen to the recordings of Joe Pass and pianist Bill Evans and eventually developed an individual jazz blues fusion guitar style.

In the early 1970s Connors moved to San Francisco. Here he played with pianist Art Lande and bassist Steve Swallow. He was heard by pianist Chick Corea who was so impressed that he signed Connors to play with his 'Return To Forever' group. This association brought international recognition for the young guitarist's talent. After leaving Corea in 1974, Connors moved to New York. Here he played with John Abercrombie and keyboard player Jan Hammer. He also recorded with vocalist Gene McDaniels and bassist Stanley Clarke.

In 1975 Connors became attracted to the classical guitar. For the next three years, inspired by the recordings of Julian Bream, he devoted most of his time to developing a classical guitar technique. In 1979 Connors decided to return to playing jazz fusion on a solid-body electric guitar. He played and recorded with the Jan Garbarek Quintet for the next two and a half years. Since that time Bill Connors has maintained a busy career as both leader and sideman.

Bill Connors

SELECTED RECORDINGS

Return To Forever	Polydor 5536
Quiet Song w/Jimmy Giuffre	Improvising Artists IA 373839
Theme To The Gaurdian	ECM 1057 CD 829 387-2
Places	ECM 1118
Of Mist And Melting	ECM 1120 CD 847 324-2
Photo With	ECM 1135
Double Up -Bill Connors Trio	Evidence ELD 22081-2
Swimming with a Hole in my Body	ELM 1158 CD 849 078-2

SELECTED READING

Profile	Guitar Player, October 1974
Interview	Guitar, October 1979
Profile	Guitar World, November 1981
Profile	Guitar Player, May 1985

ROBERT CONTI
Born-Philadelphia, USA
21 November 1945

Robert Conti

Robert Conti began to play the guitar at the age of twelve. Although he studied briefly with a local teacher, Conti is virtually self-taught. He was a childhood friend of Pat Martino and they often played and practiced together. Conti's early jazz influences were Johnny Smith, Wes Montgomery and Joe Pass

Conti's first professional work was with various commercial bands. From 1961-67 he had little involvement in jazz, spending most of his career travelling with show bands. He decided to settle in the Jacksonville, Florida area and made his living teaching guitar. From 1971-76 he gave up music and the guitar, and devoted himself to a career in securities. Since 1976 Conti has once again made his career in music, both teaching, and playing guitar in diverse jazz groups in Florida.

SELECTED RECORDINGS

Latin Love Affair	Discovery/Trend VDS-100
Solo Guitar	Discovery/Trend TR-519
Laura	Discovery/Trend TR-540
Robert Conti Jazz Quintet	Discovery/Trend DS-834
Gerald Wilson Orchestra	Discovery/Trend DS-833
Comin' On Strong	Time is J19802 CD

JULIAN CORYELL
Born-Doylestown, Pennsylvania, USA
9 April 1973

Julian Coryell is the son of famed jazz guitarist Larry Coryell. He first played the piano at the age of five, and also studied the violin, viola, bass and drums. He began to play the guitar professionally at the age of 14 performing with his father, Dave Brubeck, Herbie Mann and others. At 19 he was the youngest-ever graduate from Boston's Berklee College of Music. In 1989 he was voted Downbeat magazine's 'Outstanding Guitar Soloist'.

Coryell's jazz style is strongly influenced by rhythm and blues, country, and rock music. He recorded with the Rhythm and Blues group 'Changing Faces' and toured with the rock group 'October Project'. He recorded two CDs in Japan for Venus Records and these were well received in that country and abroad. His first USA CD was released in 1997 on the Encoded Music label.

SELECTED RECORDINGS

Jazzbo	Venus Records TKCV-79301 CD
Without You	Venus Records TKCV-3500 CD
Duality	Encoded Music N2K-10011
Twelve Frets to One Octave -Larry Coryell	Shanachie 97015 CD

Julian Coryell

Two Gibson Guitar advertisements from the 1950s

LARRY CORYELL
Born-Galveston, Texas, USA
2 April 1943

Larry Coryell is the son of two accomplished pianists. He began studying the piano at the age of 4. At the age of 12 he began to play the ukulele and then the guitar. In 1950 his family moved from Texas to Richmond, Washington and here at the age of 15 he joined a rock and roll group. Coryell had originally been attracted to the guitar styles of Chet Atkins and Chuck Berry. He started taking lessons from a teacher who introduced him to the recordings of jazz guitarists Barney Kessel, Wes Montgomery and Tal Farlow. Whilst Coryell was studying journalism at the University of Washington, Seattle, he decided that he would make a career as a jazz guitarist. At first he gigged in and around Seattle but then in 1965 moved to New York City.

His first major job in New York was in 1966 with drummer Chico Hamilton's Quintet. In 1967 he joined a group led by vibraphonist, Gary Burton. Through his appearances and recordings with this group Coryell's ability soon gained worldwide recognition. In 1968 Coryell left Burton determined to lead his own group. This he did in 1969 calling the group 'Foreplay'.

In 1970 he recorded the now famous 'Spaces' album with John McLaughlin, Chick Corea, Miroslav Vitous and Billy Cobham. In 1973 he formed his highly successful jazz-rock group 'Eleventh House'. This featured Mike Mandel, Randy Brecker and Alphonse Mouzon. In 1975, after this group broke up, Coryell decided to concentrate on playing acoustic guitar. He toured Europe that year playing solo guitar. In 1976 he formed a guitar duo with Philip Catherine. They toured and recorded together until 1977.

In 1978 Coryell toured internationally with guitarists John McLaughlin and Paco de Lucia. In 1979 he recorded with bassist Charlie Mingus and also with guitarist John Scofield. By the mid 1980s he was playing electric guitar again with a trio made up of drummer Alphonse Mouzon, and bass guitarist Bunny Brunel. Around this time he transcribed for guitar, and recorded, some Stravinsky ballets for the Japanese label Nipon Phonogram. This recording became a best seller in Japan.

Larry Coryell recent recordings prove that he is one of the most important, and most consistent, jazz/fusion guitarists of the past thirty years.

PHOTO: MAURICE J. SUMMERFIELD

Larry Coryell

SELECTED RECORDINGS

Free Spirits	ABC 593
Barefoot Boy	Flying Dutchman 10139
The Essential Coryell	Vanguard VSD 75176
Offering	Vanguard 79319
Coryell	Vanguard VSD 6547
At the Village Gate	Vanguard VSD 6573
The Restful Mind	Vanguard VSD 79353
Me Myself & I w Charles Mingus	Atlantic SD 8803
Spaces	Vanguard 79345
Basics	Vanguard 79375
Return	Vanguard 79426
Twin House w/ Philip Catherine	Atlantic 50342
Standing Ovation	Arista AN 3024
Level One	Arista AL 4052
Aspects	Arista AL 4077
Two For The Road w/Steve Khan	Arista AB 4156
Guitar Player	MCA MCA2-6002
Quiet Day In Spring	Steeplechase SCCD 311 87
Splendid w/ Philip Catherine	Elektra K52086
Together w/ Emily Remler	Concord CCD 4289
Young Django w/Stephane Grappelli	Pausa PR 7041
Shining Hour	Muse MCD 5360
Duster w/Gary Burton	RCA LSP 3835
Live From Bahia	CTI 1005-2
Advanced Jazz Guitar Instructional Video	Hot Licks
Jazz Guitar Instructional Videos 1-3	Vestapol
Blues Guitar Video	Vestapol

SELECTED READING

Profile	Jazz Magazine,December 1969
Profile	Downbeat, June 1967
Profile	Downbeat,February 1976
Profile	Guitar Player, August 1970
Profile	Guitar Player, December 1974
Profile	Guitar, April 1975
Profile	Downbeat, June 1980
Interview	Downbeat, May 1984
Profile	Guitar Player, August 1997

SELECTED MUSIC

Improvisations from Rock to Jazz	Guitar Player Productions
Larry Coryell Jazz Guitar Solos	Hal Leonard Publishing
Larry Coryell-Dragon Gate	Mel Bay Publications
Larry Coryell-Twelve Frets/One Octave	Mel Bay Publications
The Guitar of Larry Coryell	Stephan Grossman Guitar Workshops

RAY CRAWFORD
Born-RAY HOLLAND CRAWFORD
Pittsburgh, Pennsylvania, USA
7 February 1924

Ray Crawford began his musical career as a saxophonist. In 1941 he was the featured saxophonist, doubling on alto clarinet, with the famed Fletcher Henderson band. While with the Henderson band he contracted tuberculosis. He had to spend two years in a sanitorium recovering and the illness ended his career as a saxophonist. While recovering he took up the guitar. By the time he had recovered from his illness he was already playing the guitar well enough to secure professional work.

In May 1951 Crawford joined the Ahmad Jamal trio. He stayed with this group for six years. In the late 1950s he worked in clubs in the New York area and also led his own group at Minton's Playhouse. It was while he was in New York that Crawford came to the attention of band leader Gil Evans. he guitarist joined the Evans orchestra and was soon a featured soloist. Crawford also played with organist Jimmy Smith, and clarinetist Tony Scott whilst he was in the New York area.

In 1960, disenchanted with the way things were working out for him on the East Coast, Crawford moved to Los Angeles. He earned a living as a teacher and guitar player but remained in relative obscurity until the late 1970s when a Japanese company released for the first time a 1961 recording of a group led by Crawford. This recording, and those made with the Gil Evans orchestra, show Ray Crawford to be a talented jazz artist.

Ray Crawford

SELECTED RECORDINGS
One Step At A Time	United National	UND 1035
Old Wine, New Bottles Gil Evans Orchestra		
	EMI-Manhattan	CDP746 855 2
Out Of The Cool Gil Evans Orchestra MCA		MCAD 5653CD
Bluesmith w/Jimmy Smith		Verve V6-8809 LP
Smooth Groove Ray Crawford Sextet		Candid 9028
It's About Time		Dobre DR 1010

SELECTED READING
Profile	Downbeat, July 1962

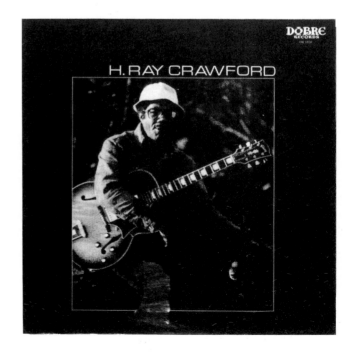

HENRI CROLLA
Born-Naples, Italy
26 February 1920
Died-Paris, France
October 1960

Both Henri Crolla's parents were musicians of Gypsy background. They left Italy in 1922 and settled on the outskirts of Paris near Porte Choisy and Porte Clichy. This was the same area where Django Reinhardt was living at the time. Crolla began to earn a living by playing the mandolin in street cafes. After changing to the guitar in his mid-teens he was hired to play alongside Matelot Ferre in the Gus Viseur Orchestra. He becomes well known through his regular appearances at the popular night spot Jimmy's Bar in Paris. Crolla's jazz guitar style was greatly influenced by Django Reinhardt.

Henri Crolla managed to continue working as a musician throughout World War II. In 1945 he played at the Schubert Club in Paris with saxophonist Andre Ekyan and pianist Leo Chauliac. In 1946 he began a fourteen-year association with the popular French singer Yves Montand. At the same time Crolla managed to continue playing jazz in various groups. In 1954 he played at the 3rd Paris Salon de Jazz in the Django Reinhardt Memorial Concert. In the same year he played with Stephane Grappelli's group at the Club St Germain. Crolla also wrote music for several French films.

Many French jazz lovers regarded Crolla as the leading jazz guitarist in France after the death of Django Reinhardt in May 1953, until Crolla's own death after an operation in 1960.

SELECTED RECORDINGS

Henri Crolla Quintet	Vega 45 P1730 LP
Les Amis de Django	Vega V30S 805 LP
Crolla/Grappelli Quartet	EMI Jazz Time 251286-2CD

Henri Crolla with Joseph Reinhardt

IAN CRUICKSHANK
Born-Ipswich, UK
24 January 1947

Ian Cruickshank has established himself as one of the foremost advocates of the jazz guitar style of Django Reinhardt and the many followers of this style.

Ian Cruickshank started to play the guitar at the age of sixteen. Self taught he started playing professionally, mainly in rhythm and blues bands, in 1969. It was not until 1977 that he first began to study the recordings of Django Reinhardt. Since that time he has established himself as one of the leading promoters of the jazz guitar style of Django Reinhardt and the many contemporary Gypsy jazz guitar stylists.

As well as leading his own 'Hot Club' style group called 'Gypsy Jazz', Cruickshank has gained wide recognition by touring extensively with Belgian Gypsy guitarist, Fapy Lafertin. Also his books and video on the Gypsy jazz guitar style have enjoyed good international sales. Cruickshank was also co-producer and music co-ordinator for the Channel 4 television documentary 'The Django Legacy'.

Ian Cruickshank

In recent times Ian Cruickshank gained recognition as the first promoter of guitarist Gary Potter, and appeared on several of his recordings. Cruickshank has now extended his jazz interest into other styles. In particular the great swing and bebop instrumentalists, and guitarists Wes Montgomery and Lenny Breau. Cruickshank has also been involved in teaching, often conducting weekend workshops, both Django style and jazz guitar in general.

SELECTED RECORDINGS

Ian Cruickshank's Gypsy Jazz	Fret Records FJC 102
Swingin' Spirits	Fret Records FJCD 107
Django meets the Duke	Fret Records FJCD 109
Gypsy Jazz Guitar Instructional Video	Starnite/Warners

SELECTED MUSIC

The Guitar Style of Django Reinhardt & The Gypsies	Music Sales Ltd
From Rock To Jazz	Music Maker Publications

SELECTED READING

Django's Gypsies	Ashley Mark Publishing

IAN CRUICKSHANK'S GYPSY JAZZ

FRET FJC 102

PIERRE CULLAZ
Born-Paris, France
21 July 1935

Pierre Cullaz was born into a musical family. His father was a well-known music critic. As a child, because of World War II, Cullaz moved to the Haute-Savoie region of France. Here, with the encouragement of his parents, he studied music and the piano. On his return to Paris, at the end of the war, he took up the guitar. He was attracted to jazz initially through hearing Al Casey's guitar work on his parents' Fats Waller recordings. He also enjoyed studying and playing classical and flamenco music.

Cullaz started his professional career as guitarist playing in various jazz clubs in Paris. Over the years he played with many important jazz artists including Art Simmons, Michel Gaudry, Eddy Louiss, Martial Solal, Claude Bolling, Quincy Jones, Sarah Vaughan and Michel Hausser. He was instrumental in founding the excellent jazz guitar quintet 'The Guitars Unlimited', with Francis Lemaguer, Raymond Gimenez, Victor Apicella and Tony Rallo. They recorded for the 'Barclay' record label.

Pierre Cullaz worked for many years as a studio guitarist but in recent years has maintained an active interest in playing jazz in France. An excellent cellist, Cullaz is also a prolific writer and arranger for the guitar. His articles have appeared over a period of many years in French music magazines.

SELECTED RECORDINGS

Claude Bolling Big Band	Decca 6.22649 AO
Les Guitars Unlimited Vols 1 & 2	Barclay 80.927/28LP
Golden Gate Quartet	EMI CDP 780573-2CD
Misty-Sarah Vaughan	Emarcy 846488-2CD

Pierre Cullaz

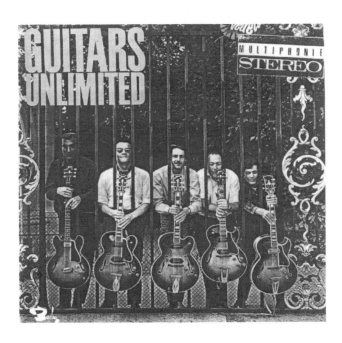

BILL DE ARANGO
Born-WILLIAM DE ARANGO,
Cleveland, Ohio,USA
20 September1921

Bill ('Buddy') De Arango started his professional musical career playing with various local Dixieland and Chicago jazz groups in 1939-42. After leaving the Army in 1944 he moved to New York City where he played as a sideman with tenor saxophonist Ben Webster on 52nd Street. In 1945 he recorded with Dizzy Gillespie and Charlie Parker. For a time he led his own group featuring vibraphonist Terry Gibbs both in New York and Chicago.

Since 1954 Bill De Arango has been out of the limelight despite a high reputation amongst jazz musicians who have heard him play. He is currently living in his home town Cleveland where he had his own music store. Until recently he still played jazz in several local clubs on an occasional basis, and in the late 1960s he managed a rock group called 'Henry Tree'.

Bill De Arango

SELECTED RECORDINGS

Greatest Of The Small Bands	Black & White RCA741106
Bill De Arango	Em Arcy MG 26020
Ben Webster Septet	Vogue Coral 10021
Dizzy Gillespie Septet	RCA CL 42787 AF
Dizzy Gillespie Sextet	RCA PM 42408
Barry Altschul Sextet	Muse MR 5176
Anything Went	GM Recordings EM 3027 CD

SELECTED READING

Profile	Jazz Journal, July 1971
Profile	Guitar Player, October 1996

ALAN de MAUSE
Born-Detroit, Michigan, USA
29 April 1938

Alan de Mause began to play the guitar at the age of ten. He went to the University of Michigan where he earned a B.A. in American literature in 1960. After leaving University he moved to New York in 1962, determined to make a career in music. Over a period of time he studied with several prominent jazz guitarists including Joe Fava, Sal Salvador, Jimmy Raney, Johnny Smith and Jim Hall. He also studied classical guitar with Albert Valdes Blain and William Matthews. At nights he played folk and jazz guitar in coffee houses around Greenwich Village. In 1990 de Mause completed courses in design and calligraphy at the School of Visual arts in New York.

Alan de Mause is well known internationally to guitarists through his jazz guitar books published by Mel Bay Publications and Music Sales Ltd. Still a New York resident he leads a triple life as a computer graphic specialist, a music teacher and as a performer. Recent years have seen him play in the orchestra for several Broadway shows, and as a member of diverse groups including 'The American Brass Quintet' and the Les Elgart Band. As an educator he was a music instructor at Columbia University for almost ten years. De Mause also has his own teaching studio and runs a study course by correspondence. In recent years, inspired by George Van Eps, de Mause has changed to playing a seven string guitar.

Alan de Mause

PHOTO: COURTESY ALAN DE MAUSE

SELECTED MUSIC

Art of Solo Jazz Guitar Vol 1	Mel Bay Publications
101 Jazz Guitar Licks	Mel Bay Publications
Jazz Guitar Etudes	Mel Bay Publications
Jazz Guitar Handbook	Mel Bay Publications
Joe Pass Virtuoso III Transcriptions	Mel Bay Publications

SELECTED READING

Interview	Just Jazz Guitar, February 1996

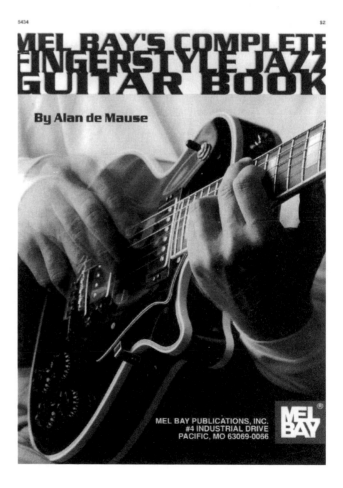

AL DI MEOLA
Born-Jersey City, New Jersey, USA
22 July 1954

Al Di Meola was raised in Bergenfield, New Jersey. He started on thc drums at the age of five and then, inspired by Elvis Presley, on the guitar at eight. By the time he was in his early teens he had already played with various school bands playing both steel and regular electric guitars. At that time country music had a great appeal for him, but when he was sixteen he heard a record by Larry Coryell. Di Meola was so impressed by Coryell's playing that he took every opportunity he could to hear him play in New York jazz clubs. He was fortunate to develop a friendship with Coryell and this helped Di Meola gain valuable knowledge and contacts. On leaving high school in 1973 Di Meola went to the Berklee College of Music in Boston. After leaving Berklee he played for a few months with the Barry Miles Quintet, but decided to return to the college to study arranging and further his musical education. In 1974 Di Meola was offered a job with the pianist Chick Corea's 'Return To Forever' group without an audition. Corea had heard some tapes made by the Barry Miles quintet featuring Di Meola on guitar. This was an amazing stroke of luck for the guitarist as at that time 'Return To Forever' was Di Meola's favourite group.

Di Meola made several best selling records with 'Return to Forever' earning himself in a very short time a high international reputation. After he left this famous jazz fusion group in the late 1970s Di Meola led several of his own groups. He then toured throughout the world in an acoustic guitar trio with John McLaughlin and Paco de Lucia. Their recordings achieved excellent sales. In the mid 1980s Di Meola was once again fronting his own group. This fusion group featured Danny Gottlieb (drums), Phil Markowitz (keyboards), Ron McClure (bass), and Airto Moreira (percussion).

Al Di Meola continues to be at the forefront of the jazz fusion movement with his innovatory ideas and virtuoso playing on both electric and acoustic guitars.

SELECTED RECORDINGS

Return To Forever/Forgotten Warrior	Columbia CBS81221
Land of the Midnight Sun	Columbia CK 34074
Elegant Gypsy	Columbia CK 34461
Splendido Hotel	Columbia CJM CK 46117
Electric Rendezvous	Columbia FC 37654
Tour De Force	Columbia FC 38373
Casino	Columbia CK 35277
Ciello E Terra	Manhattan ST53002
Friday Night In San Francisco	Columbia CK 37152
World Sinfonia	Tomato R2 79750
Kiss My Axe	Tomato R2 79751
Heart Of The Immigrants	Mesa/Bluemoon 79052

Al Di Meola

Orange & Blue	WEA 79197 CD
Di Meola plays Piazzolla	Blue Moon 2-92744 CD
Al Di Meola Instructional Video	REH/CPP

SELECTED READING

Profile	Guitar Player,October 1975
Article	Downbeat, February 1977
Interview	Guitar Player, Febuary 1978
Profile	Melody Maker, October 21st 1978
Profile	Downbeat,September 1983
Interview	Guitar Player,February 1986
Interview	Jazz Times, December1991
Profile	Downbeat, January 1992
Profile	JAZZIZ, March 1992
Interview	Jazz on CD, June 1994
Profile	Jaziz, November 1994

SELECTED MUSIC

Ciello E Terra	21 Century/Hal Leonard Publishing
Picking Techniques	21 Century/Hal Leonard Publishing
Guide To Chords/Scales/Arpeggios	21 Century/Hal Leonard
Music, Words, Pictures	Hal Leonard Publishing
Saturday Night In San Francisco	Hal Leonard Publishing

JOE DIORIO
Born-JOSEPH LOUIS DIORIO
Waterbury, Connecticut, USA
6 August 1936

Joe Diorio first became interested in jazz and the guitar at the age of nine by listening to his father's record collection. He started to play the guitar at the age of thirteen. He studied music and the guitar for three years with Fred Bredice who was a Django Reinhardt enthusiast. Diorio then began to listening to the recordings of saxophonists Charlie Parker, Sonny Rollins and John Coltrane. They were to be a great influence on him. Diorio was by that time playing regularly in Hartford and New Haven. He was then hired to play in a commercial road band. This group broke up after two years in Dayton, Ohio. From here Diorio moved to Chicago where he became involved in playing jazz again. He met and recorded with tenor saxophonist Eddie Harris. Throughout the 1960s Diorio was associated as a sideman with many jazz artists including Sam Lazar, Sonny Stitt, Bunky Green, Melvin Rhyne and Jerold Donavon. He also worked as a studio blues guitarist for Chess Records. In 1965 he led his own quartet for the Downbeat Jazz Festival in Chicago. He also worked with singer Julie London, and Chad Mitchell.

In 1969 Diorio moved to Miami, Florida. Here he worked for several years with saxophonist/trumpeter, Ira Sullivan. Whilst in Miami Diorio further developed his musical knowledge by taking part in various courses at the University of Miami. He also began to study the classical guitar, and in 1975 drawing and painting. Diorio started a succesful duo with pianist Wally Cirrilo in Miami. They played in many local clubs and made several recordings.

Since August 1977 Joe Diorio has been based in the Los Angeles area where he divides his time between record and club dates, writing instructional books for the guitar, and teaching at the Guitar Institute of Technology (GIT).

SELECTED RECORDINGS

Move On Over w/ Sonny Stitt	Cadet S730 LP
Ira Sullivan Quartet	Galaxy GXY 5137 IMS LP
Rapport w/Wally Cirillo	Spitball SB-1 LP
Solo Guitar	Spitball SB-2 LP
Soloduo	Spitball SB-3 LP
Straight Ahead w/Steve Bagby	Spitball SB-5 LP
Peaceful Journey	Spitball SB-7 LP
20th Century Impressions	J Discs JD 1 LP
Italy	MGI Records MGR 1010 LP
Lorraine Feather Quintet	Concord CJ 78 LP
Monty Budwig Septet	Concord CJ 79 LP
Earth Moon Earth	Nocturne NT 103 CD
We Will Meet Again	RAM RMCD-4501
Double Take	RAM RMCD-4502
Rare Birds w/Mick Goodrick	RAM RMCD-4505
The Breeze and I w/Ira Sullivan	RAM RMCD-4508
More than Friends	RAM RMCD-4514
Narayani	RAM RMCD-4519

Joe Diorio

To Jobim with Love	RAM RMCD-4529
Gratitude w/Maurizio Carugno	RAM RMCD-4530
Creative Jazz Guitar Instructional Video	REH CPP

SELECTED READING

Profile	Coda, June 1972
Profile	Guitar Player, August 1976
Profile	Downbeat, July 1978

SELECTED MUSIC

Intervallic Designs	REH Publications
Fusion	CPP/Belwin
The Ten Book	GIT
Single Line Improvising	CPP/Belwin
Jazz	REH Publications

DIZ DISLEY
Born-WILLIAM CHARLES DISLEY
Winnipeg, Manitoba, Canada
27 May 1931

Diz Disley

Canadian by birth, Diz Disley grew up in Wales. He began playing the banjo at an early age but after hearing Django Reinhardt in 1945 switched to the guitar.

Disley studied art at the Leeds College of Art. It was from this prominent Yorkshire college that he graduated in art and soon became known as a talented cartoonist. His work was to be seen over many years in many leading publications including the Radio Times, Spectator, Melody Maker and Jazz Journal. While at college he had played guitar with the Yorkshire Jazz Band. In the 1950s he was often a featured sideman with leading British traditional jazz bands including those of Alex Welsh, Sandy Brown and Kenny Ball. Disley also led his Hot Club-style quintets in jazz clubs throughout the UK. He was also featured with some of the most popular skiffle groups of the period. Always a devotee to the guitar style of Django Reinhardt, Disley achieved international fame in 1973 when he persuaded Stephane Grappelli to appear in clubs throughout the UK with the Diz Disley Trio. This group also included guitarist Denny Wright and bassist Johnny Hawksworth. The concert tour, which included an appearance at the Cambridge Folk Festival, was an enormous success. It led to a highly successful ten year period of working with Grappelli in concerts, clubs and on recordings in many countries of the world.

In the 1980s Diz Disley formed his own string quintet and appeared mainly in the London area. In recent times Disley lived for a while in Southern Spain but has now settled in Los Angeles where he works as an actor in the film business.

SELECTED RECORDINGS
Violinspiration Diz Disley Trio and Stephane Grappelli
MPS BAP 5063 LP
Diz Disley & The Soho String Quintette   Waterfront WF 031 LP

SACHA DISTEL
Born-Paris, France
29 January, 1933

Now known throughout the world as a popular singer, Sacha Distel, in the late 1950s was regarded by many as France's, and Europe's, leading modern jazz guitarist.

Sacha Distel is the nephew of the European big band leader, the late Ray Ventura. His father was a chemist, and his mother a singer and pianist. As a result Distel's first musical instrument was the piano. He began to play the guitar at the age of fourteen. Distel played in various college groups at the Lycee Claud Bernard in Paris. He gained national prominence by winning an amateur talent contest at the age of eighteen. From the age of nineteen he was constantly featured and recording with top jazz artists including Bernard Pfeiffer, Henri Salvador, Bobby Jaspar, Kenny Clarke and John Lewis. In 1954 and 1956 he won 'Jazz Hot' magazine's readers' poll. In 1957 he won that magazine's critics' prize, and also the International Jazz Club's prize. Whilst playing in Paris at clubs like the Club St.Germain Distel gained a lot of popular press publicity from his association with film star Brigitte Bardot. Later, on a six month trip to the USA he met and befriended saxophonists Stan Getz and Gerry Mulligan.

Sacha Distel

PHOTO: COURTESY JAZZ JOURNAL

For over two years Sacha Distel was featured in the backing group of the famous French chanteuse, Juliette Greco. It was during this time he developed his own individual singing style. In 1958 Distel made his first hit record as a vocalist and since that time has been a top line popular singer and entertainer all over the world. In 1960 he appeared in the French film, 'Les Mordus'. In recent times he has occasionally included his jazz guitar playing into some of his many television and radio programmes. He has also had as his guests on these programmes top jazz guitarists. In 1983 he made a jazz recording for the Pablo label.

SELECTED RECORDINGS

Afternoon in Paris with John Lewis	OrioleMG20036 LP
From Paris with Love (vocal)	RCA Victor LPM2611 LP
Bobby Jaspar All Stars	Barclay 84.023 LP
My Guitar and All That Jazz	Pablo 2310-892 LP
Back to Jazz	Columbia 10025 LP

TED DUNBAR
Born-EARL THEODORE DUNBAR
Port Arthur, Texas, USA 17 January 1937
Died – Kendal Park, New Jersey, USA, 29 May 1998

Ted Dunbar

Ted Dunbar, like his parents and brother was a qualified pharmacist. He qualified Cum Laude from Texas Southern University in Houston and practiced pharmacy for sixteen years.

Dunbar's first interest in jazz and music was after being taken to a Duke Ellington concert by his mother at the age of six. Shortly after he began to play the trumpet and was soon playing in the Lincoln High School Band in Port Arthur. Dunbar studied both trumpet and singing with local teachers but was primarily self-taught, gaining experience playing in local dance bands. Dunbar started to play the guitar in 1947. While at university he had the chance to play with many jazz musicians including Arnett Cobb and Don Wilkerson. In his last year at college he met guitarist Les Spann who was playing with the Dizzy Gillespie band at the time. Spann encouraged Dunbar to go and hear Wes Montgomery. This he did on a college trip to Indianapolis. Dunbar was so impressed by Montgomery's playing that he decided to move to Indianapolis to join in the local jazz scene there. The young guitarist befriended Montgomery and other leading jazz musicians including Freddie Hubbard, Slide Hampton, Leroy Vinnegar, Larry Ridley and David Baker. Baker was to prove an enormous influence on Dunbar introducing the young musician to the Lydian concept.

In 1966 Dunbar moved to Dallas and played in a quintet with Red Garland and David Newman. While in Dallas he met saxophonist Bill Harper and they began to play together regularly. When Harper moved to New York Dunbar followed, working there as a pharmacist during the day and as a musician at night. He soon found he was much in demand for club and studio work. In 1972 he gave up pharmacy to devote his whole time to music. Dunbar worked with Jimmy Heath and McCoy Tyner, the Gil Evans orchestra and in 1971 he took over the guitar chair from John McLaughlin in Tony Williams's Lifetime. This position he held for around a year.

In 1972 Dunbar began his involvement in music education when he began to teach at Rutgers University in New Brunswick, New Jersey. He soon became an Associate Professor of Music, a position he held until his death in 1998.

PHOTO: COURTESY XANADU RECORDS

SELECTED RECORDINGS

Ted Dunbar/ Opening Remarks	Xanadu 155
Ted Dunbar/ Jazz Guitarist	Xanadu 196
In Tandem w/Kenny Barron	Muse MR5140
Gentle Time Alone	Steeplechase 1298 CD

SELECTED MUSIC

A System of Tonal Convergence for Improvisors, Composers and Arrangers	Dunte Publishing
New Approaches to Jazz Guitar	Dunte Publishing
The II-V Cadence as a Creative Guitar Learning Device	Dunte Publishing

EDDIE DURAN
Born-EDWARD LORENZO DURAN
San Francisco, USA
6 September 1925

Eddie Duran

Eddie Duran was born to parents of Mexican heritage. His first instrument was the piano, but he changed to the guitar at the age of eight. Duran was self-taught until he went to junior high school, at which time he began to take harmony and theory lessons in a local music studio. Duran began to play professionally in the San Francisco area from the age of fifteen.

During World War II Duran was drafted into the Navy. After his discharge in 1946 he returned to San Francisco where he formed a band with his brothers, Manny on piano, and Carlos on bass. This group was styled after the succesful Nat `King` Cole trio. During this time Duran supplemented his income earned as a musician, by working part-time as a barber.

By the early 1950s Eddie Duran had become one of the most respected jazz musicians in the Bay Area. Over the years he worked with many of the world's most famous jazzmen including Stan Getz, George Shearing, Charlie Parker, Flip Philips and Red Norvo. For many years Duran worked and recorded with pianist, Vince Guaraldi, and vibraphonist Carl Tjader. In the late 1950s he was guitarist with the local CBS Radio band. In the 1960s he worked in many San Francisco jazz and night clubs backing top celebrities including singers Barbra Streisand and Betty Bennett, and comedians Woody Allen, Bill Cosby and Richard Pryor.

In 1976 Duran accepted an offer to join the Benny Goodman band for a USA tour. Until this time he had turned down many similar offers as he was always reluctant to leave his family. After this Duran went on tour with singer Pearl Bailey, and then again with Goodman to Japan and Bermuda.

For many years Eddie Duran was little known outside the San Francisco area except through a few recordings on the Fantasy label. But his excellent jazz guitar playing, although still relatively unknown, has had international exposure through his recordings on the Concord label.

Since 1986 Duran has worked throughout California in a duo with his wife Mad, a saxophonist and flautist. They have released several cassette recordings on the 'Loose Deuce' label.

Eddie Duran	Fantasy 3247 LP
Vince Guaraldi Trio	Fantasy 3225 LP
Vince Guaraldi Trio	Fantasy 3257 LP
Ginza	Concord CJ 94 LP
Piquant Tania Maria	Concord CCD-4151
Tania Maria Sextet – Taurus	Concord CCD-4175
Come With Me – Tania Maria	Concord CCD-4151
Let There Be Love Dee Bell/Getz	Concord CJ 206 LP
Seven Stars-Eiji Kitamura	Concord CJ 217 LP
One By One Dee Bell/Stan Getz	Concord CJ 271 LP

SELECTED READING

Profile	Guitar Player. April 1984

SELECTED RECORDINGS

B Goodman Band	Eastworld EWJ 80187 LP
Earl r s Quartet	Prestige P 24043 IMS LP

EDDIE DURHAM
Born-San Marcos, Texas, USA
19 August 1906
Died-Brooklyn, New York, USA
6 March, 1987

A prominent jazz musician of the 1930s, Eddie Durham is known mainly as a trombonist, arranger and composer, who also played the guitar. His importance to jazz guitar history is that it is generally accepted that he was the first musician to play an electrically amplified guitar. It was Durham who first demonstrated its potential to Charlie Christian in 1937.

Although Eddie Durham's first instrument was the guitar, he began to play a four-string guitar when he was ten, it was on the trombone that he gained his first professional experience. His father was a country music fiddler, and all his six brothers were musicians. Durham played with circus bands during the early 1920s touring the Southern States of America. In 1926 he joined a twelve piece jazz group called 'The Dixie Ramblers'. He was then featured with groups led by Gene Coy and Walter Page. In 1929 Durham was a member of Bennie Moten's Kansas City Band. In the following years he was associated with many of the top names in jazz including Count Basie, Andy Kirk, Cab Calloway and Jimmy Lunceford. Whilst he was with Lunceford in 1935, Durham experimented with methods to amplify his guitar. Attaching an aluminium resonator to his instrument he made the first recorded jazz solo on an 'amplified' guitar on a 1935 recording called 'Hittin' the Bottle' with the Lunceford band. Whilst he was with Count Basie, Durham played the guitar in several small band sessions for jazz promoter John Hammond. In 1938 he made some recordings with one of these groups called the 'Kansas City Six' which included tenor saxophonist Lester Young. These recordings included Durham's historic electrically amplified guitar solos. In 1937 Durham met Charlie Christian in Oklahoma City and it was there that he demonstrated his electrically amplified guitar to the young guitarist who, within two years, would help begin a new era in jazz. It was Durham who also introduced the electric guitar to Floyd Smith. On March 16, 1939 Smith made the hit record 'Floyd's Guitar Blues' with the Andy Kirk band on an electric 'steel' lap-top guitar.

After the end of World War II Durham continued his professional career in the New York city area. In the early 1950s he led a small touring band accompanying singers Wynonie Harris and Larry Darnell. In 1969 Durham played with

Eddie Durham

the Buddy Tate orchestra on both guitar and trombone. For the next few years he was active as a performer and arranger on the East Coast appearing regularly at the West End Cafe in New York. In the 1980s he was regularly featured with the Harlem Blues and Jazz Band.

Eddie Durham's greatest contribution to jazz was his compositions, and many arrangements, for the big bands of Count Basie, Artie Shaw, Glenn Miller and Jimmy Lunceford in the 1930s and 1940s. But there is little doubt that his early experiments with amplifying the guitar were a major influence on the evolution of the jazz guitar.

SELECTED RECORDINGS

Jimmy Lunceford Harlem Shout 1933-6	MCA 510018 LP
Kansas City Six	Ace of Hearts ZAHC176 LP
Eddie Durham Quartet	RCA LPL15029 LP
Kansas City Five and Six	Columbia XLF 104937 LP

SELECTED READING

Profile	Downbeat, July 1962
Profile	Jazz Magazine , February 1976
Profile	Coda, December 1977
Profile	Guitar Player. August 1979

MARK ELF
Born-Queens, New York, USA
13 December 1949

Mark Elf

Mark Elf began to play the guitar at the age of eleven. When he was seventeen he began to study with guitarist Ralph Patt who encouraged him to listen to the recordings of Jimmy Raney and Tal Farlow. Elf, his interest in jazz now kindled, went on to study with Chuck Wayne, Barry Galbraith and Jim Hall. From 1969 to 1971 he studied at the Berklee College of Music in Boston. Elf also studied classical guitar in 1972 for a year with William Matthews.

In 1969 Elf played in saxophonist Billy Mitchell's quintet. Over the next few years he played with many leading jazz musicians in the New York area including Freddie Hubbard, Joe Williams, the Adderley Brothers, Sonny Stitt, George Benson, Buddy Rich and Les McCann. In 1987 Elf was the guitarist with the 'New York All Stars', a group that included Billy Mitchell, Joe Newman, Benny Powell, Groove Holmes, Major Holley and Oliver Jackson. This all-star group toured on an Italian cruise liner in the Mediterranean and was featured at the 1987 Lugano Jazz Festival in Switzerland.

Mark Elf is one of the busiest and most respected jazz guitarists on the New York scene both as leader of his own group and as a sideman. He has also filled the guitar chair in pit orchestras for many of the top Broadway shows.

| A Minor Scramble | Jen Bay Records JBR0003 CD |
| Trickynometry | Jen Bay Records JBR0004 CD |

SELECTED READING

| Profile | Just Jazz Guitar. August 1995 |

SELECTED RECORDING

Mark Elf Trio Vol. 1	Half Note Records 00001
The Eternal Triangle	Jen Bay Records JBR00002 CD
The Mark Elf Trio	Alerce CDAEO 175
Boppin at the Blue Note	Telarc CD83320

MIKE ELLIOTT
Born-MICHAEL ELLIOTT
Chicago, Illinois, USA
1941

Michael Elliott was brought up in Colorado Springs, Colorado and it was here that he had the opportunity to study with Johnny Smith. Elliott was originally inspired by various guitar styles including those of Duane Eddy, Les Paul, Link Wray and Johnny Smith. By the time he was fifteen he was playing professionally in a country music band called 'The Starlighters'. He soon tired of country music and decided to make his living playing jazz.

In 1963 he formed his own jazz group in Colorado called "The Contemporary Quartet" but after two years Eliott decided to move to the Minneapolis area. Here he formed a new group which was called "Natural Life". They made several successful recordings together.

Elliott has worked in many areas of music including recording studios, Broadway musicals, symphony orchestras, jazz clubs and as a clinician for the Gibson Guitar company. He has worked with important jazz artists including Ramsey Lewis, Clark Terry, Howard Roberts and Les Paul.

Mike Elliott

PHOTO: MAURICE J. SUMMERFIELD

SELECTED RECORDINGS

Natural Life	ASI 5001
Atrio	ASI 5003
City Traffic Mike Elliot Trio	ASI 5007

SELECTED READING

Interview	Guitar Player, January 1978

SELECTED MUSIC

Contemporary Chord Solos	Vol 1	Hal Leonard Publishing
Contemporary Chord Solos	Vol 2	Hal Leonard Publishing

Creative Guitar

The sound of Howard Roberts and his Epiphone guitar is the unique and inventive sound of one of America's most creative musicians.

Steeped in the traditional jazz idiom and a first-call sideman for dozens of top recording stars, Howard has forged a new, completely different sound of his own that is explorative, yet unpretentious—fiery and hard-swinging, but creative. And underscoring every note is the earthy honesty of the artist himself.

For all his solo and studio work and for his own Capitol recordings, Howard plays Epiphone, a guitar that guarantees him superb sensitivity, excellent response and a beautifully dependable performance *every* time.

the choice of those who can hear the difference

ЄPIPHONE

Epiphone guitars and amplifiers are products of CMI, 7373 N. Cicero, Lincolnwood, Ill.

GEORGE BENSON
THE GEORGE BENSON QUARTET

George Benson's Amp is a Guild ThunderBird.
It cuts right through organ in his quartet.

Guild

Guitarist, composer, singer, leader of his own hard-driving jazz quartet ... George Benson ... a young genius with roots in Charlie Christian", says *Down Beat*. ... Most exciting new guitarist on the jazz scene today ... had the album caption for his first LP record. ... Simmering, steaming, boiling ... always cooking ... said the beat today for his second ... George Benson has been playing Guild ever since he was 17. Watch him fly.

For Catalog No. 7054-B, write Guild Musical Instruments, Hoboken, New Jersey 07030. Or see your music dealer now.

Hear artist MARY OSBORNE and her Gretsch "White Falcon" on the Jack Sterling Show (WCBS—New York)

On Stage—And Great!

The first note...voices hush...you are being watched, listened to, appreciated. Your talent and showmanship have paid off. So have the terrific sound and looks of your Gretsch guitar!

Have you seen and played the famous Gretsch "White Falcon" electric guitar? It's a real show-piece...now available in a new Super Project-O-Sonic electronic model (stereo sound, with two amps, *at playing level*). Well worth a special trip to your dealer's. Ask him to make one available for you, soon. Today, write for Gretsch's completely detailed Project-O-Sonic folder and complete guitar catalog.

GRETSCH THE FRED GRETSCH MFG. CO · Dept. D-24G · 60 BROADWAY, B'KLYN 11, N.Y.

FREDDIE GREEN of the Count Basie Band

Reputation Reflected

A guitarist's ability; what others think of his playing, determine how far he will go. Choice of instrument is important. Freddie Green plays a Gretsch guitar. So do a growing number of successful guitarists, like him.

If success is important to you, consider a Gretsch: guitar sound like no other...modern styling and playing features you won't find elsewhere. Whether you play Acoustic or Electromatic guitar, Gretsch has a model for you. Try one out at your dealer's soon. Today, write for Gretsch's detailed guitar catalog.

GRETSCH THE FRED GRETSCH MFG. CO., · DEPT M-109 60 BROADWAY B'KLYN 11, N. Y.

Examples of 1950s/60s advertisements featuring jazz guitarists.

Oscar Peterson Trio with Herb Ellis and Ray Brown

HERB ELLIS
Born-MITCHELL HERBERT ELLIS
Farmersville, McKinney, near Dallas, Texas, USA
4 August 1921

Herb Ellis like many other leading American jazz guitarists (including Charlie Christian, Eddie Durham, and Oscar Moore) was born in the South Western part of the USA. The blues, with a touch of country music, are a distinctive feature of his jazz guitar playing. This is most certainly due to the environment in which Ellis was brought up.

Herb Ellis first played the banjo, although it is claimed he played the harmonica at the age of four. He took up the guitar at the age of ten. Whilst he was at high school he played alto horn in the school band. Ellis studied at the North Texas State College and helped start a jazz programme there. He met and befriended many now well known jazz musicians whilst at this college including Jimmy Giuffre, Gene Roland and Harry Babasin. Ellis graduated in 1941 and joined Glen Gray's band. In 1945 he joined the Jimmy Dorsey big band for three years.

Following this Ellis formed his own instrumental/ vocal trio called 'The Softwinds'. This group, which featured Lou Carter on piano, and Johnny Frigo on bass, played together for five years. During this time Ellis wrote several successful tunes including 'Detour Ahead' and 'I Told You I Love You - Now Get Out'. Ellis's jazz talent first became internationally recognised in 1953 when he took over from Barney Kessel in the Oscar Peterson Trio. There is no doubt that during his five year stay with Peterson, and his subsequent four years accompaying the renowned jazz singer Ella Fitzgerald, Ellis developed his musical abilities as a soloist and accompanist to the full. It was during this time that he also began a long association, and friendship, with bass player Ray Brown.

Since that time Herb Ellis has led a career as one of the busiest guitarists on the international jazz scene. Over the years he has played and recorded with 'The Great Guitars' group with Barney Kessel and Charlie Byrd, in a duo with Joe Pass, and as leader of his own trios and quartets. Although for many years Ellis played in the Los Angeles studios, and was a regular member of the Don Trenner Band on the popular 'Steve Allen Television Show', he returned some time ago to a life devoted to jazz. He once again appears and records regularly with Oscar Peterson.

Herb Ellis

PHOTO: ASHLEY SUMMERFIELD

SELECTED RECORDINGS

Ellis In Wonderland	Verve MGV 8171
Nothing But The Blues	Verve 314 521 674 2CD
Herb Ellis Meets Jimmy Giuffre	Verve MGV 8311
Thank You Charlie Christian	Verve MGV 8381
The Midnight Roll	Epic LA 16034
Three Guitars in Bossa Nova Time	Epic LA 17036
Herb Ellis & Stuff Smith	Koch 3 7805 2CD
Herb Ellis/Charlie Byrd	CBS CL 2330
4 to Go w/Andre Previn	Columbia 477339 2CD
Man With Guitar	Dot DLP 3678
Oscar Peterson Trio In Concert	Verve 2683 063 (2LPs)
Oscar Peterson Trio at the Concertgebouw	Verve 314 521 649 2CD
Oscar Peterson at the Stratford Festival	Verve 2304 223
Oscar Peterson Trio Rare Performances	Kings of Jazz KLJ20022
Hello Herbie w/Oscar Peterson	MPS/BASF 20723
Jazz Concord w/Joe Pass	Concord CCD 6001
Seven Come Eleven w/Joe Pass	Concord CCD 6002
Soft Shoe	Concord CCD 6003
Two For The Road w/ Joe Pass	Pablo 2310.714
After You've Gone	Concord CCD 6006
Hot Tracks	Concord CCD 6012
Rhythm Willie w/Freddie Green	Concord CCD 6010
A Pair To Draw To	Concord CJ 17
Wind Flower w/Remo Palmier	Concord CCD 4056
Soft & Mellow	Concord CCD 4077
Herb Ellis At Montreux	Concord CJ 116
Monty Alexander Trio	Concord CCD 4136
Herb Mix	Concord CJ 181
Monty Alexander Trio – Triple Treat	Concord CCD 4193
Monty Alexander Trio	Concord CJ 253
Monty Alexander Trio	Concord CJ 287
Monty Alexander Trio – Triple Treat II	Concord CCD 4338
Great Guitars	Concord CCD 6004
At The Winery – The Great Guitars	Concord CCD 4131
At Charlies, Georgetown – Great Guitars	Concord CCD 4209
Straight Tracks – The Great Guitars	Concord CCD 4421
Herb	CBS/Sony 25AP 867 LP
Sweet And Lovely	Atlas LA 27-1028 LP
When You're Smiling	Atlas LA 27-1029 LP
Doggin' Around w/Red Mitchell	Concord CCD 4372
Oscar Peterson Quartet	Telarc CD-83304
Oscar Peterson Quartet	Telarc CD-83306
Oliver Jones Trio	Justin Time JUST 34 2CD
Roll Call	Justice JR1001 2CD
Just Friends Vol 1	Justice JR0502 2CD
Just Friends Vol 2	Justice JR0503 4CD
Poor Butterfly duo w/Barney Kessel	Concord CCD 4034
Oscar Peterson Trio at Zardi's	Pablo 2PACD 2620 118 2
Oscar Peterson Trio – Encore	Telarc CD 83356
Texas Swings	Justice JR1002 2CD
Down Home	Justice JR1003 2CD
The Soft Winds – Then & Now	Chiaroscuro CR(D) 342 CD
Return of the Great Guitars	Concord CCD 4715
Kings of Swing	Contemporary CCD 14067

Herb Ellis Instructional Video	Hot Licks
Herb Ellis Instructional Video	REH
Herb Ellis – Profile – Instructional Video	Ridge Runner
The Essential Herb Ellis – Instructional Video	Ridge Runner

SELECTED READING

Profile	Guitar Player, December 1972
Interview	Guitar Player, April 1978
Interview	Coda, April 1980
Article	Jazz Times, August 1996
Interview	Just Jazz Guitar, February 1997

SELECTED MUSIC

Herb Ellis Jazz Guitar Style	Mills Music Co
Jazz Duets with Joe Pass	Mel Bay Publishing Company
In Session MMO record/music set	Guitar Player Productions
Blues Shapes	Alfred Publishing Company
All The Shapes You Are	Warner Music
Sung Blues	Warner Music
Rhythm Shapes	Warner Music

Herb Ellis

LLOYD ELLIS
**Born-Pensacola, Florida, USA
1920
Died-Pensacola, Florida, USA
5 May 1994**

Lloyd Ellis

Lloyd Ellis began to play the guitar at the age of ten. His original interest was in country music. After hearing some jazz records, including some early Django Reinhardt releases, he decided to play jazz.

Entirely self taught, Ellis first played on an acoustic guitar. His first professional work was in Pensacola with Gene Villar`s Dixielanders. In 1940 he moved to Baton Rouge, Louisiana where, having heard recordings of Charlie Christian on electric guitar with Benny Goodman, he changed over to the amplified instrument. In 1942 Ellis went into the US Navy. After leaving the services in 1946 he worked for a while backing country/gospel singer Jimmy Davis. In late 1946 Ellis moved to California where he did studio work for two years for Mercury Records.

In the late 1960s Ellis moved to Las Vegas, staying there for eight years. For a while he played in Red Norvo`s trio with electric bass player Monk Montgomery. He also played in pit bands and stage bands in Las Vegas. In 1976 Ellis moved to New Orleans. Where he had a long association with the band led by clarinetist Pete Fountain.

Lloyd Ellis did not travel professionally outside the USA and as a result was not well-known to international jazz audiences. Jazz artists and fans who heard Ellis play spoke with the highest respect for his talent.

SELECTED RECORDINGS

The Fastest Guitar In The World	Carlton 12/104 LP
Las Vegas-3AM Lloyd Ellis Quintet	Famous Door HL-110 LP

SELECTED READING

Profile	Guitar Player, April 1986

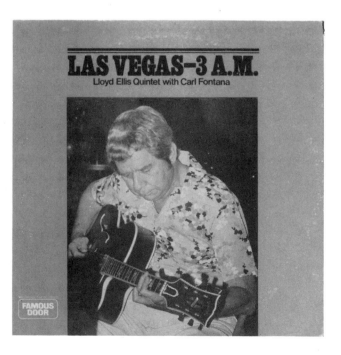

RON ESCHETE
Born-RONALD ESCHETE
Houma, Louisiana, USA
19 August 1948

Ron Eschete started playing the guitar at the age of fourteen. His early influences were blues artists such as B.B. King, Muddy Waters and Jimmy Reed. After graduating from high school in Houma, Eschete moved to New Orleans where he began his professional career as a guitarist in the bars and clubs on Bourbon Street. He then decided to further his musical education and attended the Loyola University in New Orleans from which he majored in classical guitar. While at university he also gained valuable experience playing in the school jazz lab band. He was able to pay his way through college from money earned playing in various local jazz groups and backing singers such as Frankie Laine and Joni James.

In 1968 he won the 'Outstanding Musician Award', which was presented to him by Mundell Lowe, at the Mobile Jazz Festival. In 1969 Eschete was hired by singer Buddy Greco and moved to Las Vegas to back this popular artist. In 1970 he was offered a position in Los Angeles. He accepted and since that time has established himself as one of the busiest guitarists in the recording and television studios, and jazz clubs in the Los Angeles area. He has also been on the teaching staff of the GIT (Guitar Institute of Technology) since 1978.

Ron Eschete is currently a featured soloist in a jazz group led by pianist Gene Harris. Over the last twenty years he has been associated with many other leading jazz artists including Ray Brown, Jake Hanna, Hampton Hawes, Milt Jackson, Dizzy Gillespie, Warne Marsh, Bob Cooper, Bill Mays, Al Grey and Bob Brookmeyer.

Ron Eschete

SELECTED RECORDINGS
Spirit's Samba	JAS 4003
To Let You Know I Care	Muse MR 5186
Line Up	Muse MR 5246
Stump Jumper	Bainbridge BT 6264 LP
Christmas Impressions	Bainbridge BCD 6267
Gene Harris Quartet – Listen Here	Concord CCD 4385
Gene Harris Quintet – Black & Blue	Concord CCD 4482
Gene Harris Quartet – Like a Lover	Concord CCD-4526
Mo' Strings Attached	Jazz Alliance TJA-10020 CD
A Closer Look	Concord CCD 4607
Rain or Shine	Concord CCD 4665
Soft Winds	Concord CCD 4737

SELECTED READING
Interview	Guitar Player May 1984
Interview	Just Jazz Guitar, November 1995

SELECTED MUSIC
Jazz Guitar Method	Alfred Publishing
Chord Phrases	REH Publications
Key Correlation	REH Publications

CHRISTIAN ESCOUDÉ
Born-Angouleme, France
23 September 1947

Christian Escoudé started to play the guitar as a youth. He first played professionally as a teenager in local dance bands. He was introduced to jazz in 1969 when he joined the Aime Barelli band in Monte Carlo. Within a few years he began to be recognised as one of France's oustanding young jazz guitarists. His early influences were Django Reinhardt (Escoudé's family are of gypsy origin) and Jimmy Raney. He came to national prominence when he was featured in a trio led by jazz organist, Eddy Louiss, at the Jazz-Inn club in Palais Royal.

In 1976 he won the 'Prix Django' as French Jazz Musician of the Year. After this success Escoude played and recorded with many important international jazz musicians including bassist Charlie Haden, pianist John Lewis and guitarists Larry Coryell and John McLaughlin. In 1983 he toured Switzerland and Austria in a duo with Larry Coryell.

Christian Escoudé continues to be one of France's most important jazz musicians, recording prolifically with diverse jazz artists.

Christian Escoude

PHOTO: IAN CRUICKSHANK

SELECTED RECORDINGS

Catherine/Lockwood/Escoudé Trio	JMS Productions 031 LP
Charlie Haden/Escoudé Duo	Dreyfus Jazz Line FDM 36505 2CD
Christian Escoudé-Holidays	Emarcy 514 304 2 CD
Escoudé Plays Reinhardt	Emarcy 510 132 2 CD
Gypsy Waltz	Emarcy 838 772 2 CD
Escoudé Live w/P.Michelot	Emarcy CD K7 848 573 2/4
Christian Escoudé Group	JMS 18656 2 CD
Three of a Kind	JMS 18666 2 CD
Escoudé in LA	Gitanes 518 653 2 CD
Cookin' in Hell's Kitchen	Gitanes 526 743 2 CD

SELECTED READING

Interview	Cadence, June 1995

SELECTED MUSIC

Christian Escoudé – My Book	Salhani

JOHN ETHERIDGE
Born-JOHN MICHAEL GLYN ETHERIDGE
London, England
12 January 1948

John Etheridge started to play the piano at the age of six but gave it up after two years. He bought his first guitar when he was thirteen and taught himself to play the instrument while still at school.

Etheridge went to Essex University and in the early 1970s played with various jazz-rock groups in the London area. From 1975-78 he gained some prominence as guitarist with the group 'Soft Machine'. He joined the jazz mainstream when he became lead guitarist with Stephane Grappelli's quartet. He toured extensively from 1978-81 with the famous violinist and gained international recognition for his guitar work in this quartet. In 1980-81 he toured Australia with his own group 'Second Vision' and in 1982 toured the USA with virtuoso bassist Brian Torff. 1983 saw him back in the UK touring with his own jazz trio.

Etheridge continued some involvement in rock music in the early 1980s but recent years have seen his involvement once again in jazz playing with guitarist Gary Boyle, bassist Danny Thompson and others. He is also a respected teacher and is featured on many courses both in the UK and abroad.

John Etheridge

SELECTED RECORDINGS

At The Winery Stephane Grappelli Quartet	Concord CJ 139
New World Didier Lockwood Group	MPS 7046
First Steps	Chrysalis ZCHR 1289
Ash – John Etheridge	The Jazz Label JJL 103 CD

SELECTED READING

Interview	Guitar Player March 1983
Interview	Guitar, October 1982

BUS ETRI

Born-ANTHONY ETRI
New York City, USA
1917
Died-Culver City, California, USA
21 August 1941

Due to his premature death Bus Etri is little known to jazz lovers today. Yet most of those who heard him play have no doubt that he would have become one of the jazz guitar greatest players.

Bus Etri was a cousin of guitarist Tony Mottola, and his brother Ben is a saxophonist. His first professional work was with the Hudson De Lange band in 1935, but he only came to prominence when he joined the Charlie Barnet band in 1938. His recordings with that band show him to be one of the band's best jazz soloists. After being with the band for only three years Etri was tragically killed in a car accident near Los Angeles in 1941. The car was driven by vocalist Lloyd Hundling who also died in the accident.

SELECTED RECORDINGS

Charlie Barnet And His Orchestra	DJM Records	DJML 061 LP
Charlie Barnet 1939-41 Vol 1 Black & White	RCA	PM 42041 LP
Charlie Barnet And His Orchestra	RCA	NL 89483 TIS LP
Charlie Barnet And His Orchestra	RCA	PM 45689 LP

Bus Etri with the Charlie Barnet Orchestra

KEVIN EUBANKS
Born-KEVIN TYRONE EUBANKS
Philadelphia, Pennsylvania, USA
15 November 1957

Kevin Eubanks comes from a very musical family. His mother is a Doctor of Music. Two of his uncles, Tommy and Ray Bryant, are prominent jazz musicians. His brother Robin is an excellent trombone player.

Eubanks first instrument was the violin. He studied on the violin for six years and then changed to the guitar. By the time he was thirteen he was already playing in local gigs. After graduating from high school in 1975 he went to Berklee College of Music. Here he studied with guitarist Ted Dunbar. In 1980 he graduated from Berklee with a BA in composition.

At first Eubanks was influenced by guitarist John McLaughlin. By the time he was in his early twenties Wes Montgomery was to become his major influence. During 1980 and 1981 the young guitarist played with Art Blakey's Jazz Messengers, including an appearance at the Montreux Jazz Festival with this famous group. Since that time he has developed a reputation as being one of the best of the new generation of jazz fusion guitarists and has worked with many top jazz musicians including Roy Haynes, Slide Hampton, Dave Holland and Mike Gibbs.

In May 1992 Kevin Eubanks came to national prominence in the USA when he accepted the guitar chair in the band of 'The Tonight Show' hosted by Jay Leno. The all star group featured in this popular television show is led by Branford Marsalis. Eubanks had to move to Los Angeles to take up this new position and it is from here that he plans to continue his jazz career in clubs and in the recording studios.

Kevin Eubanks

PHOTO: COURTESY KEVIN EUBANKS

| Article | Jazz Times, December 1995 |
| Article | Fingerstyle Guitar, September/October 1997 |

SELECTED MUSIC

The Creative Guitarist	Hal Leonard Publishing
Kevin Eubanks Guitar Collection	Hal Leonard Publishing

SELECTED RECORDINGS

Kevin Eubanks – Guitarist	DTM 71006 CD
Sundance	GRP A 10008 CD
Opening Night	GRP 95202 CD
Face To Face	GRP 95392 CD
The Heat of Heat	GRP 95522 CD
Shadow Prophet	GRP 95652 CD
The Searcher	GRP 95802 CD
Promise Of Tomorrow	GRP 96042 CD
Extensions-Dave Holland Quartet	ECM 841 778-2 CD
Karma	POL 34446 CD
Turning Point	Blue Note CD P 7 89170
Spirit Talk	Blue Note CD P 7 89286
Live at Bradley's	Blue Note CD P 7 30133

SELECTED READING

Interview	Guitar Player, May 1986
Profile	Downbeat, July 1992
Profile	Guitar Player, August 1992
Interview	Jazz Times July/August 1992
Profile	Jazziz, October/November 1992
Profile	Jazz The Magazine, Issue 11 1992
Profile	Jaziz, March 1994

KEVIN EUBANKS creative guitarist
by kevin eubanks & john amaral

An In-depth
Approach To
Music Concepts
And Techniques

FRANK EVANS
Born-Bristol, UK
1 October 1936

Frank Evans began playing the guitar at the age of 11. His early jazz influences were Charlie Christian and Django Reinhardt, although over the years he studied a much broader musical spectrum including classical and Eastern styles.

Evans early years as a professional guitarist were spent working in restaurants and clubs. His first professional job was in a quartet backing the singer and cabaret artist Tessie O'Shea. He then spent many years on the road in Britain and Europe with various jazz groups, including one led by saxophonist Tubby Hayes. In 1961 he decided to settle permanently in his home town of Bristol.

Since that time Frank Evans has been very involved in the Bristol music scene. He writes and arranges for local television, radio, and other commercial work. Evans still devotes much of his time to playing jazz in local clubs. He runs his own recording studio in which several of his own records have been made. These recordings, and his club appearances, have given general recognition that Frank Evans is one Britain's best jazz guitarists.

SELECTED RECORDINGS

Jazz Tete a Tete w/Tubby Hayes	77 Records	77LEU-12/21 LP
Mark Twain Suite	77 Records	77SEU-12/37 LP
Stretching Forth	Saydisc	SDL 217 LP
In An English Manner	Saydisc	SDL 233 LP
Noctuary	Blue Bag	101 LP
Soiree	Blue Bag	102 LP
Thank Evans For Little Girls	Blue Bag	104 LP

SELECTED READING

Interview	Guitar, February 1978
Profile	Guitar Player, May 1978

Frank Evans

PHOTO: COURTESY FRANK EVANS

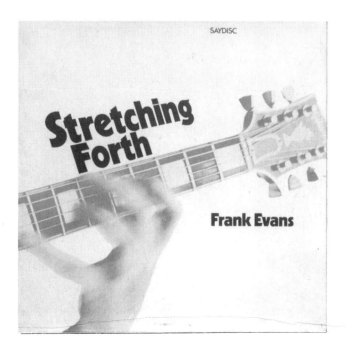

SAYDISC

Stretching Forth

Frank Evans

Tal Farlow

TAL FARLOW
Born-TALMADGE HOLT FARLOW
Greensboro, North Carolina, USA 7 June 1921
Died – New York City, USA, 25 July 1995

Talmadge Holt Farlow, is recognised as one of the great jazz guitarists of all time. He originally set out to be a commercial painter and artist and did not start playing the guitar professionally until he was twenty-two.

Farlow played the mandolin and the guitar as a hobby from the age of eight. His father played guitar, banjo, ukulele and violin, and Farlow taught himself to play hill-billy music on one of his father's instruments. In the late 1930s Farlow heard Charlie Christian on some Benny Goodman records. He was immediately attracted to Christian's jazz guitar style. He listened to the records over and over again until he could play Christian's guitar solos note-for-note.

Until 1943 Farlow worked as a sign painter and played the guitar as a hobby. With the establishment of a large US Air Force training base at Greensboro, there was a sudden demand for musicians to play at U.S.O. dances. Farlow was hired to play at some of these. One of the many musicians he played with was jazz pianist Jimmy Lyons. After the end of the war Farlow joined a group led by the well-known pianist Dardanelle. He played with her group in Baltimore and Philadelphia, and then for six months at the 'Copacabana' nightspot in New York. It was in the jazz clubs of New York's 52nd Street area that Farlow had the opportunity to hear many leading modern jazz musicians including Charlie Parker, Art Tatum, Erroll Garner and Dizzy Gillespie.

After leaving Dardanelle Farlow returned for a while to North Carolina but then returned to New York where he played with clarinetist Buddy De Franco. Tal Farlow was then hired in 1949 by vibraphonist Red Norvo to take Mundell Lowe's place in his trio. Lowe had recommended Farlow for the job . The new trio was made up by bassist Red Kelly. It was this period with Norvo's trio that Farlow partly attributes to his mastery of the phenomenal technique he now has. Red Norvo's trio, after Charles Mingus replaced Kelly on bass, became one of the most popular jazz groups of the 1950s. Their recordings were constantly amongst the best selling jazz records. Farlow appeared with the Norvo trio on the first ever USA colour television programme. Through club and concert appearances, and recordings with the trio, Farlow gained international recog-

Tal Farlow

nition for his incredible technique, brilliant improvisation, and many original musical concepts. Playing an instrument of his own design with a finger board over an inch shorter than the standard pattern, Farlow achieved a most individual sound.

Whilst with Norvo's trio Farlow developed various original rhythm techniques on the guitar, often confusing listeners into thinking that a drummer had been added to the line-up. One such technique was to play chords whilst simultaneously tapping out rhythms on the guitar body and strings with his finger tips. In 1954 Farlow left Norvo to play with Artie Shaw's Gramercy Five in New York.

In 1954 Tal Farlow won the Downbeat magazine 'New Star Award', and in 1956 their critics' poll. By this time Farlow was recognized worldwide as one of America's leading jazz artists. He was signed up by Norman Granz for the Verve label. He made several outstanding recordings for Verve as leader of groups which featured several top jazz artists of the day including Ray Brown, Chico Hamilton, Eddie Costa, Vinnie Burke and Stan Levey.

In 1958 Farlow married and that year also marked what was to be his last important public appearance for several years. It was held at the 'Composer' club in Manhattan. He then moved to his new home in Sea Bright, New Jersey on the Atlantic coast, and entered virtual semi-retirement for almost twenty years. He spent much of his time working at his old love of sign painting. Nevertheless he did not entirely neglect his playing and from time to time many of the world's top guitarists took time off to visit him, play and talk guitar. In

1968 Farlow made a brief comeback appearing to packed houses for seven weeks, with his trio, at the 'Frammis' club on Manhattan's East Side. After this brief reappearance Farlow returned again to his home in Sea Bright.

Pressure from jazz lovers all over the world, together with his own desire to play jazz again, encouraged Farlow in 1975 to start playing regularly. From that time, until his death of esophageal cancer in July 1998, he made several recordings, and played frequently at jazz clubs and festivals all over the world. His life as a jazz musician, and sign painter, was the subject of a 1982 television documentary

SELECTED RECORDINGS

Red Norvo Trio	Natural Organic 7001
Red Norvo Trio	Savoy STL2212(2LPs)
Red Norvo Small Bands	RCA ND 86278 CD
Jazz Workshop	Debut DLP-15
Oscar Pettiford Memorial Album	Prestige HBS 6101
Artie Shaw Gramercy Five	Verve 2304 208
Buddie De Franco Quintet	Verve MV 2513
Tal Farlow Quartet	Blue Note BLP5042
Early Tal	Blue Note BNP25104
Tal Farlow Plays Harold Arlen	Verve MV 2589
Tal Farlow Album	Verve MV 2584
Interpretations of Tal Farlow	Verve MV 2542
Recital	Verve MV 2586
Guitar Artistry of Tal Farlow	Verve MV 2588
Swing Guitars	Norgran 1033
Tal	Verve MV 2565
Swinging Guitar of Tal Farlow	Verve MGV 8201
This is Tal Farlow	Verve 314 537 746 2 CD
Autumn In New York	Verve MGV 8184
Buddy De Franco Quintet	Progressive 7014
Up, Up And Away w\Sonny Criss	Prestige 7530
Artie Shaw: The Last Recordings (2 CD set)	Music Masters 820 847 2 CD
Tal Farlow-Fuerst Set	Xanadu 109
Tal Farlow-Second Set	Xanadu 119
Return of Tal Farlow	Prestige 7732
Sign of the Time	Concord CCD 4026
Mostly Flute w\Sam Most	Xanadu 133
Tal Farlow Trio-Trinity	Columbia 476580 2 CD
Tal 78	Concord CJ 57
Poppin' And Burnin'	Verve 815 236-1 (2LPs)
On Stage	Concord CCD 4143
Chromatic Pallette	Concord CCD 4154
Cooking On All Burners	Concord CCD 4204
Legendary Tal Farlow	Concord CCD 4266
Tal Farlow – Giants of Jazz	CD 53247
Standards Recital Duo w/Philippe Petit	FD 151932 CD
Verve Jazz Masters (41)	Verve 314 527 365 2 CD
Chance Meeting w/Lenny Breau	Guitarehaves GR-003 CD
Talmadge Farlow Video	Stutz Cinema Ventures
Tal Farlow Instructional Video	Hot Licks
Red Norvo Trio-Video	Kultur 1278

SELECTED READING

Article	Downbeat, December 1963
Profile	Downbeat, June 1968
Profile	Coda, January 1968
Article	Guitar Player, June 1975
Appreciation	Jazz Journal, April/May/June 1981
Interview	Guitar Player, July, 1980
Interview	Crescendo, December 1981
Profile	Downbeat, January 1982
Interview	Guitar World, March 1983
Private Lesson	Guitar Player, July 1984
Profile	Jazz News January/February 1989
Interview	Guitarist, December 1989
Tal Farlow Biography Shane Hill	Razzmajazz (1987)
Profile	Downbeat, August 1995
Interview	Guitarist, November 1995
Article	Guitar Player, May 1996
Profile	Downbeat, August 1995
Interview	Just Jazz Guitar, November 1996

SELECTED MUSIC

Tal Farlow Audio Instruction Course	Hot Licks
Chordal Genius	Guitarist, September 1985
The Jazz Style of Tal Farlow	Rochinski, Hal Leonard

Tal Farlow with Red Norvo and Charles Mingus

RAPHAEL FAYS
Born-Paris, France
10 December 1959

Raphael Fays

Raphael Fays, like Django Reinhardt, was born into a Manouche family of Gypsies. He started to play the guitar at the age of twelve. His teacher was his father, guitarist Louis Fays. At first he played both jazz and classical music but Fays soon devoted most of his time to jazz. He listened to the recordings of Django Reinhardt and quickly developed a virtuoso technique, and a mastery of the 'Hot Club' style. Fays also listened to recordings by contemporary jazz guitarists, including those of Wes Montgomery, Jim Hall and Jimmy Raney, and these were to prove an influence.

Raphael Fays first real professional break came in 1975 when French country guitarist Marcel Dadi arranged to record him. Since that time Fays has been recognised as one of the finest contemporary exponents of the jazz guitar style of Django Reinhardt. He has appeared with Stephane Grappelli on French television, and performs frequently at leading jazz clubs and festivals throughout Europe.

SELECTED RECORDINGS

Raphael Fays	Sonopresse 69689 LP
Raphael Fays	Decca 6.24130 AP LP
Raphael Fays Group	Acoustic Music AMC lOlS LP
Night in Caravan	WEA 58232 LP
Raphael Fays w/Pierre Blanchard	Ricordu CDR 068
Raphael Fays	GHA 126 037 CD

SELECTED READING

Profile	Guitar, August 1981

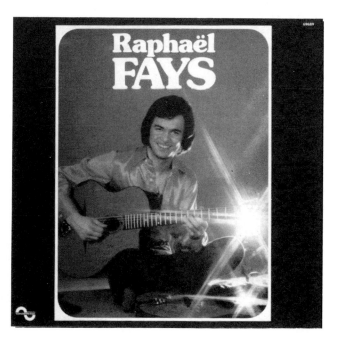

JIM FERGUSON

Born-JAMES EDWIN FERGUSON
Dayton, Ohio, USA
23 December 1948

Jim Ferguson is known to jazz guitarists all over the world for his hundreds of articles on jazz guitarists written over a period of many years in Guitar Player magazine.

Ferguson began to play the guitar at the age of fifteen, initially drawn to folk and blues music . Whilst at college he became attracted to both jazz and classical guitar. His early jazz guitar influences were Django Reinhardt and Kenny Burrell.

In the early 1970s Ferguson moved to the Santa Cruz area of California. Here he studied jazz guitar with Davis Ramey, and then George Barnes until the guitarist's death in 1977. Ferguson published a book on blues guitar and then began to work for Guitar Player magazine which is based in Cupertino, California. Over many years he worked in various capacities with this prestigious magazine, achieving the title of Associate Editor. He wrote hundreds of pedagogical features, history-oriented articles, and profiles of, or interviews with, many of the world's most famous jazz guitarists.

For a time Ferguson studied with Lenny Breau, ghost writing this unique guitarist's fingerstyle jazz column for Guitar Player.

Jim Ferguson is recognised as a leading American jazz authority. He has contributed to The New Grove Dictionary of Jazz (1988). He has compiled and annotated CD jazz guitar collections by Fantasy Records and Rhino Records and also annotated dozens of jazz guitar recordings for the Concord and Fantasy labels. With his classical guitar background he has also edited several works for this instrument for GSP Publications of San Francisco. He reviews regularly for Jazz Times magazine.

Ferguson has performed and taught in the USA, Europe and Scandinavia. He holds a Master of Fine Arts degree in music from Mills College in Oakland, California. He currently divides his time between freelance writing, college music instruction, composition and jazz and classical performance.

Jim Ferguson

PHOTO: COURTESY JIM FERGUSON

SELECTED MUSIC

All Blues for Jazz Guitar	Mel Bay Publications
All Blues Soloing for Jazz Guitar	Mel Bay Publications

SELECTED RECORDINGS

Songs for our fathers - Robin Anderson Big Band	RABB 001

ALL BLUES for JAZZ GUITAR comping styles, chords & grooves

MEL BAY

By Jim Ferguson
Guitar Master Class Publications

BOULOU FERRE
Born-Paris, France
24 April 1951

Boulou Ferre

Boulou Ferre was born into a family of Gypsy musicians. His father Pierre Matelot Ferre, and uncles Sarane and Barreau Ferre, were all prominent French guitarists. Ferre was taught by his father from the age of eight. His father was at one time a guitarist in the Quintet of the Hot Club of France accompanying Django Reinhardt. By the time Boulou Ferre was nine he was regarded as a prodigy and had given his first concert at the Musee Guimet in Paris.

Boulou Ferre studied both classical and jazz guitar techniques. As a result he was influenced by master classical guitarist, Andres Segovia, and jazz masters Charlie Parker and Dizzy Gillespie. His most important jazz guitar influences were Django Reinhardt, Wes Montgomery and Tal Farlow. In 1963 he enrolled at the Conservatoire National in Paris to study classical music. At the age of twelve Ferre made his first jazz recording under the direction of Alain Goraguer on the Barclay label. This record and another one released on the Barclay label, under the direction of Jean Boucherty, are proof of the amazing talent Boulou Ferre had as a child.

Over the years Ferre has based himself in Paris working with a variety of top jazz artists including Dexter Gordon, Stephane Grappelli, Gordon Beck, and T. Bone Walker. He has appeared many times on French television. He played at the Antibes Jazz Festival in 1965 with Bernard Lubas and Gilbert Rovere, and also starred in several concerts at Olympia, Paris in the same year.

In recent years Boulou Ferre has played on the international jazz circuit in an acoustic guitar duo with his younger brother, Elios. They play in the style of Django Reinhardt and the Quintet of the Hot Club of France, and have enjoyed great success. They play regularly at the annual Django Reinhardt Festival held in Samois, France.

SELECTED RECORDINGS

Boulou	Barclay 80311 LP
Boulou and the Paris All Stars	Barclay CBLP 2083
Nuages	Steeplechase SCS 1222 LP
Pour Django	SteepleChase SCCD 31120
Gypsy Dreams	SteepleChase SCCD 31140
Trinity	SteepleChase SCCD 31171
Confirmation	SteepleChase SCCD 31243
Guitar Legacy	SteepleChase SCCD37009/10 2CD

SELECTED READING

Interview	Vintage Guitar Magazine, February 1998

BARRY FINNERTY
Born-San Francisco, California, USA
3 December 1951

Barry Finnerty first studied classical music on the piano. His mother was a piano teacher. At the age of twelve he started to play the guitar. A year later he moved to Hong Kong with his mother who had a Fulbright Grant to teach in the former UK colony for a year. Finnerty's main music interest was in rock and roll. On his return to San Francisco he began to listen to diverse blues and rock artists including Jimi Hendrix, Jeff Beck, Jerry Garcia, Eric Clapton and Jimmy Page. At the same time he began to listen to some jazz recordings by Miles Davis, Paul Desmond and guitarist Howard Roberts.

By the time he was 17 Finnerty had decided to devote himself to jazz. In 1970 he studied for a year at the Berklee College of Music in Boston. Here he had the chance to meet and study with many top jazz artists including Mick Goodrick, Charlie Mariano and George Benson. On his return to San Francisco in 1972 Finnerty met Dave Creamer who proved to be a great influence on the guitarist's musical approach and style. In 1973 Finnerty went to New York where he joined Chico Hamilton's quintet appearing with the famous drummer at the Montreux Jazz festival a few months later. In the same year he met Pat Martino who had by now become one of his main guitar influences together with Wes Montgomery and Django Reinhardt.

In 1974 Barry Finnerty joined the Airto and Flora Purim band in Los Angeles. He had been recommended by drummer Billy Cobham. After leaving this famous band Finnerty returned to New York where he played with saxophonist Joe Farrell and flautist Hubert Laws. In 1976 he joined Ray Barretto's band. Soon after he was playing and recording with the Crusaders, staying with this famous group on and off until 1984. In 1981 Finnerty played for Miles Davis on his recording 'The Man With The Horn'. In 1984 he formed his own rock style band called the Negatives. This group performed in both Miami and New York.

Barry Finnerty combines his international career in jazz with a busy career as a session guitarist and producer in the USA. He appeared from 1984 -1996 on the Manhattan Cable television programme The Jon Hammond Show as co-producer, musical director and featured performer.

Barry Finnerty

Heavy Metal Bebop w/Brecker Bros	RCA 2119257-2 CD
Straight Ahead	Arabesque Records AJ0116 CD
Bargain Hunters	Hot Wire Records

SELECTED READING

Article	Guitar World, February 1989
Profile	Jazz Times, August 1995

SELECTED RECORDINGS

Flight Time w/Billy Cobham	Inak 8616 CD
The Man with a Horn w/Miles Davis	CBS 468701-2 CD

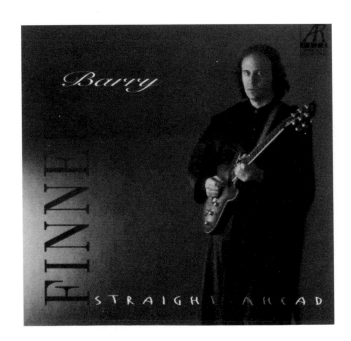

BUDDY FITE
Born-RONALD FITE
Vancouver, Washington, USA
19 June 1938

Buddy Fite

Buddy Fite began to play the guitar as a child and was influenced by the early multi-track recordings of Les Paul. His first experience as a musician was playing country music on a steel guitar. After leaving school he played professionally in a country music trio in bars and clubs in the Portland area of Oregon for over twenty years. The trio moved to Oakland, California where they were booked to play country music in a local club.

It was during this period that Fite became interested in playing jazz on a regular six string archtop guitar. After playing the Oakland club scene Fite decided to take up a job in the lumber mills of Oregon. Whilst he was in Oregon he was booked as a guitar demonstrator for the Sunn Amplifier company. The guitarist, whilst demonstrating for the Sunn company, was heard by Les Paul at the 1968 Chicago NAMM trade convention. He was so impressed by Fite's unique style that he persuaded the Sunn company to arrange for the guitarist to make what was to be the first of three recordings for the Cyclone label in Los Angeles. It was in Los Angeles that Fite was heard by singer Johnny Mathis, who immediately hired him to be his accompanist. The guitarist toured with Mathis for one and a half years. After leaving Mathis, Fite once again returned to Portland to work in the lumber mills during the day and play jazz at night. In 1972 Fite bought into a musical instrument business in Portland. Since that time, despite suffering from severe arthritis, he has continued to play in local clubs at nights attracting the admiration of his peers but remains virtually unknown to jazz lovers outside Oregon.

SELECTED RECORDINGS

Buddy Fite	Cyclone CY 4100 LP
Changes – Buddy Fite	Cyclone CY 4110 LP
Buddy Fite & Friend	Bell 6058 LP
Buddy Fite	Different Drummer DD 1001 LP
Tasty-Buddy Fite	Pinnacle PNL 7779 LP
The Hits of Yesterday	CMI 1005 LP

SELECTED READING

Profile	Guitar Player, October 1972

SELECTED MUSIC

Buddy Fite Jazz Guitar Solos	Mel Bay Publications

CHRIS FLORY
Born-CHRISTOPHER FLORY
New York City, USA
13 November 1953

Chris Flory

Chris Flory began playing the guitar at the age of twelve. He became interested in jazz at the age of seventeen. He began his professional career as a guitarist in 1974 freelancing in the Providence, Rhode Island area. He played frequently with saxophonist Scott Hamilton.

Flory moved to New York in 1976. Here he continued to work as a member of Scott Hamilton's quartet. Over the years he has backed, and recorded with, many other top jazz artists including Illinois Jacquet, Hank Jones, Bob Wilber, Buddy Tate, and Ruby Braff. In 1979 Flory joined the Benny Goodman Sextet staying with this famous group until 1983. He also appeared in Goodman's last big band concert in 1985 at Wolf Trap. In 1989 Flory made his first solo tour of Great Britain. He has toured Europe and Japan many times with Scott Hamilton.

In 1991 Flory recorded his first album as leader for the Concord label. Flory's jazz guitar style is firmly rooted in the mainstream tradition of Charlie Christian and Oscar Moore, although he cites Django Reinhardt, Bill Jennings and Wes Montgomery as influences.

SELECTED RECORDINGS

Duke Robillard Band	Demon Records Fiend CD 191
Ruby Braff Quintet	Phontastic PHONT 7568
Songs of Leo Robin	Pausa 7175 LP
Sailboat In The Moonlight w\Braff & Hamilton	Concord CCD 4296
Rosemary Clooney Sings Berlin	Concord CCD 4255
Sound Investment w/Flip Phillips	Concord CCD 4334
Maxine Sullivan-Uptown	Concord CCD 4288
Maxine Sullivan-Swingin' Street	Concord CCD 4351
Chris Flory Quartet-For All We Know	Concord CCD-4403
City Life	Concord CCD 4589
Word on the Street	Double Time DTR9 119

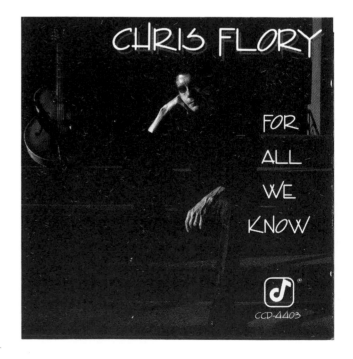

CHRIS FLORY

FOR ALL WE KNOW

CCD-4403

ROBBEN FORD
Born-ROBBEN LEE FORD
Woodlake, California, USA
16 December 1951

Robben Ford is a fusion guitarist whose style is based in the blues, yet his improvisational and technical abilities have earned him high respect amongst contemporary jazz musicians.

Ford comes from a musical background. His father was a country musician, and his brothers bluesmen. His early musical influences were Mike Bloomfield and Eric Clapton. Ford's first professional work was in 1970 in the San Francisco Bay area with the Charlie Musslewhite band. In 1971 he formed the Charles Ford Band with his brothers and they backed singer Jimmy Witherspoon 1972-74. In 1974 Ford became a member of Tom Scott's group L.A. Express. They toured nationally and recorded with singer/guitarist Joni Mitchell. This exposure led to top session work for Ford with Barbra Streisand, George Harrison, Kenny Loggins and others. Through this Ford gained wide recognition for his guitar talent. Ford has also taught at the Guitar Institute of Technology in Hollywood.

In 1978 Ford formed the successful group 'Yellowjackets' with keyboardist Russell Ferrante. In the early 1980s he worked with saxophonist Sadao Watanabe, and in 1986 joined the Miles Davis band for a USA and European concert tour.

Since that time Robben Ford has established himself as one of the most successful jazz/blues/rock fusion guitarists of the day.

Robben Ford

PHOTO: WILLIAM HAMES/COURTESY HAL LEONARD INC.

SELECTED RECORDINGS
Charles Ford Band	Arhoolie 4005 LP
Robben Ford & Jimmy Witherspoon	L.A. International GG 58003 LP
The Inside Story	Elektra 6E-169 LP
Talk To Your Daughter	Warner Bros 25647-1 CD
Love's A Heartache	Polydor (Japan) 28MM0253
Yellowjackets	Warner Bros 3573 CD
Robben Ford & The Blue Line	Jazz Door 1283 CD
Handel of Blues	Blue Thumb 7004 CD
Mystic Mile	Sector Two STC 1107 CD
Tiger Walk	Blue Thumb 7011 CD
Playin' The Blues Instructional Video	REH

SELECTED READING
Interview	Guitar Player, October 1976
Profile	Guitar World, January 1982
Interview	Guitarist, October 1988
Interview	Guitar Player, September 1988
Profile	Guitar World, November 1988
Profile	Downbeat, January 1993
Profile	Jazz Journal, May 1990
Profile	Jazz Times, March 1994
Interview	Fingerstyle Guitar, March/April 1996
Profile	Jazz Times, November 1997

SELECTED MUSIC
Rhythm/Blues Book/Cassette	REH Publications
Yellow Jackets Transcriptions	Hal Leonard Publishing
Robben Ford Blues Collection	Hal Leonard Publishing

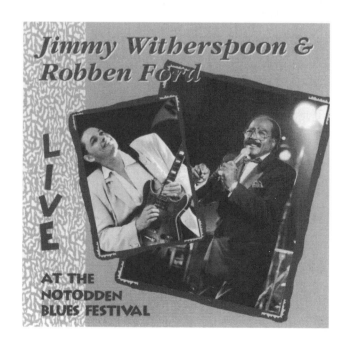

BRUCE FORMAN
Born-Springfield, Massachusetts, USA
14 May 1956

Bruce Forman

Bruce Forman began to study the piano by ear at the age of six. Although born in Massachusetts he lived in Dallas until he was thirteen, at which time his family moved to San Fransisco. It was then that Forman began to play the guitar. When he was fourteen he heard a recording by Charlie Parker which influenced him to play jazz. At first Forman was self taught but eventually he studied with guitarist Jackie King. He made excellent progress and was soon playing jazz gigs all over the Bay area of San Francisco. But it was in a New York jazz club that Forman's first real break happened. While sitting in with a group that included pianist Roland Hanna and drummer Sam Jones he was heard by an executive from Choice Records. He immediately signed Forman up for a LP record release as leader of his own group.

Further recognition came to Forman when he joined saxophonist Richie Cole's band. Since that time this extremely talented guitarist, who continues the Tal Farlow/Jimmy Raney tradition of jazz guitar, has made several excellent recordings as leader. Highly respected amongst guitarists, San Francisco based Forman has not as yet received the full international recognition his talent deserves.

SELECTED RECORDINGS

Coast To Coast	Choice	CRS 1026 LP
River Journey	Muse	MR 5251 LP
20/20 Bruce Forman Quintet	Muse	MR 5273 LP
Jimmy Knepper Quartet	Black Hawk	BKH 51001 LP
Full Circle Bruce Forman Quartet	Concord	CJ 251 LP
Dynamics Bruce Forman/George Cables Duo	Concord	CJ 259 LP
Bruce Forman Quartet	Concord	CCD 4332
Pardon Me! Bruce Forman Quartet	Concord	CCD 4368
Still Of The Night	Kamei	KR 7000CD
On The Job	Kamei	KR 7004CD

Bruce Forman-Jazz Guitar Instructional Video	GSP Videos

SELECTED MUSIC

Jazz Guitarists Handbook	GSP Publications

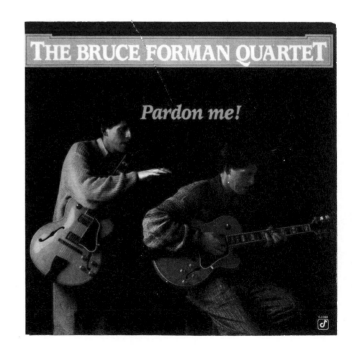

MARC FOSSET
Born-Paris, France
1949

Marc Fosset began to play the guitar at the age of eleven. His parents had taken him to see singer Yves Montand in concert. Fosset was impressed by the artistry of guitarist Didi Duprat who backed Montand on his recordings. This encouraged him to take up the guitar. At first his main influences were the rock and popular guitarists of the day, especially Hank Marvin of 'The Shadows'.

Fosset first became interested in jazz through hearing recordings of Charlie Byrd, Bill Evans and Boulou Ferre. He then listened to recordings by Django Reinhardt, Wes Montgomery, Jimmy Raney, Tal Farlow, Joe Pass and other leading mainstream guitarists. Mainly self-taught, Fosset has developed an individual jazz sound on the acoustic guitar. In recent years he has gained international recognition through his recordings and concert appearances with violinist Stephane Grappelli. Early in his career Fosset had a successful jazz duo with double bass player Patrice Caratini. Their success in France is reflected in the fact that their recordings won the prestigious award the 'Prix de l'Academie Charles-Cros'.

Marc Fosset

SELECTED RECORDINGS

Caratini/Fosset Duo-Half Nelson	OMD CD 1520
Stephanova w/Stephane Grappelli	Concord CCD 4225
Stephane Grappelli Trio in Tokyo	Denon CY-77130CD
Grappelli Plays Jerome Kern	GRP 91032CD
Marc Fosset – The Crooner	OMD CD1524
Stephane Grappelli Trio – Live	Bellaphon 660 50 007 CD
Grappelli Quartet Live Video	Castle Hendring HEN 22-2

WILLIAM L. FOWLER
Born-Salt Lake City, Utah, USA
4 July 1917

William L. Fowler

William L. Fowler is recognised as one of the foremost jazz guitar educators of the past forty years.

Fowler, whose parents were musicians, taught himself to play the guitar and banjo. After leaving high school he formed his own band and then went on to lead various music groups playing mainly country music around Utah, Nevada and Idaho. During World War II he directed stage shows and bands for the army. After the war he went on to study music at the American Conservatory in Chicago and also at the Eastman School of Music. In 1949 he earned a BA in composition and theory from the American Conservatory. In 1954 he earned a Ph.D. in composition from the University of Utah. He was then appointed as an associate professor of music at this university. In 1974 he became a Professor of Music at the University of Colorado at Denver.

For many years Dr Fowler has been involved in a multitude of music education events including jazz workshops and National Stage Band Camps. For many years he contributed, as Education Editor, several hundred columns and feature articles to Downbeat magazine. Through these the benefits of his musical expertise reached guitarists all over the world. From 1986 to 1988 he was a regular columnist for Keyboard magazine. He is the author of several important methods for jazz guitar and other instruments.

William Fowler, one of America's most distinguished and prolific music educators, still lives in Colorado. Here he continues to write on music matters and also runs his own specialist music publishing business.

SELECTED MUSIC

Tonal Shorthand	Maher Publications
Guitar Patterns for Improvisation	Maher Publications
Chord Voicing Systems	Fowler Music
Chord Progression Systems	Fowler Music
Advanced Chord Voicings	Fowler Music
Advanced Chord Progressions	Fowler Music
Fingerboard Lead Lines	Fowler Music

HEINER FRANZ
Born-Tubingen, Germany
3 July 1946

Heiner Franz

Heiner Franz first took an interest in music as a child. He was a member of a children's choir, played the flute and from the age of twelve studied the piano. After hearing some Traditional jazz recordings he gave up the piano and taught himself to play the guitar and banjo. He was soon playing in an amateur Dixieland band.

After leaving high school Franz studied Protestant Theology at Tubingen University qualifying in 1972. He became a Protestant parson in 1973. Franz had played jazz guitar in diverse groups throughout his university days, appearing in jazz clubs in South-West Germany, France, Luxembourg and Switzerland. His style was greatly influenced by Wes Montgomery, Jim Hall, Pat Martino and Joe Pass. In 1979 Franz decided to quit church service and devote himself to a career in music.

Heiner Franz went on to work as a freelance musician in jazz, the theatre, with radio orchestras, and composing and producing music for TV documentaries. By the mid 1980s he decided to concentrate on a career as a jazz guitarist. He played throughout Germany where he is regarded as one of the country's leading players. He also played in Dublin for the Irish Jazz Society with Louis Stewart, and since that time they have played frequently as a duo. In 1993 they founded the European Jazz Guitar orchestra, a five guitars plus rhythm band, which also featured Doug Raney. Heiner Franz has also established his own specialist recording company Jardis Music. His specialist range includes recordings by jazz guitarists Louis Stewart, Martin Taylor, Peter Leitch, Doug Raney, Klaus Spencker, Tobias Langguth and Heiner Franz.

In recent years Heiner Franz became involved in the design and construction of jazz guitars. He now produces these in small quantities from his workshop in Spiesen-Elversberg.

HEINER FRANZ

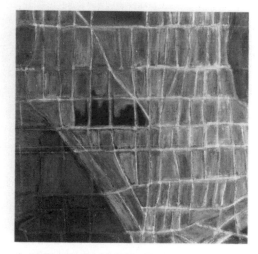

A WINDOW TO THE SOUL

SELECTED RECORDINGS

Brainstream	Rojophone 74001
A Window to the Soul	Jardis JRCD 8801
Gouache	Jardis JRCD 8903
Winter Song w/Louis Stewart	Jardis JRCD 9005
In a Mellow Tone w/Louis Stewart	Jardis JRCD 9206
European Jazz Guitar Orchestra	Jardis JRCD 9307
At First Sight w/Peter Leitch	Jardis JRCD 9611

SELECTED READING

Profile	Just Jazz Guitar, August 1995

FRED FRIED
Born-New York City, USA
2 December 1948

Although from New York City Fred Fried lived in Los Angeles for five years where he had the opportunity to study with George Van Eps, John Collins and accordionist Tommy Gumina.

On his return to New York Fried performed for four years with the Judd Woldin Trio at the top of World Trade Centre. Later he played at the Rainbow Room at the Rockefeller Centre both as a solo guitarist and with a quintet. Fried also played with many jazz groups in the New York area at the top clubs including Gregory's and Birdland.

Fred Fried has appeared with many top jazz artists both in Los Angeles and New York including Art Pepper, Derek Smith, Marty Napoleon, Mike Formanek, Gene Bertoncini, and Jay Leonhart. He has also worked with several leading popular singers including Perry Como and Tony Martin.

Fried now resides in Cape Cod, Massachusetts where he continues to work with many of New England's best jazz artists including Dick Johnson, Gary Johnson, Bob Nieske and Matt Gordy.

Fred Fried

SELECTED RECORDINGS

Fingerdance - Solo Guitar	Cutaway Records FEF 001LP
What Two Can Do w/Bill Davies	Rush Records RRAM 001 CD
Crystalline	Rush Records RRAM 002 CD
Out of my Dreams	Ballet Tree BT122CD
Cloud 3	Ballet Tree BT123CD

SELECTED READING

Interview	Just Jazz Guitar, February 1997
Interview	String Jazz News Sept/Oct 1995

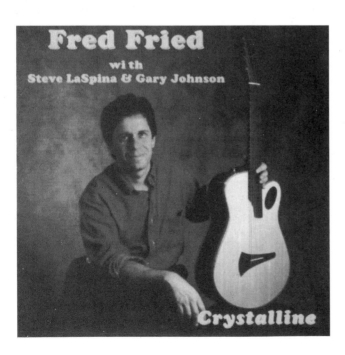

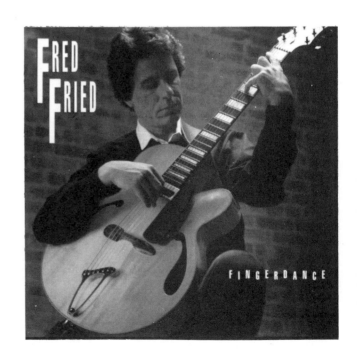

BILL FRISELL
Born-WILLIAM RICHARD FRISELL
Baltimore, Maryland, USA
18 March 1951

Bill Frisell was brought up in Denver, Colorado. Encouraged by his father, a tuba and string-bass player, Frisell began playing the clarinet and then the saxophone. He then changed to the guitar and this was to become his chosen instrument.

Frisell studied music at North Colorado University and majored there in 1971. He went on to study at the Berklee College of Music and in 1977 he was awarded a diploma in arranging and composition. He also won the prestigious Harris Stanton Guitar Award. Over a period of time Frissell studied with guitarists Jim Hall, Johnny Smith and Dale Bruning.

Within a relatively short period of time Bill Frisell has established himself as one of the most innovative, and most important, of the new breed of jazz/fusion/avant garde guitarists. His work with leading contemporary jazz musicians, in concert and on recordings, has brought him a wide international following. Frissell has played with Eberhard Weber, Mike Gibbs, Charlie Haden, Paul Motian, Paul Bley, John Scofield, Jan Garbarek amongst others. He was featured in John Zorn's hardcore group, 'Naked City'.

Bill Frisell's guitar style includes influences from mainstream jazz (Wes Montgomery), rock guitar (Jimi Hendrix), cool modern jazz (Jim Hall) through to the extremes of the avant-garde. He is heard on his many recordings playing on acoustic guitar, electric guitar, banjo and ukulele, sometimes with the aid of electric devices, in order to achieve the musical picture he wishes to paint.

In recent time he has been the winner of many jazz polls including 'Best Guitarist' – Downbeat Magazine's 1997 reader's poll.

SELECTED RECORDINGS

Before We Were Born	Nonesuch 60843 CD
Smash & Scatteration	Ryko RCD 10006
Lookout For Hope	ECM 1350 CD
Rambler	ECM 1287 CD
In Line	ECM 1247 CD
Works	ECM 837 273-2/4 CD
More News For Lulu	Hat Art CD 6055
Is That You?	Nonesuch 7559-60956-2CD
Where In The World	Nonesuch 7559-61181-2CD
Grace Under Pressure w/John Scofield	Blue Note CDP 7 98167 2
Motian In Tokyo	JMT 849 154-2 CD
This Land	Nonesuch 9-79316-2 CD
Go West	Nonesuch 9-79350-2 CD
High Sign/One Week	Nonesuch 9-79351-2 CD
Bill Frisell Quartet	Nonesuch 9-79401-2 CD
Nashville	Nonesuch 9-79415-2 CD

The Guitar Artistry of Bill Frisell Video	Warner/Rittor

Bill Frisell

PHOTO: JAQUES LOWE

SELECTED READING

Profile	Guitar Player, April 1985
Profile	Guitar World, May 1989
Profile	Downbeat, May 1989
Profile	Guitar Player, December 1990
Appreciation	Jazz Magazine (France), October 1991
Interview	Downbeat, March 1992
Profile	Jazz Times, May 1993
Profile	JAZZIZ, May 1993

AL GAFA
Born-ALEXANDER GAFA
Brooklyn, New York, USA
9 April 1941

Al Gafa is a self taught guitarist. He first began playing professionally working as a rock musician in the New York studios from 1964-69. He played with a wide variety of musicians and singers including Sammy Davis Jnr, Kai Winding, Chick Corea and Herbie Hancock. From 1970-71 he was musical director for Carmen McRae.

In 1971 Gafa joined Dizzy Gillespie's sextet and it was then that he gained international recognition as a talented jazz soloist and composer. Since leaving the Gillespie group he has led an active life in the studios and jazz clubs of New York City. In 1976 he made a recording on the Pablo label as leader of his own quartet. In recent years he has appeared in a Jazz trio at the World Trade Centre in New York, accompanied singer Sylvia Symms and toured with Johnny Hartman. He has also recorded with singer Susannah McCorkle for Concord Records.

Al Gafa

SELECTED RECORDINGS

Dizzy Gillespie Quintet	Pablo 2625-708 LP
Al Gafa Quintet	Pablo 2310-782 LP
Joe Albany Quartet	Elektra MUS K 52390 LP

SELECTED READING

Profile	Guitar Player, September 1976

Al Gafa with the Dizzy Gillespie Quintet

SLIM GAILLARD

Born-BULEE GAILLARD
Detroit, Michigan, USA
4 January 1916
Died-London, UK
26 February 1991

A multi-instrumentalist, Slim Gaillard gained prominence on the jazz scene in the late 1930s as a vocalist/guitarist in a duo with bassist Slam Stewart. 'Slim and Slam' achieved great popularity and Gaillard's bop- influenced guitar playing, though of limited ability, earned him recording dates with jazzmen of the calibre of Charlie Parker and Dizzy Gillespie. He was also featured in several films playing the guitar.

Gaillard's father was a merchant sailor and during the school holidays sometimes took his son along with him on his boat trips. By the time he was in his early twenties Gaillard was working solo in variety as a tap dancer and guitarist. In 1937 he moved to New York and, after appearing in a radio talent show, joined up with Leroy 'Slam' Stewart. Their composition 'Flat Foot Floogie', sung in Gaillard's original 'jive' talk which he called 'Vouty', became a best seller. This hit, and similar 'jive' songs, assured the duo success until Gaillard joined the US army as an airplane pilot in 1944. After leaving the forces Gaillard lived and worked in the Los Angeles area, leading his own group in various clubs. In 1947 he moved to New York and recorded further hits including, 'Cement Mixer'.

Over the next twenty years Slim Gaillard worked as a vocalist and comedian. For a time, in 1962, he had to work as a motel manager in San Diego to make a living. Gaillard returned to work as a cabaret artist, sometimes with his own band, but more often as a solo pianist. He had had a brief reunion with Slam Stewart at the Monterey Jazz Festival in 1970. In the early 1980s Gaillard was featured in numerous British television and stage shows. In 1983 he became a UK resident, and in 1989 starred in a successful four-part BBC television series, 'The World of Slim Gaillard'. Right up to the time of his death Slim Gaillard was active playing at jazz festivals and in jazz clubs.

SELECTED RECORDINGS

Slim and Slam	Vol 1 Caete LP-3
Slim and Slam	Vol 2 Caete LP-4
Slim and Slam	Tax LP-8028
Slim Gaillard and Friends	Storyville SLP809
Son of McVouty	Hep 11
Slim's Jam 1945-46	Alamac QSR2441
Slim Gaillard Rides Again	Paramount C064-924 87
Opera In Vout	Verve (France) LP 2304 55
Slim Gaillard	FolkLyric 9038
Slim Gaillard Trio	MCA LP 1508
Anytime, Anyplace, Anywhere	Hep LP 2020
Slim & Slam Complete Recordings	Affinity CD AFS 1034-3

SELECTED READING

Profile	Downbeat, June 1968
Discography	Discographical Forum Nos 49 & 50

Slim Gaillard and his Trio

PHOTO: COURTESY JAZZ JOURNAL

BARRY GALBRAITH
Born-JOSEPH BARRY GALBRAITH
Pittsburgh, Pennsylvania, USA
18 December 1919
Died New York City, USA
13 January, 1983

Barry Galbraith

PHOTO: COURTESY GUITAR PLAYER

Barry Galbraith originally started as a banjoist, but after hearing Eddie Lang's guitar artistry in the early 1930s, he changed over to the guitar. Self taught, Galbraith gained his first professional experience playing in clubs around Pittsburgh. He played with many top jazz stars such as Red Norvo and Teddy Powell but his first major professional success came in New York when he joined the Claude Thornhill Band 1941-42, and then again in 1946-47 after completing his army service.

From 1947-70 Galbraith was one of the most highly respected staff musicians working for the NBC and CBS networks. He developed a high reputation and was involved as a sideman on hundreds of recordings. The list of artists he played with reads like a 'Who's Who' of jazz and popular music. Stan Kenton, Peggy Lee, Ella Fitzgerald, Tony Bennett, Billie Holiday, Sarah Vaughan, Barbra Streisand, Michel Legrand, Tal Farlow and Benny Goodman, are only a few of the names with whom Barry Galbraith played.

A respected educator, Galbraith was involved for many years as a private teacher in New York, and also as a faculty member at New York City College. He published several excellent guitar music books through his own Vista Publishing company. Since his death these have been published by Jamie Aebersold, the specialist jazz publishing house.

SELECTED RECORDINGS

East Coast Jazz with Hal McCusick	Bethlehem BCP 16 LP
Tal Farlow Album	Norgran 1047 LP
Guitar and the Wind	Decca 9200 LP
Jimmy Hamilton Orchestra	Jazz Kings 1204 LP
Jazz at the Academy	MEA Coral CRL 57116 LP
Willie Rodriguez Jazz Quartet	Riverside RSLP 469 LP
Manhattan Jazz Septette	Jasmine JASM 1017 LP
Best of Kenny Burrell	Prestige 7448 LP
Portrait of Sheila w/Sheila Jordan	Bluenote CDP 89002-2

SELECTED READING

Interview	Guitar Player, July 1976
Article	Just Jazz Guitar, August 1996

SELECTED MUSIC

Two Part Invention	Aebersold
Fingerboard Harmony	Aebersold
Guitar Improvisation	Aebersold
Guitar Comping	Aebersold

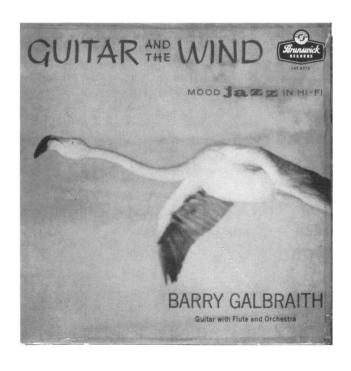

FRANK GAMBALE
Born-Canberra, A.C.T., Australia
22 December 1958

Frank Gambale began to play the guitar at the age of seven inspired by recordings of blues guitarist Eric Clapton. By the time he was thirteen Gambale had started his own band. Hearing the recorded sounds of John McLaughlin and his Mahavishnu Orchestra the young guitarist was drawn to the more sophisticated forms of jazz and jazz/rock fusion.

After leaving high school Gambale played in various Australian bands. At the same time he was much in demand as a teacher. Though already a formidable technician Gambale felt that he could not progress in his studies in Australia. So, whilst still in his early twenties, he enrolled in the Guitar Institute of Technology (GIT) in Los Angeles. His enormous talent was soon recognised and he was awarded Student Of The Year honours. In 1983 he was offered a teaching post at GIT, a position he was to hold for three years. During that time he wrote several important books on guitar technique.

Gambale became a resident of Los Angeles and his musical talent soon gained international recognition through his position as guitarist with Chick Corea's Elektric Band, and appearances with Jean-Luc Ponty and Jeff Berlin. Several solo albums and video instruction tapes have established his reputation as one of the best contemporary jazz guitarists of the 1990s.

Frank Gambale

PHOTO: COURTESY FRANK GAMBALE

SELECTED RECORDINGS
Brave New Guitar	Legato 1001 CD
A Present For The Future	Legato 1002 CD
Frank Gambale – Live	Legato 1003 CD
Chick Corea Light Years	GRP 9546 CD
Jeff Berlin Pump It	Passport PJ 88017
Note Worker	JVC VICJ 75 CD
The Great Explorers	JVC 2020-2 CD
Thunder From Down Under	JVC 3321 CD

Modes, and More Modes Instructional Video	DCI
Chopbuilder Instructional Video	REH/CPP
Modes: No More Mystery Instructional Video	REH/CPP
Monster Licks and Speed Picking Instructional Video	REH/CPP

SELECTED READING
Interview	Guitarist, January 1988
Interview	Guitar Player, June 1988
Profile	Guitar World, July 1988
Article	Jazz Times, July/August 1994

SELECTED MUSIC
Frank Gambale Technique Vols 1 & 2	Manhattan Music Publications
Speed Picking	REH Publishers
Best of Frank Gambale Recorded Versions	Hal Leonard Publishing
Artist Transcription	Hal Leonard Publishing
The Great Explorers	Hal Leonard Publishing

DICK GARCIA
Born-RICHARD JOSEPH GARCIA
New York City, USA
11 May 1931

Dick Garcia

Dick Garcia started playing the guitar at the age of nine. His father and grandfather were guitarists, and his great-grandfather reputedly once played the guitar in a command performance for the King of Spain.

Virtually a self-taught player, Garcia's first professional break came when vibraphonist Terry Gibbs heard him play in a Greenwich Village jam session. Gibbs recommended him to clarinetist Tony Scott. Garcia played with Scott throughout 1950, and then played with various jazz groups including almost a year in 1952 with George Shearing's quintet. From 1955-56 Garcia played again with Tony Scott, and then again in 1959 with the Shearing quintet. Although a very talented jazz soloist, Garcia became involved in freelance and studio work for many years in the New York City area.

SELECTED RECORDINGS

The Hi-Fi Land of Jazz	Seeco CELP428 LP
Joe Roland Quintet	Bethlehem BCP-17 LP
Message from Garcia	Dawn 1106 LP
Fourmost Guitars	ABC 109 LP

Dick Garcia with the George Shearing Quintet

HANK GARLAND
Born-WALTER LOUIS GARLAND
Cowpens, South Carolina, USA
11 November 1930

Hank 'Sugarfoot' Garland began to play the guitar at the age of six. He was first attracted to the acoustic guitar sounds on the recordings of country music stars 'The Carter Family'. He then heard some radio broadcasts by Arthur Smith playing an electric guitar and soon after Garland was playing an amplified instrument. Whilst just into his teens he was already playing in a local band led by Shorty Painter.

After a chance meeting in 1945 with country music band leader Paul Howard, Garland was hired to play with Howard's 'Cotton Pickers Band' in Nashville. The young guitarist was only fifteen years old. As a result the Musicians Union would not allow him to carry on playing professionally until he was sixteen. Garland had to return home until November 1946 when Howard immediately hired him again. Over the next few years Garland gained valuable experience as a featured soloist in several country and western bands in the Nashville area including the 'Cowboy Copas'. His interest in jazz was kindled after meeting Billy Byrd, guitarist with the Ernest Tubb Band. For many years Garland was regarded only as a country guitarist, but he often displayed his jazz artistry in some Nashville clubs. He listened to recordings of Django Reinhardt and Les Paul and these proved a great influence. Later he was also influenced by Barney Kessel, Tal Farlow and Barry Galbraith. In the early 1950s he worked as an accompanist for singer Eddy Arnold. During this time Garland had the opportunity to visit New York where he heard some of the best jazz guitarists of the day. He also studied jazz rhythm playing with Barry Galbraith on his visits to New York.

In the 1950s Garland was one of the busiest session guitarists in Nashville. He played with the top artists of the day including Jim Reeves, Patsy Cline and Tommy Jackson. In 1955 he designed the 'Byrdland' model guitar with Billy Byrd for the Gibson Guitar company. This guitar had a thin body and short scale-length and proved to be a popular model for both country and jazz players.

In 1960 he made what was to be his only jazz record as leader with vibraphone player - Gary Burton, bassist -Joe Benjamin, and drummer-Joe Morello. This record, 'Jazz Winds From A New Direction' remains as proof that Garland was destined to be a top jazz soloist. Tragically

Hank Garland

shortly after this recording was made Garland was involved in a serious car crash in 1961 that left him severely disabled. Only thirty years old, Hank Garland's professional career was suddenly brought to an end.

SELECTED RECORDINGS	
Hank Garland's Sugarfooters	Bear Family BLD15551 AH
Jazz Winds from a New Direction	Collector's Series 75027 CD
Nashville All Stars	RCA 2302 CD
Unforgetable Guitar	Columbia CL1913 LP
Velvet Guitar	Harmony HS 11028 LP
Jazz In New York	HG-1001-LPS

SELECTED READING	
Profile & Interview	Guitar Player, January 1981
Profile	Guitarist, August 1980
Article	Just Jazz Guitar, May 1996

159

ARV GARRISON

Born-ARVIN CHARLES GARRISON
Toledo, Ohio, USA
17 August 1922
Died-Toledo,Ohio, USA
30 July 1960

SELECTED RECORDINGS
Giants of Modern Jazz   Explosive 528-013 LP
Howard McGhee Sextet   Spotlite SPJ-131 LP
Charlie Parker on Dial   Spotlite   101 LP
Charlie Parker All Stars   America AM 008/10 LP
Charlie Parker Septet   Warner WB 66081 LP

Arv Garrison started to play the ukulele at the age of nine, but changed to the guitar when he was twelve.

Garrison played the guitar in various high school bands until he was eighteen. In 1941 he fronted his own group in Albany, New York. From late 1941, after playing with Don Seat in Pittsburgh, until 1948, Garrison played on both West and East coasts with his own trio. He gained a high reputation as a jazz guitarist with his fellow musicians. In 1946 he married bassist Vivien Garry. In the mid 1950s Garrison returned to Toledo where he continued to work as a guitarist until his premature death in 1960.

Arv Garrison (left), other guitarists are Barney Kessel, Tony Rizzi, Irving Ashby and Gene Sargent.

GRANT GEISSMAN
Born-Berkeley, California, USA
13 April 1953

Grant Geissman

Grant Geissman's first instrument was the piano which he played for a few months at the age of six. It was his grandfather, an amateur banjoist, who bought Geissman his first guitar when he was twelve years old. The young musician fell in love with the instrument at first playing only rock and pop music. Then at the age of fifteen Geissman began to take an interest in jazz and jazz/rock.

While he was in his senior year at high school Geissman began to study with jazz guitarist and educator Jerry Hahn. It was Hahn that opened the young guitarist's ears to the music of Charlie Parker, Miles Davis, John Coltrane and other modern jazz greats.

After graduating from high school Geissman went on to study music with Herb Patnoe, a director of the Stan Kenton Jazz Clinics, at De Anza College, Cupertino, California. He made such rapid progress that he was soon hired to teach at a summer workshop and other courses. In 1974 Grant Geissman entered the California State University at Northridge. Here he continued his music studies. As part of his course Geissman studied the classical guitar and this would later help extend his virtuosity. Whilst he was at Northridge the guitarist's reputation spread to nearby Hollywood. Here he was called on to work on commercial jingles for television and radio, and also on jazz recording dates with Tony Rizzi, Louie Bellson and others.

In 1976 he was offered the opportunity to play in concert with Chuck Mangione. This proved successful leading to more concert dates and several recording sessions with the famous trumpeter. Since that time Grant Geissman has developed a reputation as one of best of the new generation of jazz guitarists with several recordings released as leader.

SELECTED RECORDINGS

Good Stuff	Concord CJ62
Feel So Good Chuck Mangione	A & M SP 4658
Tony Rizzi & His Five Guitars	Milagro MR 1000
Flying Colors	Blue Moon R2 79165
Time Will Tell	Blue Moon R2 79178
Rustic Technology	Blue Moon R2 79189

EGBERTO GISMONTI
**Born-Carmo, Rio de Janeiro, Brazil
5 December 1947**

Egberto Gismonti comes from a musical family who played mainly popular Brazilian songs and some classical music. He began to play the piano at the age of six. He continued to study classical piano for fifteen years and then went on to study orchestration and musical analysis with Nadia Boulanger in Paris. Whilst in Paris Gismonti also studied practical orchestration and composition with composer Jean Barlaque, a student of Schoenberg and Webern.

Gismonti returned to Brazil and was much in demand as an arranger and composer. In 1966 he performed Ravel's piano concerto in G, a piece in which the composer is influenced by George Gershwin. After this concert Gismonti decided that he wished to broaden his musical career to incorporate many different styles, including jazz and Brazilian folk music. In 1967 Gismonti began to play the guitar because he wanted to play Brazilian choro music. He was self taught but was influenced by the recordings of Baden Powell and a Brazilian seven string guitar player called Deno.

In 1973 Gismonti started to play the eight string classical guitar. This instrument, with its extra range, allowed him to achieve many of the effects and sounds he wished to incorporate into his highly original music. Gismonti's individual guitar style continued to develop after he heard the recordings of Django Reinhardt, Wes Montgomery, John McLaughlin, Jimi Hendrix and other guitarists. In 1976 he spent a month with the Xingu Indians in the Amazon jungle. The influence of this period with the Indians can be heard on his first record album for the ECM label, 'Danca Das Cabecas'.

Egberto Gismonti has recorded and performed extensively in Brazil and appeared at major music festivals throughout the world. His many recordings have achieved impressive sales, some winning awards. He has worked with his own group and appeared with famous Brazilian musicians including Airto, Moreira, Flora Purim and Paul Horn. Gismonti has composed, and played on the soundtrack, of eleven films. As well as playing the guitar Gismonti plays acoustic and electric keyboards, sitar, accordion, cello, all types of flutes and other ethnic instruments.

SELECTED RECORDINGS

Danca Das Cabecas	ECM 1089 CD
Solo	ECM 1136 CD
Sol Do Meia Dia	ECM 1116 CD
Sanfona	ECM 1203/4 CD
Duas Vozes	ECM 1279 CD
Danca Dos Escravos	ECM 1387 CD
Circense	CARMO/2 849 077-2 CD
Academia de Dancas	CARMO/5 511 202-2 CD
Infancia	ECM 1428 CD
Musica de Sobre Vivencia	ECM 1509 CD
Zig Zag	ECM 1582 CD
Meeting Point	ECM 1586 CD

SELECTED READING

Profile	Guitar Player November 1978
Article	Jazz Times, August 1996

Egberto Gismonti

PHOTO: COURTESY ECM RECORDS

DAVE GOLDBERG

Born-DAVID GOLDBERG
Wallasey, Cheshire, UK
22 July 1922
Died-London, UK
21 August 1969

At the age of six Dave Goldberg's family moved to Liverpool. It was here that Goldberg at the age of fourteen took an interest in the guitar taking lessons from a well known local teacher, Harry Yould. After leaving school he began training to be a furniture salesman. He then moved to Glasgow and found that working as guitarist with the local dance band at night led by Jack Britton gave him a better income than selling furniture. He was also featured on BBC Scottish radio as guitarist with the Scottish Variety Orchestra led by Ronnie Munro.

Goldberg tried to sign up with the Royal Air Force as a musician but was turned down. He eventually joined as air crew and qualified as a pilot. He trained in the USA under the Empire Training Scheme and this gave him the opportunity to meet many jazz musicians, including guitarist Al Casey. Whilst he was in the RAF Goldberg was recommended to band leader Ted Heath who signed him up for his big band. Travelling to and from the air force camp the young guitarist (who also doubled on trombone) joined this famous band for many concerts and broadcasts.

In 1946, after he was discharged from the RAF, Goldberg continued to work with Ted Heath. In 1949 he emigrated to the USA to join his parents who had gone to live in North Hollywood the previous year. After working for nine months in and around Los Angeles he decided to return to London where he rejoined the Ted Heath Band. In 1951 he went back to California working in clubs and studios. He also worked for Universal Pictures on their film "The Glenn Miller Story". He then toured Italy with a group of dancers and musicians led by Katherine Durham. Whilst Goldberg was in Italy he wrote and directed the music for a film called "Mambo".

In 1954 Dave Goldberg once again returned to live and work in London as a free-lance musician. He maintained a busy schedule playing with dance bands led by Geraldo and Jack Parnell. At the same time he played in clubs and on recordings with most of the finest British modern jazz musicians of the time including, Ronnie Scott, Dizzy Reece and Phil Seamen. He was regarded as being one of the few British jazz guitarists who could play on a

Dave Goldberg

similar standard to that being set by the top USA jazz guitarists of the period. What should have been a very successful career came to a sudden halt in August 1969 when Goldberg was found dead in his home from a drug overdose.

SELECTED RECORDING
Progress Report: Dizzy Reece Quintet   Jasmine JASM 2013

GEORGE GOLLA
Born-Chorzow, Poland
10 May 1935

George Golla emigrated to Australia in 1950. He first played the saxophone and only took the guitar up in 1956. He made quick progress and within a short time was playing the guitar professionally in restaurants and clubs in Sydney. He played with the Gus Merzi band 1957-61, and then the Bryce Rohde quartet 1958-60. He toured Australia and New Zealand backing Dizzy Gillespie in a quintet led by Rohdes. Golla then joined the Eric Jupp studio orchestra in 1962. Since that time Golla has become one of Australia's foremost studio musicians. He has always been active as a jazz artist, and has had a long and successful association with the flute player Don Burrows. They have toured throughout Australia and internationally playing at festivals and in jazz clubs.

Golla, who plays a seven-string guitar, has made many recordings, written a wide range of compositions (including a concerto for electric guitar and symphony orchestra), and authored several guitar instruction books. He is also a respected teacher. From 1976-1990 he was a tutor in jazz studies at the New South Wales Conservatorium of Music.

George Golla

PHOTO: COURTESY GEORGE GOLLA

SELECTED RECORDINGS

George Golla	Cherry Pie CPS 1013
Easy Feelings	Cherry Pie CPS 1018
From The Top w/Don Andrews	Cherry Pie CPF 1024
Brazilian Parrot w/Don Burrows	Music is Medicine MIM 9031
Quiet Moods	Music is Medicine MIM 9048
Duo w/Don Burrows	Music is Medicine MIM 9049

MICK GOODRICK
Born-MICHAEL GOODRICK
Sharon, Pennsylvania, USA
9 June 1945

Mick Goodrick

PHOTO: COURTESY CMP RECORDS

Mick Goodrick first began to play the guitar at the age of twelve. His development on the instrument reached a standard at which he was able to attend the Berklee College of Music. He graduated from this prestigious establishment in 1967 with a B.M. in music education.

Goodrick then made his career, for a period of four years, as a teacher at Berklee. In 1971 he gained international recognition as the guitarist in a group led by vibraphonist Gary Burton. He recorded five albums with this group. After recording a solo album in 1979 and a short period as a member of bassist Charlie Haden's Liberation Music Orchestra, Goodrick returned to teaching at the New England Conservatory.

In 1987 Goodrick joined drummer Jack DeJohnette's group 'Special Edition'. He recorded two important albums with this band. He continued to play in other popular contemporary jazz groups including those led by Michael Brecker, Pat Metheny, Steve Swallow and Charlie Haden. At the same time Goodrick continued to teach in Boston and also attended guitar seminar's in Europe and the USA. In 1987 he released a critically acclaimed guitar method titled, 'The Advancing Guitarist'.

Mick Goodrick continues to live in Boston. From here his reputation as an outstanding jazz soloist and sideman, and also as a teacher, continues to grow.

SELECTED RECORDINGS

In Passing	ECM 1139
The New Gary Burton Quartet	ECM 1030
The Ray	Not Fat 04-22
Irresistible Forces Jack DeJohnette	MCA/Impulse 5992
Ballad Of The Fallen Charlie Haden	ECM 23794
Biorhythms	CMP Records CMP CD 46

SELECTED READING

Interview	Guitar Player, April 1989
Profile	Jazz Magazine (France), May 1991
Interview	Jazz Times, July/August 1992

SELECTED MUSIC

The Advancing Guitarist	Third Earth Productions

JIMMY GOURLEY
Born-JAMES PASCO GOURLEY Jnr
St Louis, Missouri, USA
9 June 1926

Jimmy Gourley started to play the guitar at the age of 10. His father had founded the Conservatory of Music in Hammond, Indiana.

One of Gourley's first jazz sessions was in 1941 at school with saxophonist Lee Konitz. He gained valuable musical experience working with the US Navy Band 1944-46. From 1946-48 he replaced Jimmy Raney in Jay Burkhart's band in Chicago. Gourley's guitar style has always been strongly influenced by Jimmy Raney. After leaving Burkhart, Gourley freelanced in Chicago with various jazz artists including Sonny Stitt, Gene Ammons, Johnny Griffin, Lou Levy, and Anita O'Day. In April 1951 Gourley decided to move to Europe where he settled in Paris. There, after a short time at music school, he joined forces with pianist, Henri Renaud. He played with him until 1954. Gourley proved to be very influential on the Parisian jazz scene. He introduced bebop to leading Parisian jazz musicians including Fats Sadi, Martial Solal, Bobby Jaspar, Jean-Louis Viale, and Rene Urtreger. He also recorded in Paris with many visiting American musicians including Zoot Sims, Lee Konitz, Bob Brookmeyer and Clifford Brown.

Towards the end of 1954 Gourley returned to USA and played for a short while with bassist Chubby Jackson in Chicago, but in December 1957 decided to return to Paris. Jimmy Gourley was featured as a regular artist at the top Parisian jazz club 'The Blue Note', 1959-65. There he often played with drummer Kenny Clarke. He then led his own quartet on tour throughout Switzerland and Italy. They also played at the Parisian club 'Chat Qui Peche'. From 1970-72 Gourley helped run the 'Half Note' jazz club in the Canary Islands, but after it closed, he returned to Paris where he played regularly at the 'Club St.Germain'. For many years Jimmy Gourley was associated with organists Lou Bennett, and Eddy Louiss. Since that time he has played and recorded, in and around Paris, although he did return briefly to the USA, in 1975 and 1986, for some club and concert dates.

Jimmy Gourley

Graffiti	Promophone PROM 14
Jimmy Gourley Quartet	Musica MUS. 3034
Left Bank Of New York	Uptown UP 27.32
Jimmy Gourley Paris Heavyweights	52 Rue Est RE CD 002
Jimmy Gourley/Richard Galliano 4	52 Rue Est RE CD 020

SELECTED RECORDINGS

Eddy Louiss Quartet	America AM6127
Gigi Gryce/Clifford Brown Sextet	Vogue 500053
Lester Young Quintet	Verve 2304489 IMS
Stan Getz Quintet	Jazz Anthology JA 5244
Stephane Grapelli (2LP's)	Festival FLD596
Lou Bennett Quartet	RCA Camden 900-078
Americans in Europe Vol.1	Impulse AS36

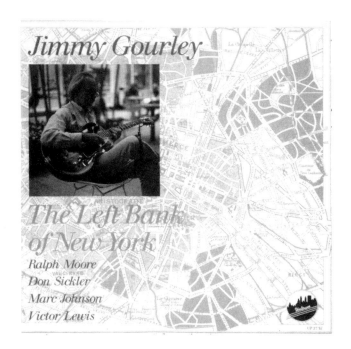

Jimmy Gourley
The Left Bank of New York
Ralph Moore
Don Sickler
Marc Johnson
Victor Lewis

FREDDIE GREEN

Born-FREDERICK WILLIAM GREEN
Charleston, South Carolina, USA
31 March 1911
Died-Las Vegas, Nevada, USA
1 March 1987

Freddie Green with Count Basie.

Freddie Green was one of the most unique guitarists in jazz history. He was the undisputed king of the rhythm guitar as opposed to the solo guitar. His fantastic rhythm guitar playing was the backbone of the legendary Count Basie band from 1937 to 1987. In many jazz lovers opinions the sound of his guitar was as much the Count Basie sound, as the Count's unique piano style.

Freddie Green played the banjo at an early age but a friend of his father, a professional trumpeter, encouraged him to change over to the guitar and study music. At the age of twelve, after the death of his parents, Green moved from Carolina to New York City to live with an aunt. After leaving school he worked as an upholsterer during the day and played the guitar at night. He studied for a short while with Allan Reuss at the guitarist's New York teaching studio. John Hammond heard Green play in a Greenwich Village club and recommended him to Count Basie as a replacement for Claude Williams. After a brief audition he was hired. From that time on Green played continually with Count Basie's band and various small groups, setting unsurpassed standards in the art of rhythm guitar, until his death in 1987. Except for one or two bars of obligato chords, he never took a solo with the Basie band in concert. He did take a few eight and sixteen bar solos on a record with singer Joe Williams as part of one of Count Basie's small groups. He never played the electric guitar. Yet Freddie Green's unique guitar sound is a legend in jazz, and has left its mark on virtually every Count Basie recording. Green was also much in demand as part of the rhythm section for recordings by many other top jazzmen including Lester Young, Lionel Hampton, Benny Carter and Benny Goodman.

SELECTED RECORDINGS

Pee Wee Russell's Rhythm Makers 1938	BYG 529-066 LP
Chairman of the Board (Basie Band)	Roulette 52032 LP
Rhythm Willie (with Herb Ellis)	Concord CJ10 LP
Mr.Rhythm	French RCA PM 42114 LP
*Joe Williams/Count Basie	Vogue VJD 553 (2LPs)
*Freddie Green solos on four tracks on this LP set.	
Natural Rhythm w/Al Cohn	ND86 465 CD
King of Rhythm – Freddie Green	Giants of Jazz 53254 CD

SUGGESTED READING

Article The Tough Straight Art	Downbeat, July 1965
Article Freddie Green-Remembered	Guitar Player, August 1987

Freddie Green

GRANT GREEN
Born-St.Louis, Missouri, USA
6 June 1931
Died-New York City, USA
31 January 1979

Grant Green first learnt to play the guitar whilst at school. At the age of thirteen he was already playing professionally with various St Louis bands. Initially he played rhythm and blues, and then rock and roll. But after hearing saxophonists Lester Young and Charlie Parker, he decided to devote his career to playing jazz. Green played in the 1950s with saxophonist Jimmy Forrest. He then played in small groups led by organists Sam Lazar (1960) and Jack McDuff (1961).

In the early 1960s tenor saxophonist Lou Donaldson heard Green play in a St.Louis club. Donaldson encouraged Green to come to New York where he was able to persuade Blue Note Records to record the young guitarist. Green's playing on his first Blue Note records received rave reviews from most jazz critics. He was hailed as the new heir to Charlie Christian's throne. Green became staff guitarist for Blue Note and recorded regularly with a wide variety of top jazz artists including Jimmy Smith, Stanley Turrentine, Yusef Lateef, Joe Henderson, Hank Mobley, Elvin Jones and Herbie Hancock. He also recorded many fine albums under his own name for Blue Note, and these display the full dimension of his swinging, single-note jazz guitar style.

Green continued to record and play in clubs in and around New York. In 1977 he was hospitalized with a serious illness, and in January 1979 died after a heart attack.

His son Greg is also a jazz guitarist and features on the 1996 CD recording 'A Tribute to Grant Green'. (Paddle Wheel KICJ 282).

SELECTED RECORDINGS

Grants First Stand	Blue Note 4064 LP
Green Street	Blue Note 4071 LP
Grantstand	Blue Note 46430 CD
Sunday Mornin'	Blue Note 52434 CD
Idle Moments	Blue Note 4154 LP
Talking About	Blue Note 4183 LP
Visions	Blue Note 4373 LP
Iron City	Cobblestone 9002 LP
Reaching Out	Black Lion 760129 CD
Born To Be Blue	Blue Note 84432 CD
Last Session	Atlantis ATS 9 LP
Complete Blue Note Recordings	Mosaic MD4-133 (4 CDs)
Latin Bit	Blue Note 37645 CD
Solid	Blue Note 33580 CD
Alive!	Blue Note 89793 CD
Matador	Blue Note 84442 CD
Complete Quartets w/Sonny Clarke	Blue Note 57194 CD

SELECTED READING

Profile	Downbeat, July 1952
Profile	Guitar Player, January 1975
Article	Guitar Player, February 1997

PHOTO: COURTESY KUDU RECORDS

Grant Green

STEVE GREENE
Born-Rochester, New York, USA
3 September 1955

Steve Greene

Steve Greene began to play the guitar at the age of ten studying under local musicians Don Ames and Dick Longale. In 1974 he started at Berklee College of Music in Boston graduating from Bard College in 1979 with Bachelor of Art degree. He then attended the Eastman School of Music where he studied with Gene Bertoncini.

Steve Greene has been influenced by a wide variety of jazz guitar styles. From Eddie Lang, Carl Kress and Django Reinhardt through to Jim Hall and Sonny Greenwich. As a result he has led several groups with different styles from Traditional Jazz to Avant Garde. Greene is also known for his compositional ability and has written for the internationally known Garth Fagan Dance Company. At this time he works out of Rochester, New York with his trio and as a soloist. He also devotes some of his time to teaching.

SELECTED RECORDING

Acoustic Living	NorthTwelve	North 12-1 CD

TED GREENE
Born-Los Angeles, California, USA
26 September 1946

PHOTO: FRANK FORTE

Ted Greene

Ted Greene is known to guitarists throughout the world for his excellent jazz guitar instruction books. Born in Hollywood he started to play the guitar from the age of ten. He has lived for some years in Woodland Hills, Los Angeles where he has devoted most of his career to teaching, giving seminars and demonstrations. His recording on the PMP (Professional Music Products) label, 'Solo Guitar', shows that he is a virtuoso player in the style of George Van Eps, with whom he studied briefly.

SELECTED RECORDINGS

Solo Guitar	PMP A-5010 LP
John Pisano-Conversation Pieces	PABLO 2310 963-2

SELECTED READING

Article-Chord Voicings	Guitar Player, June 1980

SELECTED MUSIC

Chord Chemistry	CPP/Belwin
Modern Chord Progressions	CPP/Belwin
Jazz Guitar Single Note Soloing Vols 1 & 2	CPP/Belwin

SONNY GREENWICH
Born-Hamilton, Ontario, Canada
1 January 1936

Sonny Greenwich was introduced to music by his father who was a jazz pianist. His first professional experience was as the lead guitarist in a Toronto based rhythm and blues band led by pianist Connie Maynard. At that time Greenwich was still in his early twenties. A member of the band introduced him to some recordings of Sonny Rollins and he soon developed a serious interest in jazz. In 1967 he toured with alto saxophonist John Handy. Greenwich's distinctive style has developed because of his affinity for horn players, such as Rollins and John Coltrane, rather than guitarists. In 1969 Miles Davis hired the young guitarist for a short while in Canada but work permit restrictions did not allow Greenwich to return to the USA with Davis.

Greenwich settled in Montreal and is today not very well known outside Canada. He leads his own jazz group and is respected as an original jazz artist by local and visiting jazz musicians.

Sonny Greenwich

SELECTED RECORDINGS

The Old Man and The Child	Sackville 2002
Sun Song	Radio Canada 399
Evol-utin, Love's Reverse	PM Records PMR016
From Spirituals to Swing John Handy Group	Vanguard VSD 47
Love Songs Don Thompson Band	Sackville 2003
Bird Of Paradise	Justin Time 22 2 CD
Live At Sweet Basil	Justin Time 26-1 2 CD
Standard Idioms	Kleo 1 CD
Portraits in Jazz	Radioland RACD 10006

SELECTED READING

Interview	Guitar Player, May 1979
Profile – Jazz in Canada/Miller	Nightwood Edition (1988)

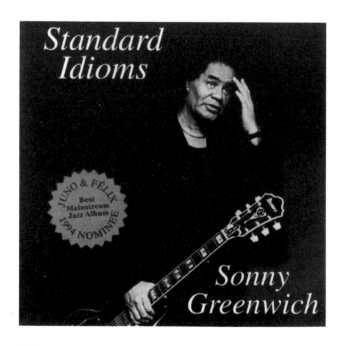

TINY GRIMES
Born-LLOYD GRIMES
Newport News, Virginia, USA
7 July 1917
Died-New York, USA
4 March 1989

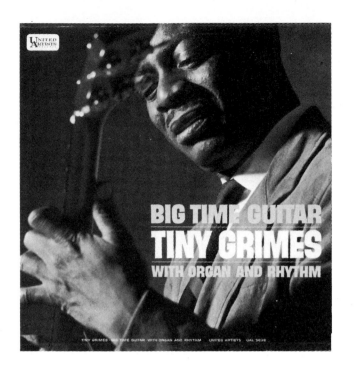

Tiny Grimes played drums in his school band, but started his professional career in 1935 as a pianist and dancer in Washington DC. In 1937 he moved to New York City where he played at the 'Rhythm Club'. He taught himself to play the four-string guitar, an instrument originally devised to ease the transition of banjo players over to the guitar. By the end of the 1930s he was playing an electric four-string guitar.

In 1940 Grimes was featured with a popular jazz and novelty group called 'The Cats and The Fiddle'. In 1941 he moved to California where he met Art Tatum during a jam session. The pianist was so impressed with Grimes's playing, he invited him to join his trio with bassist Slam Stewart. After three historical years with Tatum, Grimes returned to New York City where he worked in 52nd Street clubs as a sideman with top jazz musicians including Billie Holiday. In 1944 he recorded with Charlie Parker. Grimes then formed his own group 'The Rocking Highlanders'. This enjoyed some popular success but in 1947 Grimes moved to Cleveland. In the 1950s he settled in Philadelphia returning in the 1960s to New York City. Here he played regularly in Harlem and Greenwich Village clubs.

Tiny Grimes swinging, bluesy single-note playing became much appreciated in Europe, particularly in France. He toured there in 1968 with organist Milt Buckner, and later in 1970 with Jay McShann. During the last years of his life he was in constant demand on the East Coast of the USA, both in jazz clubs and at festivals.

SELECTED RECORDINGS

Callin' The Blues	Prestige 714 LP
Tiny in Swingville	Prestige 2002 LP
Big Time Guitar	United Artists UAL 3232 LP
Tiny Grimes & Friends	Gotham KK821 LP
Art Tatum Trio	Jazz Anthology 30 JA 5208 LP
Tiny Grimes Rocking Highlanders	Riverboat 2101 LP
Tiny Grimes Rocking Highlanders	Swingtime ST1016 LP
Tiny Grimes-Some Groovy Fours	Black & Blue 33-067 LP
Tiny Grimes and Roy Eldridge	Sonet SNTF 736 LP
Profoundly Blue	Muse 5012 LP
Frankie & Johnny Boogie	Black & Blue 33.712 LP
Arnett Cobb/Tiny Grimes Live	Frances Concert FCD133

SELECTED READING

Tribute	Downbeat, July 1969
Interview	Guitar Player, January 1981
Profile	Guitar World, March 1983

STEFAN GROSSMAN
Born-Brooklyn, New York, USA
16 April 1945

Stefan Grossman comes from a musical family. His cousin Stephen Grossman is a saxophonist who has played with Miles Davis and Elvin Jones. Another cousin Harold Grossman is a trumpet player and professor at the Berklee College of Music in Boston. Grossman's parents encouraged him to take up the guitar at the age of nine. He became interested in the blues after hearing some traditional blues music in Greenwich Village, New York. In 1960 he was encouraged by a friend to study with blues artist Rev. Gary Davis who at that time lived at Claremont Avenue in the Bronx. He went on to study the country blues techniques of Son House, Skip James, Mance Lipscomb, Fred McDowell and Mississippi John Hurt. In 1963 he formed the 'Even Dozen Jug Band'. In 1965 Grossman produced what was to be the first of many instruction blues guitar books and recordings. In 1966 he played with the bohemian/poet group 'The Fugs' and later with a blues group called 'The Chicago Loop'.

In 1967 Grossman decided to live in Europe, residing for a time both in Britain and Italy. Over the next twenty years he toured internationally with his Kicking Mule concert package. This in many ways was a blues/ragtime/traditional jazz version of Norman Granz's 'Jazz At The Philharmonic'. Grossman presented many of the top blues, ragtime and fingerpicking guitarists of the day alongside his own authentic country blues guitar sound. At the same time he established his Kicking Mule record label which featured many of the artists who appeared in concert with Grossman. The Kicking Mule company closed in 1979.

In the late 1980s Grossman returned to live in the USA. Based on the East Coast he continues to perform and write prolifically on all aspects of the blues and fingerpicking guitar. His books are currently published by Mel Bay Publications, CPP/Belwin and other leading publishers. His recordings are available on the Shanachie label. Grossman also operates his specialist international mail order service supplying a wide range of blues, ragtime and jazz music books and recordings. Although primarily a blues artist and educationalist, Grossman's outstanding work in this field as a performer, author, entrepreneur and impressario often extend into areas of jazz. In recent years his Vestapol company has released some very important jazz guitar performance and instruction videos.

Stefan Grossman

SELECTED RECORDINGS

Ragtime Cowboy Jew	Transantlantic 223 LP
Stefan Grossman 'Live'	Transantlantic 264 LP
My Creole Bell	Transantlantic 326 LP
Country Blues Guitar Festival	Kicking Mule 109 LP

SELECTED READING

Pro's Reply	Guitar Player, July 1975
Profile	Guitar Player, April 1979
Interview	Guitar International, August 1991

SELECTED MUSIC

Fingerstyle Jazz Guitar Workshop	CPP/Belwin
Rev. Gary Davis Blues Guitar	CPP/Belwin
Anthology Country Blues Guitar	CPP/Belwin
Blind Boy Fuller Transcriptions	CPP/Belwin
Fingerpicking Guitar Exercises & Hot Licks Vol 1-4	Mel Bay Publications
Folk, Blues, Jazz & Beyond	Mel Bay Publications
Complete Blues Country Guitar Book	Mel Bay Publications
Fingerpicking Blues Guitar Solos	Mel Bay Publications

MARTY GROSZ

Born-MARTIN GROSZ
Berlin, Germany
28 February 1930

Marty Grosz came to the fore in the 1970s as a fine acoustic guitar player. He is not just a rhythm guitarist, but also a soloist carrying on the tradition and styles of Dick McDonough, Carl Kress, George Van Eps and other top acoustic players of the 1930s.

Marty Grosz's father was the famous satirical artist George Grosz. With the rise of the Nazi party the Grosz family left Germany in 1932 to settle in the USA, making their home in Huntingdon, Long Island, New York. Marty Grosz started playing the ukulele at the age of eight, and then took up the guitar when he was twelve. He became interested in jazz, in particular Chicago style, and started to play with various groups around New York. In 1951, on leaving the Army, Grosz settled in Chicago where he took up the banjo. Over the next few years he played in a wide variety of jobs, usually on the banjo. Always fascinated by the guitar, he experimented with many tunings in his spare time. He ended up with one, based on a banjo tuning, not unlike the tuning used by Carl Kress. Kress tuned his guitar (low to high) B♭-F-C-G-A-D, later raising the C to a D an octave below. Grosz tunes his guitar (low to high) B♭-F-G-G-B-D.

Grosz first came to international prominence in 1974 when saxophonist Bob Wilber asked him to join the 'Soprano Summit'. The relatively enormous success of this group, both in concert and on record, brought the attention of the world's jazz lovers to the special talents of Marty Grosz.

In 1975 Grosz returned to live in New York after having lived in Chicago for eighteen years. There he formed a guitar duo with Wayne Wright. The bulk of their repertoire was based on popular acoustic guitar solos and duets from the 1930s and 1940s. In recent years Grosz has continued to play and sing all over the world in diverse classic jazz groups.

There is no doubt that Grosz, who is also a talented jazz journalist, has made an important contribution to the jazz guitar. Through his tireless efforts the legacy of the jazz artistry of the early acoustic guitar players has been drawn to the attention of new generations of jazz guitarists. The result has been a new interest in a field of the jazz guitar which to a large extent had been forgotten.

SELECTED RECORDINGS

Let Your Fingers Do The Walking w/Wayne Wright	Aviva 6000 LP
Take me to the Land of Jazz	Aviva 6001 LP
Goody Goody Duo w/ Wayne Wright	Aviva 6003 LP
Marty Grosz and His Blue Angels	Aviva 6004 LP
Marty Grosz Keepers of The Flame	Stomp Off SOS 1158 LP
Sings Of Love	Statiras SLP 8080
Swing It w/Destiny's Tots	Jazzology JCD 180
Just for Fun!	Nagel Heyer NH-CD 039

SELECTED READING

Profile	Coda, February 1977
Interview	Guitar Player, March 1978
Interview	Jazz Journal, October and November 1992
Interview	Just Jazz Guitar, August 1997
Interview	Jazz Rag, Nov/Dec 1997

Marty Grosz

RUNE GUSTAFSSON
Born-RUNE URBAN GUSTAFSSON
Gothenburg, Sweden
25 August 1933

Rune Gustafsson

Rune Gustafsson first gained national exposure in Sweden after playing in a Gothenburg based quartet led by Bert Dahlander from 1952 to 1954. He then went on to play with clarinettist Putte Wickman's band. In 1959 Gustafsson started an association of over twenty years, playing and recording with the Arne Domnerus orchestra.

Gustafsson is regarded as one of Sweden's best jazz musicians as well as being one of its busiest studio guitarists. He has recorded with top jazz artists including saxophonist Zoot Sims and bassist Niels-Henning Orsted-Pedersen.

SELECTED RECORDINGS

Killing Me Softly	Sonet SLP-2546 LP
Move	Sonet SLP-2601 LP
Sweetest Sounds w/Zoot Sims	Sonet SNTF 819 LP
Just The Way You Are w/Orsted-Pedersen	Sonet SNTF 869 LP
String Along With Basie	Sonet SNTF 1005 LP
Young Guitar	Metronome MLP 15072
Sweet and Lovely	Dragon DCD 254

FRED GUY
Born-FREDERICK GUY
Burkesville, Georgia, USA
23 May 1897
Died-Chicago, USA
22 November 1971

Fred Guy

Fred Guy started his career as a musician on the banjo. His first professional work was with the Joseph C. Smith Orchestra. Guy then led his own band at 'The Oriental' in New York. In early 1925 he joined Duke Ellington's orchestra. At first he only played the banjo with this historic band but changed to the guitar in 1934. He remained with the Duke Ellington orchestra, with hardly a break, until January 1949. Like Freddie Green, Guy was not a soloist, but an integral part of the Duke Ellington Orchestra rhythm section for almost a quarter of a century.

After Fred Guy left his orchestra, Duke Ellington never hired another guitarist. Guy gave up his career in music and went to live in Chicago. Here he became a ballroom manager in Chicago, a position he held for almost twenty years. After a long illness he committed suicide in 1971.

SELECTED RECORDINGS

Duke Ellington on V.Discs	Jazz Live BLJ8018 LP
Duke Ellington Cotton Club 1938	Jazz Anthology 30JA 5169 LP
Duke Ellington Sessions 1943-45	Jazz Anthology 30JA 5103 LP
Duke Ellington Sessions 1943-45	Jazz Anthology 30JA 51 LP

JERRY HAHN
Born-JERRY DONALD HAHN
Alma, Nebraska, USA
21 September 1940

Jerry Hahn`s family moved to Wichita, Kansas in 1947. Influenced by his father and uncle, both steel guitar players, Hahn`s first instrument was the steel guitar. By the time he was in his late teens Hahn had changed to a regular six-string guitar, and was playing country music with various local bands. After hearing recordings by leading West Coast jazz guitarists, in particular Barney Kessel, Hahn started to play jazz rather than country music.

In 1962 Hahn moved to San Francisco. Here he began playing with small commercial groups in bars and hotels. His first important jazz date was with alto-saxophonist John Handy in 1964. He then appeared with Handy at the Monterey Jazz Festival in 1965. Hahn earned a lot of praise from jazz critics and audiences for his part in that group. In 1968 he joined vibraphonist Gary Burton. He toured the world with Burton for almost a year. Hahn then formed his own group in 1970. It was called `The Jerry Hahn Brotherhood`. In 1971, after some personal problems, he decided to join the academic world of music instead of performing.

In 1973 he was appointed Professor of Music at Wichita State University. He also occasionally demonstrated for the Conn Musical Instrument Co. Hahn wrote a regular monthly column for `Guitar Player` magazine from 1974-77. In July 1986 he moved to Portland Oregon. There he began to play jazz in local clubs, and taught music at Evergreen College, and Lewis and Clarke College. He also devoted some time to composing, and has had three jazz guitar instruction books published by the Mel Bay Publishing company. In recent times he has worked as a sideman with saxophonist Benny Wallace, and mandolinist David Grisman, on the West Coast.

SELECTED RECORDINGS

John Handy Album-2	CBS BPG62881
Gary Burton Quartet	RCA PL 45319
Jerry Hahn Quintet	Arhoolie 8006
Are-Be-In	Changes LP7001
Brotherland	Columbia CS1044
Moses	Fantasy 9426
Imending Bloom w/Nancy King	Justice 0801
Time Changes	Jenja ENJ-9007 2 CD

SELECTED READING

Profile	Guitar Player, March 1971
Profile	Downbeat, June 1973
Interview	Cadence, September 1991

SELECTED MUSIC

Jazz Guitar Instruction 3 Volumes	Mel Bay Publications

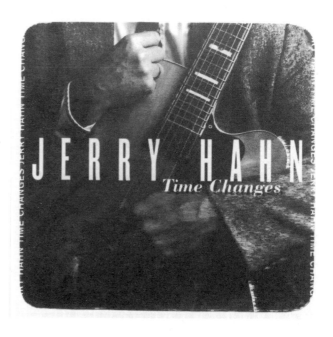

Jim Hall

JIM HALL
Born-JAMES STANLEY HALL
Buffalo, New York State, USA
4 December 1930

Jim Hall as a child was surrounded by music, His grandfather played the violin, his mother the piano, and his uncle the guitar. It was the uncle who influenced Hall to take up the guitar at the age of ten. His talent was soon evident and although it was against union rules, he started to play professionally in local dance bands at the age of thirteen. Like many of the jazz guitar greats of the 1950s and 1960s, it was the recordings of Charlie Christian that first turned Hall's attention to jazz.

Hall's family moved to Cleveland, Ohio in 1946. Having decided to make a career in music he entered, and later graduated from, the Cleveland Institute of Music. It was during this period that Hall became aware of the gypsy jazz guitar genius Django Reinhardt. Reinhardt's recordings affected the further development of his guitar style. Hall, not happy with economic prospects working as a guitarist in Cleveland, decided to move to Los Angeles in 1955. Here he felt he could both earn a living and still continue his musical studies at the University of California in Los Angeles. He was also able to study classical guitar, for a short while, with Vicente Gomez. In 1958 drummer Chico Hamilton was forming what was to be the first of his many outstanding jazz quintets. John Graas, the French horn player, recommended Hall to Hamilton. Hall got the job with what proved to be one of the most successful, and innovative, jazz groups of the day. He stayed with Hamilton for one and a half years.

This association with Chico Hamilton was to be Hall's first step up the ladder to the top of the jazz guitar tree. At the end of 1959, he joined another highly successful small group, the Jimmy Giuffre Trio. This trio was as equally innovative as the Hamilton group. Hall received well deserved praise for his part in Giuffre's trio from jazz audiences, and critics, all over the world. Now established internationally as a jazz musician of the highest calibre Hall was hired to play with top singers, including Ella Fitzgerald, and Yves Montand. He also was a featured sideman with leading jazz artists including Lee Konitz, Ben Webster and Sonny Rollins. In many cases he produced some fine and historic recordings with these players.

In 1960 Hall moved back to New York. For a while he worked as a studio musician, including a spell with the band on the popular 'Merv Griffin Show'. The late 1960s and early 1970s saw Hall once more back at the top of his profession as a jazz musician. Over the years since then, Hall has made many outstanding recordings with diverse jazz musicians. He has appeared in concert, and recorded with, bassists Ron Carter and Red Mitchell, trumpeters Art Farmer and Chet Baker, pianists Bill Evans and George Shearing, saxophonists Paul Desmond and Ornette Coleman, and many other top jazz artists. Some of these recordings contain some of the best jazz guitar playing on record, and certainly confirm the title often bestowed upon Hall, 'The Poet of Jazz'. He also recorded with a quartet, led by pianist Andre Previn, backing classical violinist, Itzhak Pearlman, and also with the Kronos string quartet. Jim Hall was awarded the prestigious JAZZPAR Prize for 1998. He accepted the honour which included a cash award of approximately $30,000, at The JAZZPAR Prize Gala Concert in Copenhagen, Denmark, on 5 April 1998.

Jim Hall is without doubt one of the most inventive, influential, and lyrical jazz musicians of the day. He continues to live in New York City and plays regularly at jazz festivals, and in jazz clubs, all over the world.

SELECTED RECORDINGS

Chico Hamilton Quintet	World Pacific WP 1209
Hamton Hawes Trio	Contemporary S7545
Jimmy Guiffre Three	Atlantic LP 1254
Jimmy Guiffre Trio – Live	FreshSounds FSCD-1026
Jim Hall Trio	Pacific CDP 46851-2
Undercurrent (Duo w/Bill Evans)	Blue Note CDP 90583-2
Intermodulation (Duo w/Bill Evans)	Verve 83371 2CD
Interplay w/Bill Evans	OJG CD 308-2
Good Friday Blues	World Pacific Jazz PJ 10
Street Swingers	World Pacific Jazz PJ 1239
Otra Vez w/Jimmy Raney	Mainstream MRL 358
It's Nice to be with You	MPS 20708
Where Would I Be?	OJC-649 CD
The Bridge-Sonny Rollins Quartet	RCA LPM/LSP 2527
Paul Desmond Quartet	Telarchive CD83319
Alone Together w/Ron Carter	Milestone MSP9045
Jim Hall-Live	Horizon A&M SP-705
Jim Hall-Concierto	CTI 65132 CD
Jim Hall-Commitment	A & M Horizon SP-715
Live in Tokyo	A & M Horizon GP 3515
Jazz Impressions of Japan	A & M Horizon GXU 1
Jim Hall/Red Mitchell Duo	Artists House AH 5
Jim Hall Trio	Concord CCD-4161
George Shearing/Jim Hall Duo	Concord CCD-4177
Jim Hall & Ron Carter Live	Concord CCD-4245
Jim Hall & Ron Carter	Concord CCD-4270
Jim Hall's Three	Concord CCD-4298
Jim Hall Quartet	Concord CCD-4384
Jim Hall Trio w/Tom Harrell	Denon CY-30002-EX CD
Power Of Three w/Michel Petrucciani	Blue Note BT-85133 CD
Jim Hall & Friends Vol 1	Musicmasters 5050-2-C CD
Jim Hall & Friends Vol 2	Limelight 820 843-2 CD
Jim Hall-Subsequently	Limelight 844 278-2 CD
Jim Hall-Youkali	CTI CTI 1001-2CD
Jim Hall-Something Special	Musicmasters 65105 2 CD
Subsequently w/Larry Golding	Musicmasters 65078 2 CD
Dedications and Inspirations	Telarc CD-83365
Dialogues	Telarc CD-83369
Textures	Telarc CD-83402
Live at Village Vanguard	Telarc CD-83408
Jim Hall-Instructional Video	Star Licks

Jim Hall with Jeff Linsky

PHOTO: MAURICE J. SUMMERFIELD

178

ALLEN HANLON
**Born-Long Island, New York, USA
10 January 1919
Died-New York, USA
6 April 1986**

Allen Hanlon's first musical instrument was the violin. He began to study the violin at the age of eight with a local teacher who insisted that the young musician had a sound grounding in theory and that he become a good sight reader.

Hanlon switched to the guitar as a teenager. He was greatly influenced by George Van Eps and other leading guitarists of the day. He made friends with the Van Eps family who lived on Long Island. They helped him in his guitar studies. After joining the local musician's union Hanlon met guitarist Allan Reuss. He gave the young guitarist the opportunity to take his place for a short while in the Benny Goodman band in 1937. Hanlon then went on to join vibraphonist Red Norvo's band. He stayed three years with this famous jazz group. In 1941 Hanlon accepted an offer to become a radio studio musician in New York but after a few weeks he left to join the Claude Thornhill band. Following this Hanlon played in a trio led by Adrian Rollini.

After the end of World War II Hanlon once again became involved in studio work and teaching the guitar. He was featured on recording sessions with singers such as Tony Bennett, Perry Como, Vic Damone and Bobby Vinton. His involvement in jazz after this was limited although in 1970 he started a jazz guitar duo with Sal Salvador and they gave many concerts in the New York area. Hanlon was also an adjunct professor for New York University.

Allen Hanlon

SELECTED RECORDINGS
Allen Hanlon Picks Le Roy Anderson   Golden Crest CR 3012
Sal Salvador & Allen Hanlon Live in Concert
         Glen Productions GPSA 5010
Bucky Pizzarelli Quintet   Monmouth Evergreen MES 7066

SELECTED READING
Interview   Guitar Player August 1977

SELECTED MUSIC
Kreutzer for Guitar   Belwin-Mills
Chemistry of Chords for Guitar   Ryckman & Beck
Scale Studies & Etudes for Guitar   Mel Bay Publishing

Sal Salvador & Allen Hanlon
LIVE IN CONCERT
AT THE
University of Bridgeport

FAREED HAQUE
Born-Chicago, Illinois, USA
28 January 1963

Fareed Haque was born to a Chilean mother and a Pakistani father. He also travelled a lot as a child and his musical style and compositions reflect the music of many lands, in particular flamenco and the music of Spain.

In 1981 Haque was the recipient of a scholarship to study jazz guitar at North Texas State University. There he studied with Jack Peterson. He went on to study classical guitar at Northwestern University from where he earned his Bachelor of Music in Performance degree in 1986. He currently heads the guitar department at North Illinois University where he is an associate professor in both jazz and classical studies. As a classical artist Haque has worked with Nigel Kennedy, Robert Conant, Edgar Meyer and many symphony orchestras in the US and abroad.

Fareed Haque

PHOTO: JIMMY KATZ

SELECTED RECORDINGS

Voices Rising	Panagea PAN C-42156 CD
Manresa	Pangaea PAN D-82012 CD
Sacred Addiction	Blue Note-89662 CD
Opaque	Blue Note 29270 CD
Deja Vu	Blue Note 52419 CD

SELECTED READING

Article	Guitar World, March 1989
Article	Downbeat, August 1989
Interview	Jazz Times, December 1989
Interview	Guitar Player, April 1994
Interview	Jazz Times, July 1994
Interview	JAZZIZ, Aug/Sept 1994

Alvino Rey, guitarist/bandleader with his 1946 orchestra.

BILL HARRIS
Born-WILLIE HARRIS
Nashville, North Carolina, USA
14 April 1925
Died-Washington, DC, USA
6 December 1988

Bill Harris

As a child Bill Harris was taught the piano by his mother and he later played the organ in his father's church. On his twelfth birthday he was given a guitar by his uncle but soon gave it up as he did not make much progress. It was eight years later, on his discharge from the army, that Harris decided to take up the guitar seriously. He initially played a steel strung guitar playing some classical pieces for his own enjoyment with a pick. Whilst studying at the Columbia School of Music in Washington, Sophocles Papas encouraged him to take up the classical guitar. He made excellent progress and in the late 1950s took part in an Andres Segovia masterclass.

Harris made his living gigging in and around Washington with various groups. Whilst playing with a rhythm and blues vocal group he was heard by Mickey Baker. He encouraged Harris in 1958 to make his first solo jazz record using classical finger style technique on a nylon string guitar. This record proved successful and is probably the first solo jazz guitar record using classical guitar technique on the classical instrument. Harris was obviously an early influence on Charlie Byrd, whose world-wide success playing jazz on the classical instrument followed very shortly after.

Bill Harris never achieved international recognition for his unique jazz talent. He continued to live in Washington D.C. where he ran his own teaching studio. He opened his 'Pigfoot' jazz club in 1975 but this closed when he found he had cancer. Despite the financial and personal problems caused by his illness, Harris continued to perform and teach until shortly before his death.

SELECTED RECORDINGS

The Harris Touch	Emarcy MG36113LP
Great Guitar Sounds	Mercury MGW16220 LP
Down in the Alley	Black & Blue 33-042 LP
Rhythm	Black & Blue 33-062 LP
The Fabulous Bill Harris	V.S.O.P. 66 CD

SELECTED READING

Profile	Jazz Journal, November 1960
Profile	Downbeat, July 1961
Profile	Downbeat, June 1968
Profile	Guitar Player, May 1975

SELECTED MUSIC

Classic Jazz	Bill Harris Publications
Instant Guitar	Bill Harris Publications
Harris Touch	Bill Harris Publications

JOHN HART
Born-Ft. Belvoir, Virginia, USA
15 June 1961

John Hart grew up in Florida where he began to play the guitar at the age of twelve. His first interest was in rock music and then, after hearing Chick Corea and Al DiMeola, jazz fusion. At the age of sixteen he heard a recording of Porgy and Bess by Miles Davis and from then on decided he wanted to be a professional jazz musician.

Hart went on to study jazz at the University of Miami, graduating in 1983. After touring with Latin pop star Jose Luis Rodriguez, Hart moved in 1984 to New York City. There he soon established himself as one of the most sought after young jazz guitarists playing and recording with diverse jazz artists including Jack McDuff, Terumasa Hino, Jimmy Smith, Mike Mainieri, Lou Donaldson and Larry Goldings. Hart was also a member of the Apollo Theatre house band.

In the early 1990s Hart recorded for the Blue Note label, and since 1995 has recorded for the Concord label.

SELECTED RECORDINGS

High Drama	Concord CCD 4688
Bridges	Concord CCD 4746
It's About Time w/ Jack McDuff	Concord CCD 4705
Pure w/Chris Potter	Concord CCD 4637

SELECTED READING

Profile	Jazz Times, July/August 1996

John Hart

SCOTT HENDERSON
Born-West Palm Beach, Florida, USA
26 August 1954

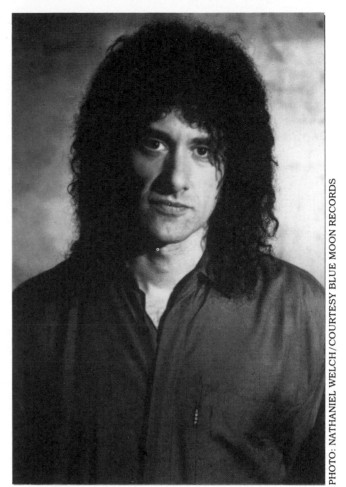

Scott Henderson

Scott Henderson began playing lead guitar in local rock and funk bands at the age of sixteen. He then decided to study music seriously and enrolled at Florida Atlantic University. Here he studied under Dr Bill Prince. After three years at university Henderson majored in music.

In 1980 the young guitarist moved to Los Angeles to continue his studies with Joe Diorio at the Guitar Institute of Technology (GIT). He graduated after a year at GIT and was immediately hired as a teacher.

Henderson's first real professional break, giving him wide recognition, was when bassist Jeff Berlin asked him to join his group 'Vox Humana'. With this group Henderson played at many jazz clubs in the Los Angeles area. On the recommendation of Allan Holdsworth he was then hired by violinist Jean-Luc Ponty for a 1982 concert tour. This led to a further three concert tours and a record session with the famous jazz-fusion violinist. Henderson then went on to work with pianist Chick Corea and this association further established his reputation as one of the most important jazz fusion guitarists of the day.

In the mid1980s Scott Henderson formed his own group,'Tribal Tech'. The guitarist described the sound of this group as 'modern electric jazz'. Since that time Henderson has continued a busy career as a leader, sideman and teacher. Scott Henderson was voted 'Best Jazz Guitarist' by Guitar World magazine's readers in April 1991, and by Guitar Player magazine's readers in January 1992.

SELECTED RECORDINGS

Spears Tribal Tech	Passport Jazz PJ 88010
Champion Vox Humana	Passport Jazz PJ 88004
Fables Jean-Luc Ponty Band	Atlantic ATC 81276-1
Chick Corca Elcktric Band	GPR CD GPR 9535
Tribal Tech	Relativity 885612-1049-4
Illicit-Tribal Tech	Blue Moon R2 79180 CD
Tore Down House	Atlantic 92722 CD
Dog Party	Rhino/Atlantic 79073 CD

Jazz Fusion Improvisation	Instructional Video	REH
Melodic Phrasing	Instructional Video	REH

SELECTED READING

Interview	Guitar Player, October 1986
Profile	Downbeat, May 1987
Interview	Guitar Extra, Spring 1991
Profile	Downbeat, December 1992
Profile	Guitar Player, September 1997

SELECTED MUSIC

Scott Henderson Guitar Book Artist Transcriptions	
	Hal Leonard Publishing
Best of Scott Henderson	Hal Leonard Publishing

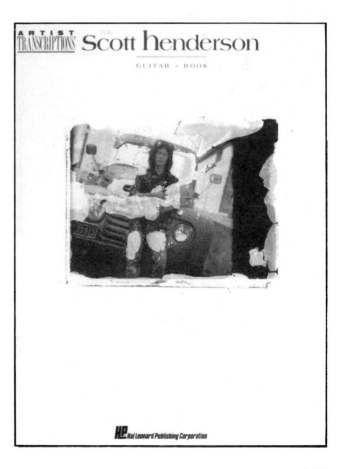

AL HENDRICKSON
Born-ALTON REYNOLDS HENDRICKSON
Eastland, Texas, USA
10 May 1920

Al Hendrickson

Although today not widely known to the general jazz listener, Al Hendrickson is highly respected by his fellow guitarists, and jazz musicians, in the USA. Over the years, from 1939 to 1980, he was one of the busiest guitarists in the Los Angeles studios. He is reputed to have played on over 5000 film sound tracks.

Hendrickson first came to prominence as guitarist with Artie Shaw's band and 'Gramercy Five' from 1942-45. He then joined the Benny Goodman band and sextet as singer/guitarist. Over a period of many years Hendrickson was the first choice as guitarist for the best big bands of the day including those of Ray Noble, Woody Herman, Johnny Mandel and Neal Hefti. He was also featured in the I962 Monterey Jazz Festival with trumpeter Dizzy Gillespie and drummer Louis Bellson.

Al Hendrickson's guitar playing can be heard in a multitude of recordings including those of the guitar groups 'Guitars Inc' and 'Guitars Unlimited'. Over the years Hendrickson has been associated with many popular artists including Nat 'King' Cole, Peggy Lee, Gordon Jenkins, Frank Sinatra, Benny Carter, Lalo Schifrin, Nelson Riddle, Phil Moore, Lena Horne and Quincy Jones. Hendrickson has written several guitar music books and methods for the Mel Bay Publishing Company.

SELECTED RECORDINGS

Artie Shaw's Gramercy Five	RCA PM 43699 LP
Benny Goodman	Jazz Anthology JA 5195 LP
Barney Kessel-To Swing or Not To Swing	Contemporary 3513 LP
Guitars Inc-Invitation	Warner Bros 1206 LP
Guitars Inc-Soft and Subtle	Warner Bros 1246 LP
Guitars Unlimited-Tender is the Night	Capitol ST173 LP
Dizzy Gillespie-Big Band 1965	Trip Jazz TRLP5584 LP
Juggernaut	Concord CCD 4040

SELECTED READING

Interview	Guitar Player, March 1988
Interview	Just Jazz Guitar, August 1997

SELECTED MUSIC

Jazz Guitar Duets	Mel Bay Publications
Deluxe Guitar Arpeggio Studies	Mel Bay Publications
Jazz Guitar Solos	Mel Bay Publications

ALLAN HOLDSWORTH
Born-Leeds, Yorkshire, England
6 August 1946

Allan Holdsworth's father was a pianist and it was he who introduced his son to music. His first instruments were the saxophone and the clarinet. Holdsworth took up the guitar at the age of seventeen and his style on the instrument was immediately influenced by his earlier experience with woodwinds. He was also interested from an early age in electronics.

Holdsworth played with various groups in the Leeds area and then moved to London in the late 1960s. By the early 1970s he had become one of the pioneers of jazz/rock fusion. He gained international recognition in 1972 as a member of trumpeter Ian Carr's group. Further fame came when he joined John Hiseman's band 'Colosseum'. He left this group in November 1973. Following this Holdsworth appeared with some of the most famous fusion groups of the day including 'Soft Machine' and Tony Williams' 'Lifetime' band. Holdsworth also worked with various bands led by drummer Bill Bruford.

In 1985 Allan Holdsworth, as leader of his own groups, enjoyed great success in concert tours of California and Japan. Since that time he has become recognised as one of the most influential, and innovative, of the jazz/rock fusion guitarists of the day. His experiments with synthesisers and electronic sound devices have extended the boundaries of contemporary jazz.

Allan Holdsworth

PHOTO: COURTESY IBANEZ GUITARS

SELECTED RECORDINGS

Velvet Darkness	CTI 6068
Sand	Enigma 3293 1
Secrets	Virgin CD ENV 536
I.O.U.	Cream CR 260-2
Metal Fatigue	Cream CR 270-2
Atavachron	Cream CR 280-2
Wardenclyff Tower	Cream CR 310-2

Allan Holdsworth Instructional Video	REH/LPP

SELECTED READING

Interview	Guitar Player, December 1980
Profile	Guitar World, September 1981
Profile	Guitar World, November 1982
Interview	Guitar Player, December 1982
Profile	Guitar World, June 1987
Interview	Guitarist, November 1987
Profile	Guitar World, May 1989
Interview	Guitar Player, March 1990
Interview	Jazz Journal, May 1992
Profile	JAZZIZ, September 1994

SELECTED MUSIC

Hold Down A Common Chord

    20th Century Music/Hal Leonard Publishing

Allan Holdsworth Chords   Centerstream

TONINHO HORTA
Born-Belo Horizonte, Brazil
2 December 1948

Toninho Horta's maternal grandfather was a musician who composed religious and popular works. Horta began to play the guitar at the age of ten, his first teacher was his mother. He was introduced to jazz by his elder brother, Paulo. He encouraged him to listen to his recordings of American jazz guitarists Barney Kessel, Tal Farlow and Wes Montgomery and those of the Duke Ellington and Stan Kenton big bands.

Horta composed his first song, 'Flor Que Cheirava Saudade', at the age of thirteen. A year later this song was recorded by a local band. During his teens he played in various bands, backed singers and also performed frequently on radio and television. In 1970 he played with Milton Nascimento in Rio de Janeiro. Following this important concert he joined a new band called 'A Tribo'. Horta, now recognised as one of Brazil's best young musicians, played regularly with that country's top popular artists. His original songs were recorded by Flora Purim, Milton Nascimento, and Sergio Mendes. In 1979 Horta's first record album, 'Terra Dos Passaros', was released.

In 1980 Horta met Pat Metheny when the American guitarist was appearing at a jazz festival in Brazil. The two soon became close friends and started playing together. Both guitarists developed a mutual admiration for each others approach to music, and have played and recorded together often since that first meeting.

Horta moved to New York for two years in the early 1980s. He studied at the Julliard School of Music for two terms, and played in New York clubs with bassist Mark Egan, and drummer Danny Gottlieb. Horta returned to Brazil and in July 1986 organised the First Brazilian Seminar of Instrumental Music in his home state of Minas Gerais. He returned to live in New York in early 1992, and played and recorded as leader of a jazz quartet with pianist Kenny Barron, bassist Gary Peacock, and drummer Billy Higgins.

Toninho Horta plays a unique style of Brazilian folk/jazz/classical/bossa nova fusion music usually on a nylon-strung classical guitar. He is one of the most distinctive new jazz guitar voices of the 1980s and 1990s.

Toninho Horta

Toninho Horta	World Pacific 93865 LP
Once I Loved	Verve 314 513 561-2 LP
Serenade	Truspace TSJD 9705 CD
Into the Night w/Jack Lee	Truspace TSJD 9701 CD

SELECTED READING

Interview	Guitar Player, January 1990
Profile	Acoustic Guitar, March/April 1993
Article	Jazz Times, July/August 1994

SELECTED RECORDINGS

Diamond Land	Verve Forecast 835 183 LP
Moonstone	Verve Forecast 839 734 LP

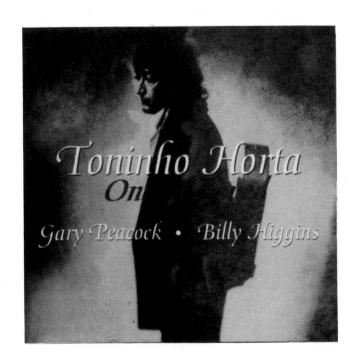

MICHAEL HOWELL
Born-Kansas City, Missouri, USA
8 October 1944

Michael Howell was first taught the guitar at the age of seven by his father. His family moved from Kansas City to Colorado. He continued his studies with a local musician, Herley Dennis. Howell studied music when he was eighteen at the Lamar Jnr. College in Colorado. In 1965 Howell decided to move to San Francisco where he studied at the local Music and Arts Institute, and with organist, Chester Thompson. He received his first important break in 1971 when he played with vibraphonist, Bobby Hutcherson and saxophonist, Harold Land. He went on to play in a ten piece band headed by Woody Shaw, and recorded with both Dizzy Gillespie and Art Blakey.

Since that time Howell has maintained a busy career as a jazz guitarist playing with many top musicians, including Sonny Rollins, Dizzy Gillespie and John Handy. He regards Wes Montgomery and Charlie Parker as his most important jazz influences.

SELECTED RECORDINGS

Dizzy Gillespie Orchestra	Pablo 2625708 LP
In the Looking Glass	Milestone M9048 LP
In the Silence	Milestone M9054 LP
Alone	Catalyst CAT 7615 LP

SELECTED READING

Profile	Guitar Player, April 1975
Profile	Downbeat, March 1975

Al Norris, guitar, with the Jimmy Lunceford rhythm section.

ADRIAN INGRAM
Born-Birmingham, UK
20 May 1950

Adrian Ingram started to play the guitar at the age of nine. When he was thirteen he heard a Wes Montgomery recording and from that moment on decided to make the guitar his career.

Ingram left school when he was fifteen and began to play professionally in a wide variety of bands. He was involved in recording work and also toured Europe and the UK in backing groups for American soul singers. In 1970 he recorded with the jazz/rock group 'Hannibal', playing lead guitar, and also composing for this seven piece band. This recording led in 1971 to two European tours with 'Hannibal'. In the same year Ingram began training to be a music teacher on a full time basis. He also began to study the classical guitar to an advanced level. In 1975 he obtained diplomas from Leeds University and the Trinity College of Music in London, after which he accepted an appointment as a full time guitar teacher in Birmingham.

The next few years saw Ingram concentrating on further study and also developing his skills as a writer on jazz and classical guitar matters. He gave many lectures, and took several jazz guitar workshops throughout the United Kingdom. In 1980 his method 'Modern Jazz Guitar Technique' was published. Since that time Ingram has been involved in several other publications for the guitar. At the same time he was still busy as a performer both in the jazz and classical fields.

In 1982, following a period as a lecturer at Huddersfield Technical College's School of Music, Adrian Ingram was appointed as full time lecturer in jazz guitar at the City of Leeds College of Music. In 1985 his definitive biography of Wes Montgomery was published. Since that time Ingram has continued to establish himself as one of the most important figures on the British jazz guitar scene. His articles and music appear frequently in many magazines including Guitarist, 20th Century Guitar and Classical Guitar. As a performer he has been played with a wide variety of jazz artists including Martin Taylor, John Etheridge, Jimmy Witherspoon, Kenny Baker, Mundell Lowe, John Pisano, Jack Wilkins, Jimmy Bruno, Jim Mullen, Don Weller, Dick Morrisey and Louis Stewart. In the educational field Ingram was a senior lecturer in guitar at the City of Leeds College of Music, and he is now a regular contributor to Just Jazz Guitar Magazine.

SELECTED RECORDINGS

Hannibal	Greentree GTR 017
A Long Time Comin'	Elderslie EM C01
Introducing the Jazz Guitar of Adrian Ingram	JJG CD-250 9298
Ben Crosland Quintet	Jazz Cat JC CD101
Adrian Ingram Quartet w/Jim Mullen	Jazz Cat JC CD102
Duets w/Andy McKenzie	Crimson IPC 010
Hands Across the Water w/Royce Campbell	String Jazz GRLD 1002

SELECTED READING

Wes Montgomery Biography	Ashley Mark Publishing Company (1985)
The Gibson ES 175	Music Maker Books (1994)
The Gibson L5	Centerstream (1997)
Interview	Just Jazz Guitar, November 1996

SELECTED MUSIC

Modern Jazz Guitar Technique	Hampton Music Publishers
Binary Guitar	Hampton Music Publishers
Jazz Guitar Workshops Vols 1 & 2	Domino
25 Graded Pieces for Plectrum Guitar	Hampton Music Publishers
Adrian Ingram Guitar Folio	Elderslie Music
Best of British	Elderslie Music
Cool Blues and Hot Jazz	Warner Bros.
Jazz Guitar Suite	Music Maker Publications
Jazz Guitar Cameos	Mel Bay Publishing

Adrian Ingram

PHOTO: COURTESY ADRIAN INGRAM

SADASHI INOUE
Born-Kobe, Japan
12 November 1956

Sadashi Inoue

Sadashi Inoue began to play on his father's classical guitar at the age of 14. He first taught himself to play by watching a guitar tuition course on television. His first real musical interest was in British Progressive Rock Music, and at the age of 18 his parents bought him an electric guitar. he was soon playing in a local rock band.

Inoue changed his musical direction after hearing some recordings of Wes Montgomery, Pat Martino, Jim Hall, Pat Metheny and Miles Davis. After graduating in 1979 with a political science degree from Doshisha University he went on to study jazz. After gaining success as a jazz guitarist in Japan, Inoue first performed in the USA with his own group in 1985. He participated in the Asian-American Jazz Festival at the Jazz Centre of New York, and at the Blue Note jazz club. Inoue stayed on in New York studying with Jim Hall at The New School in New York City. He graduated in 1994 with a Bachelor of Fine Arts degree. He now serves on the faculty of the Mannes Jazz Programme at The New School, teaching at guitar workshops and also in private lessons.

Satoshi Inoue also leads a busy life as a jazz musician in the New York area and further afield. He has toured with Frank Foster, Junior Mance, Jack McDuff, Steve Slagle and Jimmy Heath. He has been active in producing music educational material including a series of Jin Hall Master Class videos for the Rittor Music Company. He has also played for several USA television and radio shows.

SELECTED RECORDINGS

Satoshi Inoue plays Satoshi	Paddle Wheel KICJ 285 CD
Only You w/Chie Ayado	R 9690100 CD
Live at Deanna's w/Deanna Kirk	Birth Records 001NSZ93 CD

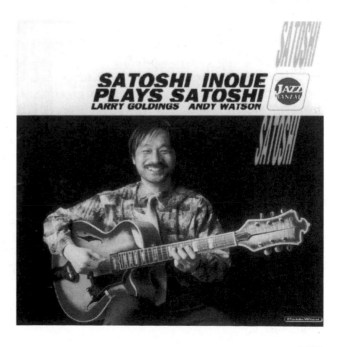

IKE ISAACS
Born-ISAAC ISAACS
Rangoon,Burma 1 December 1919
Died-Sydney, Australia
10 January 1996

Ike Isaacs

Ike Isaacs was recognized by his peers as one of the most musical guitarists in the world. In 1987 after a long career as one of the UK's top guitarists, Isaacs moved to Sydney, Australia from the United Kingdom. Here he led a busy career writing and arranging for the guitar, playing in various jazz groups, and teaching at the Australian Institute of Guitar in Sydney. Although much of his professional career over many years in the United Kingdom was spent in the television and recording studios, Isaacs always found time to play jazz.

Ike Isaacs began to play the guitar at the age of fourteen. Although he came from a very musical family, Isaacs originally played the guitar only as a hobby. He studied for a degree in chemistry at Rangoon University. In 1942 he graduated with a B.Sc., but due to the war was forced to move to India. There he was assigned to a government factory as a storekeeper. In order to enhance the low wages earned in the factory, Isaacs worked as a musician in the evenings in local hotels. In 1946 he moved to the United Kingdom and settled in London, having decided to make music and the guitar his career. His first job was with the ex-Bomber Command band led by Leslie Douglas. Isaacs left Douglas in 1947 and joined a group playing at Hatchetts Restaurant in Piccadilly. He was also the featured guitarist with the BBC Radio Show Band at that time.

Ike Isaacs first achieved recognition for his jazz guitar work when he led the resident guitar group on the popular BBC Radio programme, 'Guitar Club'. This programme was broadcast every Saturday evenings from 1955 to 1958. For many years Isaacs was involved in studio work, although he did record with groups like the Ted Heath Band. In 1975, he was offered the chance to play with the Stephane Grappelli quartet. This opportunity to be actively involved in jazz again was too good to miss, and for two years he toured the world with the famous jazz violinist. In 1977 he returned to his home in London and shared his time between the studios, various jazz gigs, teaching, and writing new works for the guitar. He also contributed a highly praised jazz guitar column in 'Crescendo' magazine for several years. He appeared often in a guitar duo with his friend, and former pupil, Martin Taylor, at venues throughout the United Kingdom. This association continued whenever Martin Taylor visited Australia, until Isaac's death in 1996.

SELECTED RECORDINGS
Guitar Club	Saga(3 EPs) ESAG7001/2/3
I Like Ike	Morgan MR116P
Lutes And Flutes	Rediffusion ZS 133
The Tender Touch	World Record Club WRCT447
Fourteen TV Themes	Decca/Eclipse ECS 2163
Music Of Michel Legrand	MFP/EMI 50047
Ike Isaacs Latin Guitars	Dansan DS 004
I Love Paris	Chapter One LRP5009
Velvet	Black Lion BLB 12187
Violinspiration w/Stephane Grappelli	MPS/BASF MPS2022545-3
After Hours Duo w/Martin Taylor	JTC Records JTC-1
Intimate Interpretations	IIM 001 CD
Ike Isaacs Instructional Video	Starnite SNT 008

SELECTED READING
Interview	Guitar, December 1977
Profile	Guitar Player, November 1976
Profile	Classical Guitar, October 1989
Profile	Just Jazz Guitar, February 1995
Tribute	Just Jazz Guitar, May 1996

SELECTED MUSIC
Guitar Moods	Kadence Music Co.
Ibanez Guitar Album	Kadence Music Co.
Glen Miller for Guitar	IMP

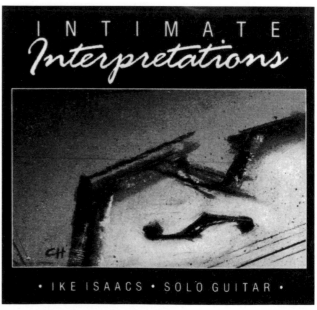

PHOTO: COURTESY IKE ISAACS

RON JACKSON
Born-RONALD WORTH JACKSON Jnr
Subic Naval Base, Philippines
27 July 1964

Ron Jackson

Ron Jackson began to play the guitar at the age of eleven. His father was in the US Army and Jackson lived in the Phillipines until he was five years old. He was attracted at first to pop, rock and rhythm and blues music. His early influences included top rock guitarists Jimi Hendrix, Jimmy Page and Richie Blackmore. By the time he was 15, he began listening to jazz recordings. Pat Metheny and George Benson made a great impact on him, and he was soon playing jazz in local jazz clubs in the Boston area. In 1982 Jackson enrolled at the Berklee College of Music where he concentrated on studying composition and arranging. He studied guitar privately with Rodney Jones, Melvin Sparks and Ted Dunbar.

In 1985 Jackson moved to Paris, France for two years. There he played electric bass performing regularly with pianist Bobby Few, saxophonist Hal Singer and Leo Wright. They concertised throughout Europe and North Africa. Jackson returned to the USA in 1987 and once again changed back to playing the guitar. Between 1982 and 1996 he won many awards and scholarships, including first place in the '1996 Heritage International Jazz Guitar Competition'. He toured with the Mingus Guitar Tribute Band which also included guitarists Larry Coryell, Jack Wilkins, Peter Leitch, David Gilmore and Russell Malone.

Since 1987 Ron Jackson has lived in New York City from where he performs, records and tours with his own jazz group, freelances in studio sessions and Broadway shows, and also teaches on a private basis.

SELECTED RECORDINGS

A Guitar Thing	Muse	MCD 5456
Thinking of You	Muse	MCD 5515
Song for Luis duo w/ Rufus Reid	Master Mix CHECD 00115	

SELECTED READING

Interview	Just Jazz Guitar, November 1996

Lonnie Johnson

LONNIE JOHNSON
Born-ALONZO JOHNSON
New Orleans, Louisiana, USA
8 February 1889
Died-Toronto, Canada 16 June 1970

Lonnie Johnson, a pioneer blues artist, was one of the greatest jazz guitarists the world has known. Fortunately due to the re-release of many of his recordings from the 1920s and 1930s, particularly his duets with Eddie Lang, guitar and jazz lovers can today fully appreciate Johnson's genius. His influence on guitarists from the 1920's to the present day, through his unique swinging blues/jazz guitar solo style is undisputed. Johnson was also an authentic singer in the blues tradition and made many fine vocal recordings throughout his long career.

As a child, Lonnie Johnson, one of thirteen children, studied the violin and guitar. He started his musical career around 1902 playing in New Orleans cafes and theatres with his brother James, a pianist. He continued his career playing with riverboat bands. In 1917 he sailed to Europe and worked for a while in theatre orchestras in London. He returned to New Orleans in 1921 only to find a flu epidemic (1918-19) had wiped out almost all his family. In 1922 he moved to St.Louis where he worked with Charlie Creath, Fate Marable and Nat Robinson. Johnson gained nationwide prominence in 1925 when he won a blues contest held in St. Louis. Part of the contest prize was a contract for the 'OKeh' record company. Over the next few years Johnson made many records both in New York City and Chicago. His most outstanding tracks at that time were probably those that he made in a guitar duo with Eddie Lang. Lang used the stage name of Blind Willie Dunn. Johnson was also featured with Duke Ellington's orchestra, Louis Armstrong's Hot Five, and many other famous jazz and blues artists of the day. From 1932-37 Johnson moved to Cleveland and played with the Putney Dandridge orchestra. He was featured occasionally on local radio shows. For a time he also worked in a tyre factory, and then a steel mill. In 1937 he moved to Chicago. From 1937-40 he worked regularly with many jazz artists including Jimmy Noone and Johnny Dodds. His great guitar talent was not fully exposed when he played and recorded with these musicians. From the mid 1940s Johnson started to play an electric guitar, but his guitar style was not as convincing on the amplified instrument. Tragically his career as a musician declined from this point, although he continued to play regularly until 1952. In 1958 he was forced to make his living for a while working as a chef in a Philadelphia hotel. Fortunately Johnson was rediscovered in 1960 by some jazz and blues enthusiasts and he was once more able to make a living singing, and playing, the blues. In early 1963 he appeared with the Duke Ellington Orchestra in New York, and in the autumn of that year he toured Europe and Great Britain as part of the blues package called the 'American Folk Blues Festival'.

In the mid-1960s Lonnie Johnson finally decided to settle in Toronto, where he became very popular with local blues fans. It was here that he died in 1970 of a heart attack, the final result of a severe accident suffered in 1969.

SELECTED RECORDINGS

Blue Guitars Vol.1	Parlophone PMC 7019 LP
Blue Guitars Vol.2	Parlophone PMC 7106 LP
Stringing the Blues	CBS BPG62143 LP
Pioneers of Jazz Guitar	Yazoo 1057 LP
Finest of Lonnie Johnson	Bethlehem BCP 6017 LP
Lonnie Johnson	RCA PM 42390 LP
Original 1927-32 Recordings	Original Jazz OJL-23 LP
Blues by Lonnie Johnson	Prestige 1007 LP
Lonnie Johnson-Live in Copenhagen	Storyville 671-162 LP
Lonnie Johnson	Xtra 1037 LP
Steppin' On The Blues	CBS 467252-2 CD
Me and My Crazy Self	Charly CD 266
Blues and Ballads w/Elmer Snowden	Bluesville OBCCD531-2
Stompin' at the Penny	Columbia/Leeacy 476720-2 CD
Blues in My Fingers	Indigo IGOCD 2009

SELECTED READING

The Devil's Music pages 177-182,	BBC Publications (1976)
Big Bill Blues Yannick Bruynoghe	Cassell (1955)
Article	Jazz Journal, January 1972
Article	Guitar Player, November 1981
Article	Guitar Extra, Spring 1991
Appreciation	Guitar Player, September 1993

SELECTED MUSIC

The Great Blues Guitar of Lonnie Johnson	Mel Bay Publications

RANDY JOHNSTON
Born-Detroit, Michigan, USA
5 December 1956

Whilst still a teenager Randy Johnston played in rock groups in Detroit and Virginia. After hearing a recording of saxophonist Charlie Parker he decided to make a career in jazz. Johnston studied at the University of Miami in Coral Gables from where he received a Bachelor of Music degree in Studio, Music and Jazz. He moved to New York from Florida in the early 1980s. Johnston has toured and recorded with some of the most respected names in jazz and blues including Lou Donaldson, Lionel Hampton, Brother Jack McDuff, Etta Jones, Lee Konitz, Warne Marsh, Tom Harrell, Houston Person and Joey DeFrancesco.

Johnston is also an important jazz educator. Since 1987 he has been a professor of jazz guitar at the University of Hartford's Hartt School of Music. From 1980-81 he taught jazz guitar at the University of Miami and 1981-87 jazz and theory at the Brooklyn Conservatory of Music. Since 1991 he has been on the faculty at Long Island University in Brooklyn, New York. Johnston has also held jazz guitar clinics and given seminars all over the USA.

Randy Johnston

SELECTED RECORDINGS

Walk On	Muse MCD 5432
Why Not!	Muse MCD 5433
The Party	Muse MCD 5451
Jubilation	Muse MCD 5495
In A-Chord	Muse MCD 5512
Somewhere in the Night	High Note 7007CD
Riding the Curve	J. Curve JCR 898CD

SELECTED READING

Interview	Jazz News November 1996

RODNEY JONES
Born-RODNEY BRUCE JONES
New Haven, Connecticut, USA
30 August 1956

Rodney Jones was born into a musical family. His uncle was an accomplished pianist and also conducted church choirs. He began to play the guitar at the age of ten years and studied with various teachers for almost seven years. After leaving high school Jones went to City College, New York to study improvisation with John Lewis.

From 1974 Jones began to lead his own small groups in the New York area, and also was a sideman with various other groups. He played not only jazz. He played on many Latin and disco recordings. In 1974 Jones had the opportunity to play with the Music Complex Orchestra led by Jackie Byard, at the Five Spot club. He then joined drummer Chico Hamilon's group for almost a year. In 1976 he gained further international recognition when he joined Dizzy Gillespie's quartet for almost three years. In 1977 he won a Certificate of Merit from the City of New Orleans. The next few years saw Jones working with many prominent jazz musicians in the USA including Chico Hamilton and Maxine Brown. He also did a world tour with the Subtle Sounds jazz group. In 1983 Jones was hired as guitarist, writer and arranger for Lena Horne. He worked with this famous singer for the next couple of years. Also in 1983 Rodney Jones was awarded a National Endowment for the Arts recording grant.

Rodney Jones

SELECTED RECORDINGS

Articulation	Timeless SJP 125 LP
When You Feel The Love	Timeless SJP 152 LP
My Funny Valentine w/Tommy Flanagan	Timeless SJP 162 CD
Dizzy Gillespie Sextet	Pablo 2310784 LP
Strut w/Hilton Ruiz	Novus RCA 83053 CD
Maceo Parker Group	Minor Music 1015 CD
The X Field	Music Masters MM65147 CD

SELECTED READING

Profile	Jazz Times, July/August 1996

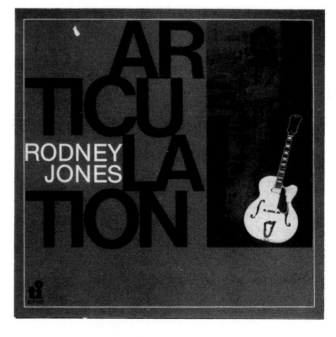

STANLEY JORDAN
Born-Chicago, Illinois, USA
31 July 1959

Stanley Jordan began playing the piano at the age of six. He started to play the guitar at the age of eleven, when his family moved to California. He soon was playing in local rock and soul bands. By the time he was 13 Jordan had already developed an interest in jazz, and was beginning to develop his unique 'touch' technique. This revolutionary guitar style was aided by the fact that he tuned his guitar in fourths (E, A, D, G, C, F, bass to treble strings). Jordan taps notes on the fingerboard, piano style, with the right hand usually playing single note lines and the left hand sounding chords. In this way he is able to play two parts on the guitar simultaneously.

At the age of 17 Jordan had perfected this new technique to such a level that he shared first place in the 1977 Reno International Jazz Festival. Following this success Jordan enrolled at Princeton University, New Jersey 1977-1981 to study music theory and composition, eventually a Bachelor of Music degree. Whilst at university he had the opportunity to play with Dizzy Gillespie and Benny Carter, as well as playing with several local jazz groups.

In 1983 Jordan released his first record album 'Touch Sensitive' on Tangent Records. This soon brought him international recognition and a recording contract with Blue Note Records. Jordan appeared at the 1984 Kool Jazz Festival in New York, the 1985 Concord Festival in California, and also the 1985 Montreux Jazz Festival in Switzerland.

Stanley Jordan

Stanley Jordan continues to advance his reputation as one of the most original jazz guitarists of the day through his recordings, and many club and concert appearances.

SELECTED RECORDINGS

Touch Sensitive	Tangent 1001
Magic Touch Stanley Jordan	Blue Note BT 85101
One Night With Blue Note	Blue Note BTDK 85117-4
Standards Stanley Jordan Vol. 1	Blue Note BT 85130
Flying Home	EMI Manhattan E1 48682
Cornucopia	Blue Note CD P 7 92356 2
Stairway to the Rainbow	Blue Note TOCJ 5531 CD
Bolero	Arista 07822 1803 2 CD
Cornucopia Video	Blue Note MVP 9912543

SELECTED READING

Interview	Guitar Player, September 1983
Interview	Guitar Player, October 1985
Profile	Downbeat, April 1985
Interview	Guitarist, August 1985
Profile	Guitar World, January 1987
Profile	Downbeat, November 1988

STEVE JORDAN
Born-STEPHEN PHILIP GIORDANO
New York City, USA
15 January 1919
Died-Alexandria, Virginia, USA
13 September 1993

Steve Jordan

Steve Jordan, although not too well known to the jazz world at large, was one of the finest exponents of rhythm guitar.

Jordan originally studied the guitar as a child with his uncle Bartolo Loguidice, father of saxophonist Don Lodice. As a teenager he played in a band led by trumpeter Vic Hunter. Jordan went on to study in New York with Allan Reuss. From the late 1930s he was featured in the rhythm section of several big bands including those led by Artie Shaw and Will Bradley. In the late 1940s Jordan spent short periods with the Stan Kenton, Glen Gray and Boyd Raeburn orchestras. He was often hired for studio work, including some sessions produced by John Hammond and the N.B.C. From 1954-57 he worked with Benny Goodman. Following this Jordan retired from music and worked as a tailor in New York and Washington.

Jordan became a resident of the Washington D.C. area in 1965 and began to play regularly with Tommy Gwaltney's group at the local Blues Alley club. In 1971 he joined the house band at this club. In 1977 he made his first recording as leader on the Fat Cats Jazz label. On this he sings and plays fine acoustic rhythm guitar backed by Bill Goodall on string bass. His biography of his life as a rhythm guitarist, co-written with Tom Scanlan, was published in 1991.

SELECTED RECORDINGS

Hi-Fi Salute to Bunny	RCA Victor LPM-1510
Ruby Braff Quartet	Epic LN-3377
Tommy Gwaltney Quartet	Blues Alley 0001
Tommy Gwaltney Trio	Laurel 163011
Here Comes Mr Jordan	Audiophone ACD-114
The Intimate Steve Jordan	B Flat Music BMP 10001
Steve Jordan Trio	B Flat Music BMP 10006

SELECTED READING

Rhythm Man Fifty Years in Jazz	University of Michigan Press (1991)
Article	Downbeat, July 1965

VIC JURIS
Born-VICTOR JURIS
Jersey City, New Jersey, USA
26 September 1953

Vic Juris

Vic Juris began to study the guitar at the age of ten with a local teacher, jazz guitarist Eddie Berg. He was originally inspired by the pop guitar greats of the day such as Duane Eddy and Chuck Berry. It was after hearing a Johnny Smith recording at his teacher's house that Juris decided he wanted to play jazz.

By the time he was eighteen Juris had an advanced technique and musical knowledge. He began to play in local jazz clubs in New York and New Jersey and was soon recognised locally, by musicians and jazz fans alike, as being a talented jazz guitarist. In 1974 he met, and impressed, saxophonist Eric Kloss who featured Juris on his 'Bodies' Warmth' recording. After this he was soon hired by other prominent jazz, and jazz/fusion musicians, including pianist Barry Miles. In 1975 Juris played with saxophonist Richie Cole and it was he who persuaded Muse Records to give the young guitarist a recording contract.

Since that time Juris has established himself as one of the busiest guitarists in the New York area. He worked for a while in a trio led by organist Don Patterson. This led to work with organists Wild Bill Davis and Jimmy Smith. In 1977 Juris went on the first of what was to be a series of regular visits to Europe. On this trip he played with the Barry Miles group at the Berlin Jazz Festival. In recent years Vic Juris has also been featured on many recording sessions with prominent artists including Mel Torme, Phil Woods, Kenny Wheeler and Michel Legrand.

SELECTED RECORDINGS

Richie Cole Septet	Muse MR 5119
Roadsong	Muse MR 5150
Vic Juris Horizon Drive	Muse MR 5206
Bleeker Street	Muse MR 5265
Bireli Lagrene Ensemble	Inak 865 CD
For The Music	Jazz Point CD JP 1034
Music of Dizzy Gillespie w/Richie Cole	Heads Up HUCD 3032
Music of Alec Wilder	Double Time DTR-118 CD

SELECTED READING

Interview	Guitar Player February 1981

RYO KAWASAKI
Born-Tokyo, Japan
25 February 1947

Ryo Kawasaki

PHOTO: TOSHI KAZAMA

Ryo Kawasaki took singing lessons when he was five years old. In junior high school he learned to play the ukulele but only started to play the guitar when he was sixteen. Inspired by the recordings of Kenny Burrell, Barney Kessel, Jim Hall, Wes Montgomery, Jimmy Raney and Grant Green, Kawasaki began to teach himself using various guitar methods. By the time he was in second year high school he was already playing in the school jazz band.

Kawasaki went on to study physics at Nippon University. During his time at university he gained valuable professional experience playing in clubs and cabarets in the evenings. The jazz groups he played with concentrated mainly on be bop and modern jazz. He also began to listen to recordings by guitarist Gabor Szabo which were to prove a major influence on his own developing jazz guitar style.

Ryo Kawasaki graduated in 1973 with a degree in physics. As he was deciding whether to be a physicist, or to make a career in music, he was offered the opportunity to make a solo recording for Polydor Records. This led to him getting regular work as a guitarist in the Tokyo studios. But after a while Kawasaki, not happy with the music he had to play in the studios, left in 1976 for the USA. He was so impressed with the opportunities in the USA that, after a short trip back to Japan, he returned to work as a professional musician. Kawasaki was hired as guitarist with the Gil Evans orchestra and this led to an offer to play with drummer Chico Hamilton. Kawasaki toured European Jazz Festivals with Joanne Brackeen and in 1979 invented his own guitar synthesiser. In the 1980's he performed regularly with his jazz-rock group 'The Golden Dragon'. He went on to create four computer music software programs. Since 1991 Ryo Kawasaki has been an artist and producer for the Japanese label One Voice.

SELECTED RECORDINGS

Juice	RCA APL1-1855
Ring Toss	Chiaroscuro CR-181
Nature's Revenge	MPS/BASF MPS 15524
Eight Mile Road	Inner City 6006
Prism	Inner City 6016
Solo Jazz Guitar	One Voice VACV-1001
My Reverie	One Voice VACV-1005 CD
Love Within the Universe	One Voice VACV-1009 CD
Mirror of My Mind	Satellites VACV-0004 CD
Little Tree	Satellites VACV-0005 CD
Sweet Life	Satellites VACV-1017 CD

SELECTED READING

Interview	Guitar Player, November 1979

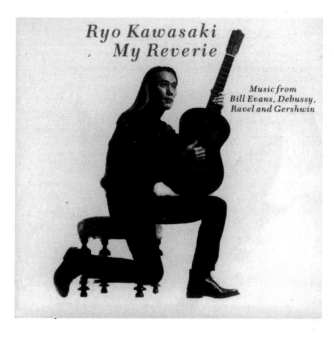

Ryo Kawasaki
My Reverie

Music from Bill Evans, Debussy, Ravel and Gershwin

PAT KELLEY
Born-Tulsa, Oklahoma, USA
12 March 1952

Pat Kelley

Pat Kelley began to play the guitar at the age of five. His first teacher was his father. He studied with various teachers in his early school years including Eldon Shamblin who worked with Bob Wills and the Texas Playboys. After leaving high school Kelley went to the University of Tulsa, Oklahoma from where he majored in music composition. He attended seminars given by Howard Roberts in Hollywood and Johnny Smith in Colorado.

Kelley moved to Los Angeles where he has worked as a studio guitarist since 1975. He has played in over 2000 sessions. From 1983-87 he was a regular band member on the Merv Griffin Show. In 1990-94 Kelley toured and recorded with George Benson. From 1992-94 he also worked with saxophonist Tom Scott on the Pat Sajak CBS television show. Since 1994 he has toured and recorded with David Benoit. Kelley has appeared in concert all over the world and played at jazz festivals in Nice, Montreux, Holland (North Sea), Newport and Montreal.

Pat Kelley currently teaches in the Studio/Jazz Guitar Department of the University of Southern California in Los Angeles and is also a prolific composer. His compositions have been recorded by George Benson, Tom Scott, Stix Hooper, Hubert Laws and many other leading musicians.

SELECTED RECORDINGS

Views of the Future	Nova 8704-2 CD
I'll Stand Up	Nova 8915-2 CD
High Heels	Denon 73764 CD
The Road Home	Positive Music PMD 78018-2 CD
Good News	ID Net AHCY-00004 CD
Voices of Heart w/Eric Marienthal	GRP GRD-9563 CD
Them Changes w/Tom Scott	GRP GRD 9613 CD
Remembering Christmas w/David Benoit	GRP GRD 9852 CD
Love Remembers w/George Benson	Warners 7599-26685-2CD

Barney Kessel with Herb Ellis

Barney Kessel with Artie Shaw's band. New York 1945. Dodo Marmarosa, piano, Roy Eldridge, trumpet and Morris Rayman, bass.

Barney Kessel

BARNEY KESSEL
Born-Muskogee, Oklahoma, USA
17 October 1923

Barney Kessel's parents were not keen on music, certainly not as far as their son was concerned. But by the time Kessel was twelve, music and the guitar were the passion of his life. By selling newspapers he was able to save enough money to buy his first guitar. Although Kessel received a few basic guitar lessons in a Federal Music Project of the WPA in the summer of 1935 he was virtually self taught. When he was fourteen he was the only white musician playing in an all black jazz orchestra in Muskogee. In 1939 Kessel's reputation was already so great that Charlie Christian came to hear him play when he came on a family visit to Oklahoma City. Meeting and playing with Charlie Christian in Oklahoma City strengthened Kessel's determination to be a professional musician.

In 1942 Kessel made his way to Los Angeles where he first worked as a dishwasher. Word soon got around about his talent and he was hired to play in a new band fronted by film comedian, Chico Marx, but actually led by drummer Ben Pollack. After a year of touring with the Marx band Kessel settled in Los Angeles, where he soon became the top guitarist on the radio networks and in the film studios. In 1944 he appeared in Norman Granz's award-winning documentary 'Jammin' the Blues', the only white musician to be featured in this historic jazz film. Over the next few years Kessel played with many famous big bands, including those of Charlie Barnet (1945, 46 and 47), Artie Shaw (1944-45), Hal McIntyre (two weeks in 1945), and later on some recording dates with Shorty Rogers (1954). He also played and recorded with the Benny Goodman Orchestra and Quintet (1958).

In 1945 Kessel made several 78rpm records under his own name with pianist Dodo Marmorosa and saxophonist Herbie Steward. Since 1943 he had been involved in the Los Angeles jazz scene playing, and recording with Charlie Parker, Howard McGhee, Wardell Gray, Sonny Criss, and many other leading modern jazz musicians. At the same time Kessel maintained a hectic, and financially rewarding, career in the Hollywood studios. He played often on radio broadcasts with Frank De Vol's orchestra. In 1952 an offer came from Oscar Peterson for Kessel to join his trio, and to take part in Norman Granz's 'Jazz at the Philharmonic' touring package . He decided to accept and over the next year Kessel toured throughout Europe and the USA. This exposure gave him further international recognition for his jazz artistry. In the

PHOTO: COLIN COOPER

Barney Kessel with Marion Montgomery.

next few years he repeatedly won every leading jazz poll, including those of 'Esquire' (1947), 'Downbeat' Readers Poll (1956-59) , 'Metronome' Readers Poll (1958-60), and 'Playboy' Readers Poll (1957-60).

In 1953 Kessel made his first long-playing record as leader of his own group on the Contemporary label. This was to be the first of many LP, and later CD, recordings by groups of all sizes led by Barney Kessel. All Kessel's records have proved over the years to be extremely influential on new generations of jazz guitarists. His 'Poll Winner's' albums with Shelley Manne (drums), and Ray Brown (bass), are particularly outstanding. These records were historic in that they made the concept of a guitar/bass/drums trio acceptable. This line up, now a regular jazz combination, was a great step forward in the evolution of the jazz guitar.

Barney Kessel is not only a brilliant soloist, but his special talents make him one of the great, and most sought after, accompanists in jazz. His recordings with singers Julie London, Sarah Vaughan, Anita O'Day, Billie Holiday, Ella Fitzgerald, Claire Austin and others are permanent proof of his exceptional ability in this important area of jazz. Kessel's many recordings with other jazz legends have included Art Tatum, Oscar Peterson, Hampton Hawes, Paul Smith, Sonny Rollins, Red Norvo, Stephane Grappelli, Lester Young, Buddy De Franco, Harry Edison, Stuff Smith, Lionel Hampton, Ruby Braff, and

203

fellow guitarists Herb Ellis, Charlie Byrd and Tal Farlow. It is a fact that the list of names of great jazz musicians that have not played with Barney Kessel since 1942 to the present day is very short indeed.

Kessel is also a prolific composer, the jazz standard 'Swedish Pastry' was an early work. He is also a talented arranger having studied with classical composer, Mario Castelnuovo-Tedesco, and composer/musicologist, Albert Harris. For many years Kessel's talent continued to be absorbed in the Los Angeles studios. From 1957-58 he became involved in producing pop recordings including some No.1 hits by Ricky Nelson, and then as a A&R man, for Verve Records. He also played on the soundtrack of several Elvis Presley films.

In 1969 Barney Kessel decided to give up his involvement in studio work to dedicate himself to a life in jazz. From that time he toured the world jazz circuit annually, playing to capacity audiences wherever he went. His guitar playing and musical genius have become a legend amongst guitarists and jazz lovers everywhere. Kessel is also a gifted educator and over the years he devoted a lot of time to presenting his famous seminar, 'The Effective Guitarist' in the USA, Europe and Australia. He has written a method for guitar, and produced four tuition videos. He also wrote a regular column in 'Guitar Player' magazine for several years and has worked as an 'Ambassador of Jazz' for the US State Department. Kessel suffered a major stroke in May 1992 which forced him to give up playing. He continues to maintain a great interest in music and still teaches selected pupils at his home in San Diego.

SELECTED RECORDINGS

Dodo Marmarosa Trio 1947	Fresh Sounds FSCD-1019
Central Avenue Breakdown; Vol 2	Onyx 215 LP
Charlie Parker on Dial	Spotlite 103 LP
Easy Like	Contemporary OJCCD-153
Plays Standards	Contemporary OJCCD-238
To Swing or not to Swing	Contemporary OJCCD-317
The Poll Winners	Contemporary OJCCD-156
Plays Carmen	Contemporary OJCCD-269
Four	Contemporary OJCCD-165
Music to Listen To	Contemporary OJCCD-746
The Poll Winners Again	Contemporary OJCCD-607
Some Like it Hot	Contemporary OJCCD-168
The Poll Winners Three	Contemporary OJCCD-692
Working Out	Contemporary C 3585 LP
Exploring the Scene	Contemporary C 3581 LP
Let's Cook	Contemporary C 3603 LP
Latin Rhythms	Reprise RP 6073 LP
Swinging Party	Contemporary C 3613 LP
On Fire	Venus TKC2-79531 CD
Feeling Free	Contemporary C 3618 LP
With Stephane Grappelli Vol 1	Black Lion 760150 CD
With Stephane Grappelli Vol 2	Black Lion 760158 CD
Swinging Easy	Polydor 2460130 LP
What's New	Mercury 135720 LP
Reflections of Rome	RCA 34012 LP
Kessel's Kit	RCA SF8098 LP
Jazz Portrait	RCA 730710 LP
Summertime in Montreux	Laser CD 15011
Two Way Conversation	Sonet S LP 2550 LP
Just Friends	Sonet SNT 685
Great Guitars – Straight Tracks	Concord CCD-4421
Great Guitars Vol.1	Concord CCD-6004
Barney Plays Kessel	Concord CCD-6009

Great Guitars Vol.2	Concord CCD-4023
Poll Winners Straight Ahead	Contemporary OJCCD-409
Soaring	Concord CCD-4033
Poor Butterfly w/ Herb Ellis	Concord CCD-4034
Kessel at Sometime-Japan	Storyville STCD-4157
Junko & Barney	Trio(Japan)PAP 9060 LP
Shiny Stockings	LOB (Japan)LDC-1004 LP
By Myself	Victor(Japan)SPX-1042 LP
Barney Kessel Trio 'Jelly Beans'	Concord CCD-4104
Barney Kessel Solo	Concord CCD-4221
Spontaneous Combustion	Contemporary C-14033-2 CD
Red Hot & Blues	Contemporary C-14044-2 CD
The Artistry of Barney Kessel	Contemporary FCD-60-021
Giants of Jazz – Barney Kessel	Giants of Jazz CD53116
It's A Blue World – Barney Kessel	Jazz Hour JHR73526 CD

Jazz Guitar Instructional Videos 3 Vols	RuMark Video
Barney Kessel – Rare Performances 1962-1991 Video	Vestapol
Legends of Jazz Guitar (Vol. 1) Video	Vestapol
Legends of Jazz Guitar (Vol. 2) Video	Vestapol
Legends of Jazz Guitar (Vol. 3) Video	Vestapol

SELECTED READING

Profile	Downbeat, July 1958
Article	Downbeat, June 1959
Profile	B.M.G., August 1959
Profile	Downbeat, January 1961
Profile	Downbeat, July 1966
Profile	Guitar Player, October 1970
Article	Guitar Player'Jan/Feb 1973
Interview	Crescendo, November 1972
Interview	Guitar, December 1972/ January 1973
Interview	Guitar, January 1977
Interview	Guitar Player, May 1982
Interview	Cadence, August 1987
Interview	Guitarist, September 1990
Blindfold Test	Jazz Times, August 1992
Just Jazz Guitar – Special Issue	June 1996

SELECTED MUSIC

The Guitar-A Tutor	Windsor Music Co.
Personal Manuscripts 1-6	Windsor Music Co.
West Coast Guitar	Leeds Music Corp.
Jazz Guitar Artistry (Vol. 1)	Ashley Mark Publishing Company
Jazz Guitar Atristry (Vol. 2)	Ashley Mark Publishing Company

STEVE KHAN
Born-STEPHEN CAHN
Los Angeles, USA
28 April 1947

Steve Khan

Steve Khan had a strong musical background. His father, the famed lyricist Sammy Cahn, encouraged his son to study the piano. This he did for almost twelve years but did not enjoy it. In the early 1960s Khan was influenced by surf music and began to play drums with a band called 'D.K. & The Cavities'. He was then offered the drum chair in another pop group called 'The Chantays'. He toured with this group for two years. It was the guitarist with 'The Chantays' that introduced Khan to the guitar style of Wes Montgomery. When 'The Chantays' broke up in 1966 Khan decided to give up the drums and devote his musical studies to the guitar.

In 1967 Khan entered the UCLA as a psychology major but soon changed his course to music and entered a period of serious study on the guitar. During his studies Khan took some time off to do some studio and club work. In 1969 he travelled to New York with vibraphonist Dave Friedman and was very impressed with the vitality of the music scene in New York. After graduating from UCLA Khan moved to New York in early 1970. He managed to get some work with Chico Hamilton and Gil Evans but mainly earned a living working in Broadway pit orchestras. As his guitar talent became more widely known he began to get more studio and club work. Over the next few years he was to be associated with leading East Coast jazz and jazz/fusion artists including the Brecker Brothers, Maynard Ferguson, Freddy Hubbard, Buddy Rich, Hubert Laws, Joe Beck, George Washington Jnr and Larry Coryell. At the same time his studio work featured his guitar on the recordings of top popular artists such as Billy Joel, James Brown, Aretha Franklin and Steely Dan.

In 1977 Khan took part in a CBS Records All-Star tour which included drummer Billy Cobham and bassist Alphonso Johnson. Since that time Khan has established his reputation further with his many recordings as leader and sideman, and also as a record producer for artists including Mike Stern, Bill Connors, Bireli Lagrene and Eliane Elias. Steve Khan has also written three important guitar music books highlighting his teaching ability.

SELECTED RECORDINGS

Tightrope	Columbia JC 34857 LP
The Blue Man	Columbia JC 35539 LP
Arrows	Columbia JC 36120 LP
Evidence	Arista AN 3023 LP
Best of Steve Khan	Columbia 36406 LP
Eye Witness	Antilles 1018
Casa Loco	Antilles 1020
Local Color	Passport 78038
Blades	Passport 88011
Public Access	GRP GRD-9599
Lets Call This	Blue Moon R2 79166
Headline	Blue Moon R2 79179

SELECTED READING

Profile	Guitar Player, March 1979
Profile	Downbeat, December 1983
Profile	Downbeat, August 1988
Interview	Guitar Player, November 1985
Interview	Guitar Player, December 1992

SELECTED MUSIC

The Wes Montgomery Folio	Plymouth Music
Pat Martino Jazz Guitar Solos	CPP/Belwin
Guitar Workshop Steve Khan	Warner Brothers

PHOTO: COURTESY STEVE KHAN

EARL KLUGH
Born-Detroit, Michigan,USA
16 September 1953

Earl Klugh first studied the piano, and then started to play the guitar when he was ten. His first interest was in folk music. When Klugh was thirteen he heard some records by Chet Atkins and suddenly realized the full harmonic and melodic potential of the guitar. This discovery was emphasised when he heard the jazz guitar artistry of George Van Eps, Wes Montgomery, George Benson, Charlie Byrd and Laurindo Almeida.

Whilst teaching the guitar in a music store in Detroit he was heard by saxophonist Yusef Lateef. Lateef was so taken by the sixteen year old playing jazz on nylon-strung classical guitar, he invited him to sit in with his group at the local Baker's Keyboard Lounge. He then featured Klugh on his Atlantic Records album, 'Suite 16'.

The following year Klugh met George Benson in Baker's Lounge. Like Lateef, Benson was fascinated by Klugh's jazz style on the classical instrument. They worked out some duets together, and in 1973 Klugh joined Benson's new quartet. This was the start of a long and close friendship between the two guitarists. They recorded two albums together on the CTI label. Klugh was then approached by Chick Corea to join his popular 'Return to Forever' group on electric guitar. He accepted and toured for two months with this famous jazz/rock group, which featured bassist Stanley Clarke and drummer Lenny White. Following this Klugh worked with singer Flora Purim, and pianist George Shearing. This gave him valuable experience working with a wide variety of top jazz musicians.

Since that time Klugh has become one of the most successful guitarists of the day. His Liberty record release, 'Crazy For You', sold over 500,000 copies. He has recorded prolifically with diverse artists including pianist/composer Bob James, George Benson and country guitarist Chet Atkins. Many of his recordings are in a commercial vein, but his recent trio recordings, with acoustic bass and drums, show that he is a very talented and original jazz musician.

SELECTED RECORDINGS

White Rabbit with George Benson	CTI 6015
Earl Klugh	Blue Note BNLA 596
Living inside your Love	Blue Note BNLA 667
Finger Paintings	Blue Note 48386 CD
Magic in your Eyes	United Artists LA 877-H
Heartstrings	United Artists LA 942-H
Dream Come True	Liberty LT-1026

Earl Klugh (left) with Bob James.

Late Night Guitar	Liberty LT-1979
Crazy For You	Liberty LT-51113
Low Ride	Capitol ST-12253
Wishful Thinking	Capitol ST-12323
Nightsongs	Capitol ST-12372
Whispers & Promises	Warners 9-25902 CD
Solo Guitar	Warners 9-26018 CD
Earl Klugh Trio Vol 1	Warners 9-26750 CD
Earl Klugh Trio Vol 2 – Sounds and Visions	Warners 9-45158 CD
Love Songs	Blue Note 53354 CD
Sudden Burst of Energy	Warners 9-45884 CD
The Journey	Warners 9-46471 CD

SELECTED READING

Profile	Downbeat, February 1977
Profile	Guitar Player, July 1977
Profile	Downbeat, March 1980
Profile	Downbeat, October 1983
Interview	Guitar Player, August 1985

WAYNE KRANTZ
Born-Corvallis, Oregon, USA
26 July 1956

Wayne Krantz

Wayne Krantz's first musical instrument was the piano which he began to play as a child. He started to play the guitar after hearing some recordings by the Beatles. He was soon playing in local rock and country groups. Shortly before graduating from high school he heard a Barney Kessel recording in his father's jazz record collection. Almost immediately jazz became Krantz's main interest, in particular the style of the leading jazz/fusion guitarists including Mick Goodrick, Pat Metheny, Mike Stern, John Scofield and Bill Frisell.

In 1982 Krantz entered the Berklee College of Music in Boston. Whilst in Boston he played in a group called D Sharpe with Bill Frisell. In 1985 Krantz graduated from Berklee. He moved to New York where he soon gained prominent recognition playing with the Carla Bley Sextet and Leni Stern Band. He toured Europe and the USA with Bley 1986-87, and with Leni Stern 1987-91. Krantz has also played with Billy Cobham, Michael Brecker, Tania Maria, Randy Brecker, Michael Formanek and Victor Bailey.

Krantz's recent CDs for Enja Records as leader of his own group confirm that Krantz is one of the leading jazz/fusion guitarists of the day.

SELECTED RECORDINGS

Leni Stern Band- Secrets	Enja ENJ 5093-2 CD
Michael Formanek - Wide Open Spaces	Enja ENJ 6032-2 CD
Michael Formanek - Extended Animation	Enja ENJ 7041-2 CD
Signals-Wayne Krantz Group	Enja ENJ 6048-2 CD
Long To Be Loose-Wayne Krantz Trio	Enja ENJ 7099-2 CD

SELECTED READING

Profile	Guitar Player, June 1996

CARL KRESS

Born-Newark, New Jersey, USA
20 October 1907
Died-Reno, Nevada, USA
10 June 1965

Carl Kress first gained prominence when he was featured with the Paul Whiteman orchestra in 1926. His first instrument was the piano which he studied for two years from the age of twelve. He then bought a banjo and within a few years began his professional career as a musician. In 1927 he recorded with two of the most outstanding musicians from the Whiteman orchestra, Bix Beiderbecke and Frankie Trumbauer. During the period 1927-29 Kress was featured on recordings with Miff Mole, the Dorsey Brothers, Red Nichols, and many other jazz artists playing both banjo and four-string guitar.

In the early 1930s Carl Kress changed over to the six-string guitar and was soon regarded as the foremost guitarist on American radio. He also recorded what are now regarded as some of the finest jazz guitar duets of the time, first in 1932 with Eddie Lang, and then in 1934 with Dick McDonough. Kress helped found the famous 'Onyx' jazz club, as a silent partner, on New York's 52nd Street. His fame at that time was mainly in and around the New York area, but his supremacy as one of the pioneers, and masters, of rhythmic chord jazz guitar playing was undisputed.

A unique feature of Kress's guitar sound was his unorthodox tuning, B flat, F, C, G, D, A instead of the conventional E, A, D, G, B, E. Many musicians who changed over from the-banjo to guitar in the early 1930s devised tunings for the guitar that facilitated their change of instruments.

In the late 1950s Kress was a member of the band supporting the Garry Moore television show. In the few years before his death in 1965, Kress began a new guitar duo with George Barnes. They made several historic recordings together which bear further testimony to the unique ability of Carl Kress. Whilst appearing with Barnes in Reno, Kress suffered a fatal heart attack.

Carl Kress

Two Guitars and A Horn w/ Geo. Barnes   Stash ST 228
10 Duets for 2 Guitars w/Geo.Barnes   Music Minus One MM03613 CD

SELECTED READING
Article   Just Jazz Guitar, November 1996

SELECTED MUSIC
Kress/McDonough Duets   Robbins Music Corporation
Carl Kress Guitar Solos   Robbins Music Corporation

SELECTED RECORDINGS

Guitar Genius in 1930's w/ Dick McDonough	JazzArchives JA-32
Guitars Anyone	Audiophile AP-87
Fun on the Frets	Yazoo L-1061
Pioneers of Jazz Guitar	Yazoo L-1057
Carl Kress Guitar Stylist	Capitol H368
Singing & Swinging w/Helen Caroll	Stereo-o-Craft RCS 505X
Town Hall Concert w/ George Barnes	United Artists UAS6335
Something Tender w/ Bud Freeman	United Artists UAJ14033
Two Guitars with George Barnes	Stash ST 222

Classics in jazz

Capitol

Carl Kress
Guitar Stylist

WALKING BEHIND MISS LUCY
JAZZ IN G • COQUETTE
SARONG NUMBER
BLONDE ON THE LOOSE
SWAN OF TONNELLE AVENUE
THE GOOSE FROM GANDER
JUST YOU, JUST ME

VOLKER KRIEGEL
Born-Darmstadt, Germany
24 December 1943

Volker Kriegel

Volker Kriegel, who is self taught, began to play the guitar at the age of fifteen. Within three years he had formed his own trio. In 1963 this group was voted Best Band at the German Amateur Jazz Festival. Kriegel also personally won the award for Best Jazz Soloist at this festival.

Kriegel entered Frankfurt University to study social science and psychology. Whilst there he became involved with local jazz musicians including Albert and Emil Manglesdorff. In 1968 US vibraphonist Dave Pike came to live in Europe and selected Kriegel for his quartet. This group had a quick success and Kriegel decided to leave university to pursue a career as a professional musician. For five years the young guitarist gained wide recognition through his guitar playing with the Dave Pike Quartet. When Pike returned to the USA in 1973 Kriegel formed his own band called Spectrum. This enjoyed success in his native Germany. In 1976 he started a new group with the title of 'The Mild Maniac Orchestra'. Kriegel's original jazz influences were Wes Montgomery, Jim Hall and Kenny Burrell. As time went by his guitar style became influenced by leading jazz/rock/fusion players including John Scofield, Pat Metheny and John McLaughlin.

Volker Kriegel has established himself as one of Europe's foremost jazz fusion guitarists. He appears at jazz festivals both in Germany and abroad, and has featured on many recordings both as leader and as a sideman

Volker Kriegel is also a talented and award winning cartoonist. His work appears in leading German newspapers and magazines. He also presents regular music programmes on German radio and television. His 1980 cartoon film "Der Falschspieler" earned international acclaim and won a prize at a Los Angeles film festival.

SELECTED RECORDINGS

Houseboat	MPS 68 206 LP
Long Distance	MPS 68 243 LP
Missing Link	MPS 88 030 LP
Star Edition	MPS 88 036 LP
Elastic Menu	MPS 15 517 LP
Volker Kriegel Trio	Atlantic ATL 60073 LP
Journal	Mood 33605 LP
Palazzo Blue	Mood 33608 LP
Schone Aussichten	Mood 33617 LP
About Time Too!	Vera Bra CD VBR 2014-2
Doldinger Jubilee Concert	Atlantic 2292-44175 CD

BIRELI LAGRENE
Born-Saverne, Alsace, France
4 September 1966

Bireli Lagrene's father and grandfather were both guitarists. Under their influence Lagrene began to play the guitar at the age of five. By the time he was seven Lagrene was already playing improvised jazz in the style of Django Reinhardt. Like Reinhardt, Lagrene was from a Gypsy family and lived the early years of his life in a horse-drawn caravan. In 1978 he won first prize at a jazz festival in Strasbourg and was featured in a television film of a Gypsy music festival.

The reports of the young guitar prodigy's incredible talent soon spread throughout Europe's jazz world and Lagrene was booked for one concert tour after another with various prominent Hot Club style groups including those led by British guitarists Diz Disley and Denny Wright. In 1982 Lagrene released his first album as leader playing in a style very reminiscent of the late Django Reinhardt.

Since that time Bireli Lagrene has developed his own distinctive style, influenced by the many top jazz artists he has worked with around the world. His latest recordings display a style with far more contemporary influences, including be bop, rock and South American, than his original recordings.

SELECTED RECORDINGS

Routes to Django	Antilles AN 1002
Bireli Swing 81	Austrophon JP 1009
Down in Town	Antilles ICT 1010
Foreign Affairs	Blue Note CD P 790 967 2
Acoustic Moments	Blue Note CD P 795 263 2
Inferno	EMI CD BLJ 48016
Live	Inak 865 CD
Standards	Blue Note CD 7802512
Bireli Lagrene Trio – Live	Dreyfus FDM36567 2 CD
My Favourite Django	Dreyfus FDM36574 2 CD

SELECTED READING

Profile	Downbeat, April 1985
Interview	Guitarist, May 1985
Interview	Guitar Player, March 1986
Profile	Downbeat, May 1989
Profile	Guitar World, January 1989
Profile	Guitarist, December 1989
Profile	Jazz Times, June 1991
Profile	Guitar International, June 1991

Django – A Jazz Tribute Video	View Video

Bireli Lagrene

PHOTO: CHRISTIAN ROSE COURTESY: DREYFUS RECORDS

NAPPY LAMARE
Born-HILTON NAPOLEON LAMARE
New Orleans, Louisiana, USA
14 June 1907
Died-Newhall, California, USA
8 May 1988

Nappy Lamare

Nappy Lamare began to study the banjo at the age of sixteen at the Warren Easton High School in New Orleans. For a short while he also played trumpet but his first professional work was playing banjo with Billy Lustig's band in the 'Little Club' in New Orleans. Lamare continued his career in New Orleans with several bands including those of Johnny Bayersdorffer, Sharkey Bonano, and Monk Hazel. Lamare then moved to New York and gained national prominence in September 1930 when he joined Ben Pollack's band on guitar. Bob Crosby formed his first band in 1935 and hired many of Pollack's best musicians, including Nappy Lamare.

In December 1942 Lamare, having joined Eddie Miller's band, moved to Hollywood. During the mid 1940s he often led his own small groups but in 1948 once more became a big band guitarist when he joined the Jimmy Dorsey Band. After leaving Dorsey, Lamare played in a night club in which he had a share. Throughout the 1950s and 1960s he was associated with drummer Ray Bauduc. In 1962 he was forced to stop working for a short while after a serious car crash. Over the next few years he worked regularly with Joe Darensbourg, Ray Bauduc and Bob Crosby. Lamare also worked in the Hollywood film studios and his guitar and banjo work was featured on the soundtracks of several Walt Disney films. In 1975 he toured Europe as part of a jazz package, and appeared at the Nice Jazz Festival in 1981. For a while Lamare led a New Orleans style jazz group at Disneyland in Anaheim.

SELECTED RECORDINGS

Bob Crosby and his Band	London HM65021 LP
Bob Crosby and his Orchestra	MCA 510134 LP
Riverboat Dandies	Capitol T877 LP
Eddie Miller's Orchestra	Affinity AFF 64 LP

SELECTED MUSIC

Blues for Guitar Five Solos	Capitol Songs Inc.

Nappy Lamare with the Bob Crosby Band.

Eddie Lang

EDDIE LANG
Born-SALVATORE MASSARO
Philadelphia, Pennsylvania, USA
25 October 1902
Died-Philadelphia, Pennsylvania, USA
26 March 1933

Eddie Lang was the son of a south Philadelphia banjo and guitar maker. Born Salvatore Massaro he decided to choose the name of a childhood basketball hero, Eddie Lang, for his professional career. He originally studied the violin and solfeggio at the age of seven with local teachers. He then began to teach himself, at the age of nine, to play the guitar on a small scale instrument built by his father. He attended the local high school with violinist, Joe Venuti. They often played together in their homes, and Venuti became Lang's closest friend until the guitarist's premature death in 1933. Their recordings were to be a major influence on Stephane Grappelli and Django Reinhardt in the early 1930s.

In 1920 Lang was hired by Philadelphia bandleader Charles Kerr. At that time he played four and six-string banjo. For the next three years Lang played with several bands in Philadelphia and Atlantic City. In 1924 Lang sat in on guitar with a novelty group, the 'Mound City Blue Blowers'. Their recording 'Arkansas Blue', which featured Lang, became a big hit. In August 1924 Lang decided to become a full time member of this group and this marked the real start of his career as America's number one jazz guitarist. The group toured England and then returned to Atlantic City. Here Joe Venuti often sat in with the group. In late 1925 Lang decided to leave the 'Mound City Blues Blowers' and to freelance with the best jazz musicians of the day.

Over the next few years Lang and Venuti were featured with many of the top bands including those of Jean Goldkette and Roger Wolfe Kahn. Eddie Lang's brilliant single note playing during the late 1920s with Venuti, Bix Beiderbecke, the Dorsey Brothers and Frank Trumbauer, marked the beginning of the guitar as a solo instrument in jazz, rather than as part of the rhythm section. Arrangers after hearing Lang, realized the potential of the guitar, and began to include important parts for the guitar in their band arrangements. Most banjo players, after hearing Lang's recordings in the late 1920s, realized the limitations of their instrument and changed over to the guitar.

The first of many historic recordings made by Venuti and Lang, 'Stringing the Blues', was made in 1926. During the period 1926-27 Lang was a featured soloist with Red Nichols and his Five Pennies. As a result Lang's enormous talent as a soloist and accompanist became widely known. His guitar work was much in demand by top band leaders of the day. Although a poor sight reader of music, Lang was fortunate to have perfect pitch and a photographic memory. Following many recording dates with Joe Venuti, Lang recorded with the legendary blues singer, Bessie Smith. Under the pseudonym of Blind Willie Dunn' Lang recorded many historic guitar duets with the outstanding New Orleans blues guitarist Lonnie Johnson. These recordings were mainly intended for a black audience and the producers thought that if Lang used his own name on the records sales would suffer.

In 1929 Paul Whiteman succeeded in hiring the Venuti/Lang team as part of his orchestra. It was during this time that Lang began a close friendship with Bing Crosby who was one of the band's vocalists. When Crosby left the Whiteman organisation in 1931 he was the nation's top male singer. He persuaded Lang to become his full-time accompanist. Eddie Lang had reached the top of his profession, and was generally regarded as the world's premier jazz guitarist. He was one of the highest paid musicians of the day. Tragically Lang died at the age of the thirty-one after complications developed following a routine tonsillectomy, bringing to an end one of the most brilliant careers in the history of jazz.

Eddie Lang, like most other legendary jazzmen who have died prematurely, left an incredible legacy. In the few years from 1924-1933, Lang laid down the path on which most jazz guitarists of the 1930s and later decades would follow.

SELECTED RECORDINGS

Boyd Senter Vol. 1	Harlequin HQ2044 LP
Jazz Guitar Virtuoso Eddie Lang	Yazoo 1059 LP
Stringing the Blues	CBS BPG62143 LP
Blue Guitars Vol.1	Parlophone PMC7019 LP
Blue Guitars Vol.2	Parlophone PMC7106 LP
Hot Strings	Black & White FPM17016 LP
Venuti/Lang/Rollini	Music For Pleasure MFP1161 LP
A Handful Of Riffs	ASV CD AJA 5061
Jazz Guitar Rarities-Eddie Lang	Suisa JZ CD 380
Joe Venuti/Eddie Lang	Jazz Portraits CD 14515
The Quintessential Eddie Lang 1925-1932	Timeless CBC 1-043 CD

SELECTED READING

Jazz Masters of the Twenties p.239-255	Hadlock Macmillan(1965)
The Guitar Players p.53-76 James Sallis	Quill(1983)
Great Guitarists p.133-136 Rich Kienzle	Facts On File (1985)
Article	Downbeat, August 1963
Profile	Guitar, February 1974
Article	Guitar Player, August 1983
Article	Guitar Player, April 1990
Article	Jazz Journal, April 1991
Article	Guitar Extra, Spring 1991

SELECTED MUSIC

Eddie Lang's Seven Compositions	Robbins Music Corporation
Eddie Lang's Fingerboard Harmony	Robbins Music Corporation

STEVE LAURY
Born-Vineland, New Jersey, USA
22 March 1953

Steve Laury

Steve Laury first began to play the guitar at the age of eleven. His first musical influences were blues guitarists such as B.B. King. After hearing some recordings by Wes Montgomery Laury decided he wanted to play jazz, and by the time he was eighteen was determined to make a career in music.

After moving to California Laury began to play with bassist Nathan East and Carl Evans. He first came to prominence as a member of the fusion group 'Fattburger'. He was lead guitarist and principal song writer for this group for five years. In 1990 he decided to go solo and signed an exclusive contract with Denon Records. His releases for this company as leader of his own group have established him as one of the leading USA jazz/fusion guitarists of the 1990s. Laury's career was brought to a sudden halt for a while after he was found to have cancer in July 1991. Fortunately intensive treatment brought him a full recovery and he is once more actively pursuing his career in contemporary jazz.

SELECTED RECORDINGS
Passion	Denon 81757 9043 2 CD
Keepin' The Faith	Denon CY-75283 CD

HARRY LEAHEY
Born-HAROLD LEAHEY
Plattsburgh, New York, USA
1 September 1935
Died-Plainfield, New Jersey, USA
12 August, 1990

Harry Leahey

Both Harry Leahey's parents were musical and it was they who encouraged their son to take an interest in music. Although he started playing the guitar at an early age, Leahey only took a serious interest in the instrument when he was thirteen. Inspired by the recordings of the leading jazz guitarists and other instrumentalists the young guitarist began to take lessons with guitarist Harry Volpe. After graduating from high school Leahey studied with Johnny Smith.

While he was in the army Leahey was fortunate to gain more playing experience including a spell with Ira Sullivan. After leaving the army Leahey got married and decided to make his living as a teacher and as a professional musician. He soon gained recognition as a fine jazz guitarist through his work with Eric Kloss, and then later in the early 1970s when he toured and recorded with the Phil Woods Quartet. Later he worked with other prominent musicians including Don Sebesky, Gerry Mulligan, Al Cohn and Michel Legrand. For many years he was affiliated to the teaching staff at the William Paterson State College in New Jersey.

Harry Leahey's two recordings as leader showed that he was talented guitarist who never gained wide recognition due to his early death from liver cancer in 1990.

SELECTED RECORDINGS
Still Waters Harry Leahey Trio	Omnisound N 1031 LP
Silver Threads Harry Leahey Duo	Omnisound N 1042 LP

214

WILLIAM G. LEAVITT
Born-WILLIAM GEORGE LEAVITT
Flint, Michigan, USA
4 October 1926
Died-Framingham, Nr. Boston, USA
4 November 1990

William Leavitt

William G. Leavitt is known to tens of thousands of jazz guitarists throughout the world by his many guitar method and musical exercise books published by the Berklee Press.

William Leavitt started playing a lap steel guitar as a youth, changing over to the regular six-string guitar in his teens. He played in local bands until he entered the US Coast Guard in 1946. Leavitt was an excellent cartoonist and did not know whether to make a career in commercial art or music. On leaving the Coast Guard in 1948 he made his decision. He entered the Berklee College of Music in Boston in its early stages as its third guitar student. He graduated in 1951 and was soon much in demand as an arranger, composer and guitarist. He worked with several top singers including Ella Fitzgerald, Andy Williams and Patti Page, and was featured in many recording sessions. He was co-author of the 1953 Les Paul and Mary Ford hit song, 'My Baby's Comin' Home'. In 1965 he was offered the position of Guitar Chairman at the Berklee school. He accepted, making his priority the provision of suitable books for teaching the guitar. The result was his three volume 'Modern Method For Guitar', reading studies and other related books. Over the years over 500,000 of the ten books for guitar written by William G. Leavitt have been sold.

Many of the top guitarists of today studied with Leavitt at Berklee. Included amongst these are John Abercrombie, Mike Stern, John Scofield, Leni Stern, Bill Frisell and Steve Vai. At the time of his death in 1990, after a stroke, he was the Berklee College of Music's Guitar Chairman Emeritus.

The contribution of William G. Leavitt to the advancement of the jazz guitar has been invaluable. Through the legacy of his methods and books this contribution will continue for the years to come.

SELECTED MUSIC

Modern Method For Guitar 3 Volumes	Berklee/Hal Leonard
Reading Studies for Guitar	Berklee/Hal Leonard
Advanced Reading Studies for Guitar	Berklee/Hal Leonard
Classical Studies For Pick Guitar	Berklee/Hal Leonard
Melodic Rhythms For Guitar	Berklee/Hal Leonard
Guitar Duets	Berklee/Hal Leonard

William Leavitt in the 1950s

PHIL LEE
Born-PHILIP ROBERT LEE
London, UK 8 April 1943

Phil Lee began to play the guitar at the age of 13. Both his parents were musical. A self-taught guitarist he joined guitarist Ivor Mairants's National Youth Orchestra at the age of 16. His first professional experience was playing in a theatre band and supporting popular pianist Joe 'Piano' Henderson. In the early 1960s he played with the John Williams Big Band. In 1964 he played in bassist Graham Collier's septet and in 1966 he joined organist Bob Stuckey's Quartet. During that time he also appeared with the Mike Gibbs' Band. From the early 1970's Lee has appeared with many leading British jazz musicians including Tony Coe, Henry Lowther, Brian Miller, Michael Garrick, Ken Baldock, Alan Ganley, Tony Faulkner and Norma Winstone. In 1979 he toured with Michel Legrand's quartet. As a freelance studio musician Lee has been one of Britain's busiest guitarists for many years. In 1983 he started teaching at the Guildhall School of Music and Drama in London.

Since the early 1980's Phil Lee has accompanied many top US jazz musicians visiting Europe, including Lee Konitz, Benny Goodman, Dardanelle, Eddie Daniels, Kenny Davern and Ken Peplowski. In recent times Lee has appeared and recorded in a duo with bassist Jeff Clyne, and played with Ron Mathewson's Sextet and the London Jazz Orchestra. He has most recently been associated with the Scott Stroman/Bobby Wellins quintet and in a duo with Martin Speake.

Phil Lee

PHOTO: ALAN BARNOWSKI

SELECTED RECORDINGS

Songs For My Father w/Graham Collier	DNA CD 001
Zeitgeist w/Tony Coe	EMC 3207
South of The Border w/Andrew Boiarsky	Spotlite SPJ LP18
Out Of Nowhere w/Dave Hancock Trio	Timeless SJP 303 CD
Twice Upon A Time w/Jeff Clyne	Cadillac SGCASCD 1
Gentle Piece w/John Horler	Spotlite SPJ - CD 542
Behind The Mask w/Pat Crumly	Spotlite SPJ - CD 554
Swingin' in London w/Dardanelle	Audiophile ACD-278
Amazing Grace w/Martin Speake	Spotlite SPJ - CD 558
New Perspectives	Spotlite SPJ - CD 559
Weaver of Dreams w/Elaine Delmar	Spotlite SPJ - CD 563

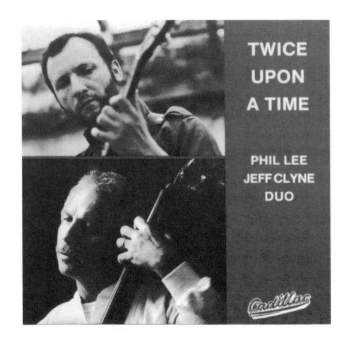

TWICE UPON A TIME

PHIL LEE JEFF CLYNE DUO

PETER LEITCH
Born-Ottawa, Canada
19 August 1944

Peter Leitch grew up in Montreal. He started to play the guitar at the age of sixteen. His main guitar influences were Kenny Burrell, Jim Hall, Wes Montgomery and Rene Thomas. He was fortunate to meet and see Thomas when the guitarist went to live in Montreal for five years from 1956. Working as a backing musician in local clubs Leitch was able to gain valuable experience working with many famous visiting jazz artists including Milt Jackson, Red Norvo and Kenny Wheeler. He first came to prominence as a jazz artist of importance after his performance on a Canadian recording with pianist Sadik Hakim in the early 1970s.

In 1983 Peter Leitch moved to New York where he soon made an impression on the local jazz scene. In 1984 he joined, and recorded with, the New York Jazz Guitar Ensemble. He also recorded with the Al Grey/Jimmy Forest Quartet, Oscar Peterson and Woody Shaw. He was a member of the Jaki Byard Big Band. His first recording in the USA as leader was on the Uptown label and featured the late Pepper Adams. In recent years Leitch has made several more recordings as leader of various trios and quartets on the Reservoir, Criss Cross and Concord labels. These have brought him the full international recognition his talent deserves.

Peter Leitch

SELECTED RECORDINGS

New York Jazz Guitar Ensemble - 4 On 6x5	Choice CRS 6831 LP
Red Zone	Reservoir RSR CD 103
Exhilaration	Reservoir RSR CD 116
On A Misty Night	Criss Cross Jazz 1026 CD
Mean What You Say	Concord CCD-4417
Peter Leitch Trio/Quartet 91	Concord CCD-4480
From Another Perspective	Concord CCD-4535
At First Sight – Duo w/Heiner Franz	Jardis JRCD9611
A Special Rapport	Reservoir RSR CD129
Duality w/John Hicks	Reservoir RSRCD134
Colors and Dimensions	Reservoir RSRCD140
Up Front	Reservoir RSRCD146
Portraits in Jazz	Radioland RACD 10006

SELECTED READING

Profile	Guitar Player, August 1993
Article	Jazz Times, July/August 1994
Interview	Just Jazz Guitar, November 1996

GAETANO LETIZIA
Born-Cleveland, Ohio, USA
27 February 1951

Gaetano (Tom) Letizia began to study jazz guitar at the age of fifteen. Over a period of years he studied jazz composition with Dr Walter Watson at Kent State University, classical guitar with Dr. Loris Chobanian at the Baldwin Wallace Conservatory, and participated in master classes with Joe Pass, Pat Martino and George Benson.

As a professional musician Letizia has given numerous jazz, classical, blues and rock concerts throughout the Mid west and East coast regions with a variety of groups. He was a member of the acclaimed Kent State University Lab Band, and was co-leader of the 20 piece Cleveland Jazz Workshop. A prolific composr Letizia has written orchestral, big band and small jazz group works, as well as jingles for commercials and industrial film scores. In recent times he has written a jazz mass, and is working on the design of a computerised composition system for Windows. He also acts as a national demonstrator for the Triggs Guitar Company.

Gaetano (Tom) Letizia

PHOTO: BILL PAPPAS

SELECTED RECORDINGS

Tom Letizia Album	TLR 001 CD
Digital Dance	TLR 002 CD
Chuckhole Blues	TLR 003 CD
Gaetano's Groove	TLR 004 CD
Dreamclipse	TLR 005 CD

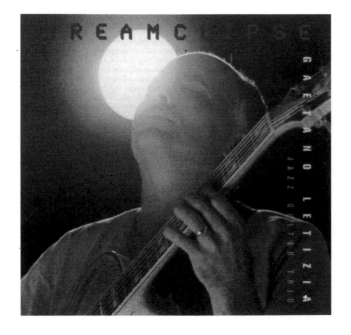

JEFF LINSKY
Born-Whittier, California, USA
12 April 1952

Jeff Linsky started to play the guitar at the age of ten. He soon developed an avid interest in both jazz and classical guitar. Although primarily self taught Linsky did have some lessons with classical/flamenco guitarist Vicente Gomez.

In his late teens Linsky moved to Hawaii and it was here that he developed his unique solo style combining jazz improvisation and swing with a classical technique. Over the years Linsky has enjoyed a busy life working as a solo artist in luxury hotels and cruise ships, but as his recordings on the Concord and Kamei labels show he has a distinctive jazz style of his own, often with a strong Latin influence.

Jeff Linsky is based mainly in the San Francisco area but has in recent years played in other major cities of the USA and Europe. His main instrument is a nylon strung small bodied requinto guitar which contributes greatly towards his distinctive sound.

Jeff Linsky

PHOTO: MAURICE J. SUMMERFIELD

SELECTED RECORDINGS
Up Late	Concord CCD-4363
Simpatico	Kamei KR 7001 CD
Solo	GSPJAZ 5000CD
Rendezvous	Kamei KR 7006 CD
Angel's Serenade	Concord CCD-4611
California	Concord CCD-4708
Passport to the Heart	Concord CCD-4764
Latin Jazz–Instructional Video	Mel Bay 97340VX

SELECTED READING
Interview	Guitar Player, August 1969
Profile	Fingerstyle Guitar, January/February 1997

SELECTED MUSIC
Jennifer's Waltz	Guitar Solo Publications

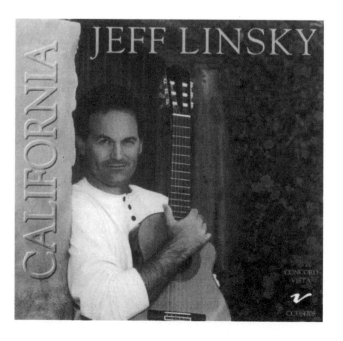

JEAN-PIERRE LLABADOR
Born-Nemours/Ghazaouat, Algeria
15 December 1952

Jean-Pierre Llabador

Both Jean-Pierre Llabador's parents were talented amateur musicians. His older brother played the guitar. The family moved to France in 1962 and over the next few years he enjoyed listeneing to popular and jazz music. When he was sixteen, inspired by some recordings of Jimi Hendrix, Llabador began to play the guitar. He took his first serious music lessons in 1972 when he attended the Montpellier Conservatoire. He gave up studying philosophy and languages at University to devote all his time to music. At the Conservatoire he studied classical guitar for three years and theory under Evelyne Haute-Labourdette.

In 1974 he founded the band 'Coincidences' with his brother Jean-Claude on keyboards. They enjoyed success and concertised all over Europe appearing in concerts with Larry Coryell, John Abercrombie and Weather Report. The band broke up after his brother's sudden death in 1978. In 1981 Llabador enrolled at the G.I.T. in Los Angeles for a year. There he studied with Joe Diorio, Pat Martino, Howard Roberts, Jay Graydon and Robben Ford.On his return to France he backed the popular singers Johnny Hallyday and Kim Wilde. In 1985 his first solo jazz guitar record was released, and in 1986 he toured with his quartet all over France appearing at jazz festivals. He also made many television and radio broadcasts. In 1992 Llabador was appointed Artistic Director of the O.J.L.R. (Region Languedoc Jazz Orchestra). In 1993 he performed in a guitar duo with Bernard Margarit, and in 1994 in the guitar quartet 'Four on Six'.

Jean-Pierre Llabador, whose individual guitar style mixes bebop and jazz fusion, is one of France's leading jazz guitarists of the 1990s.

SELECTED RECORDINGS

Coincidences	Ausfahrt EFA-06111 LP
5th Edition	Ausfahrt EFA-06144 LP

SELECTED READING

Interview	String Jazz, May/June 1995

CHUCK LOEB
Born-New York City, USA
15 December 1958

Chuck Loeb first began to play the guitar at the age of eleven. By the time he was thirteen he was playing professionally in local rock and rhythm and blues bands. He then became interested in jazz and after leaving high school went on to study at the Berklee College of Music in Boston. He also studied privately with Dennis Sandole, Jim Hall and Pat Metheny.

Since qualifying from Berklee Loeb has led a busy life as a jazz guitarist and also as a studio session musician. He has been featured on well over one thousand recording sessions for records, film scores, television programmes and commercials. He is also a prolific composer and has written several themes and soundtracks for network, cable and syndicated television series.

As a jazz artist Loeb has made five recordings as leader of his own group and has been a featured sideman on recordings of top jazz artists including Stan Getz, Eddie Daniels, Earl Klugh, Jim Hall, saxophonist Bill Evans, Bob Mintzer and others.

Chuck Loeb

PHOTO: COURTESY DMP RECORDS

SELECTED RECORDINGS

Chuck Loeb Quartet	Grapevine GVR 3304
Magic Fingers	DMP CD-472
Life Colors	DMP CD-475
Balance	DMP CD-484
Mediterranean	DMP CD-494
Stan Getz Quintet	Rare Bird BID 155501
Steps Ahead	Elektra MUS 96.0351-1
My Shining Hour	Bellaphon 53009 CD
Moon, Stars and the Setting Sun	Shanachie 5038 CD

SELECTED READING

Profile	JAZZIZ, May 1990
Profile	Jazz Times, May 1993

LORNE LOFSKY
Born-Toronto, Canada
10 May 1954

Lorne Lofsky received his first international recognition when he recorded for Norman Granz's Pablo label after a recommedation from Oscar Peterson. It was Peterson who produced this first recording in April 1980.

When Lofsky first started to play the guitar his main influences were blues and rock stars such as Jimmy Page and Eric Clapton. After hearing a jazz record by Ed Bickert and Paul Desmond he decided to enrol as a graduate of the jazz programme at York University in Toronto. Lofsky's main jazz influences were initially John Coltrane, Charlie Parker, Wynton Kelly, Bill Evans and Richy Byrack. After graduating from York University the young guitarist went to New York to study with saxophonist Lee Konitz. Following this Lofsky returned to York University to teach and also develop his career as a jazz artist in the Toronto area. He made a successful association with his fellow Canadian, guitarist Ed Bickert. They have played and recorded together on a regular basis from 1985 usually in a quartet with bassist Neil Swainson and drummer Jerry Fuller.

SELECTED RECORDINGS

It Could Happen To You Lorne Lofsky Trio	Pablo 2312-122
Lorne Lofsky/Ed Bickert Quartet	Unisson DDA-1002
This Is New - Ed Bickert/Lorne Lofsky	Concord CCD-4414
Bill, Please	Jazz Inspiration JID9307
Oscar Peterson in Paris	Telarc 2CD-83414

SELECTED READING

Profile	Jazz Times, August 1996

Lorne Lofsky

PHOTO: PHIL STERN/COURTESY PABLO RECORDS

A galaxy of French jazz guitarists. Left to right: Sacha Distel, Jean Pierre Sasson, Jimmy Gourley, Henri Crolla and Jean Bonal.

Mundell Lowe

MUNDELL LOWE
Born-Laurel, Missouri, USA
21 April 1922

Mundell Lowe first studied music with his father, a Baptist minister. He first began to play the guitar at the age of seven. Lowe left home at the age of fourteen and started to work with various bands around New Orleans. His father brought his son back home from New Orleans but Lowe persisted and was soon back on the road.

After three years in various groups, including those of Abbie Brunis and Sid Devilla, Lowe went in 1939 to Nashville. Here he joined the Pee Wee King band which was featured on the 'Grand Old Opry' radio show. He stayed with this group for about six months but once again had to return home with his father. After graduating in 1940 Lowe continued working as a musician in clubs in Louisiana, Florida, and Mississippi. In 1943 Lowe joined the army. Whilst he was stationed in Louisiana, he met another army private, John Hammond, the famous jazz critic and record producer. He was promoting jazz jam sessions and Lowe gained his first jazz experience taking part in these. It was Hammond that helped Lowe on his discharge in 1945 to gain the guitar seat in Ray McKinley's band. His two years with McKinley gave Lowe important professional experience . In 1947 he joined pianist Mary Lou Williams for a two year spell in New York City. After leaving Williams, Lowe played in several excellent small jazz groups, including those of Red Norvo, Wardell Gray, Fats Navarro, and Ellis Larkins. In 1950 he joined the NBC staff in New York. Lowe worked in the studios in New York for the next fourteen years. He also appeared and recorded with many jazz artists including Lester Young, Buck Clayton, Charlie Parker and Billie Holiday. During this period of his career Lowe developed an interest in the theatre and was hired for some small acting jobs, including a Broadway appearance in the play 'The Bird Cage'.

In 1965, after a vacation in California, Lowe decided to make his home there. Actor Jackie Cooper gave him the opportunity to write music on a regular basis for the ABC-TV series 'Love on a Rooftop'. This he did with great success. Lowe continued to write and arrange music for many other films, television and radio shows, including 'The Iron Horse', 'Wild Wild West', and 'Hawaii Five-O'. Although this involvement in the studios did not allow him to play jazz, Lowe was able to spend some time in music education. In this way he was able to train many young players in the art of the jazz guitar. In 1972, after composing the music for the highly successful film 'Billy Jack', Lowe began to freelance, including appearances in jazz clubs, in and around Los Angeles. In 1974 he toured Europe with singer Betty Bennett, and in 1975 played with the late tenor saxophonist Richie Kamuca. In the early 1980s he formed a jazz quartet called 'Transit West' with Sam Most, Monty Budwig and Nick Ceroli. They appeared at the 1983 Monterey Jazz Festival. Since that time Lowe has devoted most of his career to jazz, appearing at clubs and festivals all over the world.

SELECTED RECORDINGS '

Mundell Lowe Quintet	HMV DLP1084
Mundell Lowe Quartet	Riverside RLP204
Guitar Moods	Riverside RLP208
New Music of Alec Wilder	Riverside RLP219
A Grand Night for Swingers	Riverside RLP238
Gene Bianco Group	RCA Camden CAL-452
TV Action Jazz	RCA Camden CAL-522
Porgy and Bess	RCA Camden CDN132
Mundell Lowe All Stars	RCA Camden CAL-627
Sammy Davis Jnr & Mundell Lowe	Decca DL 8676
Satan in High Heels	Parker PLP4065
California Guitar	Famous Door HL102
Guitar Player	Dobre DR1007
The Incomparable Mundell Lowe	Dobre DR 1018
Richie	Concord CJ41
Transit West	Pausa PR 7152
Sweet'N Lovely Vol 1	Fresh Sound FSR CD-161
Sweet'N Lovely Vol 2	Fresh Sound FSR CD-162
Souvenirs	Jazz Alliance TJA 10011 CD
Old Friends w/Andre Previn	Telarc CD-83302
Uptown w/Andre Previn	Telarc CD-83303
2nd Time Around w/Sal Salvador	Westside WR2006 CD
The Return of the Great Guitars	Concord CCD-4715

SELECTED READING

Profile	Guitar Player, May/June 1972
Interview	Just Jazz Guitar, November 1995

SELECTED MUSIC

Guitar Impressions	Melrose Music Corporation
Mundell Lowe	Dick Grove Music

NICK LUCAS

Born-DOMINIC NICHOLAS
ANTHONY LUCANESE
Newark, New Jersey, USA
22 August 1897
Died-Colorado Springs, Colorado, USA
28 July 1982

Nick Lucas

Nick Lucas is reputed to have recorded the first guitar solos in the USA. His 1922 Pathe recording on acoustic guitar of his original solos 'Pickin The Guitar' and 'Teasin' The Frets' were to prove an inspiration to many guitarists over the next twenty years, including several important jazz guitarists. As a result, although Lucas was really more of a vaudeville and cabaret performer, his original guitar work was an important influence on the development of the early jazz guitar.

Nick Lucas's family were musical and he learnt music theory and harmony from an early age. He played the mandolin from the age of fifteen and by 1915 was playing guitar and mandolin with various bands, including those led by Sam Lanin and Mel Hallett, in the New York, New Jersey and Boston areas. It is claimed that Lucas pioneered the use of the guitar in the rhythm section at that time instead of the more popular banjo. In 1922 Lucas moved to Chicago where important club dates as a singer guitarist led to nationwide broadcasts on WEBH radio. His popularity on the radio as 'The Crooning Troubadour' and then as the 'The Singing Troubadour' led to a major contract with the Brunswick Record company. He was to make sixty-five singles for Brunswick.

By the mid 1920s Nick Lucas had become the premier 'pop' star of his day. The Gibson company released a 'Nick Lucas' guitar made to his own design. In 1926 he appeared in several Broadway shows and toured Europe. He sang 'Tip Toe Through The Tulips' in the 1929 film 'The Gold Diggers of 1929'. His recording of this popular song was to sell over five million copies. Lucas's success continued through the thirties into the sixties. He appeared in nightclubs, theatres, radio, films and later television as a headline performer. Nick Lucas is reputed to have sold over eighty four million records during his long career. He continued performing as a singer/guitarist until shortly before his death in 1982.

SELECTED RECORDINGS

Pioneers of Jazz Guitar	Yazoo 1057 CD
Souvenir Album	Accent ACS-5027 LP
Rose-Colored Glasses	Accent ACS-5043 LP
The Singing Troubadour	ASV Records AJA 5022 LP

SELECTED READING

Interview	Guitar Player, December 1980

SELECTED MUSIC

Nick Lucas	Guitar Method Vols 1 & 2

LAWRENCE LUCIE
Born-Emporia, Virginia, USA
18 December 1907

Lawrence Lucie was exposed to music from a child. His father was a violinist and his brother played the saxophone. They played in a hillbilly band playing for square dances. Lucie first started to play the piano at the age of seven but soon switched to the mandolin. He studied this instrument through a correspondence course. He was soon able to play in the group with his father and brother playing what would be today called bluegrass music.

In 1927 Lucie left for New York to study medicine. By that time he had already changed over to playing the banjo. Lucie then decided to make music his career and gave up his medical studies. He studied banjo with Luther Blake, a popular entertainer of the time. From there he went to study at the Brooklyn Conservatory and later to the Paramount Music Studio. It was at the Paramount that Lucie changed over to guitar, studying with Charles Ruopf and Anthony Antoine. In 1931 he was hired to play with the June Clark Band. After a few years with Clark Lucie played with violinist/arranger Lorenzo Caldwell. His first real big break in jazz came when Duke Ellington asked Lucie to deputise in his Cotton Club orchestra for Freddie Guy who had been hurt in an accident. In 1934 Lucie joined Benny Carter's new 'All Star Band' for a short while and then joined Fletcher Henderson's band. From 1934 to 1939 Lucie played rhythm guitar with the Henderson band and also one led by Lucky Millinder. In 1939 he joined the Coleman Hawkins orchestra and then later Lucie toured throughout the USA with Louis Armstrong.

In 1945 Lucie settled again in New York and formed his own group. Recent years had seen the advancement of the electric guitar so Lucie also began to use his guitar as a solo instrument. He played a wide variety of music, including be bop, with his group in many night spots and clubs all over the New York area. In the 1960's and 1970's Lucie worked in the New York recording studios and produced many albums in the rhythm and blues field, and later in rock. For a while he worked with bands led by drummers Louis Bellson and Cozy Cole. From 1971 Lucie worked as a jazz guitar teacher at the Borough of Manhattan Community College and also privately. In 1981 he appeared in a W.C. Handy Tribute Concert at the Carnegie Hall. In 1987 Lucie toured Europe with the Harlem Blues and Jazz Band.

Laurence Lucie with Velma Middleton, 1940.

SELECTED RECORDINGS

Cool and Warm Guitar	Toy T 1001 LP
Sophisticated Lady	Toy T 1003 LP
This Is It	Toy T 1005 CD
Traveling Guitars	Request 10037 LP
After Hours	Amber 202A LP
Larry Lucie and His Lucianaires	Solo 10017A LP

SELECTED READING

Interview	Guitar Player, February 1979
Interview	Storyville, August/September 1981

THIS IS IT...
...THE INNOVATOR

Lawrence Larry Lucie
GUITARIST

Nora Lee King Lucie
BASS

DOUG MACDONALD
Born-Philadelphia, Pennsylvania, USA
10 September 1953

Doug MacDonald

Doug MacDonald first began to play the guitar at the age of thirteen. He grew up in Hawaii where he played trombone in a school band. After hearing some blues recordings he decided to devote himself to the guitar. Soon after he was attracted to modern jazz and has confirmed that his early jazz influences include Thelonious Monk, Duke Ellington, Zoot Sims and Charlie Parker. The great jazz guitarists Charlie Christian, Wes Montgomery and Django Reinhardt were also to be important early influences on his musical development.

MacDonald worked as a professional musician in the early 1980s in the Las Vegas area. In 1984 he decided to settle in Los Angeles and since that time has established himself as one of the city's busiest guitarists. He has played with many top jazz musicians including Stan Getz, Joe Pass, George Shearing, Herb Ellis, Joe Williams, Sarah Vaughan, Ray Brown, Bob Cooper, Jack Sheldon and Buddy Rich.

SELECTED RECORDINGS

I've Got Minor Blues	Sharp Eleven Records
New York Session	Sharp Eleven Records
Doug MacDonald Quartet	Cexton Records CR 5678 CD
The Doug MacDonald Trio	Cexton Records CR 5680 CD
Warm Valley	Resurgent Music RM 111CD
Organizing	Resurgent Music RM 116CD

IAN MACGREGOR
Born-Droylsden, Manchester, UK
2 July 1942

Ian Macgregor

Ian Macgregor grew up in Renfrew, Scotland moving in 1960 to live in Southern England. Although he played the guitar briefly as a teenager he only began to play the instrument seriously at the age of 30. In 1979 he was a road manager for The Great Guitars when they toured the UK. In 1981 Macgregor moved to Perth, Australia. Here he began his career as one of Australia's leading personalities in the jazz guitar world. In 1989 he founded the Jazz Guitar Society of Western Australia with guitarist/vibes player Gary Lee. This non-profit organisation has over the last 18 years been instrumental in bringing some of the world's finest jazz guitarists to Australia including Joe Pass, Martin Taylor, Barney Kessel, Herb Ellis, Charlie Byrd, Peter Leitch and Emily Remler. Macgregor also produces a bi-monthly newsletter which helps promote interest in the jazz guitar.

By profession Ian Macgregor is a businessman but he also plays regularly in a local 18 piece big band and leads his jazz trio in clubs in the Perth Area.

SELECTED READING
JGSWA Newsletter   All Issues

BILLY MACKEL
Born-JOHN WILLIAM MACKEL
Baltimore, Maryland, USA
28 December 1912
Died-Baltimore, Maryland, USA
5 May 1986

Billy Mackel is well known to jazz big-band lovers through his thirty years as guitarist with the Lionel Hampton band.

Mackel's first work as a professional musician was on the banjo in the 1930s. After changing to guitar he led his own band in Baltimore until he joined the Hampton band in 1944. This position he held almost exclusively until the mid 1970s. In the 1960s he did work as an accompanist for a short while with a vocal quartet led by Billy Williams.

Billy Mackel's ability as a soloist was hardly recognised during his long stay with the Lionel Hampton band. However he made a recording for the Black & Blue label in Paris in 1977 as leader of his own quintet featuring Milt Buckner on organ and Frankie Dunlop on drums. This recording leaves positive proof of Mackel's ample ability as a jazz guitar soloist.

SELECTED RECORDINGS

Lionel Hampton And His Giants	Timeless SJP 120 LP
Lionel Hampton And His Paris All Stars	Vogue 400068DP LP
Billy Mackel At Last	Black & Blue 33.117 LP
Lionel Hampton Band Video	Milan Jazz 791 285

Billy Mackel

IVOR MAIRANTS
Born-Rypin, Poland
18 July 1908
Died-London, UK
20 February 1998

Ivor Mairants was well known throughout the world to guitarists of all styles. After over 60 years as a professional guitarist, teacher, composer and leading UK musical instrument retailer, he devoted the last few years of his life to composing and writing for the guitar.

Ivor Mairants came with his family to the United Kingdom in 1913. He took up the banjo at the age of 15 and became a professional musician at the age of 20. From the 1930s he was a featured banjoist and then guitarist of many of Britain's leading dance bands including those of Ambrose, Roy Fox, Lew Stone, Geraldo and Ted Heath. In the 1960s and 1970s his outstanding guitar playing was often heard on television, radio, film soundtracks, and on many recordings with the popular Mantovani orchestra, and with Manuel and his Music of the Mountains. His recording of the 'Adagio' from Joaquin Rodrigo's 'Concierto de Aranjuez' with Manuel sold over one million copies. His guitar quintet broadcast regularly in the late 1950s on the BBC's 'Guitar Club' series.

Of particular importance to guitarists is the fact that Ivor Mairants devoted so much of his time to writing music and instructional methods for the guitar. His solo and technique books for all styles of guitar playing, from publishers both in the UK and the USA, have enjoyed great success.

In the 1950s Ivor Mairants established his Central School of Dance Music in London. All instruments were taught at this innovative establishment, but special emphasis was given to the guitar. Several of his ex-pupils are today Britain's top guitarists. In 1958, together with his wife Lily, he opened The Ivor Mairants Musicentre. This was Britain's first specialist guitar store and it was situated in the heart of London's West End. For many years some of the world's best guitars and guitar accessories were introduced into Britain by Ivor Mairants at his store. The Ivor Mairants Musicentre became a Mecca for professional guitarists, and for amateur guitarists at all levels of ability. Because of his unique knowledge and music skills, Ivor Mairants was over the years often employed as a specialist consultant for leading instrument makers and importers.

From the 1930s Ivor Mairants was a prolific columnist in several leading music journals including Melody Maker, BMG and Classical Guitar. In 1980 his highly acclaimed biography

Ivor Mairants

PHOTO: COURTESY IVOR MAIRANTS

'My Fifty Fretting Years' was published by Ashley Mark Publishing in the UK, and in 1995 his marvellous opus, 'The Great Jazz Guitarists' -probably the most complete collection of note-for-note transcriptions of historic jazz guitar solos - was published by Music Maker Publications in Cambridge, UK.

Ivor Mairants made a unique and outstanding contribution to the world of guitar in Britain. Over the past 50 years there can be few British guitarists who have not benefited from this contribution. He was a member of the Worshipful Company of Musicians, a prestigious and ancient British guild, and a Freeman of the City of London. In 1997 The Worshipful Company of Musicians inaugurated a new annual competition The Ivor Mairants Guitar Award, which will remain an important part of the enormous legacy this irreplaceable figure has left for future generations of guitarists.

SELECTED RECORDING
Focus On Ivor Mairants	Zodiac CAS 1099

SELECTED READING
My Fifty Fretting Years- Ivor Mairants	Ashley Mark (1980)
The Great Jazz Guitarists	Music Maker Books (1994)

SELECTED MUSIC
New Swing Series-6 Solos	Bosworth & Co.
Six Evergreen Favourites	Campbell Connoly
Favourite Solos	Cavendish Music Co.
Eight Guitar Solos/Shearing Style	Robbins Music Co.
Seven Swinging Standards	Francis,Day and Hunter
Six Solos for Plectrum Guitar	Francis,Day and Hunter
Walking with Wes	Mills Music Co.
Spirit of New Orleans/Bundle of Blues	Hansen Music
Modern Chord Encyclopedia	Francis,Day and Hunter
Book of Daily Exercises	Francis,Day and Hunter
Arranging for the Guitar	Hansen Music
The Complete Guitar Experience	Mel Bay Publishing Company
Perfect Pick Technique	Ashley Mark
Famous Jazz Guitar Solos Vol 1	IMP

RUSSELL MALONE
Born-Albany, Georgia, USA
8 November 1963

Russell Malone's mother, a church organist, bought him a plastic toy guitar when he was four years old. By the time he was six Malone was playing the guitar in church. At the age of ten he began listening to the records of top country and blues guitarists. When he was 12 he saw a TV broadcast of George Benson playing with the Benny Goodman band. From that time on he devoted himself to playing and studying jazz. After graduating from high school he started his first professional gig playing in a local jazz club.

For a while Malone combined day jobs working as either a bricklayer or cook in a fast food restaurant, together with a night time job as a professional musician. He often backed visiting singers and musicians including Patti Austin, Little Anthony, Regina Belle and Peabo Bryson. In 1987 jazz organist Jimmy Smith invited him to join his trio. Malone gained further national and international prominence when in the early 1990s he recorded and toured the USA with Harry Connick Jnr's orchestra.

Russell Malone was a featured performer in Robert Altman's 1996 film 'Kansas City'. He has made several recordings as leader for Columbia Records and appeared in concert with diverse jazz artists including Benny Green, Eddie Vinson, Mulgrew Miller, Kenny Barron, Gary Mazzaroppi and Roy Hargrove. Malone has gained further international fame in recent times as the featured guitarist of singer/pianist Diana Krall's highly successful trio.

Russell Malone

PHOTO: MICHAEL HALSBAND

SELECTED RECORDINGS

Russell Malone	Columbia 472261 2 CD
Black Butterfly - Russell Malone	Columbia CK 53912 CD
Russell Malone Quartet - Wholly Cats	Venus TKCV 79302 CD
All For You w/Diana Krall	Impulse 182CD
Only Trust Your Heart w/Diana Krall	GRP 9810CD
Love Scenes w/Diana Krall	Impulse 90074CD

SELECTED READING

Profile	Downbeat, October 1993
Profile	Guitar Player, April 1994

JACK MARSHALL
Born-JACK WILTON MARSHALL
El Dorado, Kansas, USA
23 November 1921
Died-Huntington Beach, California, USA
2 September 1973

Jack Marshall began playing the ukulele at the age of ten, changing over to the guitar when he was thirteen. His first major influence was Django Reinhardt. Marshall's family moved to California in the late 1930s. In 1938 he bought his first electric guitar after his graduation from Hollywood High School. Marshall was fortunate to meet and hear Oscar Moore who at that time was the featured guitarist with the Nat 'King' Cole trio. Occasionally he would sit in for Moore. Marshall also sat in with the virtuoso jazz pianist Art Tatum, and Count Basie in the Central Avenue clubs in downtown Los Angeles.

When he was eighteen, Marshall played on a weekly radio programme with the Los Angeles City College jazz band. From 1940-42 he was a staff guitarist for the MGM studios, replacing Bobby Sherwood in November 1940. From 1942-46 he served in the US army. Whilst in the army Marshall studied both music and engineering. In 1946, after leaving the army, Marshall enrolled at the USCLA to study engineering. In the evenings he played in local jazz clubs, and also worked for the CBS. After gaining his engineering degree, Marshall began to work again for the MGM studios. When he was twenty nine he decided to study music theory and harmony with the prominent musicologist and guitarist, Albert Harris. Marshall also began to study the classical guitar. Whilst studying for a Master's Degree in structural civil engineering, he finally decided that he wanted to devote his career to writing and arranging music. Over the next few years Marshall wrote for over three hundred television programmes, and films. He wrote a guitar concerto for his cousin, the prominent classical guitarist Christopher Parkening. He edited one of Igor Stravinsky's works for guitar, and also recorded an album of Russian folk songs with this famous classical composer. His duo recordings with percussionist/jazz drummer, Shelley Manne, in the early 1960s are both innovative and brilliant. Marshall's vocal arrangements for Peggy Lee, Doris Day, Vic Damone and others have been heard on these famous singers' recordings by millions of people all over the world. He also worked and recorded with Shorty Rogers, Andre Previn, Stan Kenton, Barney Kessel, Al Hendrickson, Howard Roberts, Laurindo Almeida and many more top jazz artists.

Jack Marshall

In 1967 Marshall persuaded the owners of the Donte's club in Burbank, Los Angeles, to start a weekly guitar night. For several years the club attracted many of America's finest jazz guitarists. In September 1973, at the height of his very successful career, Marshall tragically collapsed and died from a heart attack. As a tribute to his memory Los Angeles guitarists and musicians arranged a benefit concert at Donte's. The money raised from this event helped establish a permanent music scholarship in Jack Marshall's name at the University of Southern California.

SELECTED RECORDINGS

Sounds Unheard Of Duo w/Shelley Manne	Contemporary LAC539 LP
Sounds Duo w/Shelley Manne	Capitol ST 2610 LP
18th Century Jazz	Capitol T1108 LP
Soundsville	Capitol T1194 LP
Shorty Rogers/Andre Previn Orchestra	RCA NL89308 LP

SELECTED READING

Profile	Guitar Player,	October 1972
Tribute	Guitar Player,	March 1974

SELECTED MUSIC

West Coast Guitar	Leeds Music
Bossa Nova Guitar	MCA Music
20 Popular Introductions and Endings	MCA Music
Guitar Get Together Vols.1 & 2	MCA Music
The Art of Finger Style Guitar	MCA Music

PAT MARTINO
Born-PAT AZZARA
Philadelphia, Pennsylvania, USA
25 August 1944

Pat Martino was exposed to the guitar at a very early age, as his father was a singer who also played the guitar. He listened to recordings from his father's collection including albums by Eddie Lang, Django Reinhardt, and Johnny Smith.

Martino received some lessons from a cousin and then studied with a local guitarist, Dennis Sandhole. By the time he was fifteen he was playing professionally with the rhythm and blues bands of Lloyd Price, Willis Jackson, and others. In the early 1960s Martino played in combos led by various organists including those of Jimmy Smith, Jimmy McGriff, Jack McDuff, and Richard 'Groove' Holmes. He then worked as a sideman with several jazz groups including those of saxophonists Sonny Stitt and John Handy. In 1967 Martino made the first of several recordings on the Prestige label, as leader of his own group. Within one year his exceptional technique and exciting improvisations brought great admiration from jazz critics and fans alike. At first Pat Martino's guitar style was greatly influenced by Wes Montgomery. He then made a serious study of eastern music, and then, over a period of years, developed his own distinctive jazz/rock fusion style. Martino also experimented and played with guitar synthesisers, and an electric twelve-string guitar.

In 1980 Martino suffered an aneurism on the brain. A succesful operation saved his life but he was unable to play for almost a year. It was another three years before he returned again to playing professionally. His recent recordings show that Pat Martino remains a major jazz force.

Pat Martino

Interview	Guitar Player, September 1973
Profile	Downbeat, October 1975
Interview	Coda, March 1976
Profile	Guitar Player, June 1977
Profile	Downbeat, June 1988
Interview	Guitar Player, September 1995
Article	Jazz Times, December 1995
Interview	20th Century Guitar, January 1996
Interview w/Les Paul	Downbeat, March 1997
Interview	Just Jazz Guitar, May 1997
Article	Jazz Times, August 1997

SELECTED MUSIC

Linear Expressions	REH
Pat Martino The Early Years	CPP/Belwin

SELECTED RECORDINGS

Hombre	Prestige 7513/OJC-195 CD
Strings	Prestige 7547/OJC-223 CD
East	Prestige 7562/OJC-248 CD
Desperado	Prestige 7795/OJC-397 CD
Baiyina	Prestige 7589/OJC-355 CD
The Visit	Cobblestone 9015 LP
Live	Muse 5026 CD
Consciousness	Muse 5039 CD
Exit	Muse 5075 CD
We'll be Together Again	Muse 5090 CD
Joyous Lake	Warner Bros. BS2977 LP
The Return	Muse M5328 CD
Interchange	Muse M5529 CD
Nightwings	Muse M5552 CD
All Sides Now	Blue Note 37627 CD

Creative Force Vols. 1 and 2 – Instructional Videos	REH/CPP
Analysis of a Tune Instructional Video	REH/CPP
Advanced Concepts Instructional Video	REH/CPP

SELECTED READING

Profile	Downbeat, February 1969

CARMEN MASTREN
Born-CARMEN NICHOLAS MASTANDREA
Cohoes, New York, USA
6 October 1913
Died-Valley Stream, Long Island, USA
31 March 1981

Carmen Mastren

Carmen Mastren originally began his musical career playing banjo and violin, but changed to the guitar in 1931. He came from a musical family, his four brothers were all musicians. He first played professionally in the family band. Mastren's first major break came when he joined Wingy Manone's band in 1935 in New York City. Then from 1936-40 he played with the Tommy Dorsey Band. Mastren's distinctive acoustic guitar breaks, and fill-ins, were often featured in the band's arrangements. In 1939 and 1940 he won Metronome magazine's readers' poll.

In 1941 Mastren played with Joe Marsala, and later with Ernie Holst. He worked as a member of the NBC staff until 1943 when he was drafted into the Army. During his military service Mastren was fortunate to be given the guitar seat in Glenn Miller's Air Force band. On leaving the Army in 1946 he returned to working in the New York studios.

From 1947 Carmen Mastren began to conduct and arrange, and had little connection with jazz. From 1953-70 he worked full time for the NBC in New York. From 1971, until the time of his death, he freelanced, wrote jingles for television advertisements, and was sometimes featured with the New York Jazz Repertory Company. He also appeared in 1974 in the Broadway show, 'Over Here', with the Andrews Sisters.

SELECTED RECORDINGS
Adrian Rollini and Friends	Black & White FPM1-7010 LP
Joe Marsala and His Delta Four	Affinity CD AFS 1012 LP
Tommy Dorsey and His Clambake Seven	Bluebird ND 83140 LP
Glenn Miller's Uptown Hall Gang	Esquire 302 LP
Bechet Original Sessions 1940	Jazz Anthology 30JA-5109 LP
Bechet/Spanier Quartet	Ember SE8023 LP

Carmen Mastren with the American Air Force Band

DICK McDONOUGH

Born-RICHARD TOBIN McDONOUGH
New York City, USA
30 July 1904
Died-New York City, USA
25 May 1938

Dick McDonough

Dick McDonough was the fourth of five children, of a New York clothing manufacturer. His mother was a talented pianist. As a high school student he became fascinated with his brother's mandolin and soon taught himself to play it. In his senior year at school McDonough began to play the banjo. McDonough attended Georgetown University, graduating in 1925. He then went to Columbia Law School, as his mother wanted him to be a lawyer. But his love of music made him abandon law to start a career as a professional musician on banjo, and then later on guitar.

McDonough soon became one of the busiest session men in the late 1920s and early 1930s. In 1925 he played with the orchestras of Ross Gorman and Earl Carrol. In October 1925 he made his first recording on guitar, backing vocalist Cliff Edwards (Ukulele Ike). McDonough soon developed a style of guitar playing that set unsurpassed standards until the arrival of the electric guitar at the end of the 1930s

McDonough's virtuosity on the instrument, and great musical talent, ensured that he was one of the busiest musicians in New York City. McDonough not only led his own radio and recording band, but was a featured soloist on hundreds of recordings with other bands, including those of Red Nichols and the Dorsey Brothers. In early 1934 he made the first of some historic guitar duo records with Carl Kress.

In May 1938 Dick McDonough collapsed with a ruptured ulcer in the NBC New York studios. He was rushed to hospital for an emergency operation which tragically failed to save his life.

SELECTED RECORDINGS
Dick McDonough and Carl Kress	Jazz Archives JA-32 LP
Pioneers of Jazz Guitar	Yazoo L-1057 CD
Fifty Years of Jazz Guitar	Columbia 33566 LP
Fun on the Frets	Yazoo L-1061 CD
The Guitarists 'Giants Of Jazz'	Time Life 12 LP
Dick McDonough and his Orchestra	EVA-1700 2 CD

SELECTED READING
Profile	Guitar, March 1974
Article	Guitar Player, October 1978
Profile	Guitar World, March 1986

SELECTED MUSIC
McDonough/Kress Duets	Robbins Music Corporation

Dick McDonough with Carl Kress, 1937.

235

John McLaughlin

JOHN McLAUGHLIN
**Born-Kirk Sandell, near Doncaster, UK
4 January 1942**

John McLaughlin

PHOTO: COURTESY CBS RECORDS

McLaughlin was born into a musical family. His mother was a violinist, and his three brothers and sister were musicians. Music, mainly classical, was always in the background in his home, but it was not until McLaughlin was nine that he first took a few piano lessons. Three years later he began to play the guitar, inspired by the recordings of blues guitarists Big Bill Broonzy, Muddy Waters, and Leadbelly.

At the age of fourteen McLaughlin began to listen to recordings of jazz guitarists including those of Django Reinhardt, Tal Farlow, Jim Hall and Barney Kessel. His musical development began to be directed towards modern jazz. He led his own jazz band at school, and in the next few years broadened his musical taste studying the music of Miles Davis and John Coltrane, and classical masters Bartok and Debussy. These influences all helped McLaughlin develop his very individual style and approach to music in general.

For the next six years McLaughlin gained important professional experience playing in all types of groups, mainstream to avant garde, and also in rhythm and blues bands. In his late teens McLaughlin lived in the Newcastle upon Tyne area and played in local jazz bands including Pete Deuchar's Professors of Ragtime, and Mike Carr's Quintet. He moved to London when he was twenty-one and gained his first major job with the 'Graham Bond Organization'. Other musicians in this group included bassist Jack Bruce and drummer, Ginger Baker. McLaughlin also played with artists such as Georgie Fame, Tony Oxley, John Surman and Brian Auger. During his years in London McLaughlin experimented with many of the concepts that are now regarded as everyday techniques in most jazz/rock fusion guitarists' playing. He also became interested in Eastern philosophy and religion. In the late 1960s he went to Germany for a few months. Here he played in a free jazz group led by Gunter Hampel.

In 1969 McLaughlin moved to the USA to work with drummer Tony Williams's group 'Lifetime'. Williams was a great admirer of McLaughlin's original and vigorous style, as was Miles Davis. The famous trumpeter later included McLaughlin on several of his recordings. A great turning point in McLaughlin's career ocurred in the spring of 1970 when he met the guru, Sri Chinmoy. This meeting changed McLaughlin's attitude to life. It also gave him the motivation to form his own group and play a new style of music which was greatly influenced by Indian music. The outcome was the first 'Mahavishnu' Orchestra. In this band McLaughlin usually played on a specially built twin-neck guitar. For many jazz enthuiasts the exotic sounds and rhythms of the Mahavishnu were the best thing to happen to both jazz and rock music for a long time.

From 1975 McLaughlin's love for the East and its way of life continued to influence his playing. In 1976 he formed a new group called 'Shakti'. It was made up of Indian instrumentalists and vocalists, and caused as big a sensation on the contemporary jazz scene as the original Mahavishnu orchestra had done. In this group McLaughlin played a specially built acoustic Gibson guitar, designed by Abe Wechter, which incorporated 'drones' (opcn strings), normally found on Indian instruments.

After Shakti split up in 1978 McLaughlin returned to playing electric guitar with his new jazz-rock group called, 'One Truth Band'. This group did not last long and he returned to playing an acoustic guitar in a trio with jazz guitarist Larry Coryell, and flamenco virtuoso Paco de Lucia. This trio achieved great success establishing a new format in jazz, the acoustic guitar trio blending improvised music from America, Europe and the East. This trio continued its success into the 1980s with Al DiMeola replacing Coryell.

237

In 1975 McLaughlin decided to return to Europe and make his home in Paris, France. Here he sometimes played in an acoustic guitar duo with Christian Escoude. In 1984 he appeared on the Miles Davis recording, 'You're Under Arrest'. In November 1985 he premiered Mike Gibb's guitar concerto, 'Mediterranean Concerto', with the Los Angeles Philharmonic, in Los Angeles. In the same year he formed another Mahavishnu group with drummer Billy Cobham, featuring saxophonist Bill Evans. In 1988 McLaughlin began an acoustic duo with Indian percussionist Trilok Gurtu. This duo later expanded into a trio and their 1989 concert at the Royal Festival Hall in London was released on record.

SELECTED RECORDINGS

Emergency w/Tony Williams Lifetime	Polydor 849 068
Bitches Brew w/Miles Davis	Columbia GP26
Extrapolation	Polydor 841 598
My Goals Beyond	Elektra/Musician E1-60031
John McLaughlin Electric Guitarist	Columbia JC 35326
Electric Dreams	Columbia JC 35785
Mahavishnu-Inner Worlds	Columbia 33908
Mahavishnu-Apocalypse	Columbia KC 32957
Shakti-Natural Elements	Columbia JC 34980
Love, Devotion, Surrender w/Santana	Columbia CK 32034
Where Fortune Smiles	Pye 12103
Belo Horizonte	Warner Bros BSK-3619
Music Spoken Here	Warner Bros 1-23723
Spaces w/ Larry Coryell	Vanguard VMD 79345

Friday Night in San Francisco	FC 37152
Passion, Grace & Fire	FC 38645
Live at the Royal Festival Hall	Polygram JMT 834 436-214 CD
Mediterranean Concerto	Columbia MK 45578
Que Alegria	Verve 837 280 2 CD
Time Remembered	Verve 519 861 2 CD
The Free Spirts	Philips 521-870-2 CD
The Promise	Verve 529-828-2 CD
Adventures in Radioland	Verve 519-397-2 CD
After the Rain	Verve 527-467-2 CD
The Heart of the Things	Verve 539-153-2 CD

SELECTED READING

Article	Downbeat, June 1973
Article	Downbeat, June 1974
Interview	Guitar Player, December 1972
Interview	Guitar Player, February 1975
Profile	Guitar, March 1975
Profile	Downbeat, June 1978
Interview	Guitar Player, August 1978
Profile	Downbeat, April 1982
Profile	Guitar World, March 1985
Interview	Guitar Player, September 1985
Interview	Guitarist, August 1988
Profile	Downbeat, May 1991
Interview	Jazz Times, July/August 1992
Profile	Jazz The Magazine, Issue 12 1992
Article	Downbeat, December 1993
Interview	Guitar Player, April 1996
Article	Jazz Times, May 1996

Mahavishnu Orchestra

Shakti

LOU MECCA
Born-LOUIS JOHN MECCIA
Passaic, New Jersey, USA
23 December 1926

Lou Mecca appeared briefly as a Blue Note recording artist in the 1950s. His crisp jazz guitar style was impressive and it is was a great loss to jazz world that he left the music scene in the late 1950s.

Mecca first studied the trumpet at the age of eight under the guidance of his father, a professional trumpeter with various symphony orchestras. After finding the trumpet did not suit him he changed to the guitar at the age of nine. He left high school in his fourth year to become a professional musician. He took a day job as a teacher at a music school in New Jersey and played in bars and clubs at night. Mecca also took up the trumpet again playing for a season with the Clifton Symphony Orchestra.

In 1947 Mecca met and befriended Johnny Smith. This famous guitarist proved to be a great influence on Mecca's jazz guitar style. In 1955 Mecca recorded as leader of his own quartet which featured Jack Hitchcock on vibraphone, Vinnie Burke on bass and Jimmy Campbell on drums.

However Mecca realised that as a musician he may not be able to support a family. So for six years he went to school in the evenings in New York to study to become a chiropractic physician. In the daytime he taught students and continued to perform in various clubs and private functions. In 1967 Mecca graduated from the Chiropractic Institute of New York, and for the next 25 years he practised as a physician in New Jersey and only occasionally played the guitar at various clubs. In 1992 Mecca retired from being a chiropractic physician and took a sabbatical. He taught himself to play the piano and continued to play the guitar. In 1996 Mecca moved to Florida for a year. There he made several appearances on guitar, including SUNFEST 97 with Vinnie Burke on bass, Buddy Brower on keyboard and James Martin on drums. Mecca made several appearances at the Mellon Patch Inn, Hutchinson Island, FL, and performed with several musicians at "Jazz on the Lawn" including Vinnie Burke on bass, Tony Argo on accordion and Buddy Brower on keyboard, and Tom Lund on drums.

Mecca moved back to New Jersey in 1997 and now devotes his time to his first love, music and the guitar.

SELECTED RECORDINGS
Gil Melle Quintet	Blue Note 5054 LP
Gil Melle Quintet	Blue Note 5063 LP
Lou Mecca Quartet	Blue Note 5067 LP

Lou Mecca

PHOTO: STICKLER'S PHOTOGRAPHY

Jazz on the Lawn	Mason Records 1300
Eclectic Strings	Mason Records 1313
Bridging the Gap - Lou Mecca Trio	Freehold MM-1313 276CD

SELECTED READING
Interview	Just Jazz Guitar, May 1995

PAT METHENY
Born-Lee Summit, Missouri, USA
12 August 1954

Pat Metheny has been one of the major jazz/rock guitarists since the early 1970s. Metheny's first musical instrument was the French horn. He started to play the guitar at the age of thirteen. His first jazz influences were trumpeter Miles Davis and guitarist Wes Montgomery. Whilst still at high school in Kansas City Metheny played in various jazz groups. He won a Downbeat magazine scholarship to a stage band camp. Here he met Atilla Zoller who invited him to come to New York and experience the jazz scene there at first hand. After this visit Metheny made the decision to make a career in music and jazz.

After Metheny left school he went to the University of Miami. There he taught guitar, as well as doing local club and studio work, for a year. His first major professional break came at the age of nineteen when he met vibraphonist Gary Burton in Wichita, Kansas. Burton was greatly impressed by Metheny's talent and helped him gain a teaching post at the Berklee College of Music in Boston. Burton was also instrumental in getting a recording contract for Metheny with the prominent German company ECM. Within a short period of time Metheny became one of ECM's best selling recording artists. Some of his albums for this company have sold over 100,000 copies.

After leaving Burton's group in 1977, Metheny formed his own group with keyboardist Lyle Mays. This union has proved to be one of the most successful in contemporary jazz. Since the mid 1970s Metheny has played, and recorded with, many of the finest jazz artists of the day including; Steve Swallow, Paul Bley, Jaco Patorious, Sonny Rollins, Charlie Haden, Mike Brecker, Jack DeJohnette, Dave Liebman, Ornette Coleman, and Eberhard Weber. He also backed singer Joni Mitchell for a major concert tour. Metheny has also proved to be a talented composer, and has written the musical scores for three films. By 1985 three of Metheny's twelve record albums had won Grammy awards.

In jazz terms Pat Metheny is a superstar. His concerts play to sell-out audiences all over the world, and every new record release enjoys excellent sales. A talented composer and improvisor, Metheny has become one of the most inspired and influential jazz/rock fusion guitarists of the day.

Pat Metheny

SELECTED RECORDINGS

Bright Size Life-Pat Metheny Trio	ECM 1073 CD
Water Colours-Pat Metheny Trio	ECM 1097 CD
Pat Metheny Group	ECM 1114 CD
New Chautauqua	ECM 1131 CD
American Garage	ECM 1155 CD
80/81	ECM 1180/1 2CD
As Falls Witchita, So Falls Wichita Falls	ECM 1190 CD
Offramp	ECM 1216 CD
Travels	ECM 1252/3 2CD
Rejoicing	ECM 1271 CD
First Circle	ECM 1278 CD
Works	ECM 823270-2 CD
Song X	Geffen 924096 CD
Question and Answer	Geffen 24293 CD
Secret Story	Geffen 24468 CD
Still Life (Talking)	Geffen 24145 CD
The Road To You	Geffen 24601 CD
I Can See Your House From Here	Blue Note 27765 CD
Missouri Sky Duo w/Charlie Haden	Verve 314 537 130 2 CD
Pat Metheny Quartet	Geffen 24978 CD

SELECTED READING

Profile	Guitar Player, March 1976
Profile	Crescendo, May 1978
Profile	Downbeat, July 1978
Interview	Guitar, September 1978
Profile	Guitar World, September 1980
Profile	Downbeat, November 1982
Profile	Guitar World, May 1985
Profile	The Wire, May 1985
Profile	JAZZIZ, August 1992
Profile	Jazz The Magazine, Issue 14, 1992
Interview	Guitarist, September 1992
Interview	Guitar Player, September 1992
Profile	Jazz Times, August 1993
Interview	Downbeat, June 1986
Interview	Downbeat, August 1989
Article	JAZZIZ, February 1995
Article	Downbeat, April 1995
Article	Jazz Times, April 1997
Interview	Acoustic Guitar, April 1997
Article	Downbeat, February 1998
Article	JAZZIZ, February 1998

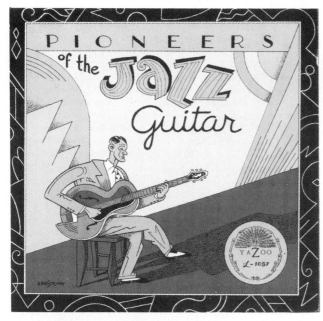

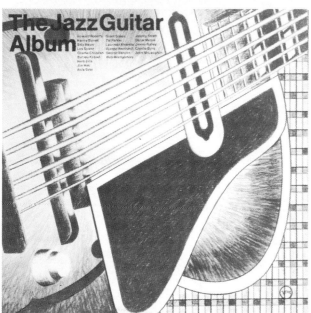

A selection of fine jazz guitar recordings from the 1920s to the present day.

Wes Montgomery

PHOTO: ROY MATHERS/COURTESY JAZZ JOURNAL

WES MONTGOMERY
Born-JOHN LESLIE MONTGOMERY
Indianapolis, Indiana, USA
6 March 1925
Died-Indianapolis, Indiana, USA
15 June 1968

Unlike most of the world's finest jazz guitarists, past or present, John Leslie 'Wes' Montgomery started to play the guitar relatively late in life. At the age of nineteen, inspired by the records of Charlie Christian, he began to play the guitar. Montgomery soon developed an incredible technique of single notes, octaves and chords which was so facile that many guitarists, prior to his emergence on the scene, would have thought it to have been technically impossible. Montgomery used his thumb, instead of a pick, on his right hand and so produced a unique and instantly recognizable sound. This unusual technique came about as a means for Montgomery to keep the volume of his guitar down whilst practising, so as not to disturb his neighbours at home.

After playing the guitar for only six months Montgomery was hired by a local band to play nothing else but Charlie Christian's solos note for note. Although not able to read music Montgomery was fortunate to have a natural ear for music, and this helped him make rapid progress. Together with his brothers, Monk on bass and Buddy on piano, he became a vital part of the Indianapolis jazz scene. Until 1959 Montgomery was virtually unknown outside of Indianapolis, even though he had spent two years on the road with Lionel Hampton's Band from 1948-50. During his time with the Hampton band he was given the nickname of 'Rev' Montgomery because he was a teetotaller. Montgomery was a devoted family man. Having seven children, the road life that was the lot of most jazz musicians did not appeal to him. Nevertheless his love of playing jazz gave him a long and arduous working day. During the day he worked in a local radio factory. In the evenings he played in the nearby Turf Bar and then moved on to play more jazz in another club, the Missile Room, into the early hours of the morning.

A chance visit to the Missile Room by jazz saxophonist Cannonball Adderly, who was on a one night stand to Indianapolis, eventually led to international recognition of Wes Montgomery's unique talent. Adderley was so taken by Montgomery's brilliant guitar playing that he immediately telephoned Orrin Keepnews, head of Riverside, the succesful jazz record company. He urged him to sign up Montgomery.

Keepnews was a bit sceptical of Adderly's adulation but coincidentally had noticed an article by the Gunther Schuller in an issue of the magazine, The Jazz Review.

In the article Schuller had written; 'The thing that it is most easy to say about Wes Montgomery is that he is an extraordinary spectacular guitarist. Listening to his solos is like teetering continually on the edge of a brink. His playing at its peak becomes unbearably exciting to the point where one feels unable to muster sufficient physical endurance to outlast it'. Within a few days Keepnews was in Indiana listening to Montgomery at the 'Turf Bar' and the 'Missile Room'. He immediately offered Montgomery a contract with Riverside and the first record was made in New York on 5 and 6 October 1959. The guitarist played with his trio from Indianapolis, which consisted of organist Melvin Rhyne and drummer Paul Parker. From then on success followed success.

In January 1960 Montgomery made what many jazz enthusiasts and historians consider to be his finest recording, 'The Incredible Jazz Guitar of Wes Montgomery'. In the following eight years Wes Montgomery became the most popular, most influential, and most recorded of jazz guitarists of the 1960s. His records constantly topped the best selling jazz charts. After leaving Riverside in 1964 Montgomery signed a contract with Verve Records. On several of these recordings he was backed by big studio orchestras with a string section, in an attempt to help attract a wider, and more popular audience. Despite the obvious commercialism of these recordings, and those produced later by Creed Taylor on the A & M label, Montgomery managed to retain his distinctive jazz style, and so keep his enormous following amongst jazz fans.

Over the years Montgomery received awards in jazz polls from Downbeat, Billboard and Playboy magazines as 'Best Guitarist' and 'Jazzman of The Year'. In 1966 he received a Grammy award for the 'Best Instrumental Jazz Performance' on his recording 'Goin' Out Of My Head'. Montgomery was profiled in Time and Newsweek magazines, rare recognition for a jazz artist. He was associated with many of the finest jazz musicians of the 1960s including Cannonball Adderley, Wynton Kelly, Paul Chambers, Jimmy Smith, Milt Jackson, Johnny Griffin, and Harold Land.

Through his many recordings, and concert and club appearances all over the world, the genius of Wes Montgomery gained full international recognition. Tragically, at the height of one of the most succesful career's in jazz, Montgomery collapsed and died in June 1968. In less than twelve years, from 1957-68, Wes Montgomery made one of the greatest contributions to jazz and to the history of jazz guitar. Even today his genius continues to be a major influence on most jazz guitarists.

SELECTED RECORDINGS

The Montgomery Brothers + Five Others	World Pacific PJ 1240
The Montgomery Brothers - Kismet World	Pacific WP1234
The Montgomery Brothers	Pacific Jazz PJ 17
Montgomeryland	Pacific Jazz PJ 5
Wes Montgomery Trio	Riverside RLP 1156
Incredible Jazz Guitar	Riverside RLP 1167
Movin' Along	Riverside RLP 942
Grooveyard	Riverside RLP 362
So Much Guitar	Riverside RLP 342
Montgomery Brothers In Canada	Fantasy 8066
Bags Meets Wes	Riverside 407
Full House	Riverside 434
Fusion	Riverside RLP 472
Boss Guitar	Riverside RLP 459
Guitar On The Go	Riverside 494
Movin' Wes	Verve 8610
Bumpin'	Verve 8625
Smokin' At The Half Note	Verve V/V68633
Willow Weep for Me	Verve 6-8765
Goin' Out Of My Head	Verve 8642
Tequila	Verve 8653
California Dreaming	Verve 8672
The Dynamic Duo w/Jimmy Smith	Verve SVLP 8678
Further Adventures w/Jimmy Smith	Verve V6 8766
A Day in the Life	A & M AMLS 2001
Down Here On The Ground	A & M (CTI) AMLS 3006
Road Song	A & M (CTI) AMLS 927
Live At Jorgies Vol 1	VGM 0001
Live At Jorgies Vol 2	VGM 0008
Impressions	Affinity AFF 13
Solitude	Affinity AFF 18
Complete Riverside Recordings 12CD Set	Riverside 12RCD-4408-2
Impressions – The Verve Jazz Sides	Verve 314-521 690-2 CD
Straight No Chaser	Bandstand BDCD 1504
Live 61	Magnetic MRCD 124
Live in Europe	Philology N97-2-CD
Body and Soul	Ronnie Scott's Jazz House JHAS-604 CD
Wes Montgomery Quartet Video	BBC625
Legends of Jazz Guitar Vol. 1 Video	Vestapol
Legends of Jazz Guitar Vol. 2 Video	Vestapol

SELECTED READING

Wes Montgomery Biography Adrian Ingram	Ashley Mark (1985)
Great Guitarists p.137-141 Kienzle	Facts On File (1985)
The Guitar Players p.213-230 Sallis	Quill (1985)
Profile	Downbeat, July 1961
Article	Downbeat, July 1964
Interview	Jazz, November 1966
Profile	Downbeat, June 1968
Appreciation	Guitar Player, July/August 1973
Appreciation	Guitar World, January 1984
Profile	Guitarist, July 1989
Article	Downbeat, May 1993
Appreciation	Guitar Player, August 1993
Profile	Guitar Player, June 1995
Article	Jazz Times, August 1995

SELECTED MUSIC

Wes Montgomery Jazz Guitar Method	Robbins Music Corp.
Wes Montgomery Jazz Guitar Solos	Almo Music Corp.
Wes Montgomery Folio trans.Steve Kahn	Gopam Enterprises
Wes Montgomery Vol 1	Jazz Improvisation Series (Japan)
Wes Montgomery Vol 2	Jazz Improvisation Series (Japan)
Wes Montgomery Artist Transcriptions	Hal Leonard
Wes Montgomery – The Early Years	Mel Bay Publishing
Wes Montgomery – Jazz Guitar Artistry	Mel Bay Publishing

Wes Montgomery

OSCAR MOORE

Born-OSCAR FREDERIC MOORE
Austin, Texas, USA
25 December 1912
Died-Las Vegas, USA
8 October 1981

Oscar Moore first played the guitar professionally in 1934, in a band with his brother Johnny Moore. Three years later he achieved international fame when he joined the Nat 'King' Cole Trio. Moore held this prestigious position for ten years with the exception of a few months in the spring of 1944 when he did some U.S. Army service.

The many recordings that Moore made with the 'King' Cole trio from 1937, are evidence of the very high standard of his jazz guitar playing. There is no doubt that his ability, and importance in jazz have been under rated. This is probably due to the fact that he emerged on to the jazz scene at around the same time as Charlie Christian. Nevertheless Oscar Moore was harmonically well ahead of his time, and was a great influence on many of his contemporaries. He won jazz polls both in 'Downbeat' and 'Metronome' magazines, from the years 1945-49. He also won 'Esquire' magazine's Silver award in 1944-45, and their Gold award in 1946-47.

In 1949 Oscar left King Cole's trio to settle in Los Angeles. There he rejoined his brother Jimmy in a group called 'The Three Blazers'. After leaving this group Moore remained on the West Coast freelancing in mainly commercial work, but also making the occasional jazz record. In the late 1950s he gave up music for a while to work as a bricklayer, but returned in the 1960s to a full time career as a guitarist.

SELECTED RECORDINGS

Nat King Cole Trio	DJM Records DJSLM 2029
Nat King Cole Trio	Music for Pleasure MFP1129
Nat King Cole Trio Live 1943	Jazz Anthology 30 JA 5219
Nat King Cole Rare Live Performances	Jazz Anthology 30JA51750
Nat King Cole Trio	Giants Of Jazz GOJ 1013
Nat King Cole Trio	Giants Of Jazz GOJ 1031
Nat King Cole Trio	Capitol M-11033
Nat King Cole Trio	Laserlight 5 CD Set 15 746-750
Nat King Cole Trio Complete Capitol Recordings	
	18 CD Set Mosaic MD-18 138
The Three Blazers	Route 66 KIX-17
Oscar Moore Trio	Vedette VDS213
Oscar Moore-1940 Era	Tampa TP22
Fabulous Guitar	Parker 830
Oscar Moore	VSOP LP 19
Oscar Moore and Friends	Fresh Sounds ESR-CD202

SELECTED MUSIC

Guitaristics-Oscar Moore Guitar Solos	Leeds Music Corp

SELECTED READING

Solo Transcription	Downbeat, September 1994

HOWARD MORGEN
Born-Jamaica, Long Island, New York, USA
17 August 1932

Howard Morgen

Howard Morgen is an outstanding teacher and arranger for the jazz guitar. He is an accomplished seven-string guitarist, playing with both pick and fingers. A former faculty member of the Manhattan School of Music, Morgen currently teaches classes at the Guitar Study Centre at The New School in New York City. He is on the faculty of the Jazz Studies Program at the C.W. Post campus of Long Island University and also teaches privately at his own studio in Great Neck. Many top popular artists have studied with Morgen including Paul Simon, James Taylor and Carly Simon.

A regular columnist for Guitar Player magazines, Morgen also wrote the fingerstyle jazz column for Guitar World magazine from 1980-1985. His arrangements and transcriptions appear frequently in Fingerstyle Guitar, Acoustic Guitar and Just Jazz Guitar magazines. Morgen has written several excellent books for jazz guitar usually concentrating on the fingerstyle approach. He is very active performing in concert and in clubs. He is also a regular lecturer at jazz clinics throughout the USA and Europe.

SELECTED RECORDING
Fingerboard Harmony Tuition Video	Bransong Music
Howard Morgen Plays Gershwin	Grace Court MMGCW001CD

SELECTED READING
Article	Guitar World, July 1980
Profile	Fingerstyle Guitar Magazine Vol.1. No.3

SELECTED MUSIC
Preparations	CPP/Belwin
Concepts	CPP/Belwin
Fingerstyle Favourites	CPP/Belwin
Fingerstyle Jazz Images For Christmas	Mel Bay Publications
10 From Guitar Player	CPP/Belwin
Fingerstyle Duke Ellington	CPP/Belwin
Songs of Paul Simon	Music Sales
The Gershwin Collection	Warners

TONY MOTTOLA
Born-ANTHONY CHARLES MOTTOLA
Kearny, New Jersey, USA
18 April 1918

Tony Mottola

Tony Mottola is well known today as one of the foremost studio guitarists of the past fifty years. His long association with singers Burl Ives and Perry Como, and more recently with Frank Sinatra, has brought him a large audience outside the field of jazz. His many easy-listening albums have also enjoyed high sales for many years. Yet his early recordings with Carl Kress show that he is a tasteful and able jazz guitarist.

Mottola first studied banjo and guitar with his father as a youth. He then went on to study classical guitar, harmony and music theory with a Professor Vallilio. His pick guitar technique was primarily self-taught by listening to the recordings of the early jazz guitar greats Eddie Lang, Django Reinhardt, Dick McDonough and Carl Kress. He made his professional debut in 1939 as guitarist with the George Hall orchestra at the Hotel Taft in New York. At the same time he began his long career as a studio musician. In 1941 he left Hall to become, on the recommendation of Carl Kress, a CBS staff musician. In the mid 1950s he won acclaim as composer and solo instrumentalist for the CBS drama show, 'Danger'. For the next ten years Mottola was guitarist for the coast-to-coast Johnny Carson television show. He arranged and played the guitar background for the film, 'Violated'. Mottola's trio for the daily television show, 'Face The Music', is reputed to have been the first group to perform exclusively on a regular basis for television.

SELECTED RECORDINGS
Fun On The Frets 1941 Duo with Carl Kress	Yazoo 1061
Percussion & Guitars	Time 52000
Tony Mottola's Quad Guitars	Project 3 PR 5078 SD
Tony Mottola & Strings	Project 3 PR 5069
String Along With Me	Project 3 LG-8217
Mr. Big	Command RS 33-807
The Guitar Artistry of Tony Mottola (2 LP set)	Project 3 PR2-6035

SELECTED READING
Interview	Guitar Player, November 1977
Interview	Just Jazz Guitar, November 1994

SELECTED MUSIC
Guitar Styles of Tony Mottola	Mel Bay Publications

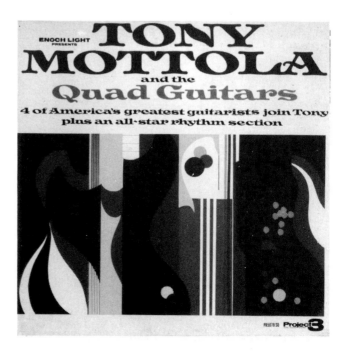

JIM MULLEN
Born-Glasgow, United Kingdom
2 November 1945

Jim Mullen started playing the guitar as a child then switched to bass in his early teens. For several years he played in local dance bands until he went back to playing the guitar and formed his own trio.

In 1969 Mullen moved from Glasgow to London and after a period of involvement with rhythm & blues bands he became associated with several popular jazz fusion groups including 'Paz', the 'Average White Band', 'Kokomo (UK)' and Herbie Mann's group. He also formed a group as co-leader with saxophonist Dick Morrisey. The Morrisey-Mullen band, which lasted until 1985, established itself as one of Britain's most successful jazz fusion groups.

Since then Jim Mullen has continued a busy life recording and playing in jazz clubs and at festivals throughout the United Kingdom and Europe. He has in recent times played with organist/pianist Mike Carr, and also once again with Dick Morrisey. His distinctive blues-oriented jazz guitar style has won him many admirers.

Jim Mullen with Mike Carr.

PHOTO: COURTESY MIKE CARR

SELECTED RECORDINGS

Thumbs Up	Coda 4 CD
Into The 90s Morrisey-Mullen Band	Embryo K 50835
Badness	Bega 27 CD
It's About Time	Bega 44 CD
Happy Hour	Cosa 29 CD
Mike Carr Trio Live	Spotlite SPJ 517
Soundbites-Jim Mullen	EFZ 1003CD
Good Times and the Blues	Cargo Gold CGCD191
Isn't It w/Guy Barker	Spotlite CPJ-CD 545

SELECTED READING

Profile	The Wire May 1985

DOUG MUNRO
**Born-Yonkers, New York, USA
9 July 1953**

Doug Munro

Doug Munro's grandfather played the banjo and the guitar. His great uncle was the famous popular composer Harry Warren. Munro was first attracted as a youth to the drums after seeing a marching band. He started lessons and by the time he was 14 he was already playing in a rock n' roll band at high school dances and in local night clubs. However at that time Munro's primary interest was in sports.

Munro chose a professional gymnastics career after leaving school but was forced to dismiss this choice after a severe spinal injury. He also was unable to play the drums or the piano so he started to play the guitar. By 1976 Munro was involved in composing popular music and also performed in a travelling musical theatre. He then enrolled at Westchester Conservatory of Music at Mercy College. Later
he earned a master's degree in jazz guitar at Purchase College.

After leaving college Munro decided to make music his career. He began to teach and in 1987 released his first solo album for producer Joe Ferry. Since that time he has made several albums for Ferry and served as an arranger and associate producer on many more. In 1989, whilst playing at the Upstairs Club in Larchmont, Munro was approached to teach music and composition at Purchase College, SUNY. He accepted this position and in 1992 the dean approached him with the concept of designing and implementing a graduate programme in Jazz Performance. The programme was established in 1993 and has been a very great success.

Doug Munro continues to lead a busy career in education as Assistant Professor Head of Jazz Studies at the Conservatory of Music at Purchase College, combined with an active live performance and recording career.

SELECTED RECORDINGS

Courageous Cats	Novus Records	NV002 CD
When Dolphins Fly	Optimism Records	OPCD 3234
Autumn in Blue	CMG Records	CMD 9002
The Blue Lady	CMG Records	CMD 8041
Shootin' Pool at Leo's	CMG Records	CMD 8050

Jazz/Blues Improvisation Tuition Video	Homespun Tapes

SELECTED READING

Interview	Just Jazz Guitar, August 1996

WOLFGANG MUTHSPIEL
Born-Judenburg, Austria
2 March 1965

Wolfgang Muthspiel's first instrument was the violin which he played from the age of six. He played in local community orchestras and was regarded as a potential classical violinist of concert stature. At the age of 15 he changed over to the classical guitar and within a short period of time had won an Austrian classical guitar competition. However after hearing some recordings by Pat Metheny and pianist Keith Jarrett he decided to make a career in jazz. He appeared at some Austrian jazz festivals in a duo with his brother, a trombonist. In 1989 Muthspiel released his first recording for the Amadeo company and this drew wide critical acclaim.

In 1990 Muthspiel began studying on a full scholarship at the Berklee College of Music in Boston. Whilst there he was heard by vibraharpist Gary Burton who immediately hired him to join his new band. This position drew international attention to Muthspiel's rising talent. His 1990 Amadeo recording featured his sextet which included flugelhornist Tom Harrell.

Wolfgang Muthspiel

SELECTED RECORDINGS

Timezones	Amadeo/Polygram	839013-2CD
Black & Blue	Amadeo/Polygram	517 653-2CD
In and Out	Amadeo/Polygram	521 385-2CD
The Promise	Amadeo/Polygram	847 023-2CD
Loaded, Like New	Amadeo/Polygram	527 727-2CD
Perspective	Amadeo/Polygram	533 466-2CD
Cool Nights w/Gary Burton	GRP	964321-2CD
The Same Breath w/Mick Goodrick	CMP Records	517 653-2CD

SELECTED READING

Profile	Guitar Player, July 1990

JIM NICHOLS
Born-Berea, Kentucky, USA
4 March 1947

Jim Nichols was raised in Virgina into a musical family. His father played with the Jimmy Dorsey and Charlie Spivak big bands, and his mother is a professional pianist. He had a few guitar lessons as a child but is basically a self-taught player from the age of ten. He listened to recordings of the leading jazz and country guitarists. As a result he has developed a jazz guitar style using right-hand country technique. In 1971 Nichols received a Bachelor of Science degree in Sociology from James Madison University, Virginia. In 1972 he moved to California to pursue a full time career in music.

In the last 25 years Jim Nichols has played with many of the world's finest jazz and country musicians including Martin Taylor, Joe Pass, Fareed Haque, Romane, Hubert Laws, Art Pepper, Toots Thielemans, Bud Shank, Louis Bellson, Chet Atkins, Della Reese and Van Morrison. He has appeared on many radio and television broadcasts including the Tonight show. As an educator Nichols has taught both jazz and country guitar styles. He was a master instructor for the Jamey Aebersold Jazz Workshops, and held has clinics in Nashville

for the Chet Atkins Appreciation Society. He has also played and taught at leading venues in France including the 1997 Django Reinhardt Festival held in Samois.

Jin Nichols lives in the Bay Area of San Francisco where he leads an active career performing and recording both as a soloist and in a duo with his vocalist wife Morning.

SELECTED RECORDINGS

Silver Morning w/Kenny Rankin	ATL 90131 LP
Lost Life w/Art Pepper	TRIO (Japan) PAP 25044 LP
Jazz & Country - Solo Guitar	GSP 5005CD
My Flame w/Morning Nichols	Kamei KR 7003CD
Unconditional Love w/Morning Nichols	Kamei KR 7007CD
Save Your Love for Me w/Morning Nichols	GSP 7008CD
Silver Morning w/Kenny Rankin	Little David LD 30LP

SELECTED READING

Article	Acoustic Guitar, April 1997
Interview	Just Jazz Guitar, November 1997

Jim Nichols

ROBIN NOLAN
Born-Danang, Vietnam
29 December 1968

Robin Nolan's British parents were both musicians who owned a jazz club 'The Speakeasy' in Kowloon, Hong Kong. His father was a guitarist and mother a singer who worked for a time in Vietnam entertaining the troops. Nolan studied the guitar with his father and a local Chinese teacher. He moved to the United Kingdom when he was nine and for a while changed to the piano. When he was 13, after hearing some recordings by the Beatles, he began to play the guitar again. He played in some 'Heavy Metal' groups and then gained a place to study jazz at the Leeds College of Music. There he was introduced to the 'Django' style of jazz guitar playing by David Eyres. Nolan also studied with Andy Watson, Trefor Owen and Adrian Ingram at Leeds.

Nolan's first professional experience included working with violinist Nigel Kennedy, and with Martin Taylor. He moved to London where he played in local jazz clubs with Dill Katz and other jazz musicians. In 1992 he formed the 'Robin Nolan Swing Quartet' with Anthony Williams, Paul Meader and Marc Meader. They moved to Amsterdam in the Netherlands later that year and gained important exposure playing on the streets of this famous city. Nolan's 'Django' style jazz trio and quartet have enjoyed great success in Europe and Canada since that time.

SELECTED RECORDINGS

Robin Nolan Trio	RNT 1 CD
Amsterdam	RNQ 2 CD
Out of Town - Robin Nolan Swing Quartet	RNQ 3CD
Robin Nolin Trio	RNT 4 CD

SELECTED READING

Interview	String Jazz, November/December 1995

Robin Nolan

ROBERT NORMANN
Born-ROBERT UNO NORMANN
Sarpsborg, Norway
27 June 1916

As a child Robert Normann was surrounded by music as most members of his family played an instrument. He taught himself to play the guitar as a youth, and then later the accordion and tenor saxophone. In 1928 he joined accordionist Sverre Samuelsen in a small dance and jazz duo.

They eventually went on to tour the cities and towns of Southern Norway managing to get work in an assortment of venues. Still only a teenager, Normann steadily gained a reputation as a virtuoso guitarist. In the early 1930s he teamed up with another accordionist, Willy Eriksen. They were a very popular duo and managed to appear on a radio broadcast. This gave Normann the break that was to establish him as Norway's foremost jazz and studio guitarist for many years to come.

Robert Normann, whose jazz guitar style is sometimes reminiscent of Django Reinhardt, was little known outside Norway until the release in 1989 of some of his recordings of the 1940s and 1950s with various Norwegian groups on the Hot Club Records label. These recordings confirm that Normann is a talented and original guitarist.

Robert Normann

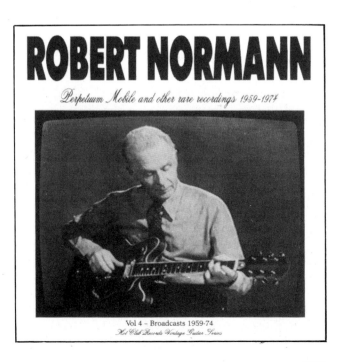*(caption vertical)* PHOTO: COURTESY HOT CLUB RECORDS

SELECTED RECORDINGS
Robert Normann Vol 1   Hot Guitar   Hot Club Records HRCD 40
Robert Normann Vol 2   Swinging Guitar Hot Club Records HRCD 41
Robert Normann Vol 3   Tricky Guitar   Hot Club Records HRCD 42
Robert Normann Vol 4   Brilliant Guitar Hot Club Records HRCD 43

SELECTED READING
Jazz Solography Robert Normann   Jan Evensmo

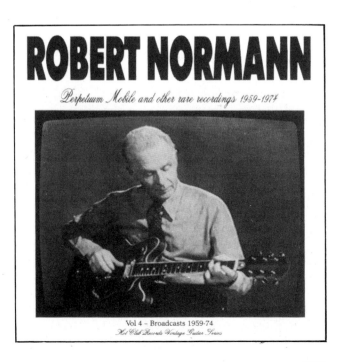

WARREN NUNES
Born-Oahu, Hawaii, USA
5 July 1937
Died-Half Moon Bay, California, USA
2 December 1999

Warren Nunes was best known to guitarists throughout the world as the author of several acclaimed jazz guitar tuition and solo arrangement books. However as his 1985 CD recording shows he was a jazz guitarist of great ability.

Nunes moved to the San Francisco area when he was twelve and became interested in the guitar at the age of sixteen. He played as a professional musician in night clubs in the Bay area for twenty years, but then decided to devote himself to a career in teaching. Nunes wrote on jazz guitar for Guitar Player magazine. A multi-instrumentalist Nunes also wrote books for the piano and saxophone.

SELECTED RECORDING
Half Moon Bay - Warren Nunes   Karlin Nunes Music 9637 CD

SELECTED MUSIC
Jazz Guitar Rhythm & Background Chords	Charles Hansen
Jazz Guitar The Blues	Charles Hansen
Jazz Guitar Chorded Solos	Charles Hansen
Jazz Guitar Solo Patterns	Charles Hansen
Jazz Guitar Portfolio	Music Trends

Warren Nunes

MARY OSBORNE
Born-Minot, North Dakota, USA
17 July 1921
Died-Bakersfield, California, USA
4 March 1992

Mary Osborne, the tenth of eleven children, had the fortune to come from a strong musical background. Both her parents were guitarists. Her father, a barber by profession, also led his own band. At the age of four Osborne could already strum the ukulele and at school she studied the violin, finally taking up the guitar at the age of nine.

Throughout her teens Osborne sang and played acoustic jazz guitar in an all-girl-trio, in local clubs in the Bismark area. At that time her influences were Eddie Lang, Django Reinhardt and Dick McDonough. On the advice of friends she went to hear Charlie Christian playing with the Al Trent Sextet in Bismark. Hearing Christian brought an immediate change in Osborne's approach to the guitar and jazz. She purchased an electric guitar similar to the one used by Christian. She was fortunate to develop a brief friendship with Christian which gave her the opportunity to study his technique.

In early 1940 Osborne played for a Pittsburgh radio station. In 1941 she was hired by Joe Venuti, and then Russ Morgan, Dick Stabile, Buddy Rogers and others. She then joined the Winifred McDonald all-girl trio, touring various states with this group, finally settling in 1945 in New York City. Here the group split up, but because of her fine ability on the guitar Osborne found many radio and recording jobs. She was also much in demand in the 52nd street jazz clubs, playing with pianist Mary Lou Williams, Coleman Hawkins and Mercer Ellington. In 1946 Osborne married trumpeter Ralph Scaffidi and they decided to live in New York City. She led her own trio and played in top jazz spots including 'Kelly's Stables'. Her jazz guitar talent became widely known and in 1946 Django Reinhardt made a point of coming to hear her play on his only visit to New York.

In 1949, after her trio broke up, Osborne decided to freelance, and soon became one of the busiest guitarists in the New York area, playing and recording with many of the top CBS studio bands. From 1962 she began a five year study of the classical guitar with Albert Valdes Blain.

In 1968 the Scaffidis moved to Bakersfield, California with their three children. Here they founded the Osborne Guitar Company.

Mary Osborne

PHOTO: COURTESY GUITAR PLAYER

Osborne taught both jazz and classical guitar, and appeared frequently in jazz venues in the Los Angeles area, including Berkeley in 1969 and at The Hollywood Bowl in 1973. In 1981 she appeared at the Kool Jazz Festival in New York and made her last jazz recording in the same year.

SELECTED RECORDINGS

Greatest of the Small Bands Black & White	RCA741106 LP
Esquire All-American Jazz	Vintage LPV544
A Girl and Her Guitar	Warwick 2004 LP
Cats vs. Chicks	MGM E255 LP
Forty Years of Women In Jazz	Jass J-CD-9/10
Now's The Time	Halcyon HAL 115 LP
Now And Then Mary Osborne	Stash ST-215
Mary Osborne A Memorial	Stash ST-CD-550

SELECTED READING

Profile	Guitar Player, February 1974

WIM OVERGAAUW
Born-JAN WILLEM OVERGAAUW
Hilversum, The Netherlands 23 November 1929
Died-Hilversum, The Netherlands
30 November 1995

Wim Overgaauw

Wim Overgaauw was the Nertherland's foremost jazz guitarist for many years. In 1951 he joined the John Krispin orchestra and then in 1958 was a founding member of the popular Pim Jacobs Trio backing singer Rita Reijs. This trio did a lot to bring jazz to Dutch schools. From 1958-72 they sometimes appeared at four or five schools a day in their ambition to make jazz better known. Overgaauw was often chosen by many leading USA jazz musicians to play in their backing group when they visited the Netherlands. Over the years he backed Stan Getz, Clark Terry, Sonny Rollins, Jimmy Raney, Lee Konitz, Sam Jones, Warne Marsh, Phil Woods, Thad Jones and Mel Lewis. He also did studio work and appeared on Dutch television with guitarists Jimmy Raney, Doug Raney, George Barnes, Joe Pass, Wes Montgomery and Barney Kessel.

As well as being an important jazz performer Wim Overgaauw spent much of his time teaching. In his capacity as jazz guitar tutor at the music conservatory in Hilversum many of the Netherlands leading jazz guitarists of the day were taught and guided by him. Included amongst his former students are Maarten van der Grinten, Martin van Itterson and Jesse van Ruller. Wim Overgaauw never received the international recognition his talent deserved, however he is without question the 'father' of modern jazz guitar in the Netherlands.

SELECTED RECORDINGS

Don't Disturb	CBS S64105 LP
Sagitarius	CBS S64566 LP
Nuages	CBS S65112 LP
Dedication	PARK LLBP 3049 LP
Blue Guitar	Polydor 2925058 LP
Round Midnight	Polydor 2925074 LP
Beboppin	Limetree MLP 198403
Toots Thielemans Group Live	Polydor 831694-2 CD
Collage	Sony/Columbia 476773 CD
Wim Overgaauw 65th Anniversary Concert	RN Discs RN009 CD

SELECTED READING

Interview	String Jazz, Jan/Feb 1995

SELECTED MUSIC

The European Jazz Guitar	Dannison Music

TREFOR OWEN

**Born-Gwalchmal, Anglesey,
Gwnedd, Wales, UK
26 August 1944**

Trefor Owen

Trefor Owen has for many years been a prominent jazz guitarist, teacher and promoter in the UK. He has taught at the Leeds College of Music and the Sandown College in Liverpool. Since 1988 he has been an examiner for the Guildhall School of Music.

Trained as a radio and television engineer Owen was for many years a semi-professional musician. Following his successes at various jazz festivals, including those held in Brecon, Cork, Belfast and Hayfield, he now devotes his career to performing and teaching jazz guitar. In recent times he has toured in various jazz guitar packages which have included Martin Taylor, Louis Stewart, Adrian Ingram and Mundell Lowe.

SELECTED RECORDINGS

Tribute to Wes Montgomery	Encore CAS 001
Wales Plays Brazil	Crimson CD

The Eddie South Band in 1937 with Isidore Langlois on guitar.

257

NATHEN PAGE
Born-Leetown, West Virginia, USA
23 August 1937

Nathen Page began to play the guitar at the age of seven. His parents were country music fans. His first introduction to jazz came when he went into the army. During his two year period with the service, he played for a while in the army band.

After leaving the army Page moved to Washington. Here he met pianist Jimmy Crawford who encouraged the guitarist to sit in with his group. This helped Page gain valuable experience. In 1965, on the recommendation of drummer Billy Hart, Page was hired by organist Jimmy Smith. He stayed with this group for five years, touring the USA and Europe. After leaving Smith he worked as a sideman with diverse artists including Roberta Flack and Herbie Mann. Page then joined Jackie McLean's quintet working mainly on the East Coast of the USA. After leaving McLean he joined Sonny Rollins, staying with the saxophonist for two years.

Nathen Page

In 1980 Nathen Page decided to move from Washington to Florida, where he now works in local clubs on piano and electric bass as well as on the guitar. He has toured Europe in recent years as a sideman with organist Lonnie Smith and has made several records as leader of his own quartet.

SELECTED RECORDINGS

Page 1	HMS 105 LP
Page 2	HMS 107 LP
Nathen Page Plays	HMS 108 LP
A Page of Ellington	HMS 110 LP
The Other Page	HMS 111 LP

SELECTED READING

Interview	Jazz Journal, April 1991

REMO PALMIER
Born-REMO PALMIERI
New York City, USA
29 March 1923

Remo Palmier

Remo Palmier first started to play the guitar at the age of eleven. He originally played the guitar professionally to pay for art studies, as he had hoped to be a professional artist.

Palmier first became interested in jazz when he heard some Tommy Dorsey recordings in 1938. He then started to listen to recordings by Django Reinhardt and Charlie Christian. He was so impressed with what he heard, in 1941 he started to study music in depth. His professional career as a musician began in December 1942 when he joined pianist Nat Jaffe's trio. Palmier soon developed a reputation as one of the most advanced East coast jazz guitarists, playing in a Charlie Christian influenced style.

In 1943 Palmier played with Coleman Hawkins, and then in 1944 with Red Norvo. He also backed singer Billie Holiday in jazz clubs on 52nd Street. In 1944 Palmier played behind Mildred Bailey on a CBS radio series and was regularly featured with the Phil Moore orchestra at the 'Cafe Society'. In 1945 Palmier recorded several times with both Dizzy Gillespie and Barney Bigard. In the same year he joined the CBS in New York working regularly on the popular Arthur Godfrey show. Having suffered a bout of double pneumonia his doctors advised him to give up club work. He remained in the NBC studios until 1972 and and as a result was not involved in jazz for many years.

In 1972 Palmier made a modest return to jazz freelancing for a period with his own quartet at various New York clubs. He played with diverse jazz artists including pianist Hank Jones and trumpeter Bobby Hackett. In 1974 he appeared with the Benny Goodman orchestra for several major jazz concerts. He recorded in October 1977 with Herb Ellis, and then in July 1978 as leader of his own quartet, for the Concord label. Since that time he has maintained a busy career as a studio musician.

SELECTED RECORDINGS
One Night in Birdland	Columbia JG34808 LP
Esquire All American Hot Jazz	Vintage LPV544 LP
Teddy Wilson Sextet	Everest FS263 LP
The Everlasting Teddy Wilson	Vernon 505 LP
Dizzy Gillespie In The Beginning	Prestige PRS 24030 LP
Windflower with Herb Ellis	Concord CCD-4056
Remo Palmier	Concord CJ76 LP

SELECTED READING
Profile	Guitar Player, August 1978

Remo Palmier (right) with Joe Puma, New York, June 1997

Joe Pass

JOE PASS

Born-JOSEPH ANTHONY JACOBI PASSALAQUA
New Brunswick, New Jersey, USA
13 January 1929
Died-Los Angeles, USA
23 May 1994

Joe Pass, the oldest of four children, spent his youth in the Italian area of Johnstown, Pennsylvania. His father Mariano Passalaqua was a steel mill worker. Pass started playing the guitar at the age of nine and received his first lessons from friends of his father. He received great encouragement from his father, took weekly lessons, and spent most of his spare time practicing and playing the guitar. By the time he was 14 Pass was already working with local bands playing at weddings and dances. He then went on to play with the bands of Tony Pastor and Charlie Barnet. As he reached his twenties he fell in love with the sounds of jazz and bebop and decided in 1949 to move to New York where he could hear the finest jazz musicians of the day.

Unfortunately whilst in New York Pass became addicted to drugs, and for the next twelve years his brilliant jazz guitar playing was not recognised due to this problem. He did work in backing groups in Las Vegas but after several arrests for narcotics had to serve time in a US Public Health Service Hospital. In 1960 Pass made the wise decision to enter Synanon, a special centre for the rehabilitation of musicians who were addicted to drugs. He stayed there for three years after which he was cured. Whilst at Synanon, Pass made a recording in 1962 with a group made up of other musicians in the hospital. It was called 'Sounds of Synanon' and jazz critics and fans were taken aback by Pass's outstanding guitar playing on this recording. After leaving Synanon Pass started working in and around Los Angeles with many top jazz names. He toured with George Shearing in 1965-67, and in 1973 went to Australia with the Benny Goodman band. In the late 1960s he made several outstanding recordings for Pacific Jazz Records.

Pass continued working in the Los Angeles studios recording with many jazz artists including Earl Bostic, Bud Shank, Gerald Wilson, Les McCann, Chet Baker, Richard 'Groove' Holmes and Johnny Griffin. Pass was also a regular at Donte's club in Los Angeles on their jazz guitar night which was held every Monday. In 1973 Norman Granz, the jazz promoter and record producer, heard Pass at Donte's. He recognized Pass's genius and immediately signed him up for his then new Pablo recording company. For many years Pass also worked with Granz's Jazz at the Philharmonic touring package, working with Oscar Peterson, Ella Fitzgerald, Milt Jackson, Count Basie, Duke Ellington, Zoot Sims and others. Pass made and continues to make many recordings for the Pablo label. He also showed phenomenal talent as a virtuoso solo artist. Using a technique incorporating the fingers of his right hand, instead of a pick, he was able to play bass lines, chords and melody lines at the same time. He recorded, and gave countless concert recitals as a solo artist. His many solo recordings for Pablo remain best sellers, and Pass became one of the company's major artists. There is no doubt that his association with Norman Granz brought Pass the international recognition and financial success his unique talents deserved.

Joe Pass was one of the all-time giants of jazz guitar. He innovated the concept of a complete concert of solo jazz guitar playing, and this inspired many guitarists to emulate him. At the same time he was a superb single-string improvisor, and, as his recordings with singers Ella Fitzgerald and Sarah Vaughan show, a brilliant accompanist.

SELECTED RECORDINGS

Sounds of Synanon	Pacific Jazz PJ 48 LP
A Sign of the Times	World Pacific WP 1844 LP
Simplicity	World Pacific WP 1865 LP
Catch Me	Fontana 688137ZL LP
For Django	United Artists UAS 29768 LP
Intercontinental	BASF BAP 5053 LP
Jazz Concord w/Herb Ellis	Concord CCD-6001
Seven Come Eleven w/Herb Ellis	Concord CCD-6002
The Trio	Pablo 2310 701 LP
Take Love Easy w/Ella Fitzgerald	Pablo 2310 702 CD
Duke Ellington's Big 4	Pablo 2310 703 LP
Virtuoso	Pablo 2310 708 LP
Live At Donte's	Pablo 2620-114 LP
Portrait of the Duke	Pablo 2310 716 LP
Dizzy Gillespie's Big 4	Pablo 2310 719 LP
Two for the Road w/Herb Ellis	Pablo 2310 714 LP
The Big 3	Pablo 2310 757 CD
Fitzgerald and Pass Again	Pablo 2310 772 CD
At Montreux 75	Pablo 2310 752 CD
A Salle Pleyel w/Oscar Peterson	Pablo 2657 015 CD
Porgy and Bess w/Oscar Peterson	Pablo 2310 779 CD
Virtuoso #2	Pablo 2310 788 CD
At Montreux 77	OJC 382/Pablo 2308 212 CD
The Good Life	Pablo 2308 701 CD
Virtuoso #3	Pablo 2310 805 CD
Tudo Bem	Pablo 2310 824 CD
North Sea Nights	Pablo 2308 221 CD
Chops	Pablo 2310 830 CD
I Remember Charlie Parker	Pablo 2312 109 CD
Speak Love w/Ella Fitzgerald	Pablo 2310 840 CD
Checkmate	Pablo 2310 865 CD
Eximous	Pablo 2310 877 CD
Blues For Two w/Zoot Sims	Pablo 2310 879 CD
We'll Be Together Again	Pablo 2310 911 CD
Ira, George & Joe	OJC 828/Pablo 2312 133 CD
Live At Long Beach College	Pablo 2308 239 CD
Blues For Fred	Pablo 2310 931 CD
One For My Baby	Pablo 2310 936-2CD
Virtuoso #4	Pablo 2640-102
Summer Nights	Pablo 2310 939-2CD
Appassionata	Pablo 2310 646-2CD
Virtuoso Live	Pablo 2310 948-2CD
Solo/Duo/Trio	Jazzette BP CD-005
What's New	Jazzette BP CD-015
Joe Pass-My Song	Telarc CD-83326
Finally w/Red Mitchell	Verve 314 512 603-2
Rose Room w/The Five Guitars	Polytone ALCR-125 CD
Sentimental Moods w/Tommy Gumina	Polytone ALCR-74 CD
Autumn Leaves w/Tommy Gumina	Polytone ALCR-85 CD
After Hours w/André Previn	Telarc CD-83302
Joe Pass and Pablo	PACD-2310-951-2
Songs for Ellen	Pablo PACD-2310-955-2

Six String Santa	Laseklight 15 470 CD
Joe Pass and Roy Clark play Hank Williams	Buster Ann Music 1001-CD
Joe Pass in Hamburg	ACT 9100-2 CD
Duets w/John Pisano	Pablo PACD 2310-959-2
Solo Jazz	Instruction Video Hot Licks
Jazz Lines	Instruction Video REH
Blues Side Of Jazz Instruction	Insctruction Video Hot Licks
Joe Pass in Concert Video	Vestapol
An Evening with Joe Pass Video	REH
Legends of Jazz Guitar Vol. 1 Video	Vestapol
Legends of Jazz Guitar Vol. 2 Video	Vestapol

JAZZ GUITAR SOLOS

By JOE PASS

SELECTED READING

Profile	Downbeat, August 1963
Profile	Downbeat, March 1975
Profile	Guitar Player, April 1976
Interview	Guitar, June 1974
Interview	Jazz Journal, May 1976
Discography	Jazz Journal, May /June 1976
Profile	Downbeat, April 1978
Profile	Coda, April 1978
Profile	Guitar Player, September 1984
Interview	Guitarist, September 1985
Private Lesson	Guitar Player, August 1986
Profile	Downbeat, May 1988
Profile	Guitarist, August 1989
Appreciation	Guitar Player, October 1994
Profile	Jazziz, February 1995
Special Issue	Just Jazz Guitar, June 1996
Transcription/Article	Downbeat, February 1997

SELECTED MUSIC

Joe Pass Guitar Style	Mel Bay Publications
Joe Pass Solos	Mel Bay Publications
Joe Pass Guitar Chords	Mel Bay Publications
Joe Pass Chord Solos	Alfred Publishing Company
Joe Pass/Herb Ellis Jazz Duets	Mel Bay Publications
Joe Pass Guitar Method	Chappell
Joe Pass Chord Solos	Jazz Improvisation Series(Japan)
Joe Pass Virtuoso	Mel Bay Publications
Joe Pass Plays The Blues	Mel Bay Publications
Joe Pass Off The Record	Mel Bay Publications
Joe Pass Note by Note	Mel Bay Publications
Joe Pass Improvising Ideas	Mel Bay Publications

Joe Pass

BOB PATTERSON

Born-ROBERT PATTERSON
Detroit, Michigan, USA
25 April 1963

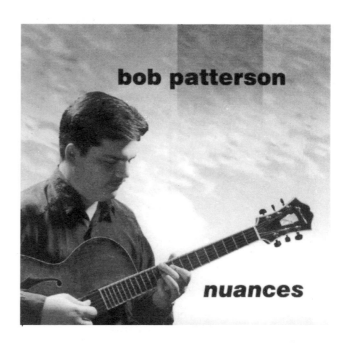

Bob Patterson is well-known to jazz guitarists throughout the world because of his excellent website 'Jazz Guitar ONLINE' (http://www.jazzguitar.com). This website, a labour of love, has proved to be an important contribution in providing information to jazz guitarists all over the world.

Patterson grew up in Flint near Detroit. His father played the banjo, his mother played piano and sang in the local church. Patterson began to play the piano at the age of five, but changed to the guitar at the age of seven. He learned to play by ear and accompanied singers in his local church. His first experience playing jazz was in high school when he played in the school band. George Benson's jazz funk hit recording 'Breezin'' was an important early influence.

In 1982 Patterson enrolled in the University of Michigan at Flint. As a music major he studied harmony and music theory. The following year he moved to Tulsa, Oklahoma where he transferred to a private religious college, Oral Roberts University. During this time Patterson gained important professional experience backing singers such as Vic Damone, Frankie Laine, Freida Payne and others. He has also done a lot of studio work, played on some live television programmes, and was involved in the local rhythm and blues scene.

In 1991 he moved to Bloomington, Indiana. Here he attended the Indiana University School of Music as a Masters student under David Baker. During this time Patterson was able to develop his improvisational skills. He also took an interest in Brazilian music. In 1994 he took a one year appointment as guitar teacher at the University of Southwest Louisiana at Lafayette. His involvement with the Internet began at this time. Subsequently he helped create a jazz guitar newsgroup. In 1995 he moved backed to Bloomington for two years. Since 1996 he has been based in Orlando, Florida playing professionally throughout the state. He is also a jazz instructor at the Shell Lake summer Jazz Camp in Wisconsin.

SELECTED RECORDING

Nuances	JGO Records BP 001 CD

SELECTED MUSIC

Jazz Guitar Soloing	Houston Publications

Les Paul

LES PAUL

Born-LESTER WILLIAM POLFUSS
Waukesha, Wisconsin, USA
9 June 1916

Les Paul is one of the most well-known names for millions of guitarists throughout the world. This is by virtue of the many solid-body electric guitars designed by him, bearing his name, and made by the Gibson company in the USA. Not many of these guitarists realize that Les Paul is also an outstanding guitarist who won many jazz polls in the late 1940s.

Les Paul fell in love with the guitar at an early age. He was self taught both on the guitar and the harmonica. Paul played the harmonica mounted on a harness of his own design, so that he could play it simultaneously with the guitar. His first professional work was really as a 'one man band', playing for tips at roadside restaurants. He called himself 'Rhubarb Red' and his reputation soon earned him some local radio broadcasts, particularly after he teamed up with Joe Wolverton whose stage name was 'Sunny Joe'.

In 1933 Paul left for Chicago where his obvious natural talent earned him many jobs in various local radio stations. His dual ability of being able to play country and western music under the name of 'Rhubarb Red', and jazz as Les Paul, ensured that he was kept very busy. It is interesting to note that in a 1934 Gibson Guitar catalogue he is shown as a Gibson player, but under the name of 'Rhubarb Red'. By 1936 Paul was concentrating on jazz and played with Art Tatum, Eddie South, Louis Armstrong and other leading jazz artists. In 1938 Paul moved from Chicago to New York. Here he led his own trio in which he now played an electric guitar. The group gained widespread popularity when it appeared on a coast-to-coast NBC radio programme with Fred Waring and his Pennsylvanians. By the mid 1940s Paul was regarded as one of the USA's foremost jazz guitarists. His style was greatly influenced by his own personal guitar hero, Django Reinhardt. In 1943 Paul moved to Los Angeles and formed a new trio which backed top stars including Bing Crosby, Rudee Vallee, Jack Benny and the Andrews Sisters. In 1944 he was chosen to appear in a Norman Granz's 'Jazz at the Philharmonic' concert in Los Angeles with J.J. Johnson, Illinois Jaquet, Nat 'King' Cole and others.

Les Paul is also renowned for his development of multi-track recording which he used to great effect on his best-selling records with singer Mary Ford. His first experiments into this field began as early as 1937, but it was not until 1946, under the persuasion of the late Bing Crosby, that Paul finally built his own studio to develop and perfect multi-track recording techniques. Multi-track recording is part and parcel of today's music scene but it was in 1948 in Paul's home studio that he made the first historic multi-track recordings of 'Lover' and 'Brazil'. When these records were released they received unprecedented commercial success. Not long after the release of these records Paul was involved in a serious car accident in which he almost lost his right arm. Miraculously his arm was saved by a doctor who was a Les Paul fan and immediately recognized the guitarist when he was brought into hospital. With the use of a metal plate the doctor was able to set the right arm in such a way that Paul could play the guitar. After his release from hospital, because of this disability, Paul was anxious to further develop his experiments with the solid-body electric guitar which he had begun in the late 1930s. He realized the compactness of the solid guitar would now suit his damaged right arm better than the conventional full-size arch-top guitar.

In 1949 he met and, in the December of that year, married singer Colleen Summers (Mary Ford). They made many very successful multi-track vocal and guitar hits together, and later had their own weekly television show. Over the years Paul became convinced that there was a demand for a solid-body guitar and by the early 1950s he persuaded the Gibson company to produce the first 'Les Paul' guitars. At first these received a cool reception from guitarists and the line was almost dropped by Gibson. But with the arrival of rock and roll in the 1960s the solid-body electric guitar suddenly became a runaway sales success. Since that time Les Paul guitars have become amongst the most popular, and the most copied, guitars the world has known.

Les Paul continues an active career in music from his home in Mahwah, New Jersey. From the mid 1960s he did have a ten year break from professional work, but since the mid 1970s has once again played and recorded with a wide variety of artists. Paul had quintuple bypass heart surgery in September 1980, but has made a full recovery. For some years he has appeared weekly with his own group at Fat Tuesday's club in New York City.

Les Paul is without doubt one of the most popular figures in the music industry, his very individual guitar style and sound still instantly recognisable. He has received three awards from the National Academy Of Recording Arts &

Sciences for his contribution to the industry. An inventive genius, Les Paul's contribution to the world of music and the guitar is exceptional.

SELECTED RECORDINGS

Jazz at the Philharmonic	Verve 2610020 LP
Les Paul Trio-Air Shots	Glendale GL 6014 LP
Les Paul Trio	Tops L 1602 LP
Les Paul Trio	Circle CLP-67
Les Paul Trio	Laserlight 15741CD
Guitar Genius	Charly CR 30243 LP
Les Paul's New Sound	Capitol 286 LP
Bye Bye Blues	Capitol 356 LP
The Hit Makers	Capitol 416 LP
Time to Dream	Capitol 862 LP
Les Paul & Mary Ford	Capitol 11308 LP
Les Paul-Now	Decca PFS 4138 LP
Chester and Lester (with Chet Atkins)	RCA PL1-1167 LP
Guitar Monsters (with Chet Atkins)	RCA PL1-2786 LP
The Legend & Legacy of Les Paul 4 CD Set	Capitol C2-91654
Les Paul Trio – Guitar Artistry	One Way MCAD 22085

Les Paul Trio Video	Millenium Jump Charly Soundie 9
The Wizard Of Waukesha Video	Direct Cinema
Les Paul and Friends Video	A Vision 50197-3
Les Paul – A Living Legend Video	BMG 80061-3

SELECTED READING

Article	Readers Digest, July 1957
Article	Guitar Player, February 1970
Profile	Guitar, February 1975
Interview	Guitar, November 1975
Profile	Guitar, December 1975
Interview	Guitar Player,December 1977
Interview	Guitar World, March & May 1983
Interview	Guitarist, January 1988
Profile	Downbeat, May 1988
Interview	Guitar Player, January 1989
Profile	Jazziz, July 1993
Interview	Just Jazz Guitar, February and May 1997
Interview w/Pat Martino	Downbeat, March 1997
Great Guitarists p.142-147 Sallis	Quill (1985)
The Gibson Les Paul Book Bacon/Day	Balafon (1993)
Les Paul An American Legend Biography	Wm. Morrow (1993)

SELECTED MUSIC

The Guitar Magic of Les Paul	Leeds Music Corp.

Les Paul with Django Reinhardt

DAN PERZ
Born-DANIEL FRANCIS PERZ
Chicago, Illinois, USA 8 May 1952

Dan Perz taught himself to play the guitar at the age of 14. After receiving a M.F.A from the Art Institute of Chicago he moved with his family to Portland, Oregon. He soon established himself as a busy jazz and blues guitarist in that area. His many CD recordings for his own Damp Records company have received exposure on college and jazz radio stations throughout the USA. Since 1982 he has specialised in playing as a solo jazz guitarist.

SELECTED RECORDINGS

Always Near	Damp Records LP
Sunrise	Damp Records LP
Cornerstone	Damp Records LP
Thoughts of You	Damp Records LP
Bemsha Swing	Damp Records LP
Swingin Them Blues	Damp Records LP
Northwest Landscapes	Damp Records CD
Can't Get Away From You	Damp Records CD
Spontaneous Combustion	Damp Records CD
Dan Perz Quartet	Damp Records CD
Don't Let Me Fall	Damp Records CD
Past Loves	Damp Records CD

Dan Perz

Historic photograph taken at the Barney Kessel Tribute. New York City. 25 June 1997.
(Back row): Peter Leitch, Bill Wurzel, Vic Juris, Howie Collins and Ray Gogarty. (4th row): Frank Vignola, John Pizzarelli, Jack Wilkins, Ron Affif, John Abercrombie, Howard Alden, Jimmy Bruno and Randall Kremer. (Smithsonian Institution). (3rd row): Gene Bertoncini, Billy Bauer, Bucky Pizzarelli, Don Arnone, Wayne Wright, Tony Mottola, Sal Salvador and Laurence Lucie. (2nd 'short' row): Charles Carlini, Producer; Remo Palmier and Joe Puma. (Front row): Mundell Lowe, Charlie Byrd, Barney Kessel, Herb Ellis, Tal Farlow and Bob Benedetto.

CARLO PES
Born-Cagliari, Italy
3 March 1927
Died-Rome, Italy
January 1995

Carlo Pes moved to Rome with his family when he was a child. A self-taught player Pes began to play with various dance bands during World War II. In 1945 he appeared at the 'Canada Club' with Bruno Martino, Enrico Simonetti, Stelio Subelli and others. He also began a long musical association with Nunzio Rotondo.

Pes spent many years in Turkey and France. Here he had the opportunity to play with Roy Eldridge, Rex Stewart, Bill Coleman, Don Byas, Django Reinhardt and other prominent jazz artists. In 1950 he recorded for the Parlophone label with his jazz trio. In 1952 he took part in the 'Salon du Jazz de Paris', leaving soon after to live in Brazil. He returned to Italy in 1956 where he renewed his association with Nunzio Rotondo playing with him at the First International Festival of Jazz at San Remo.

Pes then moved to Copenhagen, Denmark remaining there until 1962. During his stay in Scandinavia he had the opportunity to play jazz with Stan Getz, Lars Gullin, Svend Asmussen, Bo Silven and other jazz artists. On his return to Italy in 1962 he became involved in studio work writing popular songs and music for films. In 1969 he joined Barney Kessel for a concert tour of Europe, also recording with the American guitarist for the RCA (Italy) label. Pes also played in a duo with Bucky Pizzarelli at the 'Eddie Lang Jazz Guitar Festival' held in Italy.

In 1971 Pes toured Brazil and then the USA where he played with many top jazz artists including Conte Candoli, Pete Jolly, Harry Edison, Chet Baker, Stephane Grappelli and others.

Carlo Pes, regarded by many as Italy's foremost jazz guitarist, lived in Rome where he divided his career between the studios and appearances at jazz festivals and clubs until his death in 1995.

Carlo Pes

PHOTO: COURTESY CARLO PESS

SELECTED RECORDINGS

Barney Kessel	RCA Victor (Italy) 730-710
Kessel's Kit	RCA(Italy) SF 8098
What's New-Barney Kessel	Mercury (France) 135720
Duo w/ Barney Kessel	Gemelli GG ST 10025
Segtetto Swing Di Roma	G.M.30706
Easy Moments Duo w/Barney Kessel	Gemeli GGST 10025 LP
Five Continents-Italian Jazz Club	IJ-003
Swinging	HLP 211-212
Coliseum Jazz Trio Jazz	Music NPG

JACK PETERSEN
Born-Elk City, Oklahoma, USA
25 October 1933

Jack Petersen

PHOTO: SUSAN P. STANTON/COURTESY JACK PETERSEN

Jack Petersen began playing the guitar when he was fourteen. He studied with a local teacher, Bob Hames. His early influences included Charlie Christian, George Barnes and Johnny Smith. Petersen gained professional experience playing rhythm guitar in Western Swing bands before becoming involved in jazz. He attended the North Texas Teachers College at Denton, Texas as a student 1951-55 where he played cello and double bass in the college symphony orchestra, and guitar and piano in the Jazz Lab band.

After being drafted into the US army Petersen toured with the 8th Army Band from 1956-57. After leaving the forces he toured with the Hal McIntyre band from the Autumn of 1957 to Spring 1958. From 1958 Petersen became involved in studio work in the Dallas, Texas area. In 1962 he founded the Guitar Department at the Berklee College of Music, Boston. He served as its head until 1965. He returned to Dallas in 1965 where he worked with a wide variety of artists including Stan Kenton, Art Van Damme, Clark Terry, Nancy Wilson, Carl Fontana, Billy Daniels and Joe Morello. Petersen also maintained a busy career as a teacher in Texas. He was Resident Artist for twelve years at his old college, now called the North Texas State University in Denton, teaching guitar and improvisation. For many years he also taught at jazz clinics throughout the USA, and for three years was a faculty member at the Summer Music Camps in Sweden. Petersen also worked as a staff artist/clinician for the Fender Guitar Company.

Since 1988 Jack Petersen has lived in Florida where he is an associate professor teaching jazz guitar and improvisation at the University of North Florida School of Music in Jacksonville.

SELECTED RECORDINGS

Hal McIntyre Band	Roulette R 25079
Matteson-Phillips Tubajazz Consort	Mark Records MJS-57587
Superhorn	Mark Records MJS-57591
Groovey	Four Leaf Records FLC-5060

SELECTED MUSIC

Jazz Guitar Styles & Analysis	Downbeat Music Publications
The Art of Improvisation Vols 1 & 2	Music Minus One

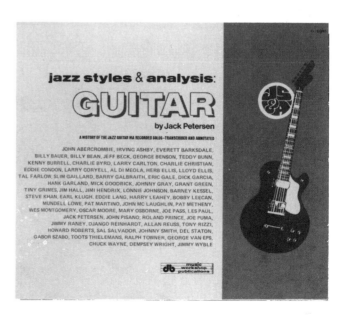

PHILIPPE PETIT
Born-Marmande, France
23 November 1954

Philippe Petit's father, who played the piano, guitar and trumpet, encouraged his son to play the trumpet from the age of five. Petit went on to study solfege and trumpet in the Conservatory in Bordeaux from the age of thirteen until he was eighteen. He had to stop playing the trumpet after an illness and then began to play the guitar. After completing his military service Petit began to play the guitar in clubs around Bordeaux. He studied music with pianist Francois Faure and also jazz with a guitarist called Jacques Raymond. At the same time he studied classical guitar with a local teacher, Henri Martin.

For some time Petit went up to Paris to study with the prominent jazz guitarist Pierre Cullaz. In 1976 he decided to move permanently to Paris. Here he continued his study of the guitar and jazz, listening to recordings and playing with local jazz musicians. In 1977 Bordeaux record dealer Alain Boucanus produced Petit's first recording, 'Parfums' on which he played solo acoustic guitar.

In recent years Petit has matured into one of France's busiest and most original jazz guitarists.

Philippe Petit

PHOTO: ERIC FEUILHERADE/COURTESY SAVAREZ STRINGS

SELECTED RECORDINGS

Parfums	Musica Records MUS 3020
Impressions of Paris with Miroslav Vitous	EPM Records FDC 5524
Standards Recital w/Tal Farlow	FD Music 15 1932

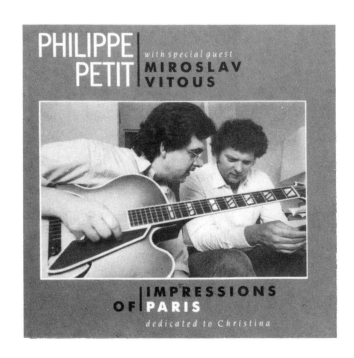

JACK PEZANELLI
Born-Worcester, Massachusetts, USA
10 October 1948

Jack Pezanelli first started to play the guitar at the age of 14 studying with an uncle. His first real musical experience was as a toddler singing with his uncles at weddings and charity functions. In 1967 he met Larry Coryell and this meeting made quite an impact on Pezanelli who at that time was already playing in diverse jazz and blues/fusion goups. From 1968-70 he attended the Berklee College of Music where his teachers were Mick Goodrick and William Leavitt.

On leaving Berklee Pezanelli joined the 14 piece Rhythm and Blues band Wayne Cochran and the C.C. Riders which at that time featured Jaco Pastorius. From 1971-72 he joined the band backing singer/entertainer Sammy Davis Jnr. In 1973 he moved to Miami, Florida where he once again joined Jaco Pastorius in Tommy Strand's Rhyhm and Blues band. From 1974-80 Pezanelli freelanced in the Miami area working with a wide variety of musicians including Lou Rawls, Mongo Santa Maria and Ira Sullivan. At that time he also studied with Joe Diorio.

In 1980 Jack Pezanelli moved to Western Massachusetts where he worked and studied with saxophonist Jimmy Giuffre. He led several of his own groups over the next five years. In 1985 he moved to Worcester, Massachusetts and 1987-88 was appointed graduate teaching assistant in the Fine Arts department at the University of Massachusetts. Since 1989 he has been an Assistant Professor at the Berklee College of Music in Boston.

Jack Pezanelli

SELECTED RECORDINGS

Pleasured Hands	Brownstone BRCD 955
It's Christmas Time	Brownstone BRCD 959

SELECTED MUSIC

Key Jazz Rhythms - Lipsius (Jack Pezanelli plays on the companion CD) Advance

JOHN PISANO
Born-New York City, U.S.A.
6 February 1931

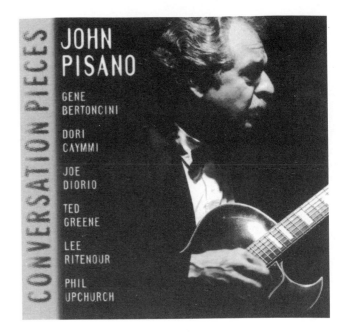

Although John Pisano did not start playing the guitar until he was fourteen he did have a good musical background. He studied the piano at the age of ten, and his father was an amateur guitarist. Whilst he was in the US Air Force 1952-55 he joined the Air Force band, and this experience made him decide to make music his career.

After leaving the Air Force Pisano joined Chico Hamilton's quintet on the recommendation of flautist Paul Horn. After touring with Hamilton 1956-58, Pisano decided to settle in Los Angeles. Here he played with Buddy DeFranco, Fred Katz, Joe Pass, and Jimmy Giuffre, and recorded some outstanding duets with fellow guitarist Billy Bean. For a period of two years he studied music at a local city college. From 1960-69 he worked as an accompanist for singer Peggy Lee. This was to prove to be a successful association.

In the mid 1960s Pisano's talents were brought to the attention of trumpeter Herb Alpert, leader of the popular 'Tijuana Brass' group. Alpert signed him up and Pisano toured the world with this band 1965-69. Pisano was also associated with composer/ songwriter Burt Bacharach, and pianist Sergio Mendes's group 'Brazil 66'. In the early 1970s he was featured with guitarists Lee Ritenour and Tony Rizzi, once more backing Peggy Lee, and also writing music. John Pisano continues to spend most of his time in and around Los Angeles where his guitar virtuosity is constantly in demand.

In recent times he has played in duo with his wife vocalist Jeanne Pisano.

SELECTED RECORDINGS

Chico Hamilton Quintet	Pacific Jazz 1225 LP
Chico Hamilton Quintet	Soul Note 121191-2 LP
Making It Duo with Billie Bean	Decca 9206 LP
Take Your Pick Duo with Billie Bean	Decca 9212 LP
Fred Katz and his Jammers	Decca 79217 LP
4,5,6-Trio	Decca 9213 LP
Under The Blanket	A & M SP 4276 LP
Summer Nights w/Joe Pass	Pablo 2310 939 2CD
Appasionata w/Joe Pass	Pablo 2310 946 2CD
The Flying Pisano's w/Jeanne Pisano	FPMusic FPM-01 CD
Duets w/Joe Pass	Pablo PACD 2310-959-2
Among Friends – John Pisano	Pablo PACD 2310-956-2
Conversation Pieces	Pablo PACD 2310-963-2
Jack Sheldon Quintet Video	Leisure MV 466

SELECTED READING

Profile	Guitar Player, November 1974
Interview	20th Century Guitar, August 1995
Interview	Just Jazz Guitar, November 1997

John Pisano

PHOTO: COURTESY JOHN PISANO

SAL SALVADOR'S PROFESSION...

is in his hands ... in his skill ... in the GRETSCH GUITAR

he has selected to bring out his superb musicianship. His "Colors in Sound" band has been hailed with raves by jazz critics since the release of his first Decca LP recordings. Creating exciting sound, with a wonderful shouting and singing quality, the band reflects Sal's unique guitar technique ... and his Gretsch "Sal Salvador Jazz Guitar" fills his every need.

The guitar capable of more subtle shadings and tonalities whether in recording session, band date or solo. Try one today ... Gretsch ... the guitar made for gifted hands.

Write to Dept. AG-7 for the FREE color-illustrated Gretsch Guitar Catalog.

The perfect companion to Sal's guitar. His Gretsch Executive model amplifier (6163). Stereophonic design with two-channel chassis playing through 15" Jensen heavy duty speaker with a high range tweeter.

GRETSCH The Fred. Gretsch Mfg. Co. 60 Broadway, Brooklyn 11, New York

Kenny Burrell

Kenny Burrell has all the technique, all the ideas, all the feeling, sensitivity, intelligence and spirit that a great jazzman needs. His ideas flow so freely, that he is everything anyone can ask in a musician. He is in tremendous demand as a sideman—probably the most recorded guitarist in the history of jazz. But his finest works are his own releases on Verve Records.

For brilliant, exciting leads, Kenny plays his Gibson Super 400 Custom and his Gibson L5 acoustic, while his quiet, emotional feelings are eloquently expressed on a Gibson Classic. As he creates and explores, he makes vast demands of his instrument, requiring a perfect performance, always. So he always plays Gibson—choice of professional artists and acknowledged world leader in fine guitars.

GUITARS AND AMPLIFIERS

Gibson

Al Caiola

Mary Osborne

Sal Salvador

WHATEVER YOUR STYLE, IT'S GRETSCH BY A MILE!

Professionals, like these top jazz artists, appreciate the full, rich sustaining tones they get in every register of their Gretsch guitars. Rave about Gretsch's new streamlined styling ... the wonderful 'new feel' of Gretsch extra-thin modeling.

Why not try a Gretsch guitar? Whatever your playing style—there's a model for you. Write for FREE, new Gretsch Guitar Catalog ... pictures over 30 different models, plus special Gretsch Electromatic Amplifiers and accessories.

GRETSCH The FRED. GRETSCH Mfg. Co., Dept. M-557, 60 Broadway, Brooklyn 11, N.Y.

MAY, 1957   11

JACK HOTOP

AND HIS GIBSON

The Joe Mooney Quartet are drawing "raves" from audiences ... and from the critics too, and Jack Hotop and his Gibson come in for their share of the applause. Smooth, easy action and brilliant response make Gibson the choice of artists who demand perfection in their guitars. Try a Gibson and note the difference!

Gibson INC. KALAMAZOO MICHIGAN

Advertisements featuring jazz guitarists from the 1950s and 1960s.

Bucky Pizzarelli

BUCKY PIZZARELLI
Born-JOHN PAUL PIZZARELLI
Paterson, New Jersey, USA
9 January 1926

Bucky and John Jnr Pizzarelli

PHOTO: COURTESY STASH RECORDS

Bucky Pizzarelli was introduced to the guitar at the age of nine by two uncles who were both guitarists. His first professional work was as a rhythm guitarist in 1941 in local dance bands. By the time Pizzarelli was seventeen he had joined Vaughan Monroe`s popular dance band. He toured with this band for about three months and then was drafted into the Army. After leaving the forces in 1946 Pizzarelli rejoined the Monroe band until 1951. In 1952 he decided to resettle in his home town of Paterson, New Jersey where he played in a local trio led by Joe Mooney. He was then offered a job by the NBC as staff guitarist for a five days a week television show. He took the position and found that he was also able to do jazz club and recording work.

Pizzarelli played with diverse groups on the East Coast including the Les Elgart band. From 1956 to 1959 he went on the road with a group called `The Three Sons`. Pizzarelli returned to studio and recording work, playing with most of the top East Coast studio guitarists including Al Caiola, Tony Mottola and Mundell Lowe. By chance in 1967 Pizzarelli heard George Van Eps playing his seven-string guitar in a New York club. Fascinated by the extra harmonies gained with the extra string Pizzarelli was determined to master the seven-stringed instrument. Whilst developing his technique on this guitar Pizzarelli renewed an old association with guitarist George Barnes, whose long time partner Carl Kress had recently died. Together they formed a new and exciting guitar duo finding they had a great rapport for each other. They played many concerts as a duo and made several excellent recordings. In 1970 Pizzarelli decided to accept an offer to join the Benny Goodman orchestra and, except for a break in 1971, stayed until 1974 with this famous band. Since that time Pizzarelli has played and made many recordings with diverse jazz artists including Joe Venuti, Stephane Grapelli, Red Norvo, Zoot Sims, Bud Freeman, Slam Stewart and others.

Bucky Pizzarelli has appeared at major international jazz festivals, and given solo recitals in jazz clubs and concerts on the seven-string guitar throughout the USA. In the last few years he has appeared and recorded frequently with his son John Pizzarelli Jnr. His son, a talented jazz guitarist in his own right, has become a very successful singer in recent years. On his recordings Pizzarelli Jnr is supported by top jazz artists including his father.

SELECTED RECORDINGS

Jazz Minus Many Men w/Vinnie Burke	Savoy MG12158
Nightwings w/Joe Venuti	Flying Dutchman BDL1-1120
Green Guitar Blues	Monmouth MES7047
Bucky Plays Bix and Kress	Monmouth MES7066
Guitars-Pure and Honest w/George Barnes	A&R Records 7100-077
Town Hall Concert	CBS S67275
A Flower for all Seasons	Choice CRS1002
Buck and Bud w/Bud Freeman	Flying Dutchman BDL1-1378
Sliding By w/Joe Venuti	Sonet SNTF734
Butch & Bucky w/Butch Miles	Dreamstreet DR-102
Benny Goodman Orchestra	Verve 820543-2
Bucky's Bunch	Monmouth MES7082
Dialogue w/Slam Stewart	Stash ST201
Duo w/Zoot Sims	Elegial STCD 8238
Doug and Bucky	Flying Fish FF043
Duet w/Stephane Grappelli	Ahead 33.755
2 x 7 = Pizzarelli	Stash ST 207
Love Songs	Stash ST 213
Cafe Pierre Trio	Monmouth MES 7093
I'm Hip John Pizzarelli Jnr	Stash ST 226
Swinging Sevens	Stash ST 239
Hit That Jive, Jack	Stash ST 256
Solo Flight	Stash ST 263
The Rhythm Encounters	Stash CD 18
A Portrait	Stash CD 551
Live w/Johhny Frigo	Chesky JD 1
New York Swing	LRC CDC 9045
Cole Porter Collective	LRC CDC 9055
New York Swing plays Rodgers and Hart	LRC CDC 9072
Nirvana	LRL CDC 9090
Live at the Vineyard w/John Pizzarelli Jnr.	Challenge CHR 7005 CD
Solos and Duets w/John Pizzarelli Jnr.	Jazz Classics JZCL-5007 CD
A Summer Thing w/Zoot Sims	Laserlight 15 754 CD

SELECTED READING

Interview	Guitar Player, June 1974
Interview	Crescendo, November 1979
Article	Just Jazz Guitar, February 1996
Interview	Just Jazz Guitar, May 1996
A Life in Music – Biography Ripmaster	Mel Bay, 1998

SELECTED MUSIC

A Touch of Class Guitar Method	Keith Perkins Publishing
Power Guitar	Camerica Publications
A Pro's Approach	Camerica Publications
A Creative Guitarist	Warner Bros. Publications
The Romance Of The Chordal Guitar Sound	Mel Bay Publications

JOHN PIZZARELLI JNR
Born-JOHN PAUL PIZZARELLI Jnr
Paterson, New Jersey, USA
6 April 1960

John Pizzarelli Jnr

John Pizzarelli Jnr is the son of famed guitarist Bucky Pizzarelli. As a child he was surrounded by music and musicians. He first started to to take tenor banjo lessons as a child with his father's uncles Bobby and Peter Domenick. As a teenager he played the guitar but his musical interest was in singing and playing rock music. With the encouragement of his father Pizzarelli began to listen to some recordings by Django Reinhardt. This changed his musical outlook and soon he was listening to and studying the recordings of all the great jazz guitarists. Pizzarelli, who is also a fine trumpeter, studied at the William Paterson College in New Jersey.

By the time he was twenty Pizzarelli was playing and singing professionally in a duo with his father. Their recordings were well received and they gained a lot of international exposure through these. In 1986 Pizzarelli joined the Tony Monte Trio and with this group was often heard on the WNEW radio station in New York. The trio's club dates in the New York area displayed full proof that John Pizzarelli Jnr is a talented jazz guitarist in his own right. He plays in a style often very reminiscent of his father.

In recent times John Pizzarelli Jnr has enjoyed great success as a jazz influenced singer with his guitar well featured on his recordings. Like his father Pizzarelli often plays a seven-string guitar.

SELECTED RECORDINGS
2 x 7 = Pizzarelli	Stash ST 207
I'm Hip Please Don't Tell My Father	Stash ST 226
Swinging Sevens	Stash ST 239
Hit That Jive, Jack	Stash ST 256
Live with Johnny Frigo	Chesky JD 01-CD
My Blue Heaven	Chesky JD 38 CD
All Of Me	BMG/Novus 63129-2 CD
Naturally	BMG/Novus 63151-2/4CD
New Standards	BMG/Novus 63172-2 CD
Dear Mr Cole	BMG/Novus 63182-2 CD
Live at the Vineyard w/Bucky Pizzarelli	Challenge CHR 70025 CD
Solos and Duets with Bucky Pizzarelli	Jazz Classics J2CL-5007 CD
John Pizzarelli Collection	Chesky JD 153 CD
John Pizzarelli Live in Montreal Video	BML 80082-3
Jazz Guitar Virtuoso Video	Mel Bay 97334VX

SELECTED READING
Profile	Downbeat, April 1992
Interview	Just Jazz Guitar, February 1995
Article	Jazz Times, August 1997

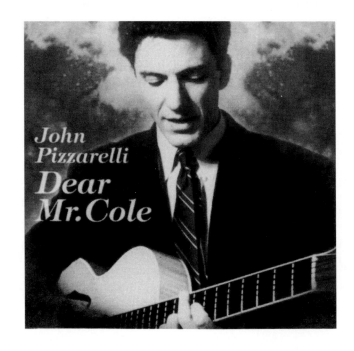

JIMMY PONDER
Born-JAMES WILLIS PONDER
Pittsburgh, USA
10 May 1946

Jimmy Ponder is a self taught guitarist. As a teenager he worked in soul music groups. He became interested in jazz after hearing some recordings of Wes Montgomery. It was this legendary guitarist who proved to be the major influence on Ponder's developing jazz guitar style. Ponder uses his right-hand thumb instead of a pick as Montgomery did.

While still at high school Ponder played professionally in an organ trio led by Bobby Jones in local Pittsburgh clubs. In 1969 he was hired to tour with organist Charles Earland. Ponder played and recorded with Earland for three years. In 1972 he moved to Newark, New Jersey where he played with organist Joe Thomas's quintet. He also commuted regularly to New York where he played in clubs such as Minton's, Small's and the Palm Cafe.

Jimmy Ponder is most often featured with organists. He has played with Lonnie Smith, Johnny 'Hammond' Smith, Groove Holmes, Jimmy McGriff, Shirley Scott, John Patton and Charles Earland. At the same time he has worked over a period of time with many other prominent jazz instrumentalists including Lou Donaldson, Donald Byrd, Sonny Stitt, Gary Bartz, Stanley Turrentine and Andrew White.

In 1990 Ponder returned to live in Pittsburgh.

SELECTED RECORDINGS

Ponder'n	CBS-51 West Q 16118
Mean Streets-No Bridges	Muse 5324 CD
Jump Jimmy Ponder	Muse 5347 CD
To Reach A Dream	Muse 5394 CD
Jimmy Ponder	LRC CDC 9031
Something to Ponder	Muse 5567 CD

SELECTED READING

Profile	Guitar Player, October 1992

Jimmy Ponder

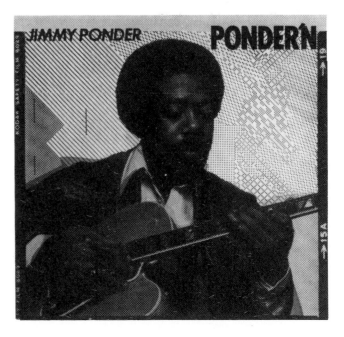

GARY POTTER
Born-Liverpool, UK
15 November 1965

Gary Potter

Gary Potter originally played a mixture of styles on the guitar. Using both pick and fingerstyles his self-taught guitar style was influenced by country, classical and jazz guitar greats. It was the guitar style of Django Reinhardt, and the many followers of the gypsy jazz guitar style, that most impressed Potter. A strong influence was Bireli Lagrene. Potter first came to the public eye outside his native Liverpool in 1985 when he sat in with Lagrene at the 100 Club in London.

Although showing great talent on the guitar in his early teens Potter initially played only in various pubs in the Liverpool area. International recognition came when he was spotted by fellow guitarist, Ian Cruickshank, who was researching for a Channel 4 television film called 'The Django Legacy'. After Potter's appearance in this successful film he was invited to appear in the annual Django Reinhardt Festival in Samois-sur-Seine, France. His success there led to many jazz club bookings, including an appearance at the Dutch 'Django Reinhardt Festival' in Rijswik for his newly formed group which also included Ian Cruickshank.

Potter, who now has several recordings to his name, seems set to be a leading British jazz guitarist.

SELECTED RECORDINGS

Now Hear This	Fret Records FJC 101
The Gary Potter Band- Live!	Fret Records FJC 103
Grace Notes Gary Potter	Fret Records FJC CD 104
Friends	HiHat HHR001 CD

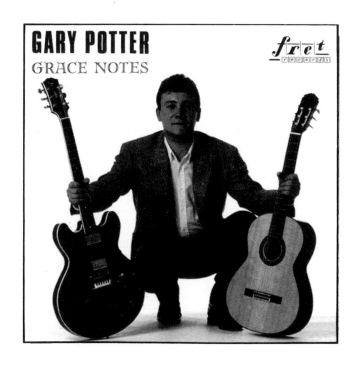

BADEN POWELL
Born-BADEN POWELL DE AQUINO
Varre-e-Sai,
Rio de Janeiro State, Brazil
6 August 1937

Baden Powell

Baden Powell is regarded by many as the foremost jazz guitarist to have come from Brazil since the start of the bossa nova boom. He certainly has been one of this idiom's most prolific and successful composers.

Powell's father was a violinist and his grandfather, a black full blood, was the conductor of Brazil's first all black orchestra. His father was also a leader of the Brazilian Boy Scouts, and a great admirer of the founder of the movement, Robert Thompson Baden Powell. As a result he named his son after the great scout leader.

Baden Powell began to play at the age of eight on a guitar belonging to his aunt. He progressed quickly and was playing professionally at the age of fifteen. He first gained national prominence in Brazil when he co-wrote `Samba Triste` with Billy Blanco in 1959. Over the next two years he was featured as a session guitarist on many bossa and samba recordings. In 1962 he teamed up with the poet/songwriter Vinicius de Moraes (1913-80). This popular Brazilian poet wrote the lyrics for more than fifty of Powell's compositions. Although Baden Powell's guitar playing is founded on traditional Brazilian music, and Afro-Brazilian rhythms, the guitarist has always said that his style was greatly influenced by jazz guitarists, including Django Reinhardt and Barney Kessel. Powell plays on a nylon-strung classical guitar, with right hand fingerstyle technique.

Although well known inside Brazil, Powell was virtually unknown outside his native country until 1966. German jazz writer Joachim Berendt, on a visit to Brazil, persuaded Powell to make his first long playing record under his own name. This was a success and Powell decided to settle in Europe. Since that time he has developed a large following for his music, and his success and popularity continue to grow. He has made many recordings as leader of his own group, and with other jazz artists including Stephane Grappelli. Powell spends much of his time in Europe although he does go back to Brazil regularly to record and give concerts. He has also played in the USA with diverse jazz artists including Stan Getz.

SELECTED RECORDINGS

Tristeza	MPS 68-093
Poema	MPS 68-089
Canto	MPS 68-157
Estudos	MPS 68-092
Images	MPS 68-091
Apaixonado	MPS 68-090
Le Monde Musical Vol.1	Barclay 80-235
Le Monde Musical Vol.2	Barclay 80-385
Aquarelles de Bresil	Barclay 80-416
Baden Powell Quartet Vol.1	Barclay 80-428
Baden Powell Quartet Vol.2	Barclay 80-429
La Coeur de Baden Powell	Festival FLD633
Stephane Grapelli/Baden Powell	Festival FLD634
Baden Powell	Fontana 6488-025
Guitar Artistry Baden Powell	Tuxedo TUX CD 5039
Live In Rio	Caju 847 111-2 CD
Live in Hamburg	Acoustic Music 319 1037 2 CD
Seresta Brasilera	Milestone 9212 CD

SELECTED READING

Profile	Guitar World, May 1982

SELECTED MUSIC

Baden Powell Guitar Solos Vol.1	Tonos Verlag
Baden Powell Guitar Solos Vol 2	Tonos Verlag

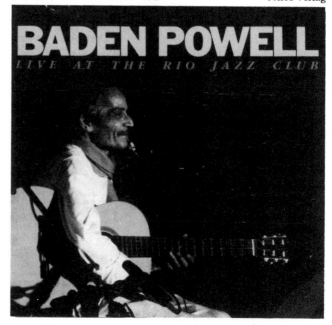

PHOTO: COURTESY CLASSICAL GUITAR

JOE PUMA
Born-JOSEPH J. PUMA
New York City, USA
13th August 1927

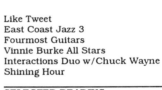

Joe Puma's father and two brothers were guitarists. Puma originally began working in 1944 as an aircraft mechanic and then as a draughtsman from 1945-47. It was in 1948, whilst living in New York, that Puma decided to become a professional musician and joined the musician's union.

For a period of five years Puma worked with a variety of small groups including those led by Cy Coleman in 1951, and Sammy Kaye in 1952. After this his guitar talent was featured in a wide assortment of jazz groups including Artie Shaw's Gramercy Five, Louis Bellson's Band and Don Elliot's quartet. In 1954 he joined singer Peggy Lee for two years, and then led his own group in 1957.

Puma continued playing in mainly small groups including that of Lee Konitz in 1958, and then in 1960 he went on tour accompanying singer Morgana King. In 1974 Puma returned to work in and around New York City and formed an outstanding, although short-lived, guitar duo with Chuck Wayne. They recorded and played together in New York jazz clubs. Since that time Puma has continued a busy career as a session guitarist, and working in jazz clubs in the New York area. His jazz talent has never received the full international recognition it deserves.

SELECTED RECORDINGS
Joe Puma Jazz	Jubilee JLP 1070
Wild Kitten	Dawn 1118

Like Tweet	Columbia CL 1618
East Coast Jazz 3	London LZ-N14033
Fourmost Guitars	ABC Paramount ABC 109
Vinnie Burke All Stars	ABC Paramount ABC 139
Interactions Duo w/Chuck Wayne	Choice CRS1004
Shining Hour	Reservoir RSR 102

SELECTED READING
Interview	Guitar Player, March 1974
Interview	Just Jazz Guitar, August 1995

SELECTED MUSIC
Joe Puma Guitar Solos	Juma Publishing Co.
Joe Puma Jazz Encounters	Mel Bay Publishing

Joe Puma with Chuck Wayne.

TONY PURRONE
Born-Bridgeport, Connecticut, USA
18 October 1954

Tony Purrone grew up in Trumbull, Connecticut. He began to play the guitar at the age of nine. At the age of 15 he was accepted by the University of Bridgeport Jazz Ensemble. Four years later, whilst still a student, he played with the Gerry Mulligan Sextet.

Purrone moved to New York University from where he graduated with a BSc in music. In 1978 Jimmy Heath invited him to join the Heath Brothers Band. Purrone toured internationally and recorded five albums with this famous group. Since 1982 Tony Purrone has played with many of the top jazz artists of the day including Lee Konitz, Al Cohn, Freddie Hubbard, Donald Byrd, Pepper Adams, Paquito D'Rivera, Sal Nistico, Frank Foster, Jon Faddis and Lionel Hampton. Purrone is also a prominent educationalist and has taught at Housatonic College, Wesleyan University in Connecticut and at Queens College in New York.

Tony Purrone

SELECTED RECORDINGS

Expansion	Quadrangle 101 LP
Electric Poetry	B & W Music BW 028 CD
New Picture w/Jimmy Heath	Landmark LM 1506 CD
Peel Pleasure w/Jimmy Heath	Landmark LM 1514 CD
Easy Flight w/Ed Thigpen	Reckless RR 9902 CD
Mr Taste w/Ed Thigpen	Justin Time JUST 43-2 CD
Set 'Em Up	Steeplechase SCCD 31389

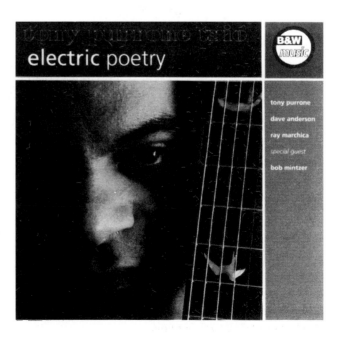

MONROE QUINN
Born-MONROE BRADFORD CHARLES QUINN
Jersey City, New Jersey, USA
8 July 1972

Monroe Quinn grew up in a musical family. His mother studied the violin and his father played the drums. His father encouraged Quinn to play the piano at the age of five. He developed an interest in jazz through listening to rehersals of a big band led by his brother Alan, an accomplished trumpeter.

At the age of eleven Quinn switched to the guitar after hearing some recordings by the great classical guitarist Andres Segovia. His first professional appearances began at the age of thirteen and since that time he has performed throughout the USA, Canada, Jamaica and in Brazil. Quinn studied for a while with Remo Palmier, and this famous jazz guitarist has proved to be a major influence.

His first CD recording as leader confirms Monroe Quinn to be one of the most promising new jazz guitar talents of the 1990s.

Monroe Quinn

PHOTO: KAREN TOWERTON

SELECTED RECORDINGS

I'll Dream of You - Monroe Quinn Quartet	MCD 7872
Live at Casey's w/Alan Quinn Big Band	ALV 89055

Examples of post 1940 jazz guitar music.

SNOOZER QUINN
Born-EDWIN MCINTOSH QUINN
McComb, Mississippi, USA
18 October 1906
Died-New Orleans, Louisiana, USA
1952

Snoozer Quinn's early recordings, which showed his true talent on the guitar, are today not available. Fortunately his old friend cornetist Johnny Wiggs recorded Quinn in 1950 when the guitarist was in hospital. Bearing in mind that Quinn was very ill, this record testifies to the fact that his reputation as a jazz guitarist of importance is correct.

Quinn played the mandolin, guitar and violin from the age of seven. His family moved to Bogalusa, Louisiana, and by his early teens he was already playing professionally in a trio in Bogalusa. At the age of seventeen he went on the road with the Paul English Travelling Shows. A little later he was featured with Claude Blanchard's orchestra in Houston. In 1925 he joined his first jazz group, Peck Kelly's Bad Boys in Shreveport. From late 1925 until 1928 Quinn played in and around New Orleans. On the recommendation of Bix Beiderbecke and Frankie Trumbauer, Quinn was hired in 1928 by Paul Whiteman. It was during the nine month period that Quinn was with Whiteman that he developed a high reputation for his guitar playing amongst his fellow musicians.

In 1929, after leaving the Whiteman band, Quinn worked for a short while with the hillbilly singer Jimmy Davis. He then returned to New Orleans were he worked with Earl Crumb's band at the Beverley Gardens. His health was not good and he had to give up full time playing in 1940. He did appear at the New Orleans National Jazz Foundation Concert in April 1948, but shortly after this, suffering from advanced tuberculosis, he went into hospital and remained there for the last part of his life

SELECTED RECORDING
The Legendary Snoozer Quinn   Fat Cat Jazz Records FCJ 104

PHOTO: COURTESY C.E.H. SMITH

Snoozer Quinn

THE LEGENDARY SNOOZER QUINN with JOHNNY WIGGS

ADAM RAFFERTY
**Born-New York City, USA
26 January 1969**

Adam Rafferty first began to play the guitar at the age of six. His first teacher was Woody Mann. Since that time Rafferty has studied with Dennis Cinelli, and pianist Mike Longo. He has also studied with classical guitarists David Starobin, Alice Artzt and Pat O'Brien. He studied composition with Anthony Newman. In 1992 Rafferty was awarded a Bachelor of Fine Arts in Music after completing his studies at the State University of New York, College of Purchase.

In recent years Rafferty has established himself as one of the busiest jazz guitarists in the New York area. He has appeared with the Dizzy Gillespie Big Band, Benny Golson's quartet, vocalist Gloria Lynn, and the Jimmy 'Preacher' Robbins Organ Trio. Rafferty is also an active guitar teacher and music educator at local university music departments and in a private capacity.

SELECTED RECORDINGS

Edelweiss		Atlantic Records
First Impressions	Consolidated Artists	CAP 905 CD

Adam Rafferty

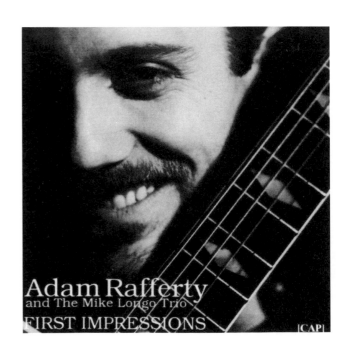

284

DOUG RANEY
Born-DOUGLAS RANEY
New York, USA
29 August 1956

Doug Raney is the son of the famed jazz guitarist Jimmy Raney. His first interest in the guitar began at the age of fourteen, not with jazz, but with rock guitarists Jeff Beck, Jimi Hendrix and Eric Clapton. He eventually began to listen to some of his father's recordings and then took informal lessons with Barry Galbraith. Raney attributes his development into a serious jazz performer after he had the opportunity to sit in with pianist Al Haig at Gregory's club in New York.

In 1977 Raney joined his father for a series of club and concert dates in New York. They went on to play in some of the major cities of Europe. It was soon obvious that Doug Raney was a great jazz guitar talent in his own right. Since the early 1980s he has performed with Dexter Gordon, Johnny Griffin, Louis Stewart, Kenny Drew, Clifford Jordan and others. He has toured Europe on numerous occasions with Chet Baker, Horace Parlan and others. He also toured Japan with Duke Jordan. Over the past 20 years Raney has made many recordings as leader of his own groups and also as a sideman for the SteepleChase, Jardis and Criss Cross record companies.

Doug Raney

PHOTO: COURTESY ENCORE PROMOTIONS

SELECTED RECORDINGS

Introducing Doug Raney	SteepleChase 31082 CD
Cuttin' Loose	Steeple Chase 31105 CD
Stolen Moments w/Jimmy Raney	SteepleChase 31118 CD
Duets w/Jimmy Raney	Steeplechase 31134 CD
Listen	SteepleChase 31144 CD
I'll Close My Eyes	SteepleChase 31166 CD
Nardis	SteepleChase 31184 CD
Blue And White	SteepleChase 31191 CD
Lazy Bird	SteepleChase 31200 CD
Guitar, Guitar, Guitar	SteepleChase 31212 CD
Something's Up	SteepleChase 31235 CD
The Doug Raney Quintet	SteepleChase 31249 CD
Everything We Love	Hot Club HCR 19 CD
Raney '81	Criss Cross 1001 CD
Meeting The Tenors	Criss Cross 1006 CD
The European Jazz Guitar Orchestra	Jardis JRCD 9307
Rancy '96	SteepleChase 31397 CD
Back In New York	SteepleChase 31409 CD

Jimmy Raney & Doug Raney
STOLEN MOMENTS

Jimmy Raney   Doug Raney   Michael Moore   Billy Hart

SteepleChase SCS 1118

Jimmy Raney

JIMMY RANEY

Born-JAMES ELBERT RANEY
Louisville, Kentucky, USA
20 August 1927
Died-Louisville, Kentucky, USA
10 May 1995

Jimmy Raney's father was a well-known sportswriter for a Louisville newspaper. His mother played the guitar and it was she that encouraged an early start on the instrument for her son at the age of ten. She gave Raney his first lessons and then later, whilst at school, he studied the classical guitar with A. J. Giancola. At the age of thirteen he began to study with local jazz guitarist Hayden Causey. He encouraged Raney to listen to the recordings of the leading jazz guitarists of the time including Charlie Christian.

By the time he was fifteen Raney was playing professionally in local bands and was determined to make a career in jazz on the guitar. In 1944 he joined the Jerry Wald band in New York. Raney developed a close friendship with the pianist in the Wald band, Al Haig. Raney went to Chicago in 1945 to live with his uncle and grandmother. From 1945-48 he played with various groups in which he played with Max Miller, Lou Levy, Cy Touff and Sandy Mosse. After a recommmendation from drummer 'Tiny' Kahn, Raney was invited to join the Woody Herman band. At that time the band included Stan Getz and Serge Chaloff. In 1949 Raney left the Herman band and took up residence in New York with guitarists Tal Farlow and Sal Salvador, and also vibraphonist Teddy Charles. Whilst in New York Raney had many opportunities to hear the leading musicians of the be bop movement including Charlie Parker and Dizzy Gillespie. Parker became his major jazz influence at that time.

For the next year or so Raney played with combos led by Artie Shaw and the Terry Gibbs. Stan Getz, by that time, had become regarded as one of the world's outstanding tenor saxophone players. After a tour of Sweden, Getz returned to the USA and formed a new quartet which featured Raney on guitar. Getz had a great respect for Raney's jazz artistry and together they played and recorded outstanding jazz 1951-52. In 1953 Raney replaced Tal Farlow in the Red Norvo Trio, touring throughout the USA and Europe. In the following year he backed jazz singer Billie Holiday. In 1954 and 1955 several jazz critics voted him ' Best Jazz Guitarist' in magazine polls. Although Raney in the early years of his career had travelled widely, he gradually developed a great dis-

like for travel, in particular for airplanes. He decided to spend most of his time at home with his wife and children.

In 1954 Raney joined Jimmy Lyon's trio at the Blue Angel in New York. For the next six years he worked in New York alternating work between Broadway shows, radio, television, and club dates. He also made several fine jazz recordings under his own name and with other artists, including Stan Getz, Bob Brookmeyer and guitarist Jim Hall. Raney then decided he could not sustain a successful career in jazz. In 1959 he took up the serious study of the cello, and he also studied composition with pianist Hal Overton. He continued working in music accompanying leading singers including Tony Bennet, Andy Williams, and Anita O'Day. He was also involved in making several valuable instructional record/music sets for the Music Minus One company in New York.

Between 1964 and 1972 little was heard of Raney as he returned to his home in Louisville and was virtually retired from the music scene. From the mid 1970s his son Doug emerged as a formidable jazz guitarist in his own right. Raney began to play in jazz clubs and record with his son. Their success encouraged Raney to start travelling on the world jazz circuit again, both as leader of his own groups, and with his son. He maintained an active career in jazz from that time until a problem with his hearing affected his ability to work.

Jimmy Raney, although never a strong chordal soloist on the guitar, was one of the all-time jazz guitar greats. His outstanding single-note playing brought him international recognition for being one of most musically creative and brilliant jazz improvisors. His playing style directly inspired many other leading jazz guitarists including René Thomas, Jimmy Gourley and Joe Puma.

SELECTED RECORDINGS

Stan Getz at Storyville (2LPs)	Vogue VJD554
Red Norvo Trio Vol.2	Vogue LDE115 LP
Red Norvo Trio	Jazz Magazine 004104 LP
Stan Getz Quintet/Quartet	Jazz Tone 1230 LP
Stan Getz Quartet at Storyville	Roulette CDP 7945072
Phil Woods – Early Quintets	Prestige OJCCD-1865-2
Early Stan	Prestige OJCCD-654-2
Immortal Concert w/Stan Getz	Giants of Jazz CD53113
Jimmy Raney visits Paris Vol. 1	BMG 74321429252 CD
Jimmy Raney Quartet	Prestige 7089 LP
Two Guitars w/Kenny Burrell	Prestige 7119 LP
Too Marvellous For Words	Biograph BLP-12060
Guitaristic	Swing CLD882
Jimmy Raney and George Wallington	Metronome ULS1607E LP
Jimmy Raney	ABC Paramount ABC 129
Fourmost Guitars	ABC Paramount ABC 109
Three Attitudes	HMV CLP1264
Street Swingers w/Jim Hall	Vogue LAE12147
Two Jims and a Zoot	Fontana TL5292
Strings and Swings	Muse 5004 LP
Strings Attached	Choice CRS1010 LP
Special Brew w/Al Haig	Spotlite LP8
Momentum	Pausa PR 7021 LP
The Influence	Xanadu 116 LP
Live in Tokyo	Xanadu 132 LP

Jimmy Raney-Solo	Xanadu 140
Jim & I w/Attila Zoller	L+R LR 40.006
Here's That Raney Day	Ahead 33.756
The Date w/Martial Solal	Stil 0703 S81
Raney' 81 w/Doug Raney	Criss Cross 1001 CD
The Master	Criss Cross 1009 CD
Wistaria	Criss Cross 1019 CD
Stolen Moments w/Doug Raney	Steeplechase SCS 1118 CD
Duets w/Doug Raney	Steeplechase SCS 1134 CD
Nardis w/Doug Raney	Steeplechase SCS 1184 CD
Complete Stan Getz Quintet Recordings	Mosaic MD3-131 CD
But Beautiful	Criss Cross 1065 CD
Jimmy Raney – Jazz Guitar Rarities	LXXVII-JZCD377

SELECTED READING

Profile	Downbeat, July 1961
Interview	Guitar Player, March 1977
Interview	Guitar, July 1977
Profile	Guitar Player, February 1988
Article	Just Jazz Guitar, May 1996

SELECTED MUSIC

For Guitarists Only (with record)	Music Minus One 4009
Jimmy Raney (with record)	Jamey Aebersold Vol 20
Play Duets with Jimmy Raney (with record)	Jamey Aebersold Vol 29
Jimmy Raney Solos	Jamey Aebersold

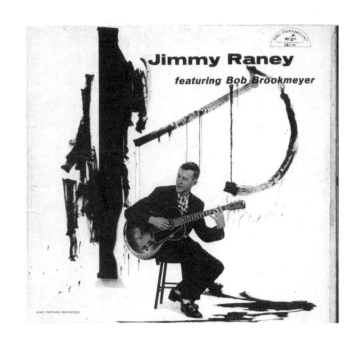

Jimmy Raney and Herb Ellis

288

ERNEST RANGLIN
Born-Manchester, Jamaica
19 June 1932

Ernest Ranglin is today hardly known outside of Jamaica, but on his few visits to Europe and the U.K. in the 1960s and 1970s he astounded jazz lovers by his amazing ability on the guitar. He briefly appeared at Ronnie Scott's jazz club in London in the mid 1960s and his jazz records made at that time on the 'Island' label bear testimony to his outstanding world class jazz guitar playing.

Ernest Ranglin's first instrument was the ukulele. He started playing the guitar in his early teens in Jamaica. He developed a high local reputation playing in a local band led by saxophonist Bertie King. During his early twenties Ranglin played in local clubs and hotels in the Bahamas. At the end of 1963 he came to Great Britain and immediately became an overnight jazz sensation.

Ranglin returned to live in Jamaica in the early 1970s where he played once again in local clubs and hotels. He did visit Germany briefly in the early 1980s to play and record with jazz pianist Monty Alexander, but decided at that time not to appear regularly on the world jazz circuit.

Since the mid-1990s Ranglin has enjoyed new popularity as the integration of 'Ska' rhythm from Jamaica into jazz has gained a large following.

Ernest Ranglin

PHOTO: HANS HARRHEIM/COURTESY JAZZ JOURNAL

SELECTED RECORDINGS
Ronnie Scott w/Strings	Fontana TL 5332
Ernest Ranglin & The GBs	Island IEP 704
Wranglin	Island ILP 909
Reflections	Island ILP 915
Ranglypso	MPS 15-440
Monty Alexander/Ernest Ranglin Duo	MPS 0068.629
Jamento-Monty Alexander Seven	Pablo 2310-826
True Blue	Rooney RR1 1202 CD
Yard Movement	Island 524232 CD
Below the Bassline	Island 24299 CD
Soul D'Ern – Ernest Ranglin	Ronnie Scott's Jazz House JHAS 611

SELECTED READING
Profile	Jazz Times, November 1996
Profile	Guitar Player, December 1996

BABIK REINHARDT
Born-Paris, France
8 June 1944

Babik Reinhardt is the son of Django Reinhardt and his second wife Sophie Zeigler (Naguine). Reinhardt and Naguine had lived together since 1928 following the breakdown of his first marriage. They married in July 1943 and in June 1944 Babik was born. Django Reinhardt also had a son by his first wife. He was the jazz guitarist Henri 'Lousson' Baumgartner (1929-1992) who played with his father in a 1948 Brussels jazz concert.

Babik Reinhardt received his first guitar at the age of three from his father. At the age of fourteen, already an accomplished player, Reinhardt began to take lessons with Eugene Vees. Vees had played in the Hot Club of France Quintet with Django Reinhardt. As a teenager Babik Reinhardt played with Larry Solero and Rene Mailhes.

In 1965 Reinhardt decided to continue in the tradition of his famous father by making his career as a jazz guitarist. His early playing in the late 1960s reflected the guitar style of Jimmy Raney and other American mainstream jazz guitarists of the 1960s. He then developed his own individual style often incorporating electronic sound devices on some of his recordings. During the early 1970s Reinhardt played with Jean-Luc Ponty. From 1976, for five years, Reinhardt gave up playing the guitar altogether. He found the constant comparisons of his playing with that of his father very difficult to come to terms with.

From 1981 Babik Reinhardt began a new career as a jazz guitarist and since that time has appeared frequently at jazz clubs and festivals throughout Europe, including the annual Django Reinhardt Festival held in Samois, France. He has toured with Larry Coryell, Christian Escoude, Birelli Lagrene and Didier Lockwood. As a solo performer he has played in the USA, South America and Europe. In 1986 he formed a successful guitar trio with Christian Escoude and Boulou Ferre.

Babik Reinhardt is now accepted internationally as one of Europe's finest contemporary jazz guitarists.

Babik Reinhardt

SELECTED RECORDINGS

Sur Le Chemin De Mon Pere	Delta DC 7008
All Love - Babik Reinhardt	Melodie 400011
Babik Reinhardt-Nuances	RDC 400182 CD
Babik Reinhardt-Live	Disques Swing 8431 CD
Three of a Kind	JMS Records JMS18662-2 CD
Vibration	RDC Records 40045-2 CD
Django – A Jazz Tribute Video	View Video

SELECTED READING

Interview	Jazz Hot, May 1993

French postal tribute to Django Reinhardt.

Magazines featuring Django Reinhardt as cover artist.

Django Reinhardt

DJANGO REINHARDT

Born-JEAN BAPTISTE REINHARDT
Liverchies, Belgium,
23 January 1910
Died-Fontainebleau, France
16 May 1953

Django Reinhardt was a legend in his own time and an even greater legend today. There are few guitarists (jazz or classical) throughout the world who have not heard of Django Reinhardt, and most guitarists will have at least one of his recordings.

Django Reinhardt was born into a Gypsy family, the son of an entertainer who worked in a travelling show. As a child Reinhardt roamed through Belgium and France in the family caravan. During this time he gained a great ability on the guitar, banjo and violin. As a young man Reinhardt worked as a street musician in the Montmartre area of Paris. His wife made wax candles in their caravan which was camped on the outskirts of Paris. On 2 November 1928 they were caught in a terrible fire in the caravan when some of the candles caught fire. Although Reinhardt and his wife succeeded in escaping, he suffered severe burns to his hands and body. After hospital treatment Reinhardt was left with two withered fingers on his left hand. For most guitarists this would have meant the end to any further thoughts of a musical career. Not Django Reinhardt. With a combination of great determination and physical strength he succeeded in developing a unique technique, and soon established himself as the most outstanding jazz guitarist of his time. Although Reinhardt could use his withered fourth and fifth fingers for some very simple chords on the first three strings, he could never use them for his outstanding single-string runs. The brilliant solos that he played, often at the most astonishing speed, were played entirely with the first two fingers of his left hand.

Reinhardt's early jazz playing has been described as 'Provencale, flaming in colourful decoration'. Yet in his later years his playing was most definitely influenced by the great American jazz musicians of the late 1940s that he heard on recordings, and during his concert tour of the USA in 1946. This tour, organised as a package with the Duke Ellington orchestra, was not a success. A most fascinating, and at times difficult personality, Reinhardt was a typical Gypsy. He was unreliable in turning up at concerts and recording sessions on time, if at all. Nevertheless Reinhardt often reached momentous heights in musical invention and artistry in concert and on his recordings. He was a natural musician, and even if he could have read music would probably still have preferred to improvise. Reinhardt had great love for all good music, including classical music. He also loved colour. This was reflected in his often garish and flamboyant dress, in his hobby of oil painting, and of course in his music.

After playing as a street musician in Paris in the early 1930s, Reinhardt was recommended as an accompanist to the popular singer Jean Sablon. He then joined forces in 1934 with violinist Stephane Grappelli, and together they formed a band that played at the Claridge Hotel in Paris. They soon came under the management of jazz enthusiast Charles Delaunay and formed the historic 'Quintet of the Hot Club of France'. The quintet's basic line up, which was originally inspired by Eddie Lang and Joe Venuti in the USA, consisted of three guitars, violin and double bass. The unique sound the quintet produced is still emulated today by many groups throughout the world. Django Reinhardt played almost exclusively throughout his career on several French made Maccaferri guitars. Easily recognized by their distinctive shape and penetrating sound, these unique instruments were made in the Selmer factory in Paris to the design of the famous Italian guitarist/luthier/engineer, Mario Maccaferri (1900-93). In his latter years Reinhardt sometimes used various American-made electric guitars which had been presented to him by the manufacturers to promote their products, but the Maccaferri guitar remained his favourite instrument and is always associated with him.

From 1935 the 'Quintet of the Hot Club of France' quickly earned international success. They made many successful recordings and toured throughout Europe and Britain playing to capacity audiences. When American jazzmen visited Paris they made a point of seeking out, and playing with, the now legendary Gypsy guitarist. It was generally recognised that Reinhardt was one of the few great original jazz musicians that Europe has ever produced. He played and recorded with several famous American jazz musicians including Coleman Hawkins, Benny Carter, Bill Coleman, Dickie Wells and Rex Stewart. The quintet is now regarded by many jazz observers as probably the most important influence in pioneering jazz in Europe and Britain 1935-39. The quintet broke up after the onset of World War II. Grappelli moved to London, and Reinhardt travelled in his caravan through parts of Europe, for the duration of the war.

After the end of World War II, Reinhardt, constantly aware of the new movements in jazz and music, played and recorded with several new small and big groups. His most famous composition 'Nuages' reached the hit parade as a popular song in several European countries in the late 1940s. This beautiful melody is still a favourite with jazz guitarists the world over. Unfortunately, as with several other great men of genius, death came all too early for Django Reinhardt. In May 1953 he suffered a stroke after an afternoon of fishing on the bank of the river Seine, and within a few hours was dead. The world had lost one of its most outstanding jazz guitarists and musicians. Today Django Reinhardt's following is greater than ever. His many records still outsell those of nearly all other jazz guitarists. Several books have been written about him, many books of transcriptions of his guitar solos are available, and music magazines regularly feature articles on him. All over the world guitarists of all ages still try to reproduce his unique sound. A recent television film, 'The Django Legacy' spotlighted dozens of fine guitarists all over Europe carrying on the tradition started in the early 1930s by Django Reinhardt and the 'Quintet of the Hot Club of France'.

SELECTED RECORDINGS

Django Reinhardt recorded for several companies, and virtually every track has been re-issued over the last few years in special sets, as well as in single, vinyl LPs, and more recently on CD. All Django Reinhardt's known recordings are listed in the special de-luxe biography of Django Reinhardt written by Charles Delaunay, and published by Ashley Mark Publishing Company in 1981

Jean Sablon & Django Reinhardt	World Records SH 368
Django Et Compagne 1934-37	Polydor 2489 188
Django Plus 1928-40	Pathe/Marconi 1727 291
Pathe/EMI Set 20 LP Records	Pathe/Marconi 054-160001/160020
Vogue Set 5 LP Records	Vogue COF03
RCA Set 3 LP Records	Black & White FXM3 7055
Decca Set 2LP Records	Decca 115-120/124
Capitol Set 2 LP Records	Capitol 10226
Barclay Set 2 LP Records	Barclay 80-929/30
50th Anniversary Hot Club Quintet 2 LP Set	Precision VJD 6950
Django	Polydor 236510 Bruxelles '48
Vogue LDM30217 Django-The Later Years	La Roulotte MA-3
Best Of Django Reinhardt LP+ Spautz Biography (In French)	Pathe Marconi BDR001
Django – Set 8 LP Records	Affinity Box Set 107
Swing In Paris 1936-40 – 5 CD Set	Affinity AFS 1003
Django – Solos/Duets/Trios	Inner City JIC 1105
Django Reinhardt & L' ATC Band	Jass J-CD628
Django Reinhardt 1947-51	Musidisc 30 CO 1504
Django Reinhardt - Nuages	Jazz Legacy 500 100
Django Reinhardt - Rythme Futur	Jazz Legacy 500 108
Django Reinhardt - Inedit Vol 1	NEC/Ultra 502 008
Django Reinhardt - Inedit Vol 2	NEC/Ultra 502 010
Django Reinhardt	DJM 22049
Django Reinhardt 1952-53	Decca 180-026
Djangologie/USA Vols 1-7CDs	Swing 8420-26(7)
Django & Co. (1928-1937)	Jazz Time 798975 2 CD
Indispensable Django Reinhardt	RCA Jazz Tribune ND70929 CD
Django Reinhardt (1935-39)	Jazz Portraits CD 14555
Djangology 10 CD Set	Blue Note 7806602 92
Gypsy Jazz	Drive Archive DE2 41050 CD
Django Reinhardt (Rome) (1949-1950)	RCA Jazz Tribune PD 71298 CD
Django Reinhardt w/Duke Ellington in Chicago	Music Masters 65110 2 CD
The Django Legacy Video	K Jazz KJ 093

SELECTED READING

Django Reinhardt Biography Delaunay	Cassell (1961)
Django Reinhardt Biography Delaunay-Special Edition	Ashley Mark Publishing Co. (1981)
Django-Mon Frere Biography Delaunay-French	Edition La Terrain
The Book of Django	Max Abrams (1973)
Django Reinhardt Special Issue	Guitar Player, November 1976
Esquire Book of Jazz	Arthur Barker Ltd (1963)
Article	Jazz Journal, June 1971
Article	Downbeat, June 1959
Appreciation	Downbeat, July 1966
Appreciation	Downbeat, February 1976
Django Reinhardt-Ein Portrait Dr.Dieter Schultz-Kohn-	Jazz Bucherei No.6'
	Jazz Magazine'(France), May 1970
Dinosaurs in the Morning p.86-91	Whitney Balliett Lippincott 1962
Jazz p.29-39 Graham Collier	Cambridge University Press (1975)
Article	Guitar Player, June 1969
Appreciation	B.M.G., March 1973
The Maccaferri-Django's Guitar	Guitar Player, April 1974
Article	Guitar, November 1973
Special Reinhardt/Grappelli Issue	Frets, October 1984
Jazz Under the Nazis Mike Zwerin	Beech Tree Books (1985)
Jazz Away From Home p.235-261	Goddard Paddington Press (1979)
Great Guitarists p. 152-157 Kienzle	Facts On File (1985)
Django Reinhardt Biography Roger Spautz (Published in German and French)	RTL, Luxembourg
Django Reinhardt Biography Schmitz/Maier (In German)	Oreos Verlag
Django Reinhardt Biography Patrick Williams (In French)	Editions du Limon
Profile	Guitarist, May 1989
Profile/Appreciation	Guitar Extra, Summer 1992
Appreciation	Jazz Hot, April & May 1993
Django Reinhardt (Book and CD)	Jazz Greats No. 13 1997
Django Reinhardt (Book and CD)	Edition Vade Retro (1997)
Django's Gypsies – Ian Cruickshank	Ashley Mark (1994)
Article	Just Jazz Guitar, November 1995
The Genius That Was Django-Cherrett	Cherrett (1997)

SELECTED MUSIC

Treasury of Django Reinhardt-76 Solos	Jewel Publishing Co.
L'Inoubliable Django 15 Solos	Francis Day SA
Magic of Django Vols 1 & 2 20 Solos	Francis Day and Hunter
Django Reinhardt 18 Solos	EMI Music
Django-Souvenir Vol.1 & 2 20 Solos	Francis Day SA
Django Reinhardt-Solos tr. Ayeroff	Amsco Publications
Django's 30 Finest Solos Note-for-Note	Paul Visvader
Django Reinhardt Swing Guitar	I.D. Music
Guitar Style of Django Reinhardt Ian Cruickshank	Music Sales Ltd
Django Reinhardt Anthology tr.Peters	Cherry Lane Music
Le Son Gitan	HL Music
Guitare Manouche	Salabert Music
Django A Souvenir Album tr.Volpe	Hansen Music

JOSEPH REINHARDT
Born-Paris, France
1 March 1912
Died-Paris, France
1982

Joseph Reinhardt

Joseph Reinhardt was the brother of the legendary jazz guitarist, Django Reinhardt. During his brother's lifetime Joseph Reinhardt played in the rhythm section in many of his brother's groups, including 'The Quintet of the Hot Club of France', with Stephane Grappelli. As a result his talents as a jazz guitar soloist were overlooked until fairly recent times.

Joseph Reinhardt, who was nicknamed Nin-Nin, started his musical career accompanying his brother, or other gypsy musicians, in the cafes of Paris in the 1920s. In 1931 Reinhardt joined Louis Vola's orchestra in Cannes in the South of France. After his return to Paris in 1932 he played with several leading jazz musicians including Frank Goudie, Arthur Briggs and Coleman Hawkins. From 1934 he became a mainstay of the rhythm section of the 'Quintet of the Hot Club of France'.

After leaving the Quintet of the Hot Club in the late 1930s Joseph Reinhardt played with several groups, including Aime Barelli's big band, and Alix Combelle's Jazz de Paris. In 1943 he formed his first group as leader with violinist Andre Hodeir. In 1947 Reinhardt began to play on electric guitar and was featured in Stephane Grappelli's Hot Four. For the next few years Reinhardt returned to life as a nomadic gypsy and was not involved in the professional music scene.

Around 1957 Reinhardt returned to Paris where he played in various clubs leading his own quintet or with other musicians. He was featured in the 1958 documentary on Django Reinhardt produced by Paul Paviot. In recent years, until his death in 1982, he was a featured soloist at the Festival Django Reinhardt held annually in Samois-sur-Seine, France. Joseph Reinhardt is buried near to his brother in Samois.

SELECTED RECORDINGS

A Django	Music Parade	LEL 223
Live in Paris 1966	Hot Club Records	HCRCD 66

EMILY REMLER

Born-New York City, USA
18 September 1957
Died-Sydney, Australia
4 May 1990

Emily Remler first started to play folk guitar at the age of ten. After a brief interest in rock music she became interested in jazz. At the age of sixteen she persuaded her parents to let her go to the Berklee School of Music in Boston to study jazz. It was there that she became influenced by the jazz guitar styles of Wes Montgomery and Pat Martino. She graduated in 1975 with a diploma in jazz studies.

In 1976 Remler moved to New Orleans and began life as a professional musician. At first she earned a living teaching and also playing in a rhythm and blues band called Little Queenie and the Percolators. She also played occasionally in a jazz group which included trumpeter Wynton Marsalis and vocalist Bobby McFerrin. The next couple of years saw Remler in the rhythm section of the band at the Fairmont-Roosevelt Hotel led by Dick Stabile. In this capacity she had the opportunity to back many top vocalists including Nancy Wilson and Rosemary Clooney.

Emily Remler's first real break came through Herb Ellis who heard her play in New Orleans in 1978. He arranged for her to appear with his quartet at the 1978 Concord Jazz Festival in California. In 1979 Remler moved to New York from where she joined the backing group for singer Astrud Gilberto. Success followed success and in 1980 Remler made her first recording as leader for the Concord Label. She then appeared at some major international jazz festivals including the Kool Festival in 1980 and the Berlin Jazz Festival in 1981.

Remler returned to Los Angeles and worked for a while in a theatre pit orchestra. She continued to record and make jazz club appearances gaining growing international recognition as one of the best young jazz guitarists of the day. During a 1990 concert tour of Australia Remler tragically collapsed and died in her hotel bedroom.

Emily Remler

SELECTED READING

Interview	Guitar Player September 1981
Profile	Downbeat, May 1982
Interview	Jazz Journal, March 1988
Profile	Downbeat, May 1989

SELECTED MUSIC

Compositions	Mel Bay Publishing

SELECTED RECORDINGS

The Firefly	Concord CJ 162
Take Two	Concord CJ 195
Transitions	Concord CJ 236
Catwalk	Concord CJ 265
Together w/Larry Coryell	Concord CJ 289
East To Wes	Concord CJ 356
Retrospective Vol.1 Standards	Concord CJ 453 CD
Retrospective Vol.2 Compositions	Concord CJ 463 CD
This Is Me!	Justice JR 0501-2 CD

Be Bop & Swing Guitar	Instructional Video	Hot Licks
Jazz & Latin Improvisation	Instructional Video	Hot Licks

ALLAN REUSS
Born-New York City, USA
15 June 1915
Died-Los Angeles, USA
4 June 1988

Allan Reuss

Allan Reuss is looked upon by many musicians as one of the best rhythm guitarists the world has known. His guitar was the mainstay of the rhythm section of some of the finest big bands from the 1930s through to the 1950s.

Reuss started playing the banjo at the age of twelve. He changed to the guitar and studied for a while with George Van Eps. It was Eps who eventually recommended that Reuss should take his place in the Benny Goodman orchestra. From 1934-38 Reuss toured with the Goodman band. In 1938 he set up his teaching studio in New York. Rhythm guitarists Freddie Green and Steve Jordan were two of his many pupils. Reuss was also hired for many studio and recording sessions in New York.

Allan Reuss played with Jack Teagarden for the first half of 1939, and then played with Paul Whiteman. In the spring of 1941 he played for a few months with Ted Weems, then with Jimmy Dorsey 1941-42, and the N.B.C. band in Chicago from 1942-43. Reuss went back to the Goodman band for a while in 1943 and then joined the Harry James band until 1944. He was rarely featured as a soloist but Reuss was capable of playing excellent rhythmic chordal and single string solos on his acoustic archtop guitar, much in the style of Dick McDonough. His superb recorded solo 'Picking for Patsy' with Jack Teagarden's orchestra in 1939 bears witness to his ability.

From 1945 Reuss freelanced and taught around the Los Angeles area for many years until his death in 1988.

SELECTED RECORDINGS
Benny Goodman and his Orchestra	Jazz Anthology 30 JA 5151 LP
Charlie Ventura 1946	Phoenix LP-6
Goodman at the Cotton Club 1938	Jazz Archives JA 12 LP
Benny Goodman Orchestra	CBS 450983-2 LP
This is Benny Goodman	RCA VPM 6063 LP
Jack Teagarden and his Big Band 1939	TAX M-8024 LP
Coleman Hawkins-Hollywood Stampede	Pathe Marconi CO6280802 LP
Gene Krupa's Swing Band	BBC CD 666
Benny Carter/Arnold Ross Quintet	Mercury 840 819-2 CD

SELECTED READING
Profile	Guitar, May 1974

SELECTED MUSIC
Allan Reuss Guitar Solos	ABC Music Corporation

THIS GUITAR FOLIO CONTAINS
ORIGINAL COMPOSITIONS
WRITTEN AND ARRANGED
BY ALLAN REUSS

····o····

CONTENTS

————— ····o···· —————

LEE RITENOUR
Born-LEE MACK RITENOUR
Los Angeles, California, USA
11 January 1952

Lee Ritenour began to play the guitar at the age of five. By the time he was ten he was already a very proficient guitarist. On the recommendation of Barney Kessel he began in 1964 to study with Duke Miller in North Hollywood. With Miller's encouragement Ritenour advanced his technique and knowledge to a very high level. At the age of twelve he was featured in a nineteen piece band called 'The Esquires'. From 1969 Ritenour began to study with leading studio and jazz guitarists including Joe Pass and Howard Roberts. He also studied with classical guitarist Christopher Parkening.

In 1973 Ritenour became involved in teaching. He had studied with Jack Marshall at the University of Southern California. After Marshall's sudden death in September 1973 Ritenour, still only twenty-one, was invited to take over his former teacher's post. Ritenour's first major international professional break came in 1974 when he joined Sergio Mendes's band, 'Brazil 77'. His travels with this successful band took him as far as Japan. On his return to Los Angeles Ritenour became one of the city's busiest studio guitarists. He also played jazz in local clubs and was often featured with guitarist John Pisano at the regular guitar night at Donte's. In 1974 he took part in the Guitar Summit at the Monterey Jazz Festival with Jim Hall, Mundell Lowe, Joe Pass and Michael Howell.

As a studio musician Lee Ritenour has played in over 3000 sessions during the last twenty years. He has backed popular singers and musicians including Barbra Streisand, Aretha Franklin, Leo Sayer, Earl Klugh, Ray Charles, George Benson, Peggy Lee, Tony Bennett, Lena Horne, Stevie Wonder, Cher, Johnny Mathis, John Denver and many others. In 1976 he recorded the first of many releases under his own name. Over the years his playing has reflected his expert musicianship and dazzling technique. Although most of his recordings have been firmly in the jazz/rock fusion camp, some of his more recent releases reflect the 1960/70s style of be bop guitarists, and a strong Wes Montgomery influence.

Lee Ritenour

SELECTED RECORDINGS

First Course	Epic PE 33947
Captain Fingers	Epic PE 34426
Guitar Player	MCA 2-6002
The Captains Journey	Elektra K52094
Feel The Night	Elektra Asylum 6E-192
Gentle Thoughts	JVC VIDC101
Lee Ritenour & His Gentle Thoughts	JVC JMI 2007-2CD

Friendship	JVC JMI 2009-2CD
Four Play	Warner 4-26656
On The Line	GRP 95242 CD
Rit 2	Elektra Musician 60186
Rio	GRP 95242 CD
Stolen Moments	GRP 96152 CD
Earth Run	GRP 95382 CD
Festival	GRP 95702 CD
Color Rit	GRP 95942 CD
Collection	GRP 96452 CD
Portrait	GRP 95532 CD
Wes Bound	GRP 97052 CD
Alive in LA	GRP 9882 CD

Guitar Secrets	Instructional Video	Rittor Music
More Guitar Secrets	Instructional Video	Rittor Music
Lee Ritenour Live Vol 1	Video	Video Arts (Japan)
Lee Ritenour w/Dave Grusin	Video	Verve 081 7863

SELECTED READING

Interview	Guitar Player, August 1975
Profile	Downbeat, March 1975
Interview	Guitar Player, February 1979
Interview	Crescendo, November 1979
Interview	Downbeat, April 1984
Interview	Guitarist, June 1988
Profile	Guitar World, November 1988
Profile	Downbeat, May 1989
Interview	Guitar Player, September 1990
Profile	Guitar Player, May 1992
Profile	Jazz Times, August 1993
Article	Jazz Times, December 1995
Interview	Fingerstyle Guitar, Nov/Dec 1997

SELECTED MUSIC

Lee Ritenour Artist Transcriptions	Hal Leonard
The Lee Ritenour Book	PMP Publications
The Lee Ritenour Collection	Columbia Pictures Publications

PHOTO: COURTESY IBANEZ GUITARS

TONY RIZZI

Born-TREFONI RIZZI
Los Angeles, California, USA
16 April 1923
Died-Newport, California, USA
2 June 1992

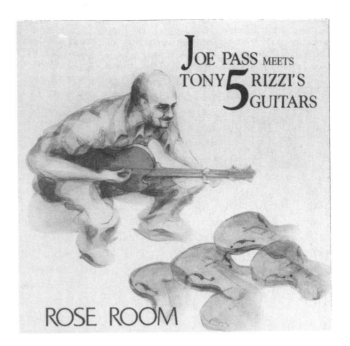

The guitar was Tony Rizzi's third musical instrument. He studied the violin for eleven years, then changed to the trumpet and finally took up the guitar when he was nineteen. After leaving the Army, Rizzi played with many name bands including those of Les Brown and Boyd Raeburn. For most of his professional career Rizzi was involved as a N.B.C. staff musician, and in television and film work. Over the years Rizzi played with diverse jazz artists and band leaders including Benny Goodman, Georgie Auld, Tommy Dorsey, Harry James, Stan Getz, Alvino Rey, and Louis Armstrong. He also took part in what is reputed to be the first recording featuring five guitars. The record track was called 'Five Guitars in Flight' and was recorded in 1946 with the Earle Spencer Orchestra. This recording also featured Barney Kessel, Arv Garrison, Irving Ashby and Gene Sargent.

Rizzi was always interested in playing jazz, especially the music of Charlie Christian. As a result he formed a band in 1973 with five guitars as lead instruments. This group played in Los Angeles clubs and made a recording devoted entirely to harmonized arrangements, by Rizzi for five guitars, of Christian's most famous solos with the Benny Goodman Orchestra.

Tony Rizzi continued as an active studio guitarist in Los Angeles until the time of his death in 1992 following an accident at his home in Huntington Beach.

SELECTED RECORDINGS

Earle Spencer Orchestra	Tops L 1532
Boyd Raeburn And His Orchestra	Savoy SV 0185
Tony Rizzi's Five Guitars Play Charlie Christian	Milagro 1000
Disco Pacific- The Five Guitars	Outstanding Records
The Five Guitars w/Joe Pass	Polytone ALCR-125

SELECTED READING

Article	Guitar Player, December 1976

Tony Rizzi (centre) with the Five Guitars.

HOWARD ROBERTS
Born-HOWARD MANCEL ROBERTS
Phoenix, Arizona, USA
2 October 1929
Died-Seattle, Washington, USA
28 June 1992

Howard Roberts

Howard Roberts taught himself to play the guitar from the age of seven. By the time he was twelve he was studying with Horace Hatchett. He inspired Roberts to listen and appreciate the full spectrum of music and the guitar, from the classics to jazz. He then studied guitar technique for a while with guitarist Howard Haitmeyer, and the Schillinger system with Fabian Andre. During World War II Roberts played professionally in and around Phoenix gaining valuable experience.

In 1950 Howard Roberts moved to Los Angeles. Soon after he arrived he went to hear Barney Kessel playing with Dave Brubeck at the Hague jazz club in Los Angeles. During the evening Kessel introduced him to Jack Marshall who was also in the audience. With Marshall's help Roberts soon established himself as one of the leading studio musicians in Los Angeles. Over the next twenty years Roberts was featured on literally thousands of recordings, and on many television and film soundtracks. In the early 1970s he became very interested in teaching and started to appear at guitar seminars all over the USA. He then formed his own publishing company called the Playback Publishing Company. In collaboration with other guitarists, including Jimmy Stewart, Roberts wrote and published several excellent jazz guitar books. He was a founder of the Guitar Institute of Technology (GIT) with Pat Hicks in 1976. Today the GIT is one of the world's prestigious educational establishments for guitarists. Roberts also became involved in guitar design and construction. The Epiphone company produced their first 'Howard Roberts' model in the late 1970s. In the early 1980s the Gibson company, having purchased the Epiphone company, released a new version of the original model as part of the Gibson range.

Howard Roberts always maintained an interest in jazz, and was active in helping establish in 1966 the jazz guitar night at Donte's club in Los Angeles. Over the years Roberts was featured with many jazz artists including Shorty Rogers, Buddy De Franco, Pete Jolly, Bud Shank, Bill Holman, Bob Cooper, Al Haig, Chico Hamilton, Gerry Mulligan, Oliver Nelson, Bobby Troup, and Dave Grusin. In 1955 he won Downbeat's 'New Star' award. He wrote an excellent monthly column for several years in Guitar Player magazine. Many of his later recordings show him as a jazz/rock fusion stylist, but his earlier recordings established him as one of the best all round jazz guitarists following in the tradition laid down by Charlie Christian.

In the last few years before his death of prostrate cancer in 1992, Roberts began to travel all over the world playing and teaching jazz. He has left guitarists the world over an invaluable legacy of jazz guitar instructional books.

SELECTED RECORDINGS

Movin' Man	VSP 29
Ten Trumpets & 2 Guitars	Mercury PPS 2016
Chico Hamilton Trio	PAcific Jazz PJ 1220
Mr.Roberts Plays Guitar	Verve MGV 8192
Velvet Groove	Verve MGV 8662
Julie is Her Name Vol.2	London HM4-V2186
Good Picking	Verve MGV8305
Art Pepper Quintet	Galaxy GCD-1016-2
Color Him Funky	Capitol ST 1887
H.R. Is A Dirty Player	Capitol SM-1961
Howard Roberts Quartet	Capitol ST 2609
Guilty	Capitol ST 2824
Thelonious Monk Orchestra	CBS 467 178-2
Antelope Freeway	ABC/Impulse ASD-9207
Equinox Express Elevator	ABC/Impulse ASD-9299
The Real Howard Roberts	Concord CJ 53
Howard Roberts Quartet	Discovery DS-812
Howard Roberts: The Magic Band	VSOP 94 CD

SELECTED READING

Profile	Guitar Player, August 1967
Profile	Downbeat, June 1967
Profile	Guitar Player, April 1970
Interview	Guitar Player, June 1979
Interview	Guitarist, March 1986

SELECTED MUSIC

Howard Roberts Chord Melody	Playback/Cherry Lane
Howard Roberts Guitar Book	Playback/Cherry Lane
Howard Roberts Sight Reading	Playback/Cherry Lane
Howard Roberts Superchops	Playback/Cherry Lane
The Accelerator	Cherry Lane
The Praxis System 3 Volumes	Advance Music

PHOTO: MAURICE J. SUMMERFIELD

DUKE ROBILLARD
Born-MICHAEL ROBILLARD
Woonsocket, Rhode Island, USA
4 October 1948

Duke Robillard first decided he wanted to play the guitar at the age of six after hearing some records by Buddy Holly and Chuck Berry. But it was not until he was twelve that he acquired his first guitar. In his early teens, he was inspired by various popular artists including Duane Eddy and 'The Ventures', as well as country music guitarists James Burton and Scotty Moore. Then his guitar style became influenced by leading blues artists including B.B. King, Buddy Guy, Otis Rush and Freddie King.

After his graduation Robillard worked for over a year in a factory. This experience made him decide to make a living as a musician. In 1967 he formed his group 'Roomful Of Blues'. Around this time his personal musical style began to be influenced by the recordings of Buddy Johnson's rhythm and blues band. Robillard then began to listen to the big band recordings of Count Basie and Duke Ellington, and also those of jazz guitarists Charlie Christian, Barney Kessel, Oscar Moore and Tiny Grimes. In 1969 he formed another blues band called 'Black Cat'. It was short lived, and after it disbanded Robillard reformed the 'Roomful Of Blues'. This group was styled on the Kansas City and Southwest swing traditions. For several years the group worked regularly in clubs around the Rhode Island and Boston areas. During this time Robillard was drawn further towards jazz when he befriended, and worked with, jazz saxophonist Scott Hamilton.

In 1978 the 'Roomful Of Blues' recorded for the Island label. Since that time Robillard has been involved in several successful groups, including 'The Pleasure Kings', 'The Legendary Blues Band' and 'The Fabulous Thunderbirds'. Duke Robillard recorded for Rounder Records. His releases for this company reflect the quality of the jazz side of his guitar playing, rather than the rhythm and blues of his earlier recordings.

Duke Robillard

Profile   Jazz Times, May 1996
Profile   Guitar Player, May 1997

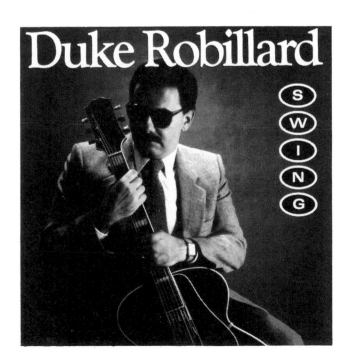

SELECTED RECORDINGS

Duke Robillard – Swing	Rounder RRCD 3103
Turn It Around	Rounder RRCD 3116
After Hours Swing Session	Network RRCD 3114
Duke Robillard plays Jazz	Bulls Eye 9597 CD
Duke Robillard plays the Blues	Bulls Eye 9598 CD
Temptation	Virgin 396052 CD
Dangerous Place	Virgin 42857 CD
Duke Robillard Instructional Video	Hot Licks

SELECTED READING

Profile	Guitar Player, September 1984
Profile	Guitar Player, October 1991

BILLY ROGERS
Born-WILLIAM ROGERS
Omaha, Nebraska, USA
2 January 1950
Died-San Francisco, California, USA
11 February 1987

Billy Rogers

Billy Rogers began to play the guitar at the age of twelve. His parents were both jazz lovers and they encouraged their son to learn music. By the age of fourteen he was already playing in a local rock group. He began to take an interest in jazz he was sixteen after hearing a friend's records of Kenny Burrell, George Benson and Grant Green. Determined to make a career in music, Rogers practised on his guitar at least eight hours a day.

Rogers joined organist Frank Edward's trio in 1967 and they played in Chicago, Detroit, Kansas City and Indianapolis. In 1971 he began playing with keyboardist Bobby Lyle. This association led to work with organist Ronnie Foster and then Jack McDuff. Rogers had by now developed a high reputation amongst his fellow musicians. In 1975 he was hired by George Shearing. Rogers stayed with the pianist's group for one and a half years.

In 1977 Rogers moved to Los Angeles. He played with saxophonist Ronnie Laws in a funk fusion band there. He then joined the highly successful group 'The Crusaders' touring with them for one and a half years. After leaving 'The Crusaders' Rogers continued to gig in and around Los Angeles with various musicians including saxophonist Plas Johnson. In 1984 he moved to San Francisco where he played with saxophonist Jules Broussard and others. In February 1987 Rogers was found dead in his San Francisco apartment from a drug overdose. Those who heard him play confirm that had Rogers not died at such a young age he would have eventually received much wider recognition for his jazz talents. A posthumous CD recording made up from private tapes, and produced by his friend Dave Stryker, certainly supports this view.

SELECTED RECORDINGS
The Genie-Bobby Lyle   Capitol ST-11627
The Guitar Artistry of Billy Rogers   Stash ST-CD-566

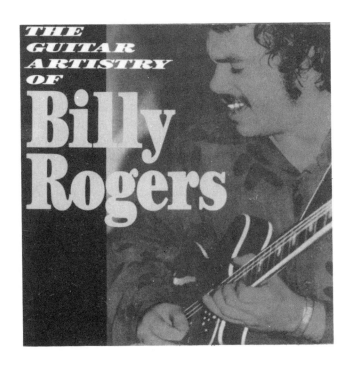

STOCHELO ROSENBERG
Born-Helmond, Holland
19 February 1968

Stochelo Rosenberg (centre) with Nous'che and Nonnie Rosenberg.

Stochelo Rosenberg was born into a Manouche Gypsy family with a long tradition of music. He began to play the guitar at the age of ten. He listened to the recordings of Django Reinhardt and after a while was able to play many of Reinhardt's solos note-for-note. Rosenberg soon achieved professional ability on the guitar and at the age of eleven made several radio broadcasts. At the age of twelve he appeared on Dutch television. For the next eight years he played with his trio to Gypsy communities in many parts of Europe, but was unknown to the general jazz audience there.

In 1989 his first recording was released on the Norwegian Hot Club label. This recording revealed Rosenberg's outstanding virtuosity and musicality. Since that time he has become a major jazz artist on the European jazz club and festival circuit, with many television and radio broadcasts. His jazz string trio, 'The Rosenberg Trio' is made up of his cousins Nous'che Rosenberg on rhythm guitar, and Nonnie Rosenberg on string-bass. The trio appeared with Stephane Grappelli in 1991 in Montreal, Canada. Following this Grappelli invited them to accompany him at his 85th birthday concert at the Carnegie Hall, New York in June 1993. Since that time they have appeared several more times with the legendary jazz violinist at jazz festivals all over Europe. The trio's recording 'Gypsy Summer' won the Dutch Edison Award as best instrumental CD of 1992. In the same year Stochelo Rosenberg won the Dutch 'Golden Guitar Award' as best guitarist.

In recent times Stochelo Rosenberg has played in concert with many of the world's finest jazz guitarists including Bireli Lagrene, Philip Catherine, Bucky Pizzarelli, Babik Reinhardt, Raphael Fays and Martin Taylor. He was also featured in the 1990 documentary television film 'The Django Legacy'.

SELECTED RECORDINGS

Seresta	Hot Club Records HCRCD 59
Gypsy Summer	Dino DNCD 1265
Impressions	Dino DNCD 1324
Rosenberg Trio-Live North Sea Jazz Festival 1992	
	Verve 519 446-2 CD
Caravan	Verve 523 030-2 CD

SELECTED READING

Profile	Just Jazz Guitar, February 1995

TERJE RYPDAL
Born-Oslo, Norway
23 August 1947

Terje Rypdal

Terge Rypdal comes from a strong musical background. His father, Jakop Rypdal is a well-known conductor of orchestras and marching bands, and his mother, Inger-Lise, was a pop singer. Terje Rypdal started playing the piano at the age of five. He began to teach himself to play rock/pop music on the guitar when he was thirteen. He went on to study composition at Oslo University, and the theory of improvisation with George Russell,

Rypdal's first professional work was in a rock group. His major influence at that time was Hank Marvin, lead guitarist with the pop/rock group 'The Shadows'. In 1968 Rypdal gained his first real jazz experience playing, and later recording, with a quartet led by Jan Garbarek. This break made Rypdal decide to make a full-time career in music. In 1969 he studied with the Norwegian composer Finn Mortenson, and for a time classical composers such as Mahler were his main musical interest. Rypdal then began to listen to recordings of USA jazz musicians including those of guitarists Charlie Christian, Wes Montgomery and Kenny Burrell.

In 1969 Terje Rypdal gained international recognition when he appeared in The German Free Jazz Festival playing in a band led by Lester Bowie. In 1972 Rypdal began to play the flute and the soprano-saxophone, but the guitar remained his main instrument. In 1975 he formed his own group called 'Odyssey' and this achieved great success both in Europe and the USA.

Since that time Terje Rypdal has made annual appearances at the most important European jazz festivals. In the mid 1980s he led a trio with Bjorn Kjellemyr and Audun Klieve. Rypdal is also recognised as a talented composer and has written guitar works for both classical orchestra and jazz ensembles.

SELECTED READING

Profile	Guitar Player, May 1977
Article	Jazz Times, August 1997
Profile	Guitar Player, September 1997

SELECTED RECORDINGS

Terje Rypdal	ECM 1016 CD
What Comes After	ECM 1031 CD
Whenever I Seem To Be Far Away	ECM 1045 CD
Odyssey	ECM 1067/68 CD
After The Rain	ECM 1-1083 CD
Waves	ECM 1110 CD
Terje Rypdal Trio	ECM 1125 CD
Descendre	ECM 1144 CD
To Be Continued	ECM 1192 CD
Eos	ECM 1263 CD
Chaser	ECM 1303 CD
Blue	ECM 1346 CD
Dream	Karusell Gold 2915 068
Undisonus	ECM 1389 CD
QED	ECM 1474 CD
If Mountains Could Sing	ECM 1556 CD
The Singles Collection	ECM 1383 CD
Skywards	ECM 1608 CD

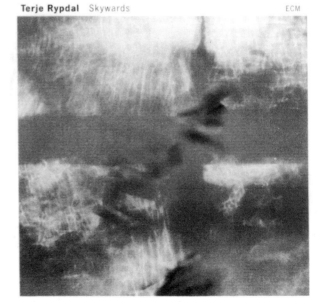

Terje Rypdal Skywards   ECM

JOHNNY ST. CYR
Born-JOHN ALEXANDER ST. CYR
New Orleans, Louisiana, USA
17 April 1890
Died-Los Angeles, California, USA
17 June 1966

Johnny St. Cyr

Johnny St. Cyr played both banjo and guitar throughout his long career in jazz. Mainly a rhythm player St. Cyr was associated with many of the great names of traditional jazz including Louis Armstrong, Kid Ory and Jelly Roll Morton.

St. Cyr's father, Jules Firmin St. Cyr played both the guitar and flute. St. Cyr began to play the guitar at an early age and began playing professionally when he was fifteen, although his main profession during the daytime was working as a plasterer. In the early 1900s he formed his own group, The Consumer's Trio, named after a local brewery. He then played in several well-known groups in New Orleans, including those of Papa Celestin, and Kid Ory. For many years St. Cyr played regularly with Armand Piron, and also on riverboats with Fate Marable and Ed Allen.

Johnny St. Cyr moved to Chicago in September 1923. There he played briefly with King Oliver and later with Darnell Howard's band. From January 1924 until November 1929 he played with Doc Cooke's Dreamland Orchestra. During this period St. Cyr was also much in demand for freelance recording sessions with the top jazz artists of the day including Louis Armstrong and Jelly Roll Morton. He returned to New Orleans in late 1929. For many years he gave up his life as a professional musician to take up plastering again, although he did play on a part-time basis at nights in local jazz clubs. In the early 1950s St. Cyr decided to return to playing music on a full time basis. He joined Paul Barbarin's band and in 1955 moved to California with him. In 1959 he was featured with the New Orleans Creole Jazz Band, and then in the early 1960s with The Young Men of New Orleans band. He was involved in a car accident in the summer of 1965 and this affected his ability to play on a regular basis. Johnny St. Cyr died in 1966 of leukaemia in Los Angeles County General Hospital.

SELECTED RECORDINGS

Jelly Roll Morton	RCA Black & White 731059 LP
Paul Barbarin Band	Storyville SLP 6008
George Lewis Session	Storyville SLP 4049
King Oliver's Jazz Band	BBC Records RP CD 607
Louis Armstrong's Hot Five	BBC Records RP CD 618
Louis Armstrong Band	CBS 463052-2 CD
Johnny St. Cyr	American Music AMCD-78

SELECTED READING
Article   Jazz Journal, September/October 1966

SAL SALVADOR
**Born-Monson, Massachussetts, USA
21 November 1925
Died – Stamford, Connecticut, USA
22 September 1999**

Sal Salvador's family moved to Stafford Springs, Connecticut in 1927. Salvador's first guitar was given to him by his father. His interest at first, in common with many of his friends, was playing hillbilly music. During the early 1940s he was drawn to jazz through the recordings of trumpeter Harry James.

Salvador first studied on an acoustic guitar, playing in the style of Dick McDonough, Carl Kress, and George Van Eps. After hearing some recordings by Charlie Christian playing with Benny Goodman he decided to change over to the electric guitar. From 1945-46 he took correspondence courses with Oscar Moore and Hy White, and also personal lessons from Eddie Smith. In 1949 Mundell Lowe, with whom Salvador was friendly, recommended him for the position of staff guitarist at New York's Radio City Music Hall. Salvador studied and developed a friendship with Johnny Smith who was also on the N.B.C. staff in New York at that time.

After leaving his Radio City job Salvador went on the road, first with vibraphonist Terry Gibbs band, then with trombonist Eddie Bert, and finally with a group called 'The Dardanelles'. On his return to New York, Salvador formed a jazz quartet with Mundell Lowe. Over the next few years he worked mainly as a studio musician with Columbia Records backing singers including Marlene Dietrich, Frankie Laine, Tony Bennett, and Rosemary Clooney.

In 1952 Salvador gained international prominence after he joined the Stan Kenton Big Band. For the next two years he was a prominent member of this famous band. In 1954 he formed his own quartet with pianist Eddie Costa. They recorded and played at top jazz clubs throughout the USA. In 1958 Salvador was a featured soloist at the Newport Jazz Festival. He then toured, and recorded for a while with his own big band 'The Colors of Sound'. This last venture coincided with the decline of the big band scene and as a result, like most other big bands at that time, had to break up. Salvador had a long association with the Gretsch Guitar Company. He helped design, and eventually played, the Gretsch 'Sal Salvador' jazz guitar for many years.

Salvador settled in the New York area where he became involved in teaching, writing jazz guitar

Sal Salvador

PHOTO: NORMAN WILSON

instruction books, and for several years played in a successful jazz guitar duo with the late Allen Hanlon. In his last few years Salvador lived in Connecticut where his time was divided between heading the guitar departments at the University of Bridgeport and Wesconn State University, private teaching, and playing with various jazz groups.

SELECTED RECORDINGS

Sal Salvador Quintet/Quartet	Blue Note BLP5035 LP
Sal Salvador Boo Boo Be Doop	Capitol Affinity AFF 68 LP
Frivolous Sal	London HA-N2043 LP
Shades Of Sal Salvador	REP 208 LP
A Tribute To The Greats	Bethlehem BCP-74 LP
Stop Smoking Or Else Blues	Roulette SR-25262 LP
Colors In Sound	Decca DL 79210 LP
Beat for this Generation	Decca DL 74026 LP
Live Duo with Allen Hanlon	Glen Productions GPSA 5010 LP
Parallelogram	Glen Productions GPSA 5016 LP
Starfingers	Beehive BH 7002 LP
Juicy Luicy	Beehive BH 7009 LP
World's Greatest Jazz Standards	Stash ST 234 LP
Sal Salvador Plays Gerry Mulligan	Stash ST 251 LP
Sal Salvador & Crystal Image	Stash ST-CD-17
2nd Time Around w/Mundell Lowe	West Side WR2006 CD

SELECTED READING

Profile	Guitar Player, July 1974
Interview	Guitar Player, June 1980
Pro's Reply	Guitar Player, September 1988
Interview	Just Jazz Guitar, May 1995
Interview	20 Century Guitar, June 1995

SELECTED MUSIC

Sal Salvador's Chord Book	Henry Adler Music
Sal Salvador's Single String Studies	Henry Adler Music
Jazz Guitar Duets	Belwin Music Inc.
Art Of Single String Soloing	Mel Bay Publications
Chordal Enrichment & Chord Substitution	Mel Bay Publications
Jazz Single String Studies	Mel Bay Publications
Four Part Harmony For Soloing & Comping	Mel Bay Publications
Sight Reading Studies for Guitar	Mel Bay Publications

GRAY SARGENT
Born-Attleboro, Massachusetts, USA
10 June 1953

Gray Sargent

Gray Sargent's family moved to Metuchan, New Jersey when he was ten years old. It was then he began to play the guitar, and by the time he was 12 he was playing in local rhythm and blues bands. Sargent became interested in jazz after hearing Count Basie, Ella Fitzgerald and Louis Armstrong play on an Ed Sullivan television show.

In the late 1960s Sargent's family moved to Weston outside of Boston. After leaving high school he attended the Berklee College of Music from 1972-74. At the same time he gained professional experience playing in diverse jazz groups in the Boston area. Sargent cites Kenny Burrell as his favourite jazz guitarist with Charlie Christian, Django Reinhardt and Barney Kessel major influences.

By the late 1970s Sargent was playing and recording with Illinois Jaquet. In 1979 he met and began playing with pianist Dave McKenna. This was the start of a successful association which continues to this day. In recent years he has made several recordings as sideman and leader of his own group for the Concord label.
He has toured regularly with saxophonist Scott Hamilton.

SELECTED RECORDINGS

No More Ouzo for Puzo w/Dave McKenna	Concord CCD-4365
Newport All-Stars	Concord CCD-4401
I Remember Bobby w/Lou Colombo	Concord CCD-4435
Concord All-Stars on Cape Cod	Concord CCD-4530
Dave McKenna & Gray Sargent Duo	Concord CCD-4552
Gray Sargent Trio-Shades of Gray	Concord CCD-4571

SELECTED READING

Profile	Jazz Times, July/August 1994

AKIO SASAJIMA
Born-Hokkaido, Japan
14 March 1952

Akio Sasajima was raise in Sapporro, Japan. He decided to play jazz guitar after hearing some recordings by Wes Montgomery. He worked professionally in jazz clubs in Japan for a while but then in 1977 went to live in Chicago with his American wife.

In 1989 Akio Sasajima moved to San Francisco from where he now leads a busy career playing and teaching jazz guitar.

SELECTED RECORDINGS
Akioustically Sound - Duo with Ron Carter	Muse MCD 5448
Humpty Dumpty	Enja Enj 8032-2 CD

Akio Sasajima

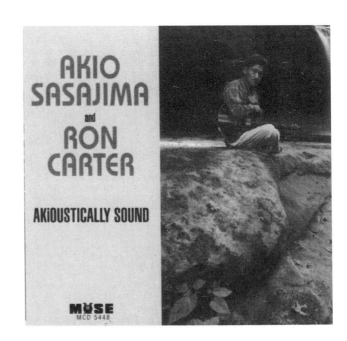

JOACHIM SCHONECKER
Born-Sarrbrucken, Germany
20 July 1966

Joachim Schonecker began to play the guitar at the age of eleven. He started to play professionally at the age of 15 with local soul and jazz groups. As he gained experience he made several TV appearances and toured through France, Denmark and Sweden.

After leaving high school Schonecker moved to Cologne where he did social service. He then moved to the Netherlands to study Jazz Guitar with Wim Overgaauw at the Hilversum Conservatorium. In 1989 he returned to Germany to continue his music studies at the Musikhochschule Koln where his teachers included Frank Haunschild, Jiggs Whigham, John Taylor and Manfred Schoof. At this time Schoneker gained more professional experience working in various pop, jazz and fusion groups.

In 1992 Schonecker founded his own bebop quartet. This band played at clubs and festivals all over Germany. In 1994 the group reduced to a trio which continues to be much in demand backing singers and horn players.

In 1995 Joachim Schonecker gained international recognition when he reached the semifinals of the prestigious Thelonious Monk Jazz Guitar Competition in Washington DC. This success led to a recording contract with Double-Time Records.

Joachim Schonecker

SELECTED RECORDINGS
Common Language   Double-Time Records DTRCD - 122

JOHN SCOFIELD
Born-Ohio, USA
26 December 1951

Shortly after his birth John Scofield's family moved to Wilton, Connecticut. It was here that Scofield grew up and began, at the age of twelve, to play the guitar. His first love was blues and rock, particularly the music of B.B. King and Otis Rush. At the age of fifteen Scofield began to study with Alan Dean, a local teacher and jazz enthusiast. He encouraged Scofield to listen to and study the guitar styles of Barney Kessel, Tal Farlow, Jim Hall and Wes Montgomery. Scofield's growing interest in jazz also turned towards the recordings of Miles Davis, John Coltrane, Freddie Hubbard and Lee Morgan.

After leaving high school in 1970 Scofield entered the Berklee School of Music in Boston. Here he had the opportunity to play and study with vibraphonist Gary Burton, and also study privately with Mick Goodrick and Jim Hall. In 1973 Scofield left Berklee, determined to be a full time professional musician.

Based in Boston, his first professional work was with Gary Burton. Scofield then went on tour with percussionist Airto. His first major break came when he was invited to join drummer Billy Cobham's jazz fusion group in January 1975. Following the break up of Cobham's band John Scofield freelanced around New York. He worked and recorded with many prominent jazz musicians including Charles Mingus and Gary Burton. In 1977 he formed his own quartet which toured Europe and appeared at the Berlin Jazz Festival.

In 1979 Scofield became a regular member of the Dave Liebman quintet. In 1982 he joined the Miles Davis band. Over the next three years Scofield toured the world with the famous trumpeter as an integral member of the group. He collaborated with Davis on several original compositions. In recent years Scofield has become recognised as one of the most important of the new generation of comtemporary jazz guitarists. His most recent recordings have featured many important jazz artists including guitarists John Abercrombie and Bill Frisell, bassist Ron Carter and drummer Jack De Johnette.

SELECTED RECORDINGS

Tributaries w/Larry Coryell	Arista AN 3017 LP
Who's Who	Arista AN 3018 LP
Bar Talk	Arista AN 3022 LP
Shinola	Enja 4004 CD
Out Like A Light	Enja 4038 CD
John Scofield Live	Inner City 3022 CD
Rough House	Inner City 3030 CD

John Scofield

PHOTO: COURTESY IBANEZ GUITARS

Electric Outlet	Gramavision 79 404 CD
Still Warm	Gramavision 79 401 CD
Blue Matter	Gramavision 79 403 CD
Loud Jazz	Gramavision 79 402 CD
Pick Hits	Gramavision 79 405 CD
Flat Out	Gramavision 79 400 CD
Three Or Four Shades Of Blue w/Charles Mingus	Atlantic 1700 CD
Time On My Hands	Blue Note 92894 CD
Meant To Be	Blue Note 95479 CD
Grace Under Pressure	Blue Note 98167 CD
What We Do	Blue Note 95862 CD
Solar w/ John Abercrombie	Quicksilver 4004 CD
Star People w/ Miles Davis	Tristar 80875 CD
Who's Who?	One Way Records 34512 CD
I Can See Your Face From Here w/Pat Metheny	Blue Note 27765 CD
Hand Jive	Blue Note 27327 CD
Quiet	Verve 533 185 CD

John Scofield On Improvisation	Instructional Video	DCI
John Scofield Jazz Funk 2 Vols	Instructional Videos	DCI

SELECTED READING

Interview	Guitar Player, September 1979
Profile	Downbeat, September 1982
Interview	Guitar Player, September 1984
Interview	Guitar Player, February 1983
Interview	Downbeat, January 1987
Profile	Downbeat, March 1989
Interview	Jazz Magazine (France), May 1991
Interview	Downbeat, April 1992
Profile	Jazziz, August/September 1992
Interview	Downbeat, April 1994
Interview	Guitar Player, February 1995
Profile	Downbeat, October 1996
Article	Jazz Times, December 1996
Article	Jazz Times, April 1997
Profile	Guitar Player, March 1997

SELECTED MUSIC

John Scofield – Artist Transcriptions	Third Earth Publications
John Scofield – Time On My Hands	CPP/Belwin

BUD SCOTT

Born-ARTHUR SCOTT
New Orleans, Louisiana, USA
11 January 1890
Died-Los Angeles, California, USA
2 July 1949

Bud Scott was mainly featured as a member of the rhythm section, on both guitar and banjo, of many jazz groups from the early part of this century. He is an important figure in the evolution of the jazz guitar as he was a direct link from the early blues singer/guitarists of the late nineteenth century right through to the middle of the twentieth century.

Bud Scott learned to play both the guitar and violin from an early age. At the age of fourteen he was playing professionally with the John Robichaux Orchestra in New Orleans. In January 1913 he took the job as featured violinist with the Billy King travelling show. In 1915 he moved to New York. There he led a varied career. He played in various theatre orchestras and played banjo with the Bob Young Band. In 1919 he sang at a Carnegie Hall concert with the Clef Club vocal group. In 1923 Scott moved to Chicago where he joined the legendary King Oliver Band. For a while he lived in California and worked for a short time with trombonist Kid Ory. Scott returned to Chicago in 1926 and rejoined King Oliver. Over the next few years he worked with many top jazz artists including Erskine Tate and Jimmie Noone.

In 1929 Scott decided to settle permanently in Los Angeles. During the early 1930s he worked with Mutt Carey's Jeffersonians, and the Leon Herriford Band. As well as doing freelance work, including working as a film-extra in the Hollywood studios, Scott led his own trio for several years. In 1944 he rejoined Kid Ory. He worked with Ory's band until late 1948, when he had to give up playing full-time due to ill health. Scott still played occasionally with Ory right up to the time of his death in 1949.

SELECTED RECORDINGS

Jelly Roll Morton Band	RCA Black & White 731059 LP
King Oliver's Creole Jazz Band	Zeta ZET 746 LP
Kid Ory's Creole Jazz Band	Good Time Jazz 12022 LP
Johnny Dodd's Band	Black & Blue BLE 59.235.2 LP

Bud Scott with the Kid Ory Band.

PHOTO: COURTESY JAZZ JOURNAL

MITCH SEIDMAN
Born-Long Branch, New York, USA
27 November 1953

Mitch Seidman began to play the guitar at the age of ten. He gained his first professional experience playing in various rock bands as a teenager. After hearing a Kenny Burrell recording he decided to play jazz. In 1973 he went to the Berklee College of Music in Boston from where he earned a bachelor's degree in composition. After leaving college in 1979 he worked for six years in New York City eventually moving to Boston. In 1993 he earned a master's degree in music education from Boston University.

Over the years Seidman has played and recorded with many top jazz artists including Harold Vick, Herb Pomeroy, Teddy Kotick, Tony Zano, Joe Hunt and Vera Auer. He is currently a frequent performer in Boston area jazz clubs and an associate professor at the Berklee College of Music. He is also a contributing editor to 20th Century Guitar Magazine. Seidman has also studied privately with Attila Zoller whom he cites as one of his major influences together with Jim Hall, Jimmy Raney and Tal Farlow.

Mitch Seidman

SELECTED RECORDINGS

Fretware - Mitch Seidman Quintet	Brownstone	BRCD 946
Ants in a Trance - Mitch Seidman Quartet	Brownstone	BRCD 9603
Until Tomorrow w/Leonard Hochman	Brownstone	BRCD 951

SELECTED READING

Interview	20th Century Guitar, April 1995
Interview	Jazz Player, June/July 1995
Interview	Cadence, February 1996

ESMOND SELWYN
Born-London, UK
19 February 1948

Esmond Selwyn first studied jazz guitar at the age of twelve with Ivor Mairants. He also studied classical guitar with Simon Munting. He later studied privately in the USA with Chuck Wayne, Sal Salvador and Allen Hanlon. An international tour in 1971 brought Selwyn's guitar playing to the attention of audiences on both sides of the Atlantic.

Since that time Selwyn has maintained a busy career as both leader of his own trio and sideman in many British jazz groups including the Don Rendell Quartet, the Robin Jones Quartet and the Jazz Turbo combo.

Esmond Selwyn is also an Honours languages graduate from Kings College in London. Alongside his career as a jazz guitarist Selwyn is well known as a journalist and teacher. He was a regular columnist for Crescendo International and also wrote a monthly column on jazz guitar for the English magazine, Guitarist.

Esmond Selwyn

PHOTO: COURTESY ESMOND SELWYN

SELECTED RECORDINGS
Eye Of The Hurricane Robin Jones Quartet   Spotlight SPJ 519
Cocktail - Melanie Marshall   Mel Records   MEL CD 021-2

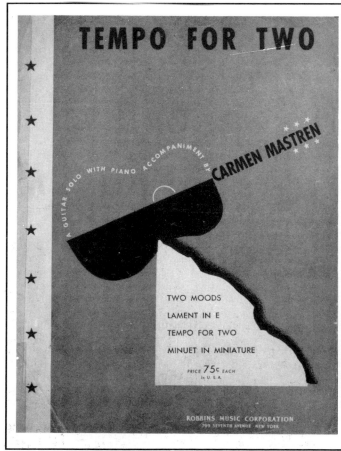

1930s jazz guitar music.

313

BOLE SETE
Born-DJALMA DE ANDRADA
Rio de Janeiro, Brazil
16 July 1928
Died-Greenbrae, California, USA
14 February 1987

Bola Sete came from a musical family. He studied theory and harmony at the National School of Music in Rio de Janeiro. His first professional work on the guitar was playing in a folk group. He became interested in jazz, after hearing some recordings of Django Reinhardt and Charlie Christian, and decided to return to the conservatory to further his music studies. Sete then became a staff guitarist for three radio stations in Rio de Janeiro. An authentic bossa nova and jazz samba interpreter, Sete played with a classical right-hand fingerstyle technique on a nylon-strung classical instrument.

In 1952 Sete took a sextet to Italy. He stayed there for almost four years playing in hotels and clubs. On his return to South America he played all over that continent, including a long stay in Buenos Aires, Argentina. In 1960 Sete decided to move to the USA. For two years he remained unrecognized by American jazz lovers and made a living by playing in various Sheraton Hotels. His break came when he was heard by trumpeter Dizzy Gillespie. He was so impressed by Sete's talent he asked him to play with his band at the 1962 Monterey Jazz Festival. Sete then recorded with Gillespie and toured the USA with his band. Soon after, the guitarist signed a contract with Fantasy records. From 1963-66 Sete played and recorded with pianist Vince Guaraldi's trio.

Bola Sete worked for several Californian radio and television stations, and in the film studios. In 1966-69 he formed his own Brazilian trio and this played successfully all over the USA. In 1971 he formed a quartet but from 1972 concentrated as a soloist both on the guitar, and the lutar (a lute shaped guitar of his own design). A talented composer Bola Sete is generally recognized as one of the most important, and individual jazz guitarists, to have come from the South American continent. Sete, for many years a devout yogi, died after a bout of pneumonia in 1987.

Bola Sete

SELECTED READING

Profile	Guitar Player, December 1967
Profile	Downbeat, July 1966
Profile	Guitar Player, February 1976

SELECTED RECORDINGS

New Wave w/Dizzy Gillespie	Mercury MGW 12318
Bola Sete-Bossa Nova	Fantasy 3349
The Incomparable Bola Sete	Fantasy 8364
Bola Sete's Tour De Force	Fantasy 8358
Vince Guaraldi & Bola Sete	Fantasy 8371
Autentico! Bola Sete Trio	Fantasy 8375
Live at Monterey	Verve SVLP 9208
Goin' To Rio Bola Sete	Columbia KC 32375
Ocean-Bola Sete Solo	Sonet SNTF 695
Jungle Suite	Dancing Cat 3005

314

PHOTO: COURTESY FANTASY RECORDS

SONNY SHARROCK
Born-WARREN HARDING SHARROCK
Ossining, New York, USA
27 August 1940
Died-Ossining, New York, USA
25 May 1994

Sonny Sharrock

Sonny Sharrock's first involvement in music was as a baritone in an amateur vocal group in his mid teens. It was not until he was twenty, in 1960, that Sharrock took up the guitar. He wanted to play the saxophone but as he suffered from asthma this was not possible. At first he taught himself with various tutor books. In 1961, after hearing some jazz radio broadcasts, he decided to enrol on the jazz course at the Berklee College of Music in Boston.

In 1962 Sharrock returned to Ossining and started to play in various jazz groups. He then gained some experience in California playing in a group with saxophonist Willie Waite. On his return to the East Coast later that year Sharrock went to a concert featuring Albert Ayler, John Coltrane and Cecil Taylor. This first exposure to 'free' jazz made the young guitarist determined to study and play this form of jazz. He then studied for a while with band-leader/pianist Sun Ra.

Sharrock then began to work with a wide variety of musicians including Nigerian percussionist Babatunde Olatunji. A short spell followed with the Byard Lancaster band. From 1965 Sharrock worked with Pharoah Sanders, Sunny Murray and Don Cherry. 1967 marked the beginning of a long association with Herbie Mann. Sharrock toured the USA and internationally with Mann, appearing at many major jazz festivals. He also recorded with Mann.

In 1973 Sonny Sharrock formed a new group with his wife, folk/jazz vocalist Lynda Chambers. In 1985 he became a member of 'Last Exit' with Peter Brotzmann, Ronald Jackson and Bill Laswell.

Sonny Sharrock claimed that he was the first guitarist to play free jazz. There are few persons who would dispute this claim.

SELECTED RECORDINGS
Guitar	Enemy ENY 102-2 CD
Seize The Rainbow	Enemy ENY 104-2 CD
Live in New York	Enemy ENY 108 CD
Highlife	Enemy ENY 119-2 CD
Monkey Pockie Boo	Affinity AFF 35 CD
Ask The Ages	Axiom CD 848 957-2

SELECTED READING
Interview	Guitar Player, February 1990
Interview	Downbeat, July 1993
Appreciation	Guitar Player, September 1994

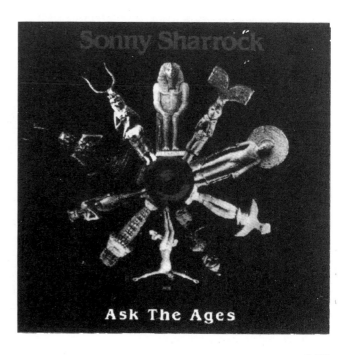

JIMMY SHIRLEY
Born-JAMES ARTHUR SHIRLEY
Union, South Carolina, USA
31 May 1913

Jimmy Shirley spent most of his childhood in Cleveland, Ohio. He received his first music education from his father. He began playing professionally in 1934 in Cincinatti with J. Frank Terry's Band, and later with Hal Draper. In 1935 he moved to Cleveland where he formed his own quartet made up of three guitars and double bass. In 1937 Shirley moved to New York where he played with Clarence Profit's trio for four years. From 1941-43 he toured with singer Ella Fitzgerald, and also played with James P. Johnson and Sidney De Paris. From 1944 Shirley began a ten year association with pianist Herman Chittison's trio. Shirley also played with his own small group in various New York jazz clubs during this time, and was featured regularly with well known jazz names including Phil Moore, Billy Williams, Vin Strong and 'Toy' Wilson. He also recorded with Artie Shaw, Coleman Hawkins and Earl Bostic.

From the early 1960s Jimmy Shirley worked regularly in and around New York on both guitar and electric bass guitar. In 1963 he played with George James' Band, and in 1967 with Buddy Tate. In 1975 he recorded for the French record company, 'Black and Blue', with his own quartet which included pianist Johnny Guarneri , and bassist Slam Stewart.

Jimmy Shirley

PHOTO: JEAN-PIERRE TAHMAZIAN/COURTESY BLACK & BLUE RECORDS

SELECTED RECORDINGS

Art Hodes' Back Room Boys	Blue Note CDP 799099-2 LP
Pete Johnson's All Stars	Savoy SV 0196 LP
China Boy-Jimmy Shirley	Black & Blue 33.081 LP
Steff and Slam	Black & Blue 33.076 LP
Slam Stewart Quartet	Black & Blue 33.109 LP
Jamming in Jazz	Blue Note 7007 LP

Two very rare jazz guitar recordings.

TED SHUMATE
Born-Meridian, Mississippi, USA
10 May 1953

Ted Shumate first exposure to music was gospel music and Delta blues. At the age of four his family moved to St Petersburg, Florida and here he was exposed to diverse Latin American music styles. After leaving high school Shumate went to Eckerd College from where he graduated with a bachelor of arts degree in Jazz studies and music composition.

In 1980 Shumate moved to California to study at the Guitar Institute of Technology in Los Angeles. Upon his graduation from the G.I.T. he was immediately hired as an instructor. He combined this career in education with playing and recording in the Los Angeles area. In 1987 he recorded with Ira Sullivan for Pausa Records and following this he toured internationally and appeared at numerous jazz festivals.

Over the years Ted Shumate has played or recorded with numerous top jazz musicians including Nat Adderley, Ira Sullivan, Jimmy Cobb, Red Rodney, Buddy DeFranco, Peter Erskine, Al DiMeola, Idrees Sulieman, Branford Marsalis and Kenny Drew Jnr.

Ted Shumate

SELECTED RECORDING
Gulfstream w/Ira Sullivan   Pausa

SELECTED MUSIC
Chord Concepts   Hal Leonard

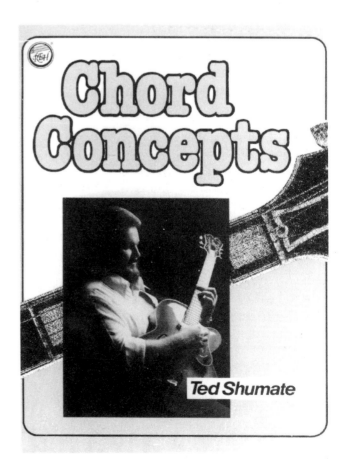

ROY SMECK

Born-Binghampton, New York, USA
6 February 1900
Died-New York City, USA
5 April 1994

Roy Smeck originally played a variety of instruments including the autoharp and the harmonica. His father sang and played the guitar. It was on one of his father's instruments that Smeck taught himself to play the guitar. Although not really a jazz artist Smeck influenced many early jazz guitarists through his many recordings and tutors. He was also the only major 1920s pick guitarist, and contemporary of Eddie Lang, Lonnie Johnson, Dick McDonough, to survive into the 1990's.

By the mid 1920s Roy Smeck was already a major recording artist for R.C.A. He had been discovered playing in a local music store by a R.K.O. theatre agent and was persuaded to go for an audition to New York City. He was immediately signed up and then started what was to be a long and highly successful music hall career as 'The Wizard of the Strings'. In 1928 he was hired by Warner Brothers to make one of the first talking movies, a seven minute film called 'Roy Smeck in his Pastime'. Smeck was not only a talented guitarist but also was a master of the banjo, ukulele and Hawaiian guitar. He was the first artist to make use of multiple recording. He made a film for Paramount playing four different instruments and by the use of overdubbing the cinema audience saw, and heard, all four instruments playing at once. Over the years Smeck was an important endorsee for various guitar manufacturers including the Gibson and Harmony companies.

From the mid 1920s to the 1950s Roy Smeck sustained a career as a top act in variety shows throughout the world. In 1937 he appeared at the London Palladium, and in 1938 was one of the first artists featured on English television. Smeck was already a radio star and had broadcast daily fifteen minute guitar lessons since 1936 for a New York radio station.

From the 1950s Roy Smeck settled in New York and for many years was involved in the teaching of all fretted instruments, and occasional cabaret, radio and television work. During his long career Smeck made over one thousand recordings and wrote 30 fretted instruments books.

SELECTED RECORDINGS

Roy Smeck Plays	Yazoo YAZ 1052 LP
South Seas Serenade	ABC-Paramount 119 LP
Melodies With Memories	ABC-Paramount 174 LP

Roy Smeck

Hi-Fi Paradise	ABC-Paramount 234 LP
Stringing Along	ABC-Paramount 412 LP
Wizard Of The Strings	ABC-Paramount 452 LP

SELECTED READING

Reminiscenses	Guitar Player, December 1972
Profile	B.M.G., September 1974
Pro's Reply	Guitar Player, September 1989

SELECTED MUSIC

Blues for Guitar-Roy Smeck	Charles Colin Publishing
Melodious Rhythms Simplified	Charles Colin Publishing

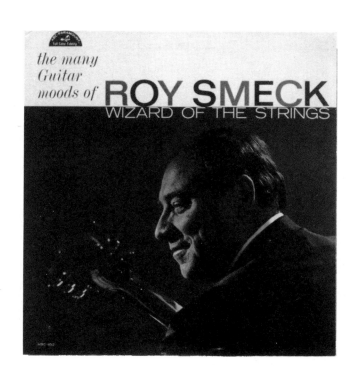

DAVID SMITH
Born-Sydney, Australia
30 November 1954

David Smith began to play the guitar as a teenager. At the age of nineteen he started playing professionally in local rock bands. He then began to take an interest in jazz. Tal Farlow and John McLaughlin were primary influences. In 1975 he went to the UK where he played in various jazz fusion bands.

Smith returned to Australia in 1979 where he played in major jazz venues. In 1983 he formed a jazz/flamenco fusion group with Spanish guitarist Miguel Rivera. They made a succesful concert tour of Australia. In 1986 he went for a few months to New York. Here he gigged frequently with Jack Wilkins, Chuck Wayne, Vic Juris and other prominent East coast jazz guitarists. Smith is regarded as one of Australia's best jazz guitarists. He plays frequently with Ike Isaacs and currently teaches at the Australian Institute of Music in Sydney.

David Smith

SELECTED RECORDINGS

The Journey	DSM-111 CD
My Funny Valentine	DSM-201 CD
Alone Together w/Jack Wilkins	DSM-112 CD

SELECTED READING

Profile	Just Jazz Guitar, August 1995

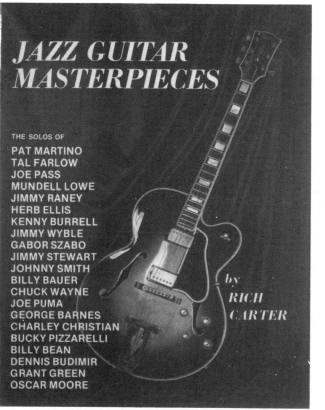

1980s jazz guitar music.

FLOYD SMITH

Born-St. Louis, Missouri, USA
25 January 1917
Died-Indianapolis, Indiana, USA
29 March 1982

Floyd Smith, the son of a railway porter who also played drums, first studied music at his local high school. A friend gave him a ukulele when he was fifteen. He made such good progress on the ukulele an uncle gave him his first guitar as a present. Smith began his professional career playing with bands around St. Louis including those of Dewey Jackson, Charley Creath, Harvey Langford and Isham Jones. In July 1934 he went on the road for two years with Eddie Johnson and his St.Louis Crackerjacks. In 1937 he joined the Jeter-Pillars Club Plantation Band to play at the Cotton Club in Cincinnati. Smith then went to New York with the Sunset Royal Entertainers.

Floyd Smith gained national prominence when, in January 1939, he joined Andy Kirk's band to play in Washington, DC. In the same year he recorded the track 'Floyd's Guitar Blues' on electric guitar with Kirk's band. This historic recording helped gain acceptance for the amplified instrument. Smith met Charlie Christian in Oklahoma City in late 1938 and they jammed together in a local club.

In May 1942 Floyd Smith was drafted into the US Army. Whilst in France in 1944 he met and played with Django Reinhardt. After the war ended he returned to work with Kirk's band from November 1946 until September 1947. For the next four years he worked with his own trio on the South Side of Chicago. In the mid 1950s Smith played in other US cities with many jazz artists including a trio with organist Wild Bill Davis and drummer Chris Columbus.

Smith played for five years with organist Bill Doggett and then settled in 1964 in Indianapolis where he led his own trio in local clubs and hotels. Smith occasionally appeared in Europe and in 1972 recorded for the French Black & Blue label with a trio featuring Davis, Columbus, and himself. A new version of 'Floyd's Guitar Blues' is included on this record.

SELECTED RECORDINGS

Andy Kirk Band-Instrumentally Speaking	MCA 510 033 LP
Floyd Smith Trio	Black & Blue 33-046 LP
Impulsions-Wild Bill Davis Trio	Black & Blue 233037 CD
Buddy Tate Quartet	Black & Blue 33-054 LP

SELECTED READING

Pro's Reply	Guitar Player, November 1979

Floyd Smith

GEORGE M. SMITH
Born-New York, USA
1912
Died-Houston, Texas, USA
1 June 1993

George M. Smith

George Smith's first instrument was the banjo. He was born and raised on New York's East Side but when he was fifteen his family moved to Los Angeles, California. After hearing some recordings by Carl Kress, Smith decided to devote all his time to playing the guitar.

Smith's first professional work was in the band backing vaudeville acts at the Paramount Theatre in Los Angeles. His first major break came when the popular singer Kate Smith asked him to be her personal accompanist for her radio broadcasts. His talents were soon recognised and he was hired as the staff guitarist at the Fox and Paramount Film Studios in Hollywood. Smith was asked to play in many styles on film soundtracks.

George Smith then embarked on a serious study of composition, theory, harmony and counterpoint at the University of New Mexico, in order to help him improve the role of the guitar both as a solo voice and in accompanying. Aware of the lack of suitable methods for guitarists he wrote his 'George M. Smith Guitar Method'. This was first published in 1942. It soon became one of the most highly respected instructional books for guitarists. Over the years it has been used by many top jazz guitarists throughout the world. Smith taught over 2000 students and some of these are amongst today's foremost guitarists. Smith also played with the Los Angeles Philharmonic Orchestra, and worked with Dimitri Tiomkin, Max Steiner, Nelson Riddle and other prominent conductors.

George M. Smith continued working as a leading studio guitarist in Los Angeles until his retirement.

SELECTED MUSIC

Modern Guitar Method	Guitarists Publications
Learning The Fingerboard	Guitarists Publications
Right Hand Technique	Guitarists Publications
Guitar Gems	Guitarists Publications

Johnny Smith

JOHNNY SMITH

Born-JOHN HENRY SMITH JNR
Birmingham, Alabama, USA
25 June 1922

Johnny Smith, one of the foremost jazz guitarists of the 1950s and 1960s, is also an accomplished performer on trumpet, violin and viola. A self taught player he cites Andres Segovia and Django Reinhardt as his major influences. Smith, whose father was a banjo player and guitarist, first developed an interest in the guitar at the age of five.

In 1935 Smith's family moved to Portland, Maine. By that time Smith was already an accomplished guitarist. He gained his first professional experience in 1939 playing in a hillbilly group, 'The Fenton Brothers'. He led his own jazz trio in Boston 1940-41 before joining the US Air Force. During the war he played cornet in the Air Force Band. After leaving the air force in 1946 he returned to Portland and played trumpet and guitar for a local radio station, as well as club work at nights. Career prospects were not good in Portland, so later that year Smith moved to New York where he became an NBC staff musician. For the next eight years he played both trumpet and guitar, and composed and arranged for the network.

Johnny Smith first gained international prominence as a jazz artist in the 1950s when he formed a quintet with tenor saxophonist Stan Getz. Their arrangement and recording of 'Moonlight in Vermont' became a jazz classic, epitomising the term 'cool' jazz. One of the best selling jazz records of 1952, this recording remains as a milestone in jazz guitar history. It is distinguished by Johnny Smith's virtuoso single note playing, and by the unique harmonies of his chords on the guitar.

From 1953-57 Johnny Smith successfully led his own group in East Coast jazz clubs, and made more than twenty recordings for the Roost label. Always interested in guitar design and construction, Smith, after working with Guild Guitars for a short while in the 1950s, has had a long association with the Gibson Guitar company. Their 'Johnny Smith' guitar has been one of their most popular jazz archtop models since its introduction in 1960. In 1957, after the sudden death of his wife, Smith decided to settle in Colorado Springs, Colorado, with his four year old daughter. He wanted to be near the rest of his family. From that time he went into virtual retirement from professional performance. Since the early 1960s he has devoted most of his time to his specialist guitar shop in Colorado Springs. In 1977 he joined Bing Crosby's backing group for a successful international concert tour, which ended shortly before the singer's death.

SELECTED RECORDINGS

Johnny Smith plays Jimmy Van Heusen	Roost 2201 LP
Johnny Smith Quartet	Roost 2203 LP
Moonlight in Vermont	Roulette CDP 7977472
The Sound of the Johnny Smith Guitar	Roost 2216 LP
Flowerdrum Song	Roost 2231 LP
Easy Listening	Roost 2233 LP
Johnny Smith Favourites	Roost 2237 LP
Johnny Smith Trio-Designed for You	Roost 2238 LP
My Dear Little Sweetheart	Roost 2239 LP
Johnny Smith With Strings	Roost 2242 LP
Johnny Smith Plus The Trio	Roost 2243 LP
Sounds of Johnny Smith	Roost 2246 LP
Man with The Blue Guitar	Roost 2248 LP
Guitar World of Johnny Smith	Roost 2254 LP
Reminiscing	Roost 2259 LP
Johnny Smith	Verve 314 537 752-CD
Kaleidoscope	Verve SVLP 9205
Johnny Smith With Jerry Southern	Roulette 52016 LP
Legends	Concord CCD-4616

SELECTED READING

Interview	Guitar Player, October 1967
Interview	Guitar Player, March 1970
Profile	Guitar, August & September 1976
Interview	Guitar Player, January 1982
Private Lesson	Guitar Player, July 1984
Interview	Just Jazz Guitar, May 1995

SELECTED MUSIC

Johnny Smith Aids to Technique	Chas Colin Publishing Co.
Johnny Smith Guitar Originals Vol.1	Chas Colin Publishing Co.
Johnny Smith Guitar Originals Vol.2	Chas Colin Publishing Co.
Johnny Smith Approach to the Guitar	Mel Bay Publications

DYNAMIC STEREO ROOST SLP 2228

THE FOURSOME VOLUME II

TERRY SMITH

Born-TERENCE SMITH
West Norwood, London, United Kingdom
20 May 1943

Terry Smith

Terry Smith's first interest in the guitar was at the age of twelve, when he started playing skiffle music. His first interest in jazz came after he heard a recording of the George Shearing Quintet featuring Chuck Wayne. He then went on to listen to recordings by Django Reinhardt, Wes Montgomery and other jazz greats.

In 1962 Smith began his professional career as a guitarist when he was hired to play in a dance band in Doncaster. By 1966 he was already recognised as one of Britain's brightest jazz guitar talents. He led a busy life in jazz clubs in the London area. In 1967 he joined the Dick Morrisey Quintet for a year. In 1969 he joined the jazz-rock combo, 'IF'. Smith stayed with this successful group for almost three years, gaining international recognition for his excellent guitar playing. In 1975 he joined another jazz-rock band called 'Zebra'. In the same year he went to live in Sweden for a few months.

On his return to London Smith formed his own quintet and once again became involved in the jazz club circuit in London. From 1966 he won the guitar category in Melody Maker's Reader's Jazz Poll for three years running. In 1968 he toured internationally with the popular singer Scott Walker.

For some years, following an accident to his hand, Smith was not able to continue his career as a musician. In recent years he has fortunately once more established himself as one of the busiest jazz guitarists on the London club scene, often playing with pianist Tony Lee.

SELECTED RECORDINGS
Fall Out   Philips   SBL 7871 LP
Terry Smith with the Tony Lee Trio   Lee Lambert LAM 002 LP

PETER SMYSER
Born-PETER MICHAEL SMYSER
Albington, Pennsylvania, USA
15 October 1967

Peter Smyser first played the guitar at the age of eight. At high school he began to study classical guitar with William Ghezzi and made excellent progress. He also studied jazz guitar with Randy Sarles during his last years at high school. Smyser had already decided to make a career in music and he went on to join a Jazz/Commercial performance programme at Temple University (1985-87) under a full academic scholarship.

For a while Smyser studied jazz guitar with Tom Giacabetti but then in 1987 decided to leave Temple University, give up classical guitar, and move on to study privately with jazz guitarist Steve Giordano. Later that year he decided to continue his music studies through intensive self-study. From the age of eleven Smyser had played in rock and pop groups but his love of jazz, inspired by the recordings of John Scofield, Pat Metheny, Wes Montgomery and others, changed his musical direction to devote his life to jazz. By the time he was 18 he was giving solo jazz guitar performances in local night spots and teaching jazz guitar privately.

Peter Smyser continues to live Pennsylvania where he maintains a busy career in jazz as both a performer and teacher.

Peter Smyser

SELECTED RECORDINGS
Out of Nowhere   PSCD 15887-2

FRED SOKOLOW
Born-FREDERICK SOKOLOW
Los Angeles, USA
14 September 1945

Fred Sokolow is one of the most prolific writers and arrangers for many styles of guitar playing and also for the banjo. He is also a vocalist and busy performer on guitar or banjo in concert, clubs and in the studios.

Sokolow grew up in a house where classical music was always in the background. He studied both piano and guitar before entering kindergarten, and was involved in various music groups throughout his school years. After leaving high school he went on to further his musical studies at the University of California at Berkley.

After leaving university Sokolow taught at Bob Baxter's Guitar Workshop in Los Angeles. It was during this time that he began to write instructional books for the guitar. Sokolow has been leader of his own jazz, bluegrass and rock bands. He has also toured as a sideman with artists such as Bobbie Gentry, Jim Stafford and the Limeliters. He continues to be much in demand as teacher and has presented guitar and banjo seminars all over the USA.

Fred Sokolow

Based in Los Angeles Sokolow is a frequent performer in jazz clubs both as a soloist or leading his own jazz trio.

SELECTED MUSIC

Complete Jazz Guitar	Almo/Columbia
Great Jazz Standards For Guitar Vol 1	CPP/Belwin
Great Jazz Standards For Guitar Vol 2	CPP/Belwin
Solos For Jazz Guitar	Carl Fischer Music
Wes Montgomery Artist Transcriptions	Hal Leonard Publishing
Lee Ritenour Artist Transcriptions	Hal Leonard Publishing
Jazzing It Up	Warner Bros

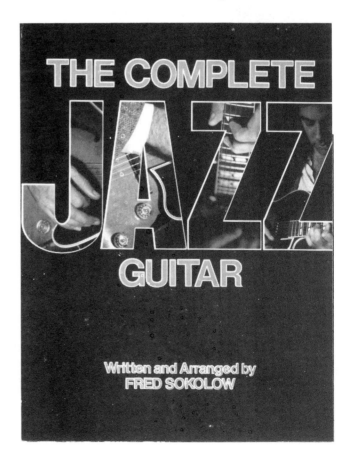

THE COMPLETE JAZZ GUITAR

Written and Arranged by FRED SOKOLOW

SOLO FLIGHT DUO

Neil Janssen
Born-Detroit , Michigan, USA
3 September 1949
Jim Lichens
Born-Yreka, California, USA
19 July 1943

Neil Janssen and Jim Lichens work as a jazz guitar duo called SOLO FLIGHT. Based in Eugene, Oregon their club work and recently released CD have won wide critical aclaim.

Neil Janssen plays the lead guitar over Lichens rhythm backing. Janssen's began to play the guitar at the age of nine. His first musical interest was in the guitar playing of Chet Atkins, Duane Edwards and Nokie Edwards of The Ventures. Over the years he changed over to jazz and cites Howard Roberts and Kenny Burrell as his main influences. He currently combines his music career in the SOLO FLIGHT duo with a daytime career as a draughtsman.

Jim Lichens early influences were also rock and country guitar players including Jimi Hendrix, Freddie King and Nokie Edwards. Like Janssen his interest soon turned to jazz and he cites many jazz guitarists as important influences including Charlie Christian, Wes Montgomery, Howard Roberts, Jim Hall and Barry Galbraith.

Neil Janssen and Jim Lichens

SELECTED RECORDINGS
Solo Flight   Oregon CD   1995

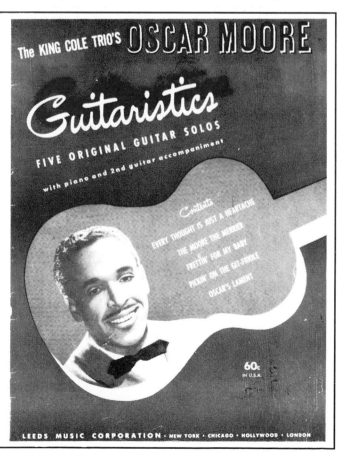

Examples of post 1940 jazz guitar music.

327

LES SPANN
Born-LESLIE L. SPANN JUNIOR
Pine Bluff, Arkansas, USA
23 May 1932

Les Spann came to prominence in the early 1960s both as a jazz guitarist and flautist but in recent years has not been in the forefront as a jazz guitarist.

Spann taught himself to play the guitar whilst at high school in Jamaica, New York. After deciding to make a career in music he went on to study at Tennessee State University, Nashville. He majored in music in 1956, having chosen the flute as his second instrument for the course. Whilst studying in Nashville he played with a local band called the 'Tennessee State Collegians'.

In August 1957, Spann returned to New York to join pianist Phineas Newborn's quartet, and later with Ronnell Bright. In August 1958 Spann gained international recognition when he was hired by Dizzy Gillespie. He toured and recorded with the trumpeter's quintet for a year. In 1959, after leaving Gillespie, Spann joined the Quincy Jones orchestra.

Les Spann

PHOTO: COURTESY GUILD GUITARS

SELECTED RECORDINGS

Dizzy Gillespie Sextet	Mercury 832574-2
Dizzy Gillespie Quintet	Verve 513875-2
Gemini-Les Spann	Jazzland JLP35
Back to Back-Ellington/Hodges	Verve 823637-2
Ben Webster & Associates	Verve 835254-2
Quincy Jones Orchestra	Verve 840040-2

SELECTED READING

Profile	Downbeat, July 1966

GEMINI ⊛ LES SPANN
FLUTE AND GUITAR
WITH JULIUS WATKINS, TOMMY FLANAGAN, SAM JONES, LOUIS HAYES/ALBERT HEATH

35 JAZZLAND

MELVIN SPARKS
Born-Houston, Texas, USA
22 March 1946

Melvin Sparks grew up in a musical enviroment. His mother ran a cafe where live jazz was played, and his brother was a drummer. Sparks first played drums but changed to the guitar at the age of eleven. His early influences were B.B. King and Chuck Berry but he soon decided that he wanted to play jazz. Grant Green, Kenny Burrell and saxophonists Charlie Parker and John Coltrane were major influences.

Sparks first professional experience was in a rock and roll show band backing singers like Sam Cooke and Jackie Wilson. However in the late 1960s he was hired by jazz organ player Jack McDuff. From that time Sparks played and recorded with many top jazz musicians including Lonnie Smith, Sonny Stitt, Charles Earland and Lou Donaldson. He appeared on many Blue Note and Prestige jazz recording sessions. From the late 1970s Sparks was lost to the jazz world as he concentrated on funk music. However in the early 1980s he made a return to jazz with the first of several recordings for the Muse Record company. In recent times he has signed to record for the Cannonball Records company.

Melvin Sparks

PHOTO: HANK SHULL

SELECTED RECORDINGS

Sparkling	Muse MR 5428 LP
Spark Plug	Prestige 10016 LP
Sparski/Akilah	BGP 64 CD
Legends of Acid Jazz	PST 24171 CD
I'm a Gittar Player	Cannonball Records CBD 27101 CD

PETER SPRAGUE
Born-Cleveland, Ohio, USA
11 October 1955

Peter Sprague

Peter Sprague spent the first part of his child-hood in Colorado. In 1963 his family moved to the Del Mar area of San Diego. Sprague took up the guitar at the age of twelve. Encouraged by his father, a jazz enthusiast, he made rapid progress. He studied with local teachers Bill Coleman and Steve O'Connor, and gained experience playing in his high school stage band. At the age of fifteen he had formed his own group, the Minor Jazz Quartet.

Sprague went on to study music at the Interlochen Arts Academy and also privately. He played in many nightspots and clubs in the San Diego area. In 1976 Sprague enrolled at the Berklee College of Music in Boston to study jazz with Pat Metheny. Sprague was greatly influenced by saxophonist Sonny Rollins. He also studied classical music at the New England Conservatory of Music with Abin Czak and Madam Challof. He also studied for a short while in New York with the Japanese fusion guitarist Yoshiaki Masuo.

In 1979 Sprague returned to San Diego and played in many groups, both as leader and as a sideman. His reputation as a guitarist of note earned him a contract with Xanadu Records. These recordings, and his later ones on the Concord label, have given Peter Sprague the international recognition his talent deserves.

SELECTED RECORDINGS

Free Bop with Charles McPherson	Xanadu 169
Peter Sprague/Dance of the Universe	Xanadu 176
Peter Sprague/The Path	Xanadu 183
Bird Raga	Xanadu 184
The Message Sent On The Wind	Xanadu 193
Musica Del Mar	Concord CJ 237
Na Pali Coast	Concord CJ 277
Brazil	Nova 9141
Soliloquy	SBE Records SBE CD 004

SELECTED READING

Interview	Guitar Player July 1986

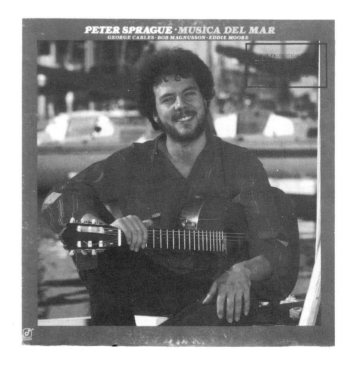

LENI STERN
Born-MAGDALENA THORA
Munich, Germany
28 April 1952

Born into a musical family, Leni Stern first learned to play the piano at the age of seven. She started to play the guitar at the age of fourteen and soon found she had a naural talent for composition. After leaving school she enrolled at the Falckenburg Schauspelschule, from which she majored in drama. After leaving drama school she went on to found her own theatre company and also acted as its musical director. Although Stern enjoyed success as an actress — she appeared regularly in the popular German television show 'Goldener Sontag' — her love of jazz and the guitar was still a major part of her life.

Leni Stern

Stern had originally been drawn to the guitar through the music of Jimi Hendrix, Joni Mitchell and the Beatles, but she soon became attracted to the jazz guitar styles of Jim Hall and Wes Montgomery. Her musical taste continued to expand through listening to the recordings of Bill Evans, Keith Jarrett, Ralph Towner and Pat Metheny. She studied composition with Ton van der Geld in Germany, and it was he who persuaded her to pursue a career in music and enroll at the Berklee College of Music in Boston. This she did, as a composition major, in 1977. Stern became a good friend of Bill Frisell soon after her arrival in the USA and he agreed to teach her privately. It was Frisell who introduced her to Mike Stern, who was also studying at Berklee at the time. In 1980 they married and moved to New York, where Mike Stern had been booked to play with the Miles Davis band.

Leni Stern was soon making a name in the New York area as a jazz guitarist in her own right. She played with her own ensembles, which included prominent contemporary jazz artists such as Paul Motian, Harvey Swartz, Bob Berg, Larry Willis and Bill Frisell.

Stern continues to develop an international reputation through her recordings, as one of the foremost contemporary jazz/fusion guitarists and composers.

SELECTED RECORDINGS
Clairvoyance	Passport PJ 88015 CD
The Next Day	Passport PJ 88035 CD
Secrets	Enja 5093 CD
Closer to the Light	Enja 6034 CD
Ten Songs	Lipstick CD-LIP 89009-2
Like One	Lipstick 89017 CD
Black Guitar	Prudence 398-535 CD

SELECTED READING
Profile	Guitar Player, March 1993
Profile	Jazz Times, May 1994
Profile	Jazziz, July 1994

MIKE STERN
Born-MICHAEL STERN
Boston, USA
10 January 1953

Mike Stern

Mike Stern began to play the guitar at the age of twelve. When he was eighteen he entered the Berklee College of Music in Boston. Here he studied with Pat Metheny and Mick Goodrick.

Stern claims a wide range of influences. From Jimi Hendrix, Eric Clapton and B.B. King, to Bill Evans, Sonny Rollins and John Coltrane. His main guitar influences are Wes Montgomery and Jim Hall. In 1976, on the recommendation of Pat Metheny, Stern was asked to join the group 'Blood, Sweat and Tears'. He played with this successful band for two years after which he returned to Boston to continue his jazz studies with Charley Banacos. Stern credits Banacos with helping him appreciate straight ahead jazz.

Stern played for a while with drummer Billy Cobham's band and then in 1981 gained full international recognition when he joined Miles Davis. He left the Miles Davis band in 1983 but went back for another year in 1985. The next few years saw Stern playing with a lot of top jazz and jazz fusion musicians including Jaco Pastorius, Michael Brecker and David Sanborn. In 1989 Stern formed a new group with Bob Berg. This band toured extensively in the USA and abroad.

Mike Stern, who is married to jazz fusion guitarist Leni Stern, is one the world's foremost contemporary guitarists.

SELECTED RECORDINGS
Upside Downside	Atlantic 7-81656-1 CD
Time In Place	Atlantic 7-81840 CD
Jigsaw	Atlantic 7-82027 CD
Odds Or Evens	Atlantic 7-82297-2 CD
Standards (And Other Songs)	Atlantic 7-82419-2 CD
Summertime w/Dieter Ilg	Lipstick LIP 89006 CD
Is What It Is	Atlantic 82571-2 CD
Give and Take	Atlantic 83036 2 CD

SELECTED READING
Interview	Guitar Player, November 1982
Interview	Guitar Player, March 1987
Fusion Guitar Article	Guitar Extra, Fall 1990
Interview Mike & Leni Stern	Guitar Player, March 1993
Profile	Jazz Times, December 1992
Profile	Jazziz, July 1994

SELECTED MUSIC
Mike Stern Jazz Guitar Solos	Corybant Publications
Mike Stern Artist Transcriptions	Hal Leonard Publishing
Mike Stern Band Transcriptions	ID Publications

JIMMY STEWART
Born-JAMES OTTO STEWART
San Francisco, California, USA
8 September 1937

Jimmy Stewart is well known to jazz guitarists throughout the world for the excellent monthly column he wrote for many years in Guitar Player magazine, and also for his guitar instruction books, his work with Howard Robert's guitar books, and a Wes Montgomery guitar method. Stewart is also a talented guitarist in his own right has worked for many years as a top session guitarist in the Los Angeles studios.

Stewart began to play the guitar when he was eight, having studied the piano from an early age with his mother. His first guitar teacher was Kenny Burke. He then studied from the age of eleven with Paul Miller for five years. By the time he was fifteen Stewart was playing professionally in the Lake Tahoe resort area. In the following year he worked backing vocalists in and around the San Francisco area. He also took an interest at that time in arranging for big bands, studying later with Bud Young.

Stewart went to the College of San Mateo, after graduating from San Francisco High School, and in 1956 earned an Associate of Arts degree. From 1957 he freelanced on guitar, banjo and mandolin until he was drafted into the army in 1958. Whilst he was in the army Stewart studied classical guitar with Richard Pick at the Chicago School of Music.

Stewart returned to San Francisco after his discharge. He was now not only accomplished on most fretted instruments, but had also gained an excellent knowledge of arranging, and the theoretical aspects of music. In the mid 1960s Stewart began a friendship with the Hungarian born jazz guitarist Gabor Szabo. In 1967 he joined Szabo's group for a three year association backing him usually on a nylon-string classical guitar.

Jimmy Stewart has continued to work as one of the busiest guitarists in the USA. After leaving Szabo he formed his own jazz quartet and made a successful debut in 1969 at Donte's Guitar Night in Los Angeles. Since 1968 Stewart has been a prolific author of many guitar instruction and music books. As a composer he has written works for electric guitar and orchestra(1971), a sonata for solo violin (1972), and a suite for trombone and string quintet dedicated to the late Jack Marshall. As a studio musician Stewart has backed Andy Williams, Barbra

Jimmy Stewart

PHOTO: DENNIS TRANTHAM

Streisand, Ray Charles, Sammy Davis Jnr, Burt Bacharach, Chita Rivera and others. In 1975 he joined the staff of Dick Grove's Music Workshops, and in 1978-80 was a member of the faculty of University of Southern California.

SELECTED RECORDINGS

The Sorcerer w/Gabor Szabo	Impulse M1PL506
Once Around The Block	Fantasy 3368
Faces w/Gabor Szabo	Mercury SRM 1141
Fire Flower	Catalyst 7621
Partners w/Sonny Stitt	Catalyst 7630
The Touch	Black.Hawk BKH 50301-1
Street Jazz	Techeku
Memorabilia	J'Bird Records 6 1746 80079 2 CD

SELECTED READING

Profile	Guitar Player, December 1970
Profile	Guitar Player, September 1980

SELECTED MUSIC

Jazz Riffs For Guitar	Cherry Lane Publications
Jazz Harmony	Cherry Lane Publications
The Complete Jazz Guitarist	Mel Bay Publications
The Art History and Style of Jazz Guitar	CPP/Belwin Publishing
Heavy Metal Guitar	CPP/Belwin Publishing
Mode Mania	CPP/Belwin Publishing
Blues Trax	CPP/Belwin Publishing
Power Trax	CPP/Belwin Publishing
The Working Guitarist Vol. 1	Alexander Publishing
Evolution of Jazz Guitar	Mel Bay Publications
Rock Guitar	Alfred Publishing
Rock Guitar	GPI/Hal Leonard Publications
Basic Guitar	GPI/Hal Leonard Publications
Contemporary Rhythm Playing for the Guitarist	
	Apophis Music Publishing
A Tribute to Classical Guitar	GPI Publications
Studio Guitar	Apophis Music Publishing
Orchestration and Arranging	Apophis Music Publishing
Guitar for Songwriters	Grove Publications
Pentatonic Madness	Apophis Music Publishing
Sight Reading for the Guitarist	Apophis Music Publishing
Ear Training for the Guitarist	Apophis Music Publishing
15 Guitar Etudes	Apophis Music Publishing
Jazz Guitar	Apophis Music Publishing
Chord/Melody	Apophis Music Publishing
Carol Kaye's Basslines Five	Gwyn Publishing
The Howard Roberts Guitar Book	Playback Music Publications
Wes Montgomery Jazz Guitar Method	Robbins Music Publishing

Louis Stewart

LOUIS STEWART

Born-Waterford, Eire
5 January 1944

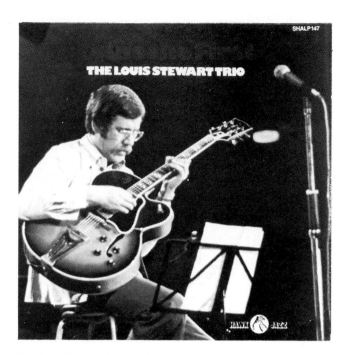

Louis Stewart's early musical experience was on the piano but when he was fifteen, after hearing a Les Paul record, he decided to buy a guitar. Sometime later he heard a Barney Kessel recording on a local radio jazz programme and this convinced Stewart that jazz was the music he wanted to play. He soon developed a reputation in and around Dublin as a world class jazz guitarist.

In 1961 Stewart was a member of a band that visited America. After three years doing showband work he joined a jazz trio led by pianist Noel Kelehan. His association with Kelehan proved very beneficial, for in the mid 1960s many visiting American jazz musicians to Ireland, including saxophonists Gerry Mulligan and Lee Konitz, played with the trio. In 1968 Stewart was featured with the Jim Doherty Quartet at the Montreux Jazz Festival, and received the Press Award as the outstanding European Soloist. Shortly after this Stewart decided to move to London where he joined a quartet led by saxophonist Tubby Hayes. Playing with this outstanding saxophonist gave Stewart international exposure to jazz audiences he could not get living in Ireland. Whilst playing with Hayes, Stewart was heard by Benny Goodman who subsequently invited him to join his big band for three European tours. This gave Stewart many more valuable new jazz contacts, particularly with American jazz musicians.

In 1971 Louis Stewart returned to Dublin and spent much of his time in television and recording work. The music he wrote for television included a composition for the award winning programme 'A Week in the Life of Martin Cluxton'. In 1975 Stewart joined Ronnie Scott's new quartet and soon became a major figure in London's jazz scene. His excellent guitar playing with Scott's quartet, on his solo and duo albums in the 1970s and 1980s, and on recordings with George Shearing, Clark Terry, Ken Moule, Martin Taylor, Heiner Franz and others in recent years has earned him a well-deserved reputation as one of the world's foremost jazz guitarists. In recent years Louis Stewart has worked mostly in Germany and Norway, but has appeared in other parts of Europe with various jazz musicians including Jim Hall, Mundell Lowe, Tal Farlow and Stephane Grappelli.

SELECTED RECORDINGS

Louis the First	Hawk Jazz SHALP 147
Baubles,Bangles and Beads	Wave LP 12
Out on his Own	Livia LRLPl
Milesian Source Louis Stewart	Pye NSPL 18555

Windows-George Shearing Trio	MPS 15.488
500 Miles High-George Shearing Trio	MPS 15.504
Swing Of Things-George Shearing Trio	MPS 15.537
Benny Goodman Today	London SPB 21
Benny Goodman Orchestra	Verve 820543-2
Drums & Friends w/John Wadham	Livia LRLP2
Alone Together w/Brian Dunning	Livia LRLP 5
Out on his Own – Solo Guitar	Jardis JRCD 9612
Louis Stewart/Martin Taylor Duo	Jardis JRCD 9613
Louis Stewart Quartet	Livia LAM 103 LP
Good News-Louis Stewart Quartet	Villa VR CD 001 LP
String-Time	Villa VR CD 003 LP
Three For The Road w/Spike Robinson	Hep 2045 LP
Louis Stewart/Heiner Franz Duo	Jardis JRCD 9005
Louis Stewart/Heiner Franz Duo	Jardis JRCD 9206
George Shearing Quintet	Telarc CD 83325
The European Jazz Guitar Orchestra	Jardis JRCDE 9307
Paper Moon w/George Shearing	Telarc CD 83375
Overdrive	HEP CD2057
A Real Corker w/Spike Robinson	Capri 74043 2 CD
Paper Moon w/Laila Dalseth	Gemini GMCD 86

SELECTED READING

Interview	Guitar, January 1975
Article	Archtop, Nov/Dec 1987

RICK STONE
Born-Cleveland, Ohio, USA
13 August 1955

Rick Stone

Rick Stone began to play the guitar at the age of nine. During the mid 1970s, while studying music at Cuyahoga Community College, he became interested in jazz after hearing a live Sonny Stitt concert on a radio broadcast. In 1978 Stone enrolled at the Berklee College of Music in Boston. In 1980 he completed his Bachelor of Music Degree and returned to Cleveland. Here he worked regularly at the 'Theatrical Restaurant' and 'Swingo's Keg and Quarter'.

In 1982 Stone moved to New York and studied with pianist Barry Harris. He gained valuable experience working as a copyist for Harris and playing with top jazz artists including Art Blakey, Lionel Hampton and Tommy Flanagan. He also joined in many jam sessions at 'Mr Harris' Jazz Cultural Theatre'.

In 1985 Stone released his first record album as leader on the Jazzane label. From 1966-88 he worked regularly with the Jimmy Robinson All-Star Band at the University of the Streets in New York's East Village. This group included saxophonist Clarence 'C' Sharpe and trumpeter Tommy Turrentine. In 1989 Stone resumed his formal education earning a Master of Arts in Jazz Performance at the Aaron Copeland School of Music at Queens College. He studied there with saxophonist Jimmy Heath, trumpeter Donald Byrd, and guitarists Ted Dunbar and Tony Purrone.

Rick Stone's playing has received wide critical praise. He currently leads his own jazz quartet at top East Coast jazz spots including the 'Blue Note' and 'Birdland' clubs in New York. He also teaches courses in Advanced Jazz Theory and Advanced Guitar at the JazzMobile workshop programme in New York. In October 1991 he presented a concert entitled 'A Tribute to the Masters of Modern Jazz Guitar' at Carnegie Hall's Weill Recital Hall in New York.

SELECTED RECORDINGS

Blues For Nobody	Jazzand J2001
Far East-Rick Stone Quartet	Jazzand JCD002

JOHN STOWELL
**Born-Bedford Village,
New York, USA
30 July 1950**

John Stowell first studied the guitar in Connecticut with Linc Chamberland. He went on to study with the noted jazz educator John Mehegan. After several years of playing in East Coast jazz clubs Stowell began a seven year association with bass player Don Friesen. They toured throughout the USA, Canada, Australia and Europe, and made six recordings.

Stowell moved to Oregon during this time. He met flute player Paul Horn there and this led to a concert tour of Russia with a jazz group including Horn and Friesen. In 1979 Stowell won the 'Talent Deserving Wider Recognition' category in Downbeat magazine's critics' Poll. He has also played with many other prominent jazz musicians including Milt Jackson, Art Farmer, Herb Ellis, Scott Hamilton, Conte Condoli, Bill Watrous and Billy Hart.

A talented and original guitarist, Stowell is also a respected educator. He has given clinics at colleges throughout the USA including the Manhattan School of Music, Berklee School of Music, USCLA and the Dick Grove School in Los Angeles.

SELECTED RECORDINGS

Star Dance w/Paul McCandless	Inner City IC 1019 LP
Waterfall Rainbow w/Ralph Towner	Inner City IC 1027 LP
Golden Delicious	Inner City IC 1030 LP
Through The Listening Glass	Inner City IC 1061 LP
Other Mansions w/ David Friesen	Inner City IC 1086 LP
Lines & Spaces w/Lynn Skinner	GSPJAZZ 5001CD

John Stowell

PHOTO: MAURICE J. SUMMERFIELD

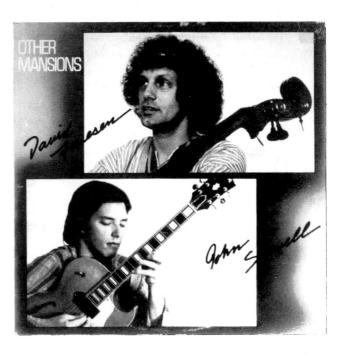

CLINT STRONG
Born-Fort Worth, Texas, USA
14 March 1965

Clint Strong began to play the guitar at the age of nine. His father is an amateur jazz guitarist. He studied privately with several teachers in Oklahoma and Texas, and also attended some Howard Roberts's guitar seminars. Strong began to play as a professional in his teens in local clubs and jazz venues. He gained valuable experience working with Bill Swift, Red Garland, James Clay, Colin Bailey, Paul Guerrero, Marchel Ivery and others.

In 1983 Strong enrolled in North Texas State University. He studied there for two semesters with Jack Peterson. In mid-1984 he left college. In 1985 he joined country artist Merle Haggard's band 'The Strangers', and toured and recorded with him until 1994. From 1994 to 1996 Strong worked with Ray Price.

Because of his involvement for several years with the country music scene, Strong is not well-known to jazz audiences. Yet his recordings are evidence that he is one of the best jazz guitarists to have appeared on the US scene in recent years. Based in Reno, Nevada he currently teaches at the University of Nevada. He also plays with his own jazz trio in local clubs with vocalist CeCe Gable and pianist JoAnn Grauer.

Clint Strong

SELECTED RECORDINGS
Marchel Ivery Meets Joey DeFrancesco
Leaning House Jazz BB-004CD
Mastering Jazz Licks Instructional Video REH 839/CPP 1507

DAVE STRYKER
Born-Omaha, Nebraska, USA
30 March 1957

Dave Stryker

PHOTO: LESLEY PEACOCK

Dave Stryker began to play the guitar at the age of ten. By the time he was twelve he was playing in a local rock band. After hearing some recordings by George Benson and John Coltrane Stryker began to take an interest in jazz. In 1978 he moved to Los Angeles. There he studied with the jazz guitarist Billy Rogers and played professionally in diverse groups around the Los Angeles area.

In 1980 Stryker moved to New York. In the same year he received a National Endowment of the Arts Jazz Study Grant. He soon became one of the busiest jazz guitarists on the New York scene. In 1984 he joined the band of organist Brother Jack McDuff . In the following year Stryker toured the USA, Canada and Jamaica with this group. He then worked with two more famous jazz organ players Lonnie Smith and Jimmy Smith. In June 1986 he joined tenor saxophonist Stanley Turrentine's group to play at major jazz spots throughout the USA. This association with Turrentine lasted right through to 1995. Stryker also appeared with Dizzy Gillespie, Kevin Mahogany and Freddie Hubbard.

Dave Stryker is also a talented teacher and clinician. He has given master classes at the Manhattan School of Music, The New School, William Paterson College, Northern Illinois University, The University of Nebraska and other prestigious educational establishments. Based in New York Dave Stryker is one of the leading and most widely recorded jazz guitarists of the 1990s.

SELECTED RECORDINGS

First Strike	Someday SMC-1011
Strike Zone	SteepleChase 31277 CD
Guitar on Top	Ken Music 019
Blue Degrees	SteepleChase 31315 CD
Passage	SteepleChase 31330 CD
Full Moon	SteepleChase 31345 CD
Stardust	SteepleChase 31362 CD
Nomad	SteepleChase 31371 CD
The Greeting	SteepleChase 31387 CD
Blue To The Bone	SteepleChase 31400 CD
Guitar Artistry of Billy Rogers	Stash 566 CD
A Tribute to Grant Green	Paddle Wheel KJCJ 283 CD
'T' Time w/ Stanley Turrentine	MusicMAsters 65124-2 CD

SELECTED READING

Article	Downbeat, July 1992
Article	Jazz Times, August 1992
Article	Guitar Player, February 1993
Article	Jazz Times, April 1996

SELECTED MUSIC

The Music of Dave Stryker	SteepleChase Music

RORY STUART
Born-New York City, USA
9 January 1956

Rory Stuart

Rory Stuart began to play the guitar when he was thirteen. His mother had bought a guitar for herself but encouraged her son to study on the instrument as well. Stuart was introduced to jazz by multi-instrumentalist Jacki Byard who taught for a while at his school. Stuart did change over to the classical guitar when he went into high school but after a while returned to playing jazz.

After leaving school Stuart decided to make his living as a jazz guitarist. His obvious talent soon earned him a lot of club work. He gained further recognition through his concert tours with saxophonists Steve Coleman and Glenn Wilson, and organists Brother Jack McDuff, Charles Earland, and Bill Doggett.

In 1982 Rory Stuart formed his own quartet as leader. This group's recordings achieved high critical praise, and he has continued to play successfully in the New York area for the last ten years. Stuart claims a wide variety of music influences from John Coltrane to Thelonious Monk, and Jimi Hendrix to Tuck Andress. Although largely self taught, he does pay tribute to the time he studied with guitarist Dave Creamer. As well as playing with his own group Stuart has played as a sideman with many other jazz artists including Charlie Rouse, Larry Coryell, Vinny Golia, Errol Parker and Geri Allen.

SELECTED RECORDINGS

Nightwork Rory Stuart Quartet	Cadence Jazz Records 1016
Hurricane Rory Stuart Quartet	Sunnyside 1021
Lee's Keys Please- Cadence All Stars	Timeless 284 CD
Bittersweet Rory Stuart & Glenn Wilson	Sunnyside SSC 1957 CD

SELECTED READING

Interview	Cadence, January 1984
Interview	Guitar Player, March 1988

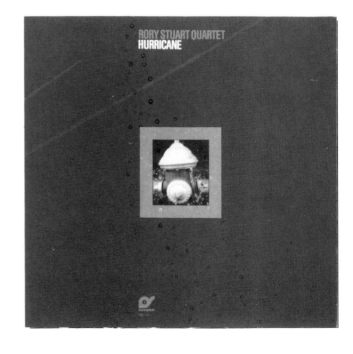

GABOR SZABO
Born-Budapest, Hungary
8 March 1936
Died-Budapest, Hungary
26 February 1982

Gabor Szabo

Gabor Szabo received his first guitar at the age of fourteen as a gift from his father. For the next four years Szabo devoted all his spare time to the guitar and taught himself to play to a high level. From 1954-56 he played professionally with various groups in Budapest, and wrote music for films and radio. He gained his first knowledge of jazz through recordings and from radio broadcasts. On 22 November 1956 he left Hungary as a freedom fighter during the uprising there, and arrived as a refugee in the USA. Szabo was fortunate to become a pupil at the Berklee School of Jazz from 1957-59. He soon gained exposure playing with various jazz groups including one led by Japanese pianist Toshiko. From 1961-65 Szabo gained international prominence as a member of Chico Hamilton's quartet. In late 1965 he was featured in Charles Lloyd's Quartet. In 1964 Downbeat magazine voted him 'Best New Jazz Guitarist' jointly with Atilla Zoller. From 1966-68 he fronted, and recorded with, his own group which featured guitarist Jimmy Stewart. A change in the style of Szabo's playing began in 1969 as he became influenced by the blues, eastern music, and also heavy rock.

For many years Gabor Szabo was based in Los Angeles working successfully with different groups, and in the television studios. One of his groups, 'The Perfect Circle' had a repertoire ranging from pseudo-classical music to hard rock.

SELECTED RECORDINGS

Chico Hamilton-Passin'Thru	Impulse A 29
The Sorcerer	Impulse M1PL506
Gypsy 66	Impulse A9105
Spellbinder	Impulse A9123
The California Dreamers	Impulse 9151
Man From Two Worlds-Chico Hamilton	Inpulse GRD-127
Blowin' Some Old Smoke	Buddah BTS 2051L
Magical Connection	Blue Thumb BTS23
Jazz Raga	Impulse A9128
Gabor Szabo - Greatest Hits	Impulse AS9204-2
Faces	Mercury SRM1-1141
Bacchanal	Skye SK-3
Dreams	Skye SK-7
Gabor Szabo 1969	Skye SK-9
Lena & Gabor w/Lena Horne	Skye SK-15
Gabor Szabo Sextet	DCC DJZ 605

SELECTED READING

Profile	Downbeat, October 1967
Interview	Guitar Player, December 1969
Profile	Guitar Player, July 1975
Interview	Crescendo, November 1979

Martin Taylor

MARTIN TAYLOR
Born-Harlow, Essex, United Kingdom
20 October 1956

Martin Taylor began to play the guitar at the age of four. His father, Buck Taylor, gave him a half-size guitar and introduced him to the recordings of Django Reinhardt. By the time he was twelve Taylor was playing in his father's band in the London area.

Taylor left school at the age of fifteen. He was already a guitarist of great talent and in 1971 was hired to play in the Lennie Hastings Band. In 1972 he joined the Harry Bence band for two years working for the Cunard Line on ships working out of New York. On his return to London Taylor teamed up with Ike Isaacs, who at that time was one of the best British studio and jazz guitarists. His association with Isaacs, and other London based jazz musicians, helped Taylor achieve the virtuoso technique and superb musicality he now displays with such natural ease. He started to gain wide recognition through his appearances in London jazz spots in a guitar duo with Ike Isaacs. In 1979 he replaced Diz Disley in Stephane Grappelli's quartet after Disley broke his wrist in a road accident. A long association with Grappelli began. Taylor appeared in concert all over the world with the legendary jazz violinist. He also made many recordings, and television and radio broadcasts, with Grappelli.

Since that time Martin Taylor has been recognised as one of the greatest jazz guitarists to have appeared on the international scene in recent years. In 1981 he recorded for Concord Records in California. Following this he toured the USA five times, teaming up with the late Emily Remler for two coast-to-coast tours. Taylor has toured extensively, and recorded, with clarinetist Buddy De Franco. For two years (1986-87) he toured throughout Europe and the United Kingdom with the brilliant Irish guitarist, Louis Stewart. In recent times Taylor has appeared with Barney Kessel and Charlie Byrd as part of their 'Great Guitars' group.

Martin Taylor has also developed a phenomenal right hand fingerstyle technique, as well as the usual pick technique, so that he now quite often records as a solo artist. His outstanding abilities have made Martin Taylor one of the busiest jazz musicians in the world today. He appears regularly in every continent at leading jazz clubs and festivals. He won the 'Top Guitarist Award' in the annual British Jazz Awards every year from 1987.

PHOTO: COURTESY MARTIN TAYLOR

Martin Taylor and George Benson.

SELECTED RECORDINGS

After Hours Duo w/Ike Isaacs	Antoria JTC-1
Taylor Made	Wave LP 17
Triple Libra	Wave LP 24
London Reprise w/Spike Robinson	Capri 44360 LP
At The Winery-Stephane Grappelli 4	Concord CCD-4139
Vintage 1981-Stephane Grappelli 4	Concord CCD-4169
Skye Boat-Martin Taylor	Concord CCD-4184
On Tour- Buddy de Franco Quintet	HEP Records 2023
Groovin'-Buddy de Franco Quintet	HEP Records 2030
A Tribute To Art Tatum	CP LP 2070
Sarabanda-Martin Taylor Group	GAIA Records 13 9018 1
Don't Fret-Martin Taylor	Linn Records AKD 014CD
Change Of Heart	Linn Records AKD 016CD
Artistry - Martin Taylor	Linn Records AKD 020CD
Reunion w/Stephane Grappelli	Linn Records CKD 022CD
Spirit of Django	Linn Records AKD 030CD
Years Apart Spirit of Django	Linn Record ALG058
Portraits	LINN AKD 048CD
Just Friends w/Barbara Jay	Spotlite SPJ-CD5J7
Two's Company	Linn Records AKD 081CD
Gypsy	Linn Records AKD 090CD
Celebrating Grappelli	Linn Records AKD 094CD

Live In San Francisco w/S.Grappelli Video	Castle Hendring
Live In New Orleans w/S.Grappelli Video	Castle Hendring
Martin Taylor Instructional Video	Starnite
Martin Taylor in Concert	Vestapol

SELECTED READING

Interview	Guitar Player, January 1984
Interview	Guitarist, September 1985
Interview	Guitarist, July 1987
Profile	Jazz News, May/June 1989
Interview	Jazz News, February 1991
Interview	Guitarist, September 1993
Interview	Just Jazz Guitar, November 1994
Interview	Fingerstyle Guitar, March/April 1997

SELECTED MUSIC

Jazz Guitar Artistry of Martin Taylor	Ashley Mark Publishing

TOMMY TEDESCO
Born-Niagara Falls, New York, USA
30 July 1930
Died-Northridge, California, USA
10 November 1997

Tommy Tedesco.

Tommy Tedesco was probably the most recorded guitarist in the history of the music. He appeared on countless television and radio shows, on the soundtracks of dozens of major cinema and television films, and also on hundreds of recordings backing the most famous singers and musicians of the day. He was known to guitarists throughout the world through his regular column in Guitar Player magazine, his tuition books and recordings as leader of his own groups.

Tedesco, encouraged by his father, started to play the guitar at the age of ten. At first he was not keen on the instrument and gave it up when he was thirteen. Three years later he took it up again and then began what was to be one of the most successful careers in the instrument's history. Band-leader Ralph Marterie hired the young guitarist. In 1953 Tedesco came with the Marterie band to the West Coast and he decided to settle in Los Angeles. He played mainly in jazz clubs in and around Los Angeles. He worked with Chico Hamilton, Buddy De Franco, Shorty Rogers, Shelly Manne, Art Pepper, Bob Cooper and many other West Coast jazz players. From around 1955 Tedesco decided to pursue a career in the cinema, television and recording studios. For the next twenty five years Tedesco was not involved in jazz but in the late 1970s he decided to return to his jazz roots. From that time he became a regular performer at jazz clubs in the Los Angeles area and also, over a period of years, recorded several albums as leader of his own jazz group.

Tommy Tedesco was always involved in music education. For many years he was Director of the Studio Guitar Programme at the G.I.T. (Guitar Institute of Technology) in Hollywood. His two instructional books, 'For Guitarists Only' and 'Anatomy of A Guitar Player' were been well received by guitarists all over the world. For his studio work Tedesco received the Emeritus Award from the National Academy of Recording Arts and Sciences. He was voted Best Studio Guitarist for several years in a row in the prestigious Guitar Player magazine's Annual Readers' Poll.

SELECTED RECORDINGS

Autumn	Discovery Trend TR514 LP
Alone At Last	Discovery Trend TR517 LP
When Do We Start	Discovery Trend DS789 LP
My Desiree	Discovery Trend DSCD-959
Carnival Time	Discovery Trend TR534 LP
Roumanis – Jazz Rhapsody	Capri 75002-2 CD

Playing Guitar For A Living	Instructional Video	Hot Licks

SELECTED READING

Interview	Guitar Player, February 1980
Interview	Downbeat, May 1983
Interview	Guitarist, May 1986
Appreciation	Guitar Player, February 1998
Appreciation	Just Jazz Guitar, February 1998

SELECTED MUSIC

For Guitarists Only	Dale Zdenek Publishers
Anatomy of a Guitar Player	Mel Bay Publications
Ten	GIT Publications

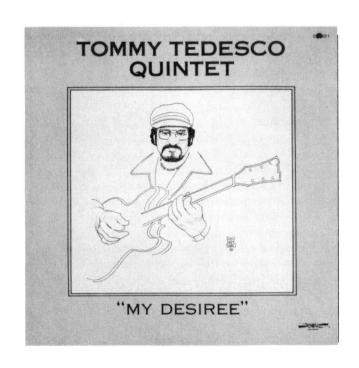

TOOTS THIELEMANS
Born-JEAN BAPTISTE THIELEMANS
Brussels, Belgium
29 April 1922

Toots Thielmans

Known throughout the world as the foremost harmonica player in jazz, 'Toots' Thielemans is also a very fine jazz guitarist. Thielmans began playing the accordion at the age of three. He started to play the harmonica in 1939 whilst studying mathematics at college. He then decided to take up the guitar after hearing some Django Reinhardt records.

Self taught on the guitar Thielemans began playing professionally in 1944 in US Army G.I. clubs. In 1949 he shared the bill with Charlie Parker at the Paris International Jazz Festival. Although he visited the United States in 1947 it was not until late 1951 that he decided to settle in America. His decision came after a successful tour with the Benny Goodman sextet in 1950 which helped establish him in the USA. Thielemans worked for a while with singer Dinah Washington and then in early 1953 he was offered the guitar seat with the George Shearing quintet. He stayed with Shearing until 1959. The following year he formed his own jazz group.

In the mid 1960s Thielemans worked as a staff musician in New York City. He worked in these studios until 1969. During this time he worked closely on several projects with bandleader/composer Quincy Jones. He then toured Russia in 1972 with his own group. Since that time Toots Thielemans has become an international jazz star and continues a highly successful career playing harmonica and guitar in concert, and in jazz clubs, all over the world.

Toots Thieleman's guitar style is instantly recognizable as he often whistles and hums in unison with his own guitar improvisations, much in the manner of bassist Slam Stewart. He is also a talented composer. His most famous compositions being the jazz standard 'Bluesette', and the background music for the American television series, 'Sesame Street'.

SELECTED RECORDINGS
Too Much! Toots	Philips PHM200-188 LP
The Whistler and his Guitar	ABC Paramount ABC482 LP
Time Out for Toots	Decca 9204 LP
Captured Alive	Choice CR1007 LP
Spotlight on Toots	Polydor 2484055 LP
Toots Thielemans Quartet	Concord CCD 4355
Oscar Peterson Big Six	Pablo 2310747-2 CD
Toots & Svent	AM Records SP 3613CD

SELECTED READING
Profile	Downbeat, July 1958
Profile	Downbeat, November 1971
Profile	Guitar Player, January 1979
Article	Downbeat, August 1993

RENÉ THOMAS

**Born-Liege, Belgium
25 February 1927
Died-Santander, Spain
3 January 1975**

René Thomas began studying the guitar at the age of ten. He did have some lessons at first but was mainly self taught. He started playing the guitar professionally in the early 1950s freelancing in Belgium and France. Thomas first gained prominence in 1955 after he played with prominent visiting American jazz musicians in Paris, including trumpeter Chet Baker. He was also closely associated in Paris with the French saxophonist Bobby Jaspar.

Thomas decided to emigrate in 1958 to New York settling later in Montreal, Canada for two years. Whilst in New York, in 1958, Thomas recorded with saxophonist Sonny Rollins, and pianist Toshiko Akiyoshi. Thomas's guitar playing made a great impression on jazz lovers and musicians in the New York area. From 1969-71 Thomas toured and recorded with saxophonist Stan Getz.

Until his premature death in 1975 from a heart attack, Thomas worked mainly in Europe, often with organist Eddy Louiss and drummer Kenny Clarke. René Thomas was a world class jazz guitarist whose style, originally influenced by Django Reinhardt and later to a much greater extent by Jimmy Raney, was one that retained its own brilliant individuality.

SELECTED RECORDINGS

René Thomas/Bobby Jaspar Quintet	RCA Victor (Italy) TML10324
Meeting Mr Thomas	Barclay 84 091
Guitar Groove	Jazzland JL 927S
Songbook in Europe w/Lucky Thompson	MPS 15231
Chet Baker is Back	RCA (Italy) RCA10307
Eddy Louiss Trio	RCA CY 3004
René Thomas Modern Group	Polydor 2445 036
Thomas/Jaspar Quintet	RCA NL 70730
René Thomas Live Paris 1964	Jeal RJD 512 CD
René Thomas-Guitar Genius Vol.1	RTBF AMC 16001 CD
René Thomas-Guitar Genius Vol.2	RTBF AMC 50022 CD
Hommage to René Thomas	Timeless STP 398 CD

Rene Thomas with Stan Getz.

PHOTO: LUCIANO MARCHESELLI/COURTESY JAZZ JOURNAL

RALPH TOWNER
Born-Chehalis, Washington, USA
1 March 1940

Ralph Towner started playing the guitar at the relatively late age of twenty two. His early musical education began on the piano at the age of three. His mother was a church organist and piano teacher. His father, who died when his son was three, played the trumpet. In 1959 Towner went to the University of Oregon to study music. His main instrument at that time was the trumpet. In his last year at college he became attracted to the guitar and from that time on he devoted most of his time to an intensive study of the instrument. Whilst at college Towner met bass player Glen Moore. He also began to listen to recordings by pianist Bill Evans, and these proved to be a major influence on his musical development.

After leaving the University of Oregon in 1963, Towner went to Vienna, Austria to study for one year at the Academy of Music and Dramatic Arts with classical guitarist Karl Scheit. Towner returned to the University of Oregon 1964-66 to do post-graduate work after which he studied for a further year with Scheit in Vienna.

Towner returned to the USA in 1968 and settled in New York where he worked at first as a pianist. He worked with diverse musical artists including singer Astrud Gilberto, bassist Dave Holland, Miles Davis and Keith Jarrett. Towner first came to prominence in 1970 when he joined the 'Paul Winter Consort' playing a twelve-string guitar, an instrument he used on several of his subsequent jazz recordings. He left the consort in 1971 and formed a new group, a quartet with Glen Moore, Colin Walcott and Paul McCandless called 'Oregon'. This group developed a very beautiful and individual sound generated by Towner's intellectual and distinctive approach to music. It mixed folk, classical, jazz and ethnic music forms into an acoustic chamber-group.

During the late 1970s and early 1980s Towner began a successful association with John Abercrombie in an acoustic jazz guitar duo. In 1981 he settled in Seattle, Washington. Since that time Towner, a major figure in the history of the guitar in jazz, has continued composing and playing in a style that he helped introduce as a leader of the group 'Oregon'. He has composed over one hundred recorded pieces, an orchestral piece for the St. Paul Chamber Orchestra in Minnesota, and a symphonic piece for eighty instruments commissioned by the Cabrillo Music Festival. Towner has also com-

Ralph Towner

PHOTO: JAMES GUDEMAN COURTESY: ECM RECORDS

posed and performed works for several dance groups, and also written film scores.

SELECTED RECORDINGS

Oregon-Our First Concert	Vanguard VSD 79432
Oregon-Winter Light	Vanguard VSD 79350
Oregon-In Concert	Vanguard VSD 79358
Trios/Solos w/Glen Moore	ECM 1025 CD
Diary	ECM 1032 CD
Matchbook w/Gary Burton	ECM 1056 CD
Sargasso Sea w/John Abercrombie	ECM 1080 CD
Dis w/Jan Garbarek	ECM 1093 CD
Solstice	ECM 1060 CD
Sounds and Shadows	ECM 1095 CD
Batik	ECM 1121 CD
Old Friends, New Friends	ECM 1153 CD
Solo Concert	ECM 1173 CD
Five Years Later w/John Abercrombie	ECM 1207 CD
Blue Sun	ECM 1250 CD
Oregon-Crossing	ECM 1291 CD
City Of Eyes	ECM 1388 CD
Open Letter	ECM 1462 CD
Always, Never & Forever	Intuition 2073-2
Out Of The Woods	Discovery 71004 CD
Roots In The Sky	Discovery 71005 CD
Lost and Found	ECM 1563 CD
Oracle	ECM 78118 21490-2 CD
Ana – Solo Guitar	ECM 1611 CD
Oregon Live 1987 Video	Proscenium Entertainment

SELECTED READING

Profile	Downbeat, June 1975
Profile	Guitar Player, December 1975
Profile	Guitar, January 1979
Profile	Downbeat, May 1983
Article	Jazz Times, May 1996

SELECTED MUSIC

Improvisation And Performance Techniques for Classical and Acoustic Guitar — 21st Century Music Productions.

JAMES 'BLOOD' ULMER
Born-St. Matthews, South Carolina, USA
2 February 1942

James Ulmer started to play the guitar at the age of seven. His father, a guitarist, taught him until he was thirteen. He also taught his son to sing and Ulmer became a member of his father's gospel group. The young musician sang baritone and played guitar with the group. At the age of thirteen he gave up the guitar and started to play the piano and the saxophone. He returned to guitar at the age of eighteen.

After leaving high school Ulmer moved north to Pittsburgh. It was here that he picked up the nickname 'Youngblood' which later was shortened to 'Blood'. The young guitarist joined a popular dance band called 'The Savoys'. This led to a job with another popular band called 'The Del-Vikings'. Whilst in Pittsburgh Ulmer met the fifteen year old George Benson, who was already a young guitar prodigy. Benson gave him some lessons and guidance so helping Ulmer develop an interest in jazz. Ulmer continued to play professionaly in the popular music field as guitarist with Jewel Brenner's 'Swing Kings'.

In 1963 Ulmer moved to Columbus, Ohio, where he formed his own group called 'Blood and The Bloodbrothers'. They became the house band at a local club, backing artists such as Dionne Warwick and Chuck Jackson. In 1965 Ulmer toured Europe with a group led by organist, Hank Marr. A member of the group was tenor saxophonist George Adams. He was to prove a great influence on Ulmer, introducing him to the music of John Coltrane and Miles Davis and also giving him an introduction to free jazz.

In 1973 Ulmer moved to Detroit, where he taught guitar at the Metropolitan Art Complex. He also formed two new groups. The first, the James Ulmer Trio, played regular modern jazz. The second group, 'Focus Novii', concentrated on free jazz and Ulmer's very original compositions. After a while he became disillusioned with the scene in Detroit and moved to New York. Here he quickly formed a new group, which was booked to play at Minton's Playhouse in Harlem. Ulmer stayed there for nine months. Although the group was booked to play the blues, he used the opportunity to play free jazz. After Minton's, he worked briefly with groups led by drummers Art Blakey and Rashied Ali. Ulmer was then introduced to Ornette Coleman. The saxophonist was very impressed with Ulmer's musical ideas and invited him to study with him. Ulmer also toured Europe with the Coleman group. This collaboration was to be the turning point for

James 'Blood' Ulmer

Ulmer to achieve the style of jazz playing he had been searching for.

In 1978 Ulmer released his album 'Tales of Captain Black'. This innovative recording , which features saxophonist Ornette Coleman and Denardo Coleman on drums, displayed the full range of Blood's free jazz guitar style. This landmark recording led to more featuring many of the leading free jazz musicians of the day including Oliver Lake and David Murray. In 1971 Ulmer formed, and recorded with, his 'Music Revelation Ensemble'. The success of his earlier recordings led to a major contract with Columbia Records. He recorded three albums on guitar and as a vocalist for this prestigious label, all of which were well received by the critics. Regardless of this critical success, the recordings, because of their specialist nature, did not achieve the sales anticipated by Columbia. Since leaving Columbia James 'Blood' Ulmer has released several recordings, including three by his new group 'Phalanx'. He in no way compromises on the free form of jazz that has distinguished him from most other jazz guitarists. He often appears in Europe and Japan and is set to further strengthen his unique place in jazz guitar history.

SELECTED RECORDINGS

Tales of Captain Black	Artists House AH 7
Are You Glad To Be In America?	Rough Trade RT 16
Eye Level	Rough Trade RT 128
Freelancing	Columbia CBS 85224
Black Rock	Columbia CBS 25064
America, Do You Remember The Love?	Blue Note CDP 746 755 2
Revealing	In & Out NN 70072 CD
James 'Blood' Ulmer-Phalanx	DIW DIW-801 CD
Music Speaks Louder Than Words	Koch Jazz 3-7833 CD

SELECTED READING

Interview	Guitar World, January 1981
Profile	Guitar Player, May 1990
Profile	Downbeat, April 1994
Profile	Jazz Times, May 1994

PHIL UPCHURCH
Born-Chicago, Illinois, USA
19 July 1941

Phil Upchurch originally started at the age of eleven on a ukulele given to him by his father who was a pianist. He changed over to the guitar when he was thirteen and was virtually self taught. He gained a lot of experience on both electric bass and guitar with various Chicago bands. Upchurch's first real professional break came when he played with rhythm and blues singer Dee Clark. His work with this artist soon earned him many bookings in the Chicago recording studios backing top artists including jazz stars Dizzy Gillespie, Stan Getz and Ramsey Lewis. In 1961 Upchurch recorded a hit blues instrumental called, 'You Can't Sit Down'.

Upchurch was drafted into the US Army in 1965 and was based in Germany. During his time there he played regularly with various small jazz groups. Upchurch left the forces in 1968 and returned to Chicago where his guitar playing was once more much in demand. He worked with several important jazz artists including Cannonball Adderley and Grover Washington. Upchurch was also staff guitarist for Chess Records backing blues artists such as Muddy Waters and Howlin' Wolf. In 1970 he toured the USA with pianist Ramsey Lewis. In 1971 he settled briefly in California where he worked with Quincy Jones. In 1972 he toured Japan with Jones.

Upchurch became a close friend of guitarist George Benson in the early 1960s. They finally came to work together in 1974 when Upchurch backed Benson on his CTI release, 'Bad Benson'. This recording was the first of several, including Benson's 1976 Grammy Award winning album 'Breezin', on which Upchurch backed Benson.

In 1977 Phil Upchurch settled permanently in Los Angeles. Here he is actively involved in jazz club and studio work. He is also associated with the Polytone Musical Instrument Company as a sales executive and clinician.

Phil Upchurch

SELECTED READING

Profile	Downbeat, June 1969
Profile	Downbeat, June 1974
Profile	Guitar Player, December 1969
Profile	Guitar World, September 1981
Profile	Guitar Player, February 1985

SELECTED MUSIC

Twelve by Twelve	Mel Bay Publishing

SELECTED RECORDINGS

Feeling Blue	Milestone MSP 9010
Upchurch	Cadet LPS 826
The Way I Feel	Cadet LPS 840
Darkness, Darkness	Blue Thumb BTS 605
Lovin' A Feeling	BlueThumb BTS 606
Upchurch/Tennyson	Motown Kudu KU-2251
Phil Upchurch	Marlin X 798
Free & Easy	JAM 007
Revelation	JAM 011
Name Of The Game	JAM 017
Companions	JAM 021
Midnite Blue	Electric Bird KICJ 53CD
Love is Strange	Bean Bag BB 55552 CD
What Ever Happened to the Blues	Bean Bag BB 55566 CD

VINNY VALENTINO
Born-Fairfax, Virginia, USA
20 June 1964

Vinny Valentino began to play the guitar at the age of six. As a youth his interest lay in rock and roll music. But when he was sixteen he went to a George Benson concert and from that time Valentino decided to play jazz.

Valentino, who earned a jazz degree from Howard University, has performed with George Benson, Russell Malone, Jimmy McGriff, Charlie Byrd, Buck Hill, among many others. In 1991 he received a grant from the Virginia Commission for the Arts and the National Endowment for the Arts for the commissioned trio guitar work 'New Music for Three Jazz Guitars'. He toured with Paul Bollenback and Rick Molina to perform the work.

Vinny Valentino maintains a busy career performing in concert and at clubs throughout the USA.

SELECTED RECORDINGS

Vinny Valentino & Here No Evil	PAR Records PAR 2016 CD
Now & Again - Vinny Valentino	DMP CD - 3003

SELECTED READING

Profile	Jazz Times, July/August 1993

Vinny Valentino

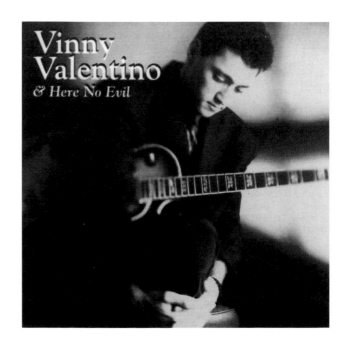

MAARTEN van der GRINTEN
Born-Geleen, The Netherlands
19 December 1963

Maarten van der Grinten

Maarten van der Grinten first played the drums at the age of nine. He took up the guitar at the age of 12. From 1982-87 he studied at the Hilversum Conservatory graduating with the highest honours. In 1987 he was awarded the Loosdrecht Festival Promotion Prize and in 1988 he was awarded a scholarship to study at the Manhattan School of Music in New York for one year. Whilst in the USA van der Grinten began to take a serious in interest in composing.

In 1991, after his return to the Netherlands, van der Grinten won the Max van Praag Award for outstanding accompaniment at the Loosdrecht Jazz Festival. Since that time he has established himself as one of Europe's best jazz guitarists. He has played with leading Dutch jazz musicians including Wim Overgaauw, Ack van Rooyen and John Engels, and also with visiting jazz artists such as Clark Terry and Toots Thielemans. He has played with the WDR Big Band, The Metropole Orchestra, the Willem Breuker Kollektief and the New Concert Band.

Maarten van der Grinten is a member of the European Jazz Guitar Orchestra which includes Louis Stewart and Doug Raney, and Picks Might Fly a jazz guitar quartet which also features Jesse van Ruller. He currently leads two jazz groups, Dig d'Diz with baritone saxophonist Jan Menu and bassist Jan Voogd, and the Van der Grinter/Herman Quartet with saxophonist Benjamin Herman. He works regularly with jazz singers Greetje Kauffeld, Laura Fygi and Soesja Citroen. Van der Grinten is currently head of the guitar department of the jazz faculty at the Conservatory of Amsterdam.

SELECTED RECORDINGS

DIG d'DIZ 'One'	Riff 85005-2 CD
Van der Grinten/Herman Quartet	Riff 85020-2 CD
European Jazz Orchestra	Jardis JRCD 9307
Van der Grinten/Herman Quartet	A-Records AL 73005 CD
The Real Thing w'Greetje Kauffeld	Riff 850031/2 CD
Wim Overgauuw 65th Anniversary Concert	
	Radio Netherlands RN 009 CD

351

George Van Eps

GEORGE VAN EPS

Born - GEORGE ABEL VAN EPS
Plainfield, New Jersey, USA
7 August 1913
Died – Newport Beach, California, USA,
29 November 1998

George Van Eps was regarded by most leading guitarists as one of the 'fathers' of the modern pick guitar. His harmonies and musical concepts are legendary.

George Van Eps came from a very musical family. His father was Fred Van Eps, the most famous five-string banjoist of his day. His mother was an excellent classical and ragtime pianist. Van Eps's first instrument was the banjo which he began to play at the age of nine, after a bout of rheumatic fever had forced him to leave school. By the time he was twelve he was already a member of the Plainfield Musicians Union. Although the minimum age for the union was sixteen, Van Eps was given a special concession because of his exceptional musical talent. At the age of fourteen, inspired by Eddie Lang, he changed over to the guitar.

Van Eps played with the Smith Ballew band from 1929-31, and with the Freddy Martin outfit 1931-33. His first real break came in 1934 when he joined Benny Goodman's orchestra. This brought his guitar talents to the attention of jazz lovers all over the world. Van Eps has also been a prominent teacher. One of his many pupils was Allan Reuss who later took his place in the Benny Goodman Orchestra. In 1936 Van Eps joined the Ray Noble band, an association that lasted on and off until 1941. During this period he moved to Hollywood where he became one of the busiest guitarists in the Los Angeles film and radio studios.

During World War II Van Eps left the music profession for a short time to help his father in his recording equipment factory in Plainfield, New Jersey. The factory was an important supplier of items necessary for the war effort. In 1944 Van Eps was once more playing with the Ray Noble band and involved in all types of studio work. He was also prominently featured on many recordings with the Paul Weston orchestra.

George Van Eps played and recorded from 1938 on a seven- string guitar, an instrument that he designed in the late 1930s. The Epiphone Guitar company agreed to build him a guitar to his design and in 1938 Van Eps received his first seven-string guitar from them. From that time he only played the seven-string guitar, which has an extra bass string tuned to a low A. In more recent times he was involved in a line of seven-string guitars produced by the Gretsch Guitar Company to his original designs. His continuous promotion of, and experimentation with, the seven-string guitar has been a great inspiration to many other guitarists including Bucky Pizzarelli, Howard Morgen, Ted Greene and Howard Alden. Van Eps also designed a string damper which helps eliminate feedback. He described his approach to solo guitar playing as treating the instrument as a 'lap' piano.

For a few years Van Eps retired from the music business. In 1955 he opened, together with his wife, a model shop in Glendale, California. This business closed in 1963 and from that time Van Eps's involvement with the guitar has gradually become stronger than ever. His highly acclaimed three volume 'Harmonic Mechanisms for Guitar' has been published by Mel Bay Publications. In recent years he made three recordings with guitarist Howard Alden for the Concord Label. He also toured internationally giving concerts and master classes until his death in November 1998.

George Van Eps's music and methods, recorded work, teaching ability, and his design and promotion of the seven-string guitar, are a lasting testimony to his enormous and unique talents. They will ensure the name of George Van Eps will always be a legend amongst jazz guitarists.

SELECTED RECORDINGS

George Van Eps-1949 w/Eddie Miller		Jump 12-6 LP
Carefree w/Paul Weston Orchestra	Columbia	1261 LP
Solo Mood w/Paul Weston Orchestra	Columbia	CL879 LP
Mood for Twelve w/Paul Weston Orchestra	Columbia	CL693 LP
Mellow Guitar	Columbia	CL 929 LP
Soliloquy	Capitol	ST 267 LP
My Guitar	Capitol	ST 2533 LP
Seven String Guitar	Capitol	ST 2783 LP
Fun on the Frets	Yazoo	1061 CD
13 Strings w/Howard Alden	Concord	CCD-4464
Hand-Crafted Swing w/Howard Alden	Concord	CCD-4513
Seven & Seven w/Howard Alden	Concord	CCD-4584
Legends	Concord	CCD-4616

SELECTED READING

Profile	Guitar Player, December 1967
Interview	Downbeat, July 1964
Interview	Guitar Player, March 1970
Profile	B.M.G., September 1970
Profile	Guitar, April 1974
George Van Eps-The Seven String Guitar	Gretsch Guitar Co.
Interview	Guitar Player, August 1981
Profile	Guitar Player, January 1994
Article	Just Jazz Guitar, August 1995

SELECTED MUSIC

George Van Eps Method	Epiphone Music Co.
George Van Eps 3 Solos	Epiphone Music Co.
George Van Eps 6 Solos	Plymouth Music Co.
Harmonic Mechanisms For Guitar 3 Vols	Mel Bay Publications
George Van Eps Guitar Solos	Mel Bay Publications

JESSE van RULLER
Born-Amsterdam, The Netherlands
21 January 1972

Jesse van Ruller came to international note as the winner of the prestigious 1995 Thelonious Monk Award held in Washington, DC. Van Ruller began to play the guitar at the age of seven. He learnt classical guitar at his local school, and then took up electric guitar when he was 11. He was influenced by pop music at this time. When he was 15 he heard Eef Albers and Peter Tiehuis, a Dutch jazz guitar duo. From that time on he became absorbed in the world of jazz. Van Ruller, after studying privately with jazz/fusion guitarist Bernhard Reinke, became a student of Wim Overgaauw at the Hilversum Conservatorium. He graduated Cum Laude. In 1995 he received a masters degree in music at the University of Miami, Florida, USA.

Since that time Jesse van Ruller has made a great impression on all who have heard him play. He appears regularly with his own jazz quartet, and teaches at the Hilversum Conservatorium and at clinics throughout the Netherlands. He has appeared in concert with many top jazz artists including Christian McBride, Ralph Moore, Tom Harrell, George Duke and Kenny Washington. Van Ruller has also appeared with the EBU Big Band.

Jesse van Ruller

PHOTO:EDWIN GLASSER. COURTESY : JAN MENU PRODUCTIONS

SELECTED RECORDINGS

European Quintet	Blue Music BM 1002 CD
Herbs, Fruits, Balms and Spices	Blue Music BM 1004 CD

SELECTED READING

Interview	Just Jazz Guitar, November 1996

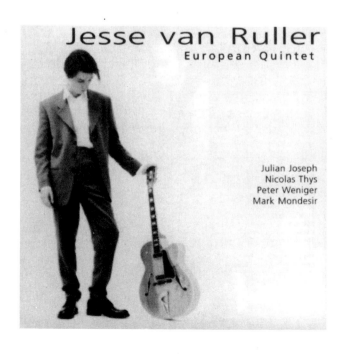

Jesse van Ruller
European Quintet

Julian Joseph
Nicolas Thys
Peter Weniger
Mark Mondesir

FRANK VIGNOLA
Born-Long Island, New York, USA
30 December 1965

Frank Vignola began to play the guitar at the age of five. His father played both the guitar and the banjo. At the age of six Vignola was impressed on hearing some recordings by Django Reinhardt. He decided this was the style of music he would prefer to play. He studied for a while with guitarist Jimmy George. By the time Vignola was in his teens he was playing in a 'Hot Club' style group.

Vignola attended the Cultural Arts Centre on Long Island, New York. He graduated from this establishment with honours. Whilst he was there he played in various progressive rock groups. At the age of fifteen he won a competition sponsored by the McDonald's Corporation to appear in their State Jazz Band. Since that time Vignola has toured or performed with many top jazz artists including Les Paul, Milt Hinton, Dick Hyman, Claude Bolling, Jon Hendricks and Dick Wellstood.

In 1988 he formed a group called 'Frank Vignola & The Hot Club' which played in the style of Django Reinhardt. Since that time the group has played at the Newport and Ottawa Jazz Festivals, The Smithsonian and New York's Town Hall. Vignola currently co-leads the group 'Travelin Light' with jazz tuba player Sam Pilafian. This 1930s style group has enjoyed great club, concert and recording success during the last year.

Frank Vignola recently signed a contract with Concord Records. His first release with this company reflect his committment to the 1930s acoustic guitar style.

Frank Vignola

SELECTED RECORDINGS

Travelin Light w/Sam Pilafian	Telarc CD-80281
Makin Whoopee w/Sam Pilafian	Telarc CD-83324
Xmas with Travelin Light	Telarc CD-83330
Ken Peplowski Quintet	Concord CCD-4517
Appel Direct-Frank Vignola	Concord CCD-4576
Look Right, Jog Left	Concord CCD-4718

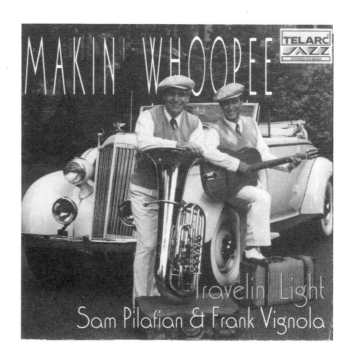

AL VIOLA
Born-ALFONSO ALFRED VIOLA
Brooklyn, New York, USA
16 June 1919

Al Viola

Al Viola was fortunate in that both his mother and elder brother were good amateur musicians who played various fretted instruments. Viola was attracted to the guitar and his initial influences were Carl Kress, Dick McDonough and George Van Eps. Eventually it was the electric guitar of Charlie Christian that had a major impact on the young guitarist. Viola was lucky in that he was able to hear Christian play at Minton's Playhouse and at other New York jazz clubs. He also heard Oscar Moore playing with Nat 'King' Cole's Trio at Kelly's Stables in New York. It was Moore that helped Viola obtain his first electric guitar.

In 1941 Viola was drafted into the US Army. He was assigned to the Camp Kohler band in Sacramento where he played the guitar in a trio called 'The Three Sergeants'. The original pianist of this group, Louis Ventrella was eventually replaced by Page Cavanaugh. After the end of World War II the trio stayed together, now calling itself 'The Page Cavanaugh Trio'. From 1947-49 the trio became a highly successful vocal/instrumental-group.

Since 1949, after leaving the trio, Viola has led a rewarding and varied music career. He settled in California and played with pianist Bobby Troup from 1950-54, the Ray Anthony Orchestra 1955-56, and in 1957 with the Harry James band. For many years he was closely associated with singer Frank Sinatra, accompanying him in a 1973 concert at the White House in Washington DC. Viola, one of Hollywood's busiest studio musicians, has also devoted a lot of his time to the study of music including a course in harmony and theory at the California Academy of Music. He has also studied, and plays, the classical guitar.

SELECTED RECORDINGS

Guitars	Liberty 3112 LP
Imagination	Liberty 3155 LP
Solo Guitar	Mode 121 LP
Guitar Vol.II	Liberty LST 7127 LP
Alone Again	Legend 1002 LP
Guitar Lament	World Pacific WP1408 LP
The Intimate Miss Christy	Capitol T1953 LP
Prelude To A Kiss	PBR International PBR 11 LP
Al Viola-Salutations F.S	PBR International GXF 3180 LP
The Digital Page w/Page Cavanaugh	Star Line 9001 CD

SELECTED MUSIC

Guitar Lament	Leeds Music Corporation
20 Preludes	Mel Bay Publications

SELECTED READING

Profile	Guitar Player, April 1977
Profile	Guitar Player, October 1994
Interview	Just Jazz Guitar, February 1997

ULF WAKENIUS
Born-Halmstad, Sweden
16 April 1958

Ulf Wakenius began to play the guitar at the age of ten. His first interest was in the blues and rock music. He then took an interest in other guitar styles including jazz, classical and flamenco. A busy sideman for many years backing top jazz artists including Airto Moreira, Flora Purim, Johnny Griffin, Herbie Hancock, Peter Erskine, Joe Henderson and Larry Coryell, Wakenius first came to international recognition as a member of the brilliant jazz duo, Guitars Unlimited, with Peter Almqvist. This duo was originally formed in 1980.

In recent years Ulf Wakenius has established himself as one of the world's best jazz guitarists. He has recorded and toured with the Ray Brown Trio, the Niels-Henning Orsted Pedersen Trio, and is currently a member of the Oscar Peterson Quartet.

Ulf Wakenius

SELECTED RECORDINGS

Enchanted Moments	Dragon 278 CD
Those Who Were– Duo w/Niels Pedersen	Verve 533-232 CD
Venture	Bellaphon CDLR 45052
Seven Steps to Heaven w/Ray Brown Trio	Telarc CD-83384

WITH GUITARS UNLIMITED

Introducing Guitars Unlimited	Sonet SNTF-923 LP
Acoustic Shokk	Sonet SNTF-953 LP
Lets Vamos	Sonet SNTF-978 LP
Three for the Road	Sonet SNTCD-1006
Phraserace	COOP 8303 CD
Extraordinaire	Musik Musik MM18 CD

SELECTED READING

Article	String Jazz, November/December 1995

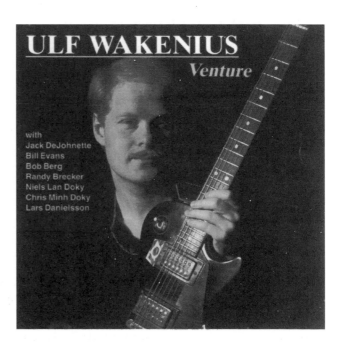

KAZUMI WATANABE
Born-Tokyo, Japan
14 October 1953

Kazumi Watanabe first began to play the guitar at the age of thirteen. His first musical interest lay with guitar pop groups such as 'The Shadows' and 'The Ventures'. As his musical and technical skills developed, he discovered the guitar styles of Jimi Hendrix and Eric Clapton, and then Larry Coryell and John McLaughlin. By the time he was seventeen Watanabe had established himself as a jazz and jazz/rock guitarist, working with top Japanese musicians such as Sadao Watanabe, bassist Isao Suzuki and drummer Motohiko Hino. In 1970 he recorded his first album.

Watanabe continued to gain wider recognition for his guitar playing, particularly in the USA. In 1980 he recorded a jazz/fusion album with a group of New York jazz musicians which included drummer Steve Jordan and vibraphonist Mike Mainieri. More well received recordings led to a USA tour in 1985.

Kazumi Watanabe is a guitarist who can play with equal mastery in the fields of swing, bop, funk and high-energy rock. He often incorporates the use of guitar synthesisers into his work, making him a leader in the area of high technology guitar playing.

Kazumi Watanabe

SELECTED RECORDINGS

Mobo Splash	Gramavision GR 18-8602-1
Mobo Club	Gramavision GR 18-8506-1
Mobo II	Gramavision GR 18-8404-1
Pandora	Gramavision R2 79472
To Chi Ka	Better Days YX-7265-ND
Kylyn Live	Denon 35C38-7135
Mermaid Boulevard w/Lee Ritenour	Inner City ICT 10533

SELECTED READING

Interview	Guitar Player, April 1986
Profile	Guitar World, December 1988

MITCH WATKINS
Born-McAllen, Texas, USA
1 August 1952

Mitch Watkins

Mich Watkins studied the piano from the age of eight. He became interested in the guitar at the age of twelve after playing on a friend's guitar. He was originally inspired by rock guitarists Jimi Hendrix and Jeff Beck. Watkins then became interested in jazz at the age of twenty after hearing some recordings by Larry Coryell, John McLaughlin and other jazz fusion guitarists.

After graduating from high school Watkins went to the TCU College in Fort Worth, Texas with the intention of becoming a choral conductor. An offer to tour with a rock group made him decide to postpone his studies for a year and a half. In 1975 he entered the University of Texas at Austin for a four year course in composition. Whilst at university he helped form a highly acclaimed jazz fusion group called `Passenger`, and also worked frequently in local studios where he was called upon to play all types of music on various fretted instruments.

In the 1980s Watkins worked as a sideman with Canadian poet Leonard Cohen (1980 & 1985), rock star Joe Ely (1983-85), saxophonist Bennie Wallace (1986-88) and singer Jennifer Warnes (1987). In 1988 he toured Germany and recorded with jazz organist Barbara Dennerlein. In 1989 he toured the USA and recorded with country singer K.T. Oslin.

Mitch Watkins currently lives in Austin, Texas where he continues a busy career as a jazz fusion and studio guitarist. He records frequently for the German company Enja both as a sideman and leader.

SELECTED RECORDINGS

Barbara Dennerlein-Straight Ahead	Enja-5077 2 CD
Barbara Dennerlein-Hot Stuff	Enja-6050 2 CD
Barbara Dennerlein-That's Me	Enja-7043 2 CD
Underneath It All	Enja ENJ-5099 2 CD
Curves	Enja ENJ-6054 2 CD
Strings With Wings	Enja TIP-8888 14 2 CD
Paul Glasse	Amazing Records AMCD-1022

SELECTED READING

Profile	Jazz Times, April 1991
Profile	Guitar Player, June 1991
Profile	Downbeat, October 1993

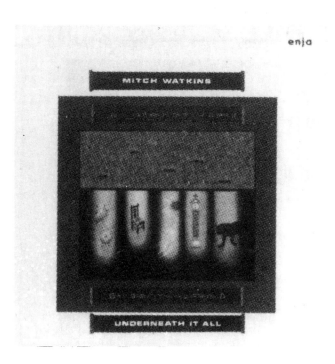

Chuck Wayne

CHUCK WAYNE

Born-CHARLES JAGELKA
New York City, USA
27 February 1923
Died-Jackson, New Jersey, USA
29 July 1997

Chuck Wayne originally started playing the mandolin in a Russian balalaika band. His father was a cabinet maker who had emigrated from Czechoslovkia. When the neck of his mandolin warped Wayne threw it in a furnace and soon after, at the age of 16 he bought his first guitar. A self-taught player Wayne was recognised by his peers as one of the all-time jazz guitar greats.

In 1941 Wayne, whilst working as a liftman during the day, started to play with various groups in and around New York City. His first professional work was on 52nd Street with Clarence Profit and Nat Jaffe. He soon gained a reputation as a talented guitarist. In 1942 Wayne was drafted into the army. On leaving the forces in 1944 he began on one of the most illustrious careers in jazz.

From 1944-46 Wayne played with Joe Marsala. For the next two years he played with diverse jazz groups including Woody Herman's band. International recognition for Wayne's exceptional jazz guitar playing came when he joined the George Shearing Quintet in 1949. He stayed with this historic jazz group for three years. In 1952 Wayne left Shearing and led his own group in New York City. From 1954-57 he was the musical director and accompanist for singer

Tony Bennett. In 1960 Wayne became a staff musician in the CBS studios in New York. Although he still did occasional jazz work it was not until 1973 that he became prominent again in jazz circles after he formed a guitar duo with Joe Puma. They played in jazz clubs in the New York area, and also recorded for the Choice label.

Chuck Wayne continued to live in New York until his death where his career was divided between playing jazz in local clubs, teaching and studio work. A virtuoso performer, Wayne never received the wide spread fame and international recognition his unique talent on the guitar deserved.

SELECTED RECORDINGS

An Evening With George Shearing	MGM E 3122 LP
Woody Herman Herd	Harmony HL 7083 LP
String Fever	Vik LX 1098 LP
The Jazz Guitarist	Savoy SV-0189CD
Tapestry	Focus FM 333 LP
Morning Mist	Prestige PR 7367 LP
Interactions w/Joe Puma	Choice CRS-1004 LP
Joe Bushkin & Friends	Reprise RS-6119 LP
Tony Bennett-Cloud 7	Columbia CL 621 LP
Four Most Guitars	ABC Paramount ABC109 LP
The Guitar Album	CBS 67275 LP
Travelling	Progressive 7008 LP
Duke Jordan Quartet	SteepleChase SCS-1053
Good Vibes w/Warren Chiasson	Audiophile ACD 236
George Shearing Quintet Video	Charly VID JAM 15

SELECTED READING

Profile	Guitar Player, February 1970
Interview	Guitar Player, March 1974
Profile	Guitar, November 1974
Profile	Guitar World, September 1980
Profile	Guitar World, May 1982
Article	Just Jazz Guitar, November 1997

SELECTED MUSIC

Guitar Arpeggio Dictionary	Henry Adler Inc. Mel Bay Publishing
Jazz Guitar Scales	Second Floor Music

Chuck Wayne and Jimmy Raney.

PHOTO: MAURICE J. SUMMERFIELD

HY WHITE
Born-HYMAN WHITE
Boston, Massachusetts, USA
17 December 1915

Hy White

Hy White's first instrument was the violin which he started to play from the age of nine. Whilst still at school he formed a band with some friends called 'Hy White and his Jazz Pals'. Whilst with this band he began to play the banjo changing over to the guitar when he was sixteen. After leaving school White played in and around Boston working with Rollie Rogers and Ted Rolfe. White at that time began to study the guitar at an advanced level in Boston with guitar teacher George Cohen. In 1938 White decided to move to New York. After a successful audition in late 1939 he joined the original Woody Herman band. He gained a lot of international exposure as a member of the Herman band, particularly after the band's hit recording of 'Woodchopper's Ball' sold over a million copies in 1939. In 1940 White started using an electric guitar for the first time. In 1944 he became a staff musician at the CBS studios in New York, and later that year joined the Les Brown Band.

For many years, from the late 1940s onwards, Hy White freelanced around the New York area. He recorded with the bands of Gene Krupa, the Dorsey Brothers, and others. He also backed many top singers including Bing Crosby, Doris Day, Frank Sinatra and Pearl Bailey. For many years White has lived in the New York area. In 1946 he opened his first teaching studio on West 48th Street and since that time has devoted much of his time to teaching. For many years he maintained a high profile in the studios including fifteen years on the 'Ed Sullivan Television Show' from 1957.

SELECTED RECORDINGS
Woody Herman's First Herd	Joker SM3059
Woody Herman & His Orchestra	Affinity AFS 1008
Les Brown Orchestra 1944-6	Hindsight HSR 103
Coleman Hawkins All Stars	EPM Musique FDC 5159

SELECTED READING
Profile	Guitar Player, June 1978

SELECTED MUSIC
Guitar Digest-Hy White	Edwin H. Morris Publishers
Hy White Originals 10 Solos	Chas. Colins Music Co.
Hy White Guitar Method Book 1	MCA Music
Hy White Guitar Method Book 2	MCA Music
Folklore for Guitar Hy White	MCA Music

MARK WHITFIELD
Born-Lindenhurst, Long Island, New York, USA
6 October 1966

Mark Whitfield

Mark Whitfield's first musical instrument was the alto saxophone, which he played in the fourth grade. He then took up the string bass and played classical music with the school orchestra. His parents were keen big-band jazz fans, so he was exposed at home to the recordings of Count Basie and Duke Ellington. Whitfield played the bass for eight years and at the same time taught himself the guitar.

Although Whitfield earned a scholarship to study medicine, he decided to make music and the guitar his career. His family had moved to Seattle and the young guitarist was very impressed by the jazz guitar style of Joe Pass after hearing a 1982 live concert by the virtuoso guitarist. At the age of sixteen he went to the Berklee College of Music in Boston. Here he discovered the recordings of the other jazz guitar greats including Charlie Christian, Wes Montgomery, Grant Green, George Benson and Django Reinhardt. These greatly influenced his developing jazz guitar style.

In 1987 Whitfield graduated from Berklee and moved to New York to begin life as a professional musician. After appearing with various groups on the Gotham club circuit he was booked to play with organist Brother Jack Mc Duff's combo. This led to appearances with Art Blakey, Jimmy Smith, Roy Haynes, Carmen McRae and Betty Carter. George Benson had the opportunity to hear him playing with McDuff, and was so impressed that he recommended his record company, Warner Brothers, to give Whitfield an exclusive recording contract. His first three recordings as leader of his own group for Warner Brothers have shown that Whitfield has the potential to be one of the best of the new generation of jazz guitarists emanating from the USA.

SELECTED RECORDINGS

The Marksman	Warner Brothers 26321 CD
Patrice	Warner Brothers 26659 CD
Mark Whitfield	Warner Brothers 9 45210-2 CD
True Blue	Verve 314 523 591 CD
7th Ave. Stroll	Verve 314 529 223 CD
Forever Love	Verve 314 533 921 CD
Finger Painting w/Christian McBride	Verve 314 537 856 CD

SELECTED READING

Interview	Guitar Player, April 1991
Interview	Guitar Extra, Summer 1991
Profile	Downbeat, May 1991
Profile	Jazz Times, December 1991
Profile	Jazz The Magazine, Issue 15 1992
Article	Downbeat, December 1995

JACK WILKINS
**Born-Brooklyn, New York, USA
3 June 1944**

Jack Wilkins

Jack Wilkins comes from a musical family, his father played the saxophone, and his mother the piano. Wilkins started playing the guitar at the age of fourteen studying with Joe Monti. At that time he played in rock and roll groups at school dances. After hearing some Johnny Smith records Wilkins decided he wanted to play jazz. He started taking lessons from a local teacher Sid Margolies. In 1962 Wilkins began to study privately with jazz musicologist John Mehegan. At the same time he studied classical guitar with Rodrigo Riera.

In 1963 Wilkins formed a jazz group which included Barry Manilow on piano. Wilkins played the vibraphone in this group. After an introduction by guitar maker Dan Armstrong, Wilkins was hired to play in the Les and Larry Elgart band. This led to work with other big bands including those of Sammy Kaye and Warren Covington. Wilkins gave up big band work for a time and was involved in studio work, and playing in pit orchestras for several Broadway shows. In 1973 he joined drummer Buddy Rich's septet. He stayed with this band until 1975.

Since that time Jack Wilkins has been regular performer in New York jazz clubs as leader of his own groups, and as a sideman with many top jazz artists including Stan Getz, Dizzy Gillespie, Earl Hines, Michael Moore, Mel Torme and Sarah Vaughan. In 1982-83 he worked with the vocal group 'Manhattan Transfer'. As well as maintaining a high profile in the New York studios Wilkins, since the early 1980s, has taught at the Manhattan School of Music in New York.

SELECTED RECORDINGS

Captain Blued-Jack Wilkins	Greenestreet GS 2004 LP
Jack Wilkins-Windows	Mainstream MRL 396 LP
Guitar Players	Mainstream MRL 410 LP
Jack Wilkins Quartet – Merge	Chiaroscuro CR 156 CD
Jack Wilkins Quintet	Chiaroscuro CR 185
Something Like A Bird w/Charles Mingus	Atlantic SD 8804
Jack Wilkins-Merge	Chiaroscuro CR(D)156 CD
Bob Brookmeyer Band Live	Gryphon G-2-785
Alien Army	Musicmasters 5049-2-CD
Call Him Reckless	Musicmasters 60211
Mexico	CTI CD R 279481
Keep in Touch	Claves CD50-1295
Trioart	Arabesque AJ0135CD

SELECTED READING

Profile	Guitar Player, May 1978
Interview	Guitar Player, January 1988
Interview	Just Jazz Guitar, August 1995

SELECTED MUSIC

Jack Wilkins – Windows	Hal Leonard Publishing

JACK WILKINS—KENNY DREW JR. QUARTET
KEEP IN TOUCH

**JACK WILKINS, GUITAR
KENNY DREW JR., PIANO
ANDY MCKEE, BASS
AKIRA TANA, DRUMS**

DEMPSEY WRIGHT
Born-Calumet, Oklahoma, USA
14 July 1929

Although Dempsey Wright started to play the guitar at the age of four, his first professional work as a musician was on the violin. From the age of twelve he played violin in local string bands. He started to become interested in jazz after hearing some recordings by Stephane Grappelli, Stuff Smith and Eddie South. Wright only returned to playing the guitar in 1948 after leaving Oklahoma's Eastern A & M Junior College, when he joined a western band led by Otto Swink. Another guitarist in the group, Gene Thomas, kindled his interest in playing jazz guitar.

In 1953 Wright moved to California, where his first job was as guitarist with a band led by pianist Frankie Carle. After this he joined a Special Services company for a tour of service bases in Japan and Korea in 1955-56. On his return to Los Angeles bassist/cellist Harry Babasin hired Wright to play both violin and guitar in his 'Jazzpickers' group. This unorthodox group, which spotlighted Babasin playing jazz on the cello, achieved success both in concert and on record. Wright gained, for the first time, international exposure to his jazz guitar talents during the two years (1957-58) he was with 'The Jazzpickers'. In 1959 Dempsey Wright played mainly in clubs in the Los Angeles area with a trio led by pianist Freddie Slack. In 1959 he toured with the Chico Hamilton Quintet.

Wright's 1958 recording as a leader of a quintet featuring Richie Kamuca, Victor Feldman, Stan Levey and Ben Tucker confirms that he was one of the best jazz guitar talents of the 1950s.

Dempsey Wright

SELECTED RECORDINGS
The Wright Approach	Andex S 3006 LP
The Jazzpickers	Mode MOD LP119
The Jazzpickers	EmArcy MG36123 LP
The Jazzpickers	Calliope CAL 3023 LP

DENNY WRIGHT
Born-DENYS JUSTIN FREETH WRIGHT
Brockley, Kent, UK
6 May 1924
Died-London, UK
8 February 1992

Denny Wright

PHOTO: BERNARD LONG/COURTESY ROBERT MASTERS

Denny Wright first started to play the guitar at the age of seven after hearing his brother's recordings of American jazz guitarists. He turned semi-professional in 1939, playing in his brother's band. In 1940 he joined trumpeter Cyril Blake's band on a full time basis at the Jig Club in London. It was during his spell with Blake's band that he started to play an electric guitar.

During the war Wright served with the Auxilary Fire Service but continued to play with various groups in the London area, including clarinettist Carl Barriteau's band. After the war ended, Wright played in diverse groups around London. In 1950 he played for Kenny Graham's Afro-Cubists and the BBC Show Band. He helped found a 'Hot Club of France' style group as well as being musical director for several night clubs.

In the late 1950s and early 1960s Denny Wright achieved a lot of popular success as lead guitarist with Lonnie Donegan's skiffle group, and then in a similar group led by Johnny Duncan. In the late 1960s he became musical director for the popular 'Music For Pleasure' record label. In 1973 he returned to playing jazz when he became a member of Diz Disley's trio, which was often booked to back Stephane Grappelli. In 1978 Wright formed the jazz combo 'Velvet' which featured guitarist Ike Isaacs, bassist Len Skeat and trumpeter Digby Fairweather. They toured and recorded together for four years. In 1981 they won the 'Small Group' award in Jazz Journal magazine's annual poll. In 1983 Denny Wright was voted 'Musician of the Year' by the BBC Jazz Society. In the same year he reformed his 'Hot Club of London' group, in which he played until his death in 1992.

SELECTED RECORDINGS

Velvet	Black Lion BLB 12187 LP
Digby Fairweather Sextet	Black Lion BL CD 760505
Stephane Grappelli Live	Black Lion BL CD 760139
Combo	One-Up EMI OU 2202 LP
Denny Wright/Don Harper Quintet	Pizza Express PE 5505 LP

WAYNE WRIGHT
Born-Cincinatti, Ohio, USA
4 September 1932

Wayne Wright's family moved in 1939 to Detroit, Michigan. At the age of twelve he was attracted by members of his neighbour's family who played various fretted instruments. He soon received a banjo/ukulele as a present from his parents. One of his musical neighbour's taught him how to play this basic fretted instrument. Wright made such progress on the banjo/ukulele that the neighbour gave him one of his old guitars. Wright soon made excellent progress. His first musical interest was in folk and country music. After hearing some Django Reinhardt and Tal Farlow recordings in a local record shop, Wright decided to devote himself to playing jazz.

As a teenager Wright played with local musicians, and whenever possible went to hear the leading jazz players of the day. He then had the opportunity to play with other local young jazz musicians in a group organised by Kenny Burrell. Wright soon developed a close relationship with Burrell, sitting in with his group at Kline's Showbar.

In 1961 Wright moved to New York. Here he took over Kenny Burrell's place in the pit band of the Broadway show, 'How To Succeed In Business'. He worked with many top singers including Peggy Lee, Tony Bennett and Tony Martin. He also appeared with many top jazz artists including Gerry Mulligan, Benny Goodman, Lloyd Glenn and Big Joe Turner. Wright also played frequently in local jazz clubs. This exposure led to an offer for him to make up a quintet with George Barnes and Ruby Braff. This group was very successful. Through his concert appearances and recordings with Barnes and Braff, Wright gained international recognition for his excellent rhythm guitar work. In 1976 Wright formed a guitar duo with Marty Grosz. Their recordings confirm Wright's talent both as a soloist and accompanist.

Wayne Wright currently lives in New York and divides his time between music, computers, and the American Guitar Museum on Long Island.

Wayne Wright

SELECTED READING
Article   Just Jazz Guitar, August 1996

SELECTED RECORDINGS
Benny Goodman Orchestra	Decca 6.28451 DP
Buddy Rich Big Band	LRC CDC 8511
Barnes/Braff Quartet	Chiaroscuro CR 121
Barnes/Braff Quartet Live	Chiaroscuro CR126
Barnes/Braff Quartet Play Fred Astaire	RCA SF 8442
Barnes/Braff Quartet Play Gershwin	Concord CJ 5
Barnes/Braff Quartet Play Rodgers & Hart	Concord CJ 7
Flip Phillips Sextet	Concord CCD4358
Marty Grosz/Wayne Wright Duo	Aviva 6000
Goody Goody Grosz/Wright Duo	Aviva 6003
Wayne Wright-Spring Is Here	Alphora Records ALH-105

JIMMY WYBLE
Born-JAMES OTIS WYBLE
Port Arthur, Texas, USA
25 January 1922

Jimmy Wyble

Jimmy Wyble began to play the guitar at the age of seven, but only began to take the instrument seriously when he was thirteen. By the late 1930s he was playing around Houston with various country music bands. In 1940, after hearing some recordings of Django Reinhardt and Charlie Christian, Wyble began to take an interest in jazz. From 1941-42 he was a staff musician for a Houston radio station. In 1944, after serving in the US Army, he joined the famed western swing band led by Bob Wills.

Wyble's first professional involvement as a jazz performer came in the late 1940s when he moved to Los Angeles. At first he worked in the film studios. This gave him the opportunity to work and play with many top jazz players who were also working in the studios. Wyble first gained international prominence as a jazz guitarist in 1956 when he joined vibraphonist Red Norvo's group. He stayed with Norvo for eight years, touring throughout the USA and abroad. During this time Wyble also played with the Benny Goodman band.

Since 1967 Jimmy Wyble has been mainly involved in the Los Angeles studios as a freelance guitarist, working for several television and radio networks and on film soundtrack recordings. For a while he was member of Tony Rizzi's group, 'The Five Guitars'. Wyble has also devoted some of his time to teaching, both privately and at the University of Southern California.

SELECTED RECORDINGS

Jimmy Wyble Quintet-Diane	Vantage LP-502
Classical Jazz	Jazz Chronicles JCS 77 1&2 LP
Wind Jammer w/Red Norvo	Dot 25-126 LP
Five Guitars Play Charlie Christian	Milagro 1000 LP
Jimmy Wyble and Love Bros	Jazz Chronicles JCS 77 3&4 LP
Jimmy Wyble-Jazz Etudes	Jazz Chronicles JCS 781 LP

SELECTED READING

Profile	Guitar Player, June 1977
Profile	Guitar World, November 1982
Interview	Just Jazz Guitar, May 1967

SELECTED MUSIC

Classical/Country	Playback Publishing Co.
Two Line Improvisation	Mel Bay Publishing
Jazz Guitar Duets	Mel Bay Publishing

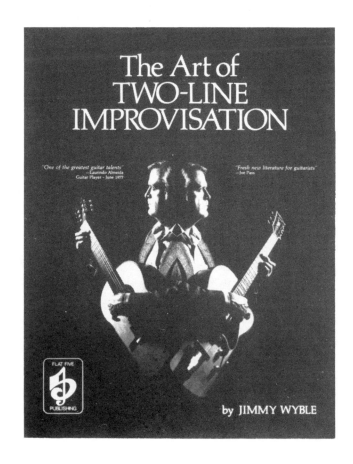

ROBERT YELIN

Born-ROBERT BRUCE YELIN
Yonkers, New York, USA
25 September 1944

Robert Yelin with his 14-string Buscarino.

Robert Yelin's family moved to New Rochelle, New York when he was nine. He began to take an interest in the guitar at the age of 15 after hearing some records by rock and roll guitarists Chuck Berry and Bo Diddley. Yelin went for lessons to Gus DeGazio a local teacher who played him Johnny Smith's famous recording of 'Moonlight in Vermont'. From that moment he realised this was the type of music he wanted to play. He continued his guitar studies with DeGazio but now devoted himself to jazz. It was at this time that Yelin started his unique collection of recordings by the great jazz guitarists. He studied technique and harmony for three years with Augie Lamont, and advanced his jazz technique by seeing the leading guitarists of the day, including Kenny Burrell, Jim Hall and Chuck Wayne, playing in New York jazz clubs.

By the time Yelin was 18 he was playing solo jazz guitar in restaurants. At the age of 20 he decided to become a full-time professional musician. For the next 15 years Yelin played at many top New York jazz spots including The Village Gate and Sweet Basil's. He combined this career with a day time one in the family clothing manufacturing business. He is also a prolific arranger for and writer on the guitar. From 1968-82 he wrote over 30 articles for Guitar Player magazine, and some other guitar magazines. He has also written for Downbeat and Cadence magazines. From 1982 Yelin was a professor at the University of Colorado where he taught the history of jazz and supervised the jazz guitar ensemble there.

In 1983 Yelin developed diabetes and muscular dystrophy. The problems from these illnesses brought his playing career to an end. Fortunately with a combination of excellent medical attention and personal will-power Yelin has since 1996 been able to play again. Robert Yelin is a unique figure in the jazz guitar world. As well as being a talented player he has one of the world's largest collections of jazz guitar audio and video recordings. His video collection has been a great source of reference to scholars and jazz guitar enthusiasts alike. Yelin has written over 2000 chord melody arrangements which he has supplied to guitarists all over the world through his specialist mail order service.

Robert Yelin conceived the idea of a 14-string archtop guitar tuned like a 12-string guitar with the addition of two extra A's (an octave apart) in the bass. He commisioned luthier John Buscarino to build him the guitar. This unique instrument was completed by Buscarino in November 1998.

SELECTED RECORDINGS

Song For My Wife	ChordMaster 101 LP
Night Rain	Capri Records 1981 LP

SELECTED READING

Article - My Story	Just Jazz Guitar, May 1995
Article - 14-String Archtop	Just Jazz Guitar, August 1999

PHOTO: MICHAEL B. LLOYD C.P.P. COURTESY LLOYD'S STUDIO

RICHIE ZELLON
Born-Lima, Peru
28 December 1954

Richie Zellon was born in Peru to Brazilian and American parents. He initially studied classical composition in Peru with Edgar Valcarcel, conductor of the Lima Symphony Orchestra. Zellon then decided he wanted to study jazz and for this purpose moved to Boston to study at the Berklee College of Music.

After leaving Berklee Zellon spent several years teaching privately and presenting Latin Jazz clinics at institutions throughout the USA and Latin America. Zellon's distinctive guitar style has been influenced by both rock star Jimi Hendrix and jazz guitar greats Wes Montgomery and Pat Martino. In 1995 he established Songosaurus Music, a record label devoted to the promotion of new Latin Jazz artists. Zellon now devotes most of his time to producing CD recordings for this record label which have featured many top jazz artists including Paquito D'Rivera, Alex Acuna, Bob Moses, Paul Wertico, John Pattitucci and Jerry Bergonzi.

SELECTED RECORDINGS

Retrato en Blanco Y Negro	Fonovox
Cafe Con Leche	Songosaurus 724772 CD
The Nazca Lines	Songosaurus 724773 CD
Metal Caribe	Songosaurus 724778 CD

Richie Zellon

370

ATTILA ZOLLER
Born-ATTILA CORNELIUS ZOLLER
Visegrad, Hungary
13 June 1927
Died-Townsend, Vermont, USA
25 January 1998

Atilla Zoller

Attila Zoller had a strong musical background. His father was a music teacher and conductor who taught his son to play the violin from the age of four. When Zoller was nine he began to play the trumpet. He played this instrument for seven years in his school's symphony orchestra. In 1945 Zoller went to Budapest to try and become a professional musician. This he realized would be difficult as a trumpeter so he decided to take up the guitar. By 1947 he had made so much progress on the guitar he was hired to play with one of the top commercial bands in Budapest. In 1948, realizing that the political climate in Hungary was going to make things difficult, Zoller decided to move to Vienna. Here he joined up with accordionist Vera Auer. Their quartet played in a jazz style, and they worked together successfully for five years. In 1951 their quartet won the Combo Prize at a jazz contest held in Vienna, even though their usual programme consisted mainly of dance and cabaret music.

By 1954 Zoller had decided to devote his career to jazz and he moved to West Germany. There he played with pianist Jutta Hipp for one year and then with saxophonist Hans Koller from 1956-59. Whilst in Germany Zoller had many opportunities to play with visiting American jazz musicians including Bud Shank, Bob Cooper, Tony Scott, Oscar Pettiford, and Lee Konitz. Zoller met up again in 1956 with Konitz on a brief trip to New York. In 1959 Zoller decided to emigrate to the USA. For a while he was sponsored by the Framus instrument company. On the recommendation of Jim Hall and John Lewis he received a scholarship to the Lenox School of Jazz in Massachusetts. After leaving Lenox, where his room mates were Ornette Coleman and Don Cherry, Zoller worked for a short while with drummer Chico Hamilton. In 1962 flautist Herbie Mann asked him to join his group and they worked together for three years. In 1965 Zoller formed a quartet with pianist Don Friedman which was based in New York City. In 1966 he worked with Red Norvo in Canada, and then in 1967 for six weeks with the Benny Goodman band.

From the early 1970s Zoller appeared frequently at European jazz festivals, clubs, and on television and radio broadcasts. In 1968 he was co-leader of a trio with Lee Konitz and Albert Mangelsdorff. In 1970 he accompanied singer Astrud Gilberto for a tour of Japan. In 1972 he returned to Japan as part of a guitar festival with Jim Hall and Kenny Burrell.

Attila Zoller's distinctive guitar style was greatly influenced by free jazz, and to a certain extent by the jazz/rock fusion movement. Zoller, a very individual and talented guitarist, devoted a lot of his time to the development of new innovations for musical instruments, including his 'Bi-directional' pickup for guitar and bass, pickups for vibraphones, and the production of his own guitar string line. He also organised jazz guitar clinics in the USA and Europe.

SELECTED RECORDINGS

Legendary Oscar Pettiford	Black Lion BLP 30185 LP
Zo-Ko-Ma	MPS 15-170 LP
The Horizon Beyond	Emarcy 25013 LP
Katz & Maus	Saba 15112 LP
Gypsy Cry	Embryo SD 523 LP
Attila Zoller	Inner City 3008 LP
Dream Bells	Enja 2078 1 CD
Common Cause	Enja 3043-3 CD
Jim & I-Duo w/Jimmy Raney	L+R Records LR 40.006 LP
Duologue	Far East ETJ-65022 LP
Conjunction	Enja ENJ 3051-1 CD
Memories Of Pannonia	Enja ENJ 5027-1 CD
Overcome	Enja ENJ 5053-2 CD
Zo-Ko-So	MPS CD 843 107-2
Lasting Love – Solo Guitar	Acoustic Music 319 1131 2 CD

SELECTED READING

Profile	Downbeat, July 1965
Profile	Guitar Player, December 1979

BARRY ZWEIG

Born-Detroit, Michigan, USA
7 February 1942

Barry Zweig's mother was a jazz fan and she encouraged her son to study music from a very early age. His first instrument was a ukulele given to him as a present for his fifth birthday. After his family moved to North Hollywood, California in 1950 Zweig began to study the violin and he played this instrument until he was 18.

He first began to play the guitar at the age of 15. His first major influence was Barny Kessel. Zweig was fortunate that he had the opportunity of hearing Kessel play live in clubs in and around Los Angeles. He credits Barney Kessel with being very helpful in giving him important advise as he embalked on a career in music. He studied with Horace Hatchett and Johnny Smith.

Zweig played on the Dinah Shore Show for five years and appeared on the Tonight Show with Doc Severinsen. He has been one of the busiest jazz guitarists in the Los Angeles area for many years playing or recording with many top jazz artists including Eddie Miller, Buddy Rich, Peggy Lee, Jack Sheldon, Bill Holman, Frank Capp, Sammy Davis Jnr, Natalie Cole, Leroy Vinegar, Gene Estes and Dave Pell. Zweig also devotes a lot of his time to teaching and has many students in the North Hollywood area.

Barry Zweig

SELECTED RECORDINGS

On The Edge w/Gene Estes	Progressive PCD-7095
Lefty Leaps In	USA 940CD

Fred Guy with the Duke Ellington Orchestra 1935.

THE JAZZ GUITAR
The Other Jazz Guitarists

This section of the book is a brief photographic tribute to some of the many fine guitarists throughout the world who are, or have been, involved with playing jazz on a regular or occasional basis. Their devotion and love of both jazz and the guitar has also made an important contribution to the evolution of the jazz guitar. Some of these guitarists may never receive international recognition. Others almost certainly will and as a result they will be included in the main biographical section of future editions of this book.

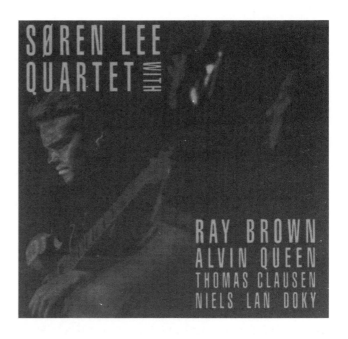

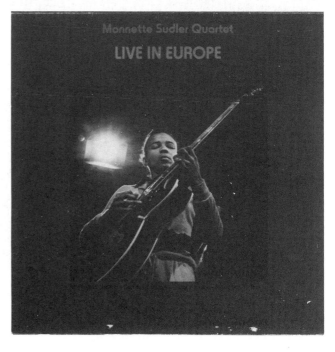

PHOTO: MAURICE J. SUMMERFIELD

Judd Proctor

Deidre Cartwright

Ron Moore

Willie Payne

374

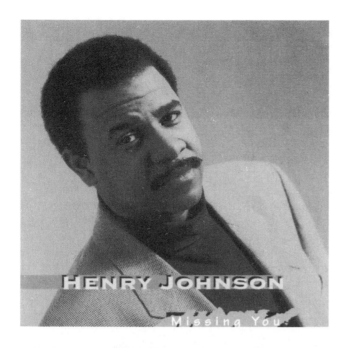

HENRY JOHNSON
Missing You

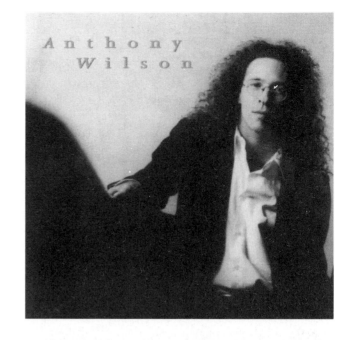

Anthony Wilson

steve masakowski **what it was**

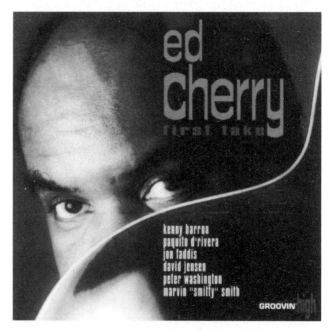

ed Cherry
first take

kenny barron
paquito d'rivera
jon faddis
david jensen
peter washington
marvin "smitty" smith

GROOVIN' high

RUDY LINKA ALWAYS DOUBLE CZECH!

john goldie

TÚRN & TWIST

with
Ewen Vernal &
Jim Drummond

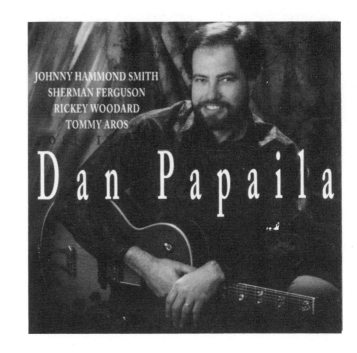

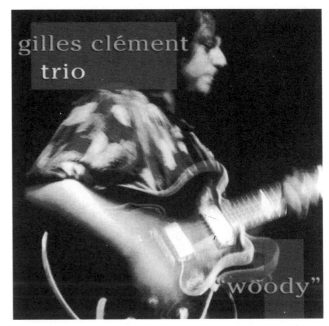

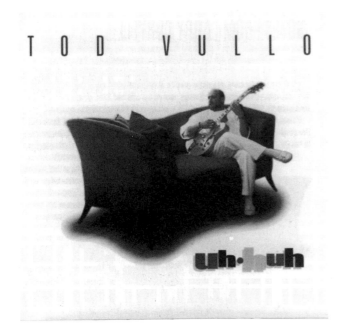

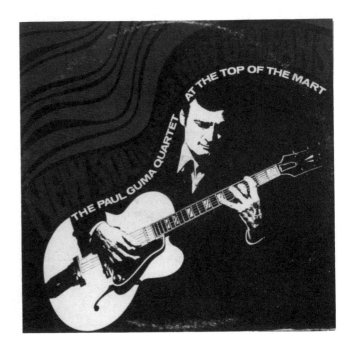

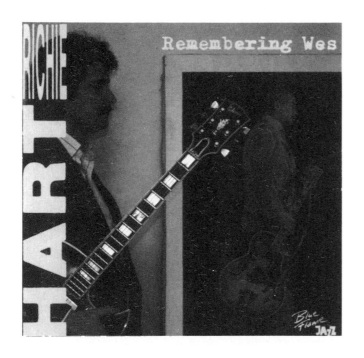

RICHIE HART
Remembering Wes

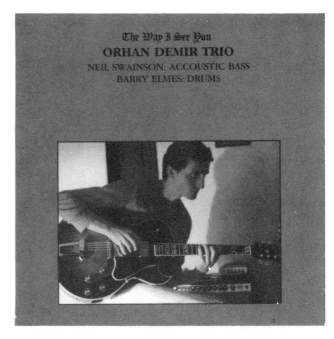

The Way I See You
ORHAN DEMIR TRIO
NEIL SWAINSON: ACCOUSTIC BASS
BARRY ELMES: DRUMS

Bill Jennings
Leo Parker Quintet
Billy in the Lion's Den

Jazz-Samba
Ao Vivo

Dan Axelrod

With
Fred Lite
Lee Hudson
Ed Paolantonio
special guest
Tal Farlow

NEW AXE

PHOENIX JAZZ

introducing the jazz guitar
of   CHARLIE BUSH
REVELATION

local
living
legend

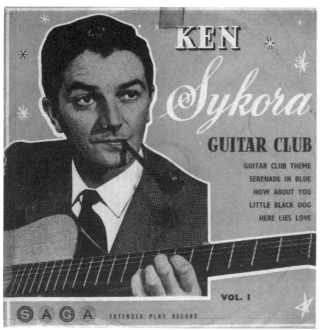

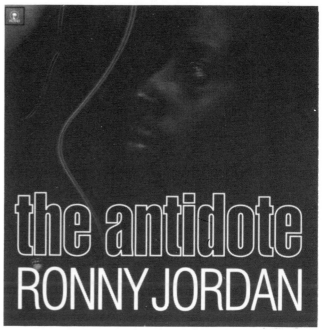

THE JAZZ GUITAR
Its Instruments

That special sound is from Johnny Smith's guitar and the listening is easy . . . easy, exciting and deeply moving. Johnny is a musician with a creative sensitivity which deepens and enriches the music he plays . . . and dramatically communicates his feelings to the listener. The Johnny Smith sound was first heard in New England, it soon reached New York and ranged from the Ed Sullivan Show to the Dave Garroway Show to appearances with Dmitri Metropolis. Johnny has also made many hit records, including *Moonlight in Vermont*, "the best jazz recording in 1953" . . . he's played and arranged for Benny Goodman and Frances Langford . . . and worked the "big" spots across the country including Storyville, Birdland, The Blue Note and The Embers. But Johnny Smith's quest for expression did not end with a sound, it extended to a guitar . . . a treasured Gibson*. This dynamically different instrument offers the rounded, balanced, resonant tones as well as brilliant sustain, fast action and easy handling that are truly ***Gibson***

easy listenin'

Johnny Smith

The all-new Gibson electric acoustic "Johnny Smith Model"

Gibson, Inc., Kalamazoo, Mich.

A 1961 Gibson Guitar advertisement for their highly successful 'Johnny Smith model'.

THE JAZZ GUITAR
ITS INSTRUMENTS

In a book covering the subject of the evolution of the guitar in jazz and its players, it would be wrong not to include details some of the actual instruments used over the years by leading jazz guitarists.

The manufacture of steel-strung guitars suitable for jazz has until recent times always been dominated by makers in the USA. The most important of these for many years was the Gibson company. To a lesser extent guitars made by Epiphone (now owned by Gibson), Guild, and C.F. Martin have also been used for many years by jazz players. In more recent times the exclusive hand-made guitars of the late John D'Angelico and his successor the late Jimmy D'Aquisto, Robert Benedetto and other fine individual makers have been the first choice of many jazz guitarists. There are of course many other American guitar makers, both past and present. Harmony, Stella, Rickenbacker, Fender, Stromberg, Ovation and Gretsch have all been used by guitarists over the years but their popularity amongst jazz players, with a few prominent exceptions, has been limited. This is in spite of the fact that Rickenbacker and Fender have made many valuable contributions to the development of the guitar's electronics. With the exception of the unique Maccaferri/Selmer guitar made in France during the 1930s, an instrument used almost exclusively over the years by Django Reinhardt and the other guitarists of the Hot Club of France, European makers have not made much impact on jazz guitarists. Levin in Sweden and Hofner in Germany were popular in Europe during the 1950s and 1960s. With the rise of the Japanese guitar industry since the mid 1960s two makers, Ibanez and Yamaha, have developed ranges of fine quality jazz guitars and these are now sold all over the world. The long established Maton company in Australia continues its tradition of making fine jazz archtop guitars.

At this time Gibson, D'Aquisto and Benedetto seem to be the guitars currently played by most leading jazz guitarists. A brief history of Gibson, C.F.Martin, Epiphone, Guild, Maccaferri, D'Angelico, D'Aquisto and Benedetto is given below.

GIBSON

The Gibson Company was founded in 1902 by Orville H. Gibson (1856-1918). He was born in

Advanced Model
CARVED TOP AND BACK

- Body size—17" wide and 21" long.
- Northern maple back and rim; mahogany neck; genuine air seasoned spruce top; rosewood fingerboard.
- Chocolate brown finish with golden sunburst shading on top.
- Fingerboard and peghead inlaid with attractive pearl designs; top and bottom edges of body, peghead, fingerboard and finger-rest bound with white ivoroid.
- Elevated brown celluloid fingerrest; side position marks; rosewood adjustable bridge; nickel plated individual Grover machine heads, and new design extension tailpiece; 19 frets; white end pin.
- Exclusive Gibson Adjustable Truss Rod neck construction.

PRICE $125.00

CASES

No. 606 — Strong three ply construction — covered with strong waterproof imitation black leather — purple flannel lining. $18.00.

No. 600 — Covered with heavy waterproof Aeroplane Cloth — sturdy luggage catches — heavy American Beauty silk plush lining. $28.00.

Case Cover: Tan zipper waterproof cover — leather bindings — metal bumpers. $15.00.

STYLE L-7

Gibson L7, as featured in Gibson 1937 catalogue.

Chataugay, New York; his father John Gibson had originally emigrated from England. He started as a shoe store assistant in Kalamazoo, Michigan. He also worked part time as an instrument maker, working in his own private workshop. It was his original conception that the carved top principle of violin making could be applied to mandolin and guitar making. The results of his experiments were very successful and the reputation of his fine instruments soon spread far and wide. In 1902 Gibson made an agreement with five Kalamazoo businessmen and the Gibson Mandolin-Guitar Mfg. Company was formed.

A vast range of fine guitars, mandolins, harp-guitars, and later banjos, were manufactured by the fast growing Gibson company. In 1919, just over a year after the death of its founder, the Gibson company was fortunate to add to it's staff the brilliant Lloyd Loar, a fine musician, composer and acoustical engineer. He perfected and developed the original ideas of Orville Gibson in relation to the arch-top guitar. The L5 and L7 guitars were conceived and developed by Loar. They became amongst the most sought after instruments by jazz guitarists for many years to come. Loar left Gibson in 1924 after a dispute over his wish to produce electrically amplified guitars. He formed the Vivi-Tone Company which produced electric guitars more than a decade before they would become accepted as a legitimate instrument, but he was not commercially successful. The mid 1930s saw the development by Gibson of the Super 400 guitar and then the first important production electric jazz guitar the ES150. This guitar was used by Charlie Christian, Oscar Moore and later by many other jazz guitarists c. the time. In 1944 the now highly successful Gibson company was purchased by the Chicago Musical Instrument Company who enlarged the Gibson factory. Over the years many new models were developed and introduced on to the market. Electronics, particularly with the help of Les Paul, were improved to a very high level. Since the early 1950s the Gibson ES 175 guitar has been a favourite for jazz guitarists all over the world. Throughout its long history Gibson has always associated itself with jazz guitarists. In the 1920s Eddie Lang, and in the 1930s Carl Kress and Dick McDonough were Gibson endorsees. In the 1950s and 1960s several Gibson guitars bore the names of top jazz artists including Johnny Smith, Howard Roberts, Tal Farlow and Barney Kessel. In the 1970s Gibson continued this tradition with developments such as the special acoustic guitar with sitar like drones which it built for John McLaughlin. The contribution of Gibson to the development of the jazz guitar has been a unique and vital one. The Chicago

Gibson Super 400

Gibson ES 175D

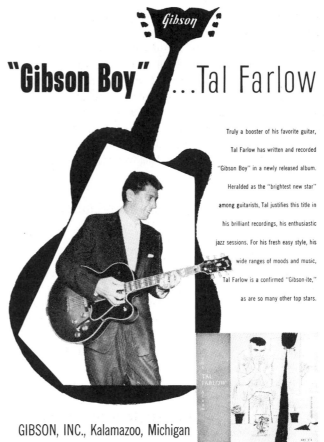

Examples of Gibson Guitar advertisements from the 1950s and l960s featuring jazz guitarists.

Musical Instrument Company also purchased the Epiphone company in 1957. On 22 December 1969 Gibson Guitars became part of ECL Industries (Norlin) a concern which distributed a vast range of products, including musical instruments, in most countries of the world. In January 1985 the Gibson Guitar Corporation became an independent business again aftcr it was purchascd by a group headed by Henry Juszkiewicz. Since that time the new management has continued Gibson's long tradition of making excellent jazz guitars. In 1993 it instigated a special campaign to promote its most famous jazz guitars including the Johnny Smith and Tal Farlow models.

SELECTED READING

The Gibson Story Julius Bellson	Gibson Co. (1973)
American Guitars-An Illustrated History Tom Wheeler	
	Harper & Row (1982)
The Gibson Super 400 Van Hoose	GPI Books (1991)
Gibson Electrics Vol 1 Duchossoir	Mediapresse (1981)
Guitar History Vol # 3	Bold Strummer (1991)
The Gibson ES175 Ingram	Music Maker Books (1993)
Gibson Guitars– 100 years of an American Icon Carter	GPE (1996)
The Gibson	Rittor Music (1996)
The Gibson L5 Ingram	Centerstream (1997)

ES-150 MODEL

Another guitar miracle by Gibson—a true, undistorted tone amplified by electricity.

The guitar itself is a full sized Gibson—you hold it, tune it and play it just as you would any guitar, and in appearance it is only slightly different—but strike the strings lightly and you have a tone that can be amplified to any volume you desire. Adjust the tone control and you change the tonal color from a rich bass to a brilliant treble.

The pick-up unit is built inside the guitar and perfectly adjusted at the Gibson factory for balanced tone.

ELECTRIC TENOR GUITAR

STYLE EST-150

Same as ES-150 but with Four String Tenor Neck and Fingerboard

PRICE: Instrument and 15 foot cord $77.50

PICK-UP UNIT

With the exception of the attractively bound coil and tone and volume controls, the entire unit is built inside the guitar body—finest steel magnets which give the maximum in power and long life—the super-sensitive pole-piece is chrome plated—tone and volume controls conveniently placed for instant regulation.

15 foot shielded cord with fool-proof shielded plugs and spring protectors—detaches from guitar when not in use.

INSTRUMENT

Grand auditorium body—carved spruce top—northern maple back and rim—mahogany neck and rosewood fingerboard—chocolate brown finish with golden sunburst—white ivoroid binding on top and bottom of body—ebony adjustable bridge—brown celluloid fingerrest—individual nickel machine heads with white buttons—exclusive Gibson Adjustable Truss Rod neck—19 frets.

PRICE: Instrument and 15 foot cord $77.50

CASE: No. 514 Heavy Faultless construction — waterproof imitation black leather covering — purple flannel lining — $13.50.
No. 534 Aeroplane cloth covering—heavy Faultless construction—purple flannel lining. $15.00.
CASE COVER: Tan Zipper waterproof cover — leather bindings — metal bumpers. $12.50.
AMPLIFIER: The ES-150 is designed to be used with the EH-150 amplifier illustrated on page 35. Price: $75.00.

[38]

Gibson ES 150 the guitar made famous by Charlie Christian and Oscar Moore.

C. F. MARTIN

Christian Frederick Martin was born on 31 January, 1796 in Markneukirchen, Germany. As a teenager he learnt the art of guitar making in the workshop of the famous luthier Johann Stauffer in Vienna, Austria. Martin later set up his own workshop in Mark Neukirchen but after a dispute with local guilds emigrated in 1833 to New York. Here he made the first American made C.F.Martin guitars in a small workshop situated at 196 Hudson Street. In 1839 the business moved to Nazareth, Pennsylvania, from where it has flourished as a family business right up to the present day. The Martin Company makes the world's most famous flat top steel-strung guitars. It's few attempts at producing arch-top guitars have never been a commercial success. As a result the Martin guitar has not often been used by jazz guitarists, although it has been a favourite for blues singer/guitarists since the end of the nineteenth century right up to the present day, and as such has made an important contribution to jazz.

SELECTED READING
Martin Guitars History   Longworth   Colonial Press (1975)
The C.F.Martin Story   Music Trades Magazine, March, 1993
The Martin Dreadnought Story   Frets, May 1988
The Martin Book – Carter   Balafon, (1995)
Martin Guitars   Washburn/Johnson   Rodale Press (1997)

C.F. Martin 000-28

EPIPHONE

The Epiphone company was established in New York in 1873 by Anastasios Stathopoulo, a violin maker and luthier of high repute. After the death of its founder the Epiphone company prospered for many years under the management of Epi Stathopoulo and his two brothers. Their instrument range consisted of many guitars, banjos and mandolins not unlike the range being produced at that time by the Gibson company in Kalamazoo. Many professional guitarists in the 1930s regarded the Epiphone arch-top guitar as an equal to those produced in the Gibson workshops. With the advent of the electric guitar the Gibson company took the initiative and strode ahead of Epiphone in the instrument market. Gibson finally purchased the Epiphone company in 1957 after the death of Epi Stathopoulo. Many of Epiphone's top craftsmen left and joined the then recently formed Guild company owned by Albert Dronge. Since the 1970s most Epiphone guitars were made in Japan, and later Korea, for Norlin Inc. Epiphone is still a division of the Gibson Guitar company and has several jazz models in it's range, including a Joe Pass signature model.

SELECTED READING
Epiphone– The Complete History   Carter   Hal Leonard (1995)
Epiphone– The House of Stathopoulo   Fish/Fried   Amsco (1996)

Epiphone Broadway

DJANGO REINHARDT

"LE ROI DE LA GUITARE"

RETOUR DE LONDRES, OU IL A OBTENU
UN SUCCÈS SANS PRÉCÉDENT
AVEC SA GUITARE FRANÇAISE

Studio Tronchet

...car c'est
une

Selmer

Example of Selmer advertisement for the Maccaferri guitar from the mid 1930s.

MACCAFERRI

Mario Maccaferri was born 20 May 1900 in Cento near Bologna, Italy. As a young man he was not only a brilliant instrument maker but also a classical guitarist of concert standard. Maccaferri felt he could apply some of the principles of violin and mandolin construction to the guitar. When he was in London in the late 1920s he showed his hand-made guitars with his original innovations to the directors of the Selmer Musical Instrument Company of London. They were so impressed they immediately recommended Selmer of Paris that they put the Maccaferri guitar into production. The result was a three year association beginning in 1930 between Maccaferri and Selmer. During these three years Maccaferri controlled the production of his guitars in Selmer's Paris factory which he had designed for them. Within a short time these distinctive and beautiful instruments were the most popular guitars in Europe for dance band and jazz guitarists. The most famous of these were Django Reinhardt and the members of his group the Quintet of the Hot Club of France. In 1933, after a dispute with the management, Maccaferri left the Selmer company. They continued producing the guitar under the Selmer brand, but changed the original 'D' sound hole to a small oval sound hole, and also made the neck fourteen frets clear of the body, instead of the original twelve. The production of all Selmer/Maccaferri models ceased at the end of the 1930s.

Mario Maccaferri continued to have a long and successful career in other trades. In 1939 he left France for the USA. Here he applied his great engineering skills to the plastics industry. He made many succesful products in plastic including saxophone reeds, wall tiles and a best-selling ukulele that sold well over a million and a half pieces. Maccaferri's love for the guitar always remained. He even tried to make a range of professional guitars, including electric guitars, out of plastic in the 1950s. Although over $100,000 was invested in the project, it was eventually abandoned. In the 1980s Maccaferri began a long association with British musical instrument distributors, Summerfields of Newcastle. Over the years, since the late 1970s, several lines of guitars based on Maccaferri's original 1930s design were made in Japan for distribution by Summerfields. These instruments proved extremely popular, particularly amongst followers of the music of Django Reinhardt and other gypsy jazz guitarists. In his latter years Mario Maccaferri continued to work full time on a project to manufacture professional quality violins out of plastic, right up to his death on 16 April, 1993.

Selmer/Maccaferri factory, Paris, France 1931

PHOTO: COURTESY MARIO MACCAFERRI

SELECTED READING

Profile	Guitar Player, April 1974
Profile	Guitar, May 1975
Interview	Guitar, January 1976
Interview	Classical Guitar, September 1984
Interview	Guitar Player, February 1986
Profile	Acoustic Guitar, April 1992
Profile	Guitarmaker, September 1992
Tribute	Guitarmaker, September 1993
Article	Vintage Gallery, April 1994
Article	Vintage Guitar Magazine, March/April 1995

The Story of the Selmer Maccaferri Guitar
           François Charle Charle Pub. (1999)

Mario Maccaferri with a selection of his all-plastic guitars.

PHOTO: COURTESY MARIO MACCAFERRI

387

GUILD

The Guild Guitar company was founded in 1952 in New York City by Alfred Dronge a former professional guitarist and musical instrument retailer. Dronge started with five guitar makers, two of whom had been top men with the Epiphone Company. Over the next few years the Guild company, under Dronge's demanding management, built up a fine reputation for its instruments. It also gained in 1957 several more of the Epiphone company's expert craftsmen when Epiphone was purchased by C.M.I. In 1956 Guild moved to Hoboken, New Jersey. Here the company continued to expand its production under the guidance of its founder Albert Dronge who ensured that the quality of their guitars was of the highest standard. After the death of Dronge in a plane crash Guild became in 1967 a division of Avnet Inc., a public company with diverse interests. Its guitars were made in a new factory at Westerly, Rhode Island. Under the new management Guild maintained it's reputation for its excellent instruments. Guild jazz guitars, particularly their Artist Award model, have over the years been much sought after. In 1986 the Guild Company was purchased by a private consortium but after business difficulties was purchased by the U.S. Music Corporation. This company, which also owned Randall Amplifiers, continued Guild's tradition of making high quality jazz guitars in 1996. Guild was purchased by the Fender company.

Guild Artist Award

SELECTED READING

The Guild Guitar Bouk and Moust	Guitarchives (1995)
Guild Guitars Beesley	Bold Strummer (1995)

D'ANGELICO

John D'Angelico was born in 1905 in New York City. His family had emigrated from Naples, Italy. In 1914 he was apprenticed to his granduncle Ciani, a luthier who had a workshop situated on Kenmare Street in New York. At first D'Angelico studied violin making. After the death of his granduncle he stayed on to manage the workshop for his aunt. In 1932 he decided to open his own workshop on Manhattan's Lower East Side. It was at this time that D'Angelico began making quality hand made arch-top guitars using the Gibson L5 as his model. Within a short period of time he was making his own very individual guitars. The excellent qualities of his magnificent instruments soon earned him orders from many of the top players in the USA and around the world. D'Angelico tragically died at the age of 59 on 1 September, 1964. Fortunately he had passed his unique knowledge on to his apprentice Jimmy D'Aquisto, who had joined him in 1952. D'Aquisto still continues the traditions of his teacher to this day. Original D'Angelico 'New Yorker' guitars are now rare collector's items and are much sought after by jazz guitarists the world over.

SELECTED READING

Article	Guitar Player, January 1973
Aquired Of The Angels-D'Angelico & D'Aquisto Schmidt	
	Scarecrow Press (1991)

John D'Angelico in his workshop

D'AQUISTO

Jimmy D'Aquisto is regarded by many guitarists throughout the world as one of the greatest archtop guitar maker of all time. He added many of his own ideas to those learnt from his teacher, the master luthier John D'Angelico.

James L. D'Aquisto was born in Brooklyn, New York, 9 November, 1935. He became interested in the guitar and jazz as a teenager. He studied with New York guitarist Anthony Antone. A friend told D'Aquisto in 1952 about John D'Angelico, and soon the young guitarist became a frequent visitor at the luthier's workshop. D'Aquisto immediately accepted an offer from D'Angelico to become his apprentice in 1952. He soon showed that he was a talented maker in his own right, nicknamed 'The Kid' by D'Angelico's regular customers. After D'Angelico died in 1964 his family told D'Aquisto that the luthier had wished that his apprentice should continue the business after his death. They offered to sell him the business, the goodwill, and the right to call himself 'the successor to D'Angelico'. He borrowed the necessary money and accepted their offer. D'Aquisto overcame many business problems in his first years as an independent maker, and established himself as one of the great jazz guitar makers. He died 18 April 1995 in California whilst working on the Fender line of his D'Aquisto guitars.

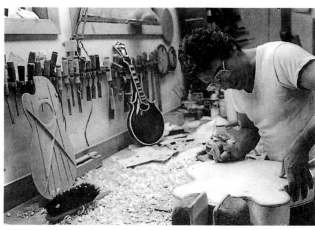

Jimmy D'Aquisto

SELECTED READING
Article   Guitar Player, February 1970
Article   Guitar Player, September 1978
Article   Frets, December 1980
Aquired Of The Angels D'Angelico & D'Aquisto Schmidt
                                         Scarecrow Press (1991)
Appreciation   20 Century Guitar, June 1995

D'Aquisto New Yorker-1995 Model.

BENEDETTO

Robert Benedetto is widely acknowledged as today's foremost maker of archtop guitars. Over a 30 year career, he has crafted 675 instruments, including over 400 archtops.

Benedetto was born 22 October 1946 in New York, USA into a family of artists, wood carvers and musicians. His father and grandfather were master cabinet makers (his grandfather carved the piano legs for the Steinway Piano Company). His uncles played guitar and mandolin and the young Benedetto was exposed to music and wood craftsmanship early on.

Benedetto made his first archtop guitar in 1968. Playing guitar professionally by age 13, he lived and played nearby the busy New York/New Jersey jazz scene. This gave him many opportunities to meet other jazz guitarists. He made guitars for some of them, including Bucky Pizzarelli and Chuck Wayne, both of whom guided him with refinements in jazz guitar construction. He also began repairing and restoring older archtops. His reputation grew as he crafted guitars for other noted players, including Johnny Smith, Jack Wilkins, Ron Eschete, Cal Collins, Joe Diorio, and later, Howard Alden, John Pizzarelli and Jimmy Bruno.

He has the distinction of being the only archtop maker in history to also be a prolific violinmaker.

He started making violins in 1983, Stephane Grappelli purchased one in 1993.

A veteran innovator, in 1982 Benedetto led the movement to strip away unnecessary bindings and inlays on the archtop guitar. He is the originator of the solid ebony tailpiece and the 'honey blonde' finish, and pioneered the use of natural wood veneers for the headstock. He is also well known for refining the 7-String guitar and is that unique model's most prolific maker. In 1992, he started a line of 'Benedetto Jazz Pickups' and also currently markets his ebony tailpiece.

In 1992, he pioneered archtop guitar construction courses and in 1994 authored the landmark book, Making an Archtop Guitar. His companion video, Archtop Guitar Design & Construction, followed in 1996. That same year he and wife Cindy began sponsoring 'Benedetto Players' concerts. A second book on archtop construction as well as a third on The Benedetto Players are in the works. Benedetto writes a regular column for Just Jazz Guitar magazine.

Currently living in East Stroudsburg, Pennsylvania Robert Benedetto works alone, making 12 archtops and 6 violins annually.

SELECTED READING
Making an Archtop Guitar– Benedetto   Centerstream (1994)

Robert Benedetto

PHOTO.: JOHN BENDER

GUITAR STRINGS

All guitars need excellent strings to sound their best. Since the 1920s some string manufacturers have spent a lot of time and money in perfecting their strings for all styles of guitars. Most of the great guitar string makers are presently based in the USA. Amongst the many famous brands used by jazz guitarists in the 1990s are Gibson, GHS, La Bella and D'Addario. There are some other strings sets, branded with well known jazz guitarmakers' names, on the market, but they are usually made for these famous instrument makers by one of the established stringmakers such as GHS and D'Addario. Here is a profile of D'Addario currently reputed to be the largest, and one of the most innovative, of the world's stringmakers.

D'ADDARIO

The D'Addario family business of string making goes back eight generations. They first started making strings in the town of Salle in the province of Pescara, Italy. Charles D'Addario emigrated to the USA in 1909 and continued the family tradition, first by importing and distributing strings and then, in 1916, by making them in a small workshop in Long Island City. At that time the business concentrated on violin strings.

John D'Addario joined his father in 1935, and became interested in other aspects of string making. In 1938 they began to make their first steel guitar strings for jazz and western guitars. Their business grew at a rapid rate from then, and after John's son, John Jnr, joined them in the late 1960s they changed their trading name to Darco Music Strings. The company prospered and was bought out by the Martin Guitar Company in 1970. In September 1974 John D'Addario, after leaving the Darco business, was joined by his youngest son James. Together with John Jnr they began to produce strings again as J. D'Addario & Company Inc. Since that time the D'Addario company has become one of the largest string-making companies in the world, making strings for virtually every stringed instrument. Since 1974 they have maintained a special interest in strings for the jazz guitarist, working with many of the world's finest players. They have introduced many new manufacturing techniques, including laser technology. Their extensive jazz guitar string range includes wound strings with their innovation the 'half-round' process. These are round-wound strings, smoothed to give a 'polished' feel but retaining the brightness of original strings, two qualities often wanted by jazz guitarists.

SELECTED READING

Meet the D'Addarios	Guitar Player, February 1976
The D'Addario Foundation	Guitar Player, November 1983
Strings- A Special Issue	Frets, November 1984

John D'Addario Jnr (Right) and Jimmy D'Addario.

PHOTO: COURTESY J. D'ADDARIO & CO.INC.

391

There are several excellent books and articles which deal in detail with the fascinating subject of the history and construction of guitars, including of course those instruments used by jazz artists. Some of these books are listed below.

SELECTED GENERAL READING

The History and Development of the American Guitar   Ken Achard
                    Musical New Services/Bold Strummer (1979)
The Guitar Book   Tom Wheeler   Harper & Row (1974)
American Guitars-An Illustrated History   Tom Wheeler
                                    Harper & Row (1982)
The Electric Guitar   Donald Brosnac   Panjandrum (1975)
Guitars-From Renaissance To Rock   Tom and Mary Evans
                                    Paddington (1977)
The Tsumura Collection   Kodansha/Harper & Row (1987)
Rickenbacker Guitars History   McGuinn   Centerstream (1987)
The Ultimate Guitar Book   Tony Bacon   Dorling Kindersley (1991)
Gretsch Guitars History   Jay Scott   Centerstream (1992)
The Gretsch Book   Bacon & Day   Balafon (1996)
Kay Guitars History   Jay Scott   Seventh String Press (1992)
Hofner Guitars History   Giltrap   IMP (1993)
Acoustic Guitars And Fretted Instruments   Gruhn   GPI Books (1993)
Steel String Guitar Construction   Irving Sloane   Dutton (1975)
The Gibson   Rittor Music (1996)
Gibson Guitars-100 Years of an American Icon W.Carter   GPG (1994)
Epiphone-The Complete History   W.Carter   Hal Leonard (1995)
Epiphone: The House of Stathopoulo   Fisch/Fred   Amsco (1996)
The Gibson Super 400   T.Van Hoose   Miller Freeman (1991)
The Gibson ES175   Adrian Ingram   Music Maker (1994)
The Chinery Collection   Balafon (1996)
Classic Guitars of the 50's   Balafon (1996)
Classic Guitars of the 60's   Balafon (1997)
The Gibson L5   Adrian Ingram   Centerstream (1997)
The Guild Guitar Book 1952-1977   Hans Moust GuitArchives (1995)
Guild Guitars   Ted Beesley   Bold Strummer (1995)
Making an Archtop Guitar   Benedetto   Centerstream (1994)

Also recommended reading are reprints of various Gibson, Epiphone and Martin Guitar catalogues, available from specialist dealers.

Tal Farlow, Bob Benedetto and Kenny Burrell backstage after Barney Kessel Tribute, New York City, 25 June 1997.

At the Smithsonian Institution, Washington DC: Debut of Scott Chinery's "Blue Guitar" exhibit, November 1997: John and Bucky Pizzarelli entertain the press: John on Linda Manzer's 'Blue Absynthe' and Bucky on Robert Benedetto's 'La Cremona Azzurra.'

A PHOTO GALLERY OF CONTEMPORARY ARCHTOP GUITARS

Moll

Grimes

Zimnicki

Monteleone

Megas

Mapson

Foster

Mortoro

Hollenbeck

Campellone

Comins

Lacey

Napolitano

De Cava

Zeidler

Unger

JAZZ GUITAR MAKERS –

A SELECTED ADDRESS LIST

BARNEY: P.O.Box 128, Southbury, CT 06488, USA.
BENEDETTO: RRI, Box 1347, East Stroudsburg, PA 18301, USA.
BUSCARINO: 9075-B 130th Avenue, Florida 34643, USA
CAMPELLONE: 725 Branch Avenue, Providence, RI 02904, USA.
COMINS: P.O.Box 611, Willow Grove, PA 19090, USA.
CROW: 13541 N.115, Longmont, CO 80501, USA.
DE CAVA: 369 Nichols Avenue, Stratford, CT 06497, USA.
FAVINO: Les Gaouats, 31160 Castelbiague, France.
FENDER: 7975 North Hayden Road, Scottsdale, AZ 85258, USA.
FOSTER: 76353 Eugene Wallace Road, Covington, LA 70435, USA.
GIBSON: 1818 Elm Hill Pike, Nashville, TN 37210, USA.
GRETSCH: P.O.Box 2468, Savannah, GA 31402, USA.
GRIMES: P.O.Box 537, Kula, HI 96790, USA.
GUDELSKY: 2963 Gopher Canyon Road, Vista, CA 92084, USA.
GUILD: Division of FENDER.
HERITAGE: 225 Parsons Street, Kalamazoo, MI 49007, USA.
HOLLENBECK: 160 Half Moon Street, Lincoln, IL 62656, USA.
IBANEZ: P.O.Box 886, Bensalem, PA 19020, USA.
KIRK SAND: 1027B North Coast Hwy, Laguna Beach, CA 92651, USA.
LACEY: P.O.Box 24646, Nashville, TN 37202, USA.
MANZER: 65 Metcalfe Street, Toronto, Ontario, Canada, M4X 1R9.
MAPSON: 3230 South Susan Street, Santa Ana, CA 92704, USA.
MATON: P.O.Box 5, Canterbury, Victoria, Australia.
MEGAS: 1070 Van Dyke, San Francisco, CA 94124, USA.
MOLL: 720 E.Cherokee, Springfield, MO 65807-2706, USA.
MONTELEONE: P.O.Box 52, Islip, NY 11751, USA.
MORTORO: P.O.Box 161225, Miami, FL 33116-1225, USA.
NAPOLITANO: 531 Old York Road, Allentown, NJ 08501, USA.
RIBBECKE: P.O.Box 1581, Santa Rosa, CA 95042, USA.
UNGER: R.D.6, Box 6379B, Stroudsburg, PA 18360, USA.
WALKER: 314 Pendleton Hill Road, North Stowington, CT 06359, USA.
ZEIDLER: 1441 S.Broad Street, Philadelphia, PA 19147, USA.
ZIMNICKI: 15106 Garfield, Allen Park, MI 48101, USA.

Buscarino

SOURCES OF INFORMATION AND SUPPLY

JAZZ AND GUITAR MAGAZINES

Downbeat
102 N. Haven Road
Elmhurst
Illinois 60126-2970, USA

The Wire
45-46 Poland Street
London
W1V 3DF, UK

Jazz Wise
2b Gleneagle Mews
Ambleside Avenue
London SW16 6AE, UK

Jazz Express
29 Romilly Street
London
W1V 6HP, UK

Just Jazz Guitar
PO Box 76053
Atlanta
Georgia 30358, USA

Crescendo & Jazz Music
28 Lambs Conduit St
London
WC1N 3LE

Guitar Player
411 Borel Avenue #100
San Mateo
CA 94402
USA

Cadence Magazine
Cadence Bldg.
Redwood
NY 13679-9612, USA

IAJRC Journal
PO Box 855
Tenafly
NJ 07670, USA

Jazz Times
8737 Colesville Road, Fifth Floor
Silver Spring
Maryland 20910-3921, USA

Jazz Hot
BP 405
75969 Paris, France

Jazz Journal
3 & 3A Forest Road,
Loughton, Essex
IG10 1DR, UK

Straight No Chaser
41 Coronet Street
London
N1 6HD, UK

Jazz At Ronnie Scott's
47 Frith Street
London
W1V 6HT, UK

Jazz UK
26 The Balcony
Castle Arcade
Cardiff CF1 2BY, UK

The Jazz Rag
PO Box 944
Edgbaston, Birmingham
B16 8UT, UK

Coda
P.O.Box 1002
Station O
Toronto, Canada M4A 2N4

Guitarist
30 Monmouth St
Bath
BA1 2BW, UK

Vintage Jazz Mart
P.O. Box 8184
Radnor,
PA 19087, USA

Hot Club News
Klausner Winkel 6
90482 Nürnberg
Germany

JAZZIZ
3620 N.W. 43rd Street
Gainesville
FL 32606, USA

Jazz Magazine
63 Champs-Elysees
75008 Paris, France

Akustic Gitarre
Hunteburger Weg 181
49086 Osnabrük
Germany

The Jazz Report
14 London St
Toronto, Ontario
Canada M6G 1MG

Jazz Thing
Moltkestr, 88
50859 Köln
Germany

Jazz Podium
Vogelsangstrasse 32
70197 Stuttgart
Germany

Jazz Forum
Nowogrodzka 49
00-695 Warszawa
Poland

Musica Jazz
Viale Sarca 236
20126 Milano
Italy

Staccato
Akazienweg 57
50827 Köln
Germany

20th Century Guitar
135 Oser Avenue
Hauppauge
NY 1178, USA

Vintage Guitar
PO Box 7301
Bismark
ND 58507, USA

Gitarre Actuell
Postfach 13 07 07
D-20107 Hambugh
Germany

JAZZ GUITAR – RECORD, MUSIC AND BOOK SHOPS

UNITED KINGDOM

Ray's Jazz Shop
108 Shaftesbury Avenue
London WC2

Recordings, Books and
Magazines.
New and Secondhand

Ivor Mairants Music Centre
56 Rathbone Place
London W1P 1AB

Guitars-New &
Secondhand. Books &
Music.

Tower Records
1 Piccadilly
London, W1R 8TR

Recordings, Books and
Magazines

Tower Records have branches in other major UK cities. Check local telephone book.

Mole Jazz
311 Grays Inn Road
London
WL1X 8PX

Recordings, Books and
Magazines.
New and Secondhand

Foyles
119 Charing Cross Road
London
WC2

Books & Music-New

HMV Shop
150 & 363 Oxford Street
London
W1N 0DJ

Recordings, Books and
Magazines.
New and Secondhand

HMV have branches in other major UK cities. Check local telephone book.

Virgin Records
14-16 Oxford Street
London
W1R

Recordings, Books and
Magazines.

Virgin have branches in other major UK cities, Paris and the USA. Check local telephone book.

Chappells
20 New Bond Street
London
W1

Books and Music.
Guitars-New and
Secondhand

James Asman's Jazz Centre
3A New Row
St.Martin's Lane
London
WC2

Recordings-New &
Secondhand

Acorn Music
Pete Russell's Hot Record Store Ltd
P.O. BOX 17
Sidmouth
Devon EX10 9EH

Recordings, Books
and Magazines.
New and Secondhand.

Jazz Wise
2b Gleneagle Mews
London
SW16 6AE

Music, Books and
Recordings.
Mail order only.

J.G.Windows
1-7 Central Arcade
Newcastle Upon Tyne
NE1 5BP

Recordings,Music &
Books. Guitars.

Ashley Mark Publishing Company
1 & 2 Vance Court
Trans Britannia Enterprise Park
Blaydon on Tyne
NE21 5NH

Music, Books and
Recordings.
Mail order only.

GERMANY

Berklee Publications
D8000 Munchen 71
Postfach 710 267

Music,Methods and Books
Mail order service.

Phonohaus
Rossmarket 7
Hauptmarkt
Frankfurt on Main

Recordings-New

FRANCE

FNAC
Several stores in Paris
including rue de Rennes &
Les Halles Forum Centre.

Recordings & Books

Disque & Musique
165, rue de Rennes
75006
Paris

Recordings

Oscar Music
20 rue Duperre
75009 Paris

Music, Books and
video recordings.

U.S.A

Tower Records 692 Broadway New York	Recordings, Books, Magazines.
Tower Records Sunset Boulevard Los Angeles	Recordings, Books, Magazines.

Plus many other TOWER RECORD stores in most major cities throughout the USA. Check local telephone book.

Jamey Aebersold P.O. Box 1244-D New Albany IN 47151-1244 USA	Music, Books and Recordings.
Sam Goody's 1290 Ave of the Americas New York	Recordings-New
Robert Yelin 2901 Clint Moore Rd. #316 Boca Raton FL. 33496 USA	Videos and Cassettes of Radio and Television Broadcasts.
Record Hunter 507 Fifth Avenue, New York, NY 10017	Recordings-New and Secondhand.
Jazz Record Center 236 West 26th Street, Room 804 New York, NY 10001	Recordings-New and Secondhand.
Rose Discount Record Store 165 West Madison Chicago	Recordings-New
Manny's 156 West 48th Street and 1600 Broadway New York NY 10019	Guitars and Music
Sam Ash 163 West 48th Street New York NY 10036	Guitars and Music

CANADA

L'Atelier Grigorian 70 Yorkville Avenue Toronto, Ontario M5R 1B9	Recordings

JAPAN

Jazz Record Mart 6182 Goi Ichihara City Chiba Ken 290	Recordings

JAZZ RECORDINGS & BOOKS – SET PRICE SALE AND AUCTION – By Mail Only

Gary Alderman P.O.Box 9164 Madison WI 53715 USA	Recordings and Books
Leon Leavitt P.O. Box 38395 Los Angeles CA 90038 USA	Recordings-Second Hand
William Carraro 25 Aberdeen Street Malverne New York 11565 USA	Recordings-Second Hand

Guitar Records
P.O. Box 422
New Ellenton
SC 29808
USA

Recordings. New and
Secondhand

Mole Jazz
311 Grays Inn Road
London
WC1X 8PX
United Kingdom

Recordings New &
Secondhand

Garon Records
P.O. Box 112
Bury St Edmunds
Suffolk
IP28 6BX
United Kingdom

Recordings New &
Secondhand.

Rare Records
1R Exchange Suite
31022030 Sherman Way
Canoga Park
CA1314
USA

Recordings-New and
Secondhand

Cadence Record Mail Order
Cadence Building
Redwood
NY 13679
USA

Recordings-New

Stash-Daybreak Mail Order
140 W.22nd Street
12th Floor
New York
NY 10011
USA

Recordings-New

COLLEGES WITH JAZZ GUITAR COURSES

Berklee College of Music,
1140 Boylston Street,
Boston
MA02215 USA

Guitar Institute of Technology,
5858 Hollywood Boulevard,
CA90028 USA

Eastman School of Music,
University of Rochester,
26 Gibb Street, Rochester,
NY14604 USA

Manhattan School of Music,
120 Claremont Avenue,
New York,
NY 10027-4698, USA

Jazz BFA Program,
The New School,
66 Fifth Avenue,
New York,
NY 1011, USA

William Paterson College,
Wayne, New Jersey 07470,
USA

USC School of Music,
Jazz Guitar Department,
RAMO Hall 112,
Los Angeles, CA 90089-0851,
USA.

City Of Leeds College of Music,
Cookridge Street, Leeds,
Yorkshire,
United Kingdom

400

INDEX

THE INSTRUMENT MAKERS

A selection of fine jazz guitar duo recordings from the 1920s to the present day.